SPSS for Social Scientists
Second Edition

SPSS for Social Scientists

Second Edition

CIARAN ACTON

ROBERT MILLER

with

JOHN MALTBY

and

DEIRDRE FULLERTON

palgrave
macmillan

First published 2009 by
PALGRAVE MACMILLAN

Palgrave Macmillan in the UK is an imprint of Macmillan Publishers Limited,
registered in England, company number 785998, of Houndmills, Basingstoke,
Hampshire RG21 6XS.

Palgrave Macmillan in the US is a division of St Martin's Press LLC,
175 Fifth Avenue, New York, NY 10010.

Palgrave Macmillan is the global academic imprint of the above companies
and has companies and representatives throughout the world.

Palgrave® and Macmillan® are registered trademarks in the United States,
the United Kingdom, Europe and other countries

ISBN-13: 978-0-230-20993-0
ISBN-10: 0-230-20993-9

This book is printed on paper suitable for recycling and made from fully
managed and sustained forest sources. Logging, pulping and manufacturing
processes are expected to conform to the environmental regulations of the
country of origin.

A catalogue record for this book is available from the British Library.

A catalog record for this book is available from the Library of Congress.

10 9 8 7 6 5 4 3 2
18 17 16 15 14 13 12 11 10

Printed and bound in Great Britain by CPI Antony Rowe

Contents

List of Figures

Preface

Statistics and quantitative methods courses in the social sciences often suffer from an inability to make a link between the skills they seek to impart and present-day society. These courses can be made more attractive to students by illustrating analytic methods with examples from the contemporary world and involving students in computer analyses of real data. As teachers of statistics and quantitative methods courses with over half a century of experience between us, we are very aware of the need for relevant data sets that are interesting to students in the social sciences. The availability of data from the Work Orientations module of the International Social Survey Program (ISSP) brought with it the possibility of utilizing genuinely global research data that could be harnessed for the teaching of techniques of social science data analysis. This use is particularly appropriate given the commitment of the organizers of the ISSP to disseminating their data to the widest possible audiences.

As well as providing 'raw material' of statistical analysis exercises and research methods training courses, the data sets constitute significant bodies of information about over thirty contemporary national societies. They can provide the basis for the substantive consideration of social structure and orientations to work that can form part of social sciences courses literally across the globe.

Acknowledgements

We are grateful for the support and interest in the development of the textbook shown by the International Social Survey Program, in particular that they made the data available for the construction of the practice data sets that accompany this text.

SPSS, Inc. has allowed us to reproduce windows and output generated by the SPSS program. This obviously was essential for this text and we are most appreciative of their permission.

Finally, students at the Queen's University, Belfast over the years have provided essential feedback that allowed us to identify areas where the text could be improved. We are grateful for their tolerance and good humour.

Introduction

The use and analysis of numeric data in the social sciences has a chequered history. During a period from the latter decades of the nineteenth century through to the middle of the twentieth, the quantification of social data and the development of means of analysis were crucial in the efforts of the social sciences to secure acceptance as legitimate academic disciplines. From the end of the Second World War and coincident with academic recognition, the quantitative perspective in the social sciences enjoyed a golden period that reached its culmination in the late 1960s and early 1970s when the computerized analysis of social data became generalized. The advent of computerization in the social sciences had a transforming effect, greatly expanding both the scope of issues that could be investigated using quantitative issues and the depth of investigation that could be carried out. Computer 'packages', sets of computer programs for the statistical analysis of social data with special 'user-friendly' interfaces to allow social scientists to run the programs without a special knowledge of their mathematical construction, were instrumental in the expansion of computerized data analysis beyond a small set of specialists. SPSS, then known as the Statistical Package for the Social Sciences, was the most popular of these. It remains so today.

THE SCHISM BETWEEN QUANTITATIVE AND QUALITATIVE PERSPECTIVES

Ironically (or perhaps predictably) the point in time when the quantitative perspective was at its most hegemonic was also the period that saw the beginnings of a serious backlash as qualitative methods began to reassert themselves. From this period, a schism developed between quantitative and qualitative practitioners that ran across all of the social sciences. In some disciplines such as geography, quantification dominated; in others like anthropology, qualitative research reigned; while in other disciplines, such as sociology, the split was roughly even. A characteristic common across all social science disciplines throughout the decades of the 1970s and 1980s, however, was a lack of contact across the schism.

Thankfully, this period of mutual incomprehension seems to be drawing to an end. At the beginning of the millennium, practitioners of both quantitative and qualitative methods began to develop a mutual appreciation of the 'opposing' camp. This was driven by developments of both perspective and technology.

In the recent past, the mainstream of quantitative research maintained a condescending view of qualitative research. Qualitative research was tolerated as useful for carrying out preliminary exploratory investigations of social phenomena, but only as a precursor to 'serious' quantitative hypothesis-testing investigation. However, more thoughtful quantitative researchers now realize that, while quantitative analysis can answer many types of questions very well – establishing *when* and *how who* did *what where* – it tends to fall down over the crucial question of *why*. To put it another way, quantitative methods are very effective at establishing the veracity of empirical social facts, but are less effective at establishing the motivations or reasoning employed by social actors. As a result triangulated research designs, in which qualitative methods are seen not just as a preliminary but also as a crucial final stage necessary to add context to empirical quantitative findings, are becoming common.

For its part, qualitative research has become more tolerant of the quantitative perspective. Qualitative researchers laboured under a dominant quantitative perspective during the 1960s and 1970s. Part of their reaction to their second-class status was aggressive anti-quantification. As they became established in positions of power and status equal to those of their quantitative counterparts, qualitative researchers felt more secure and became in turn more tolerant of quantitative information.

Technological innovation has promoted the accommodation of the two perspectives. Only a few decades ago computers were seen as hostile and esoteric devices for use only by mathematical specialists. The effects of the spread of computer use to the general population and especially the universal take-up of word-processing technology with a resultant loss of computer phobia among qualitative social scientists should not be underestimated.

Of more direct salience is the recent impact of computerization upon *qualitative* analysis. The advent of specialist qualitative data management and analysis packages has transformed qualitative research over the last decade. While doubts still remain about the extent to which a completely holistic qualitative view can be reflected in a numerical analysis, today it would be difficult to find a serious qualitative researcher who does not have an appreciation of the practical benefits of computerization for their own work. A side effect of this take-up of computers by qualitative researchers has been to render them more open to quantification.

A happy irony of technological innovation has been that as computing power and complexity has increased, the human/machine interface has simplified. This applies as much to quantitative data analysis packages in the social sciences as elsewhere. The use of a quantitative computer package today does not require any special mathematical expertise or ability, with the result that the constituency of academics with at least some capacity for social science computing has expanded. Increased ease of access has meant that more social scientists are able to 'crossover' between qualitative and quantitative techniques. SPSS, the most popular and widely used social science data analysis package, with its Windows format and extensive Help facilities, is a prime example of the more accessible packages of the new millennium.

The end result of all these changes has been that the recent mutual suspicion and incomprehension between quantitative and qualitative social scientists has abated greatly, being replaced with a more relaxed and tolerant atmosphere.

TWO QUANTITATIVE PERSPECTIVES

The empirical

It is a misnomer to speak of a single quantitative perspective. Instead, the use of quantitative data in the social sciences can be seen to fall into two broad modes of working. While these perspectives overlap, they in fact are based upon quite different premises. The first perspective, which can be termed the *empirical*, has beginnings which can be traced at least as far back as the first modern censuses carried out at the beginning of the nineteenth century. The advent of the industrial revolution and the rise of bureaucratic state apparatuses brought about the first modern collations of information drawn from the general population.

The core features of this empirical perspective are the control, manipulation, depiction, and presentation of large amounts of data. Its clearest present-day examples would be the published tabulation tables of a large-scale census or a multi-coloured three-dimensional graph or chart that depicts similar tabular information in a figurative form. The basic task of the empirical perspective is relatively simple, making use of gross computing power to carry out the reliable processing of bulk information into manageable formats. Information is sorted using common-sense sets of categories. Care should be taken in the presentation of the resulting sorts to facilitate the recognition of patterns by the scanning human eye. There is no data analysis in the sense of seeking to depict linkages or associations between bits of information statistically or attempting to model social processes. At its most advanced in the empirical mode, the clever presentation of information allows the researcher to see or notice features that are not readily apparent in raw data or in less ingenious presentation. SPSS has the capacity to carry out analyses in the empirical mode with great efficiency through its procedures for generating tables in a variety of formats, its facilities for data manipulation, its multiple classification analysis procedures, and its variety of ways for generating graphs and charts and using exploratory data analysis (EDA) techniques to depict data.

The positivist

The second perspective, which can be termed the *positivist*, has beginnings in the writings of Emile Durkheim and the first attempts to depict social processes through the modelling of social data. While in practice there is much overlap between the positivist and empirical approaches to data analysis, they in fact employ quite different 'logics' of discovery. All statistical testing which gives its results in the form of probability or significance levels or in terms of a hypothesized relationship or association being found or not confirmed by data is making use of the positivist mode of analysis. The basic perspective underpinning the positivist model of data analysis stretches from quite basic statistical procedures that can be done easily by a beginning student up through sophisticated statistical modelling at the frontiers of social science.

The exact steps involved in positivist statistical testing will be introduced in detail in Module 4, Hypothesis-Testing and *t*-Tests, and then applied in many of the other modules in this text, but here let us here consider the general ideas behind the perspective. The positivist view at its most extreme can be found in the idea of the *social fact* as propounded by Emile Durkheim. Durkheim began by noting that much social behaviour which seems highly individualistic and idiosyncratic from the point of view of a lone individual in fact conforms to quite regular and predictable patterns if the occurrence of the behaviour is looked at for a large aggregate of people. The example of individual behaviour that he chose to examine was suicide, collecting information on suicide rates from different countries and noting how the rates varied in regular ways (for instance, that single people were more likely to commit suicide than married people). However, let us pick something a bit more cheerful – love.

Popularly, falling in love is seen as almost random. Images abound such as of Cupid firing his darts randomly or of love at first sight when two strangers' eyes meet across a crowded room. Lonely people long for the one perfect soulmate that exists somewhere for them. Perhaps we are being a bit cynical and mocking here, but the point holds – people fall in love and the experience is by definition an intensely personal one. At the same time, oddly, falling in love conforms to very definite patterns of age and social groupings. If we take a cohort of 'typical' university students – those who entered straight from their secondary education – they will be aged between about 19 and 22 and, even though they have been socially active for almost a decade, most will not be in love or in a permanent partnership that is intended to last a lifetime. If we follow up the same cohort a decade or so later, most will be in a permanent relationship, probably married, and probably with children or expecting children soon. If we look at the characteristics of the partners that go to make up each couple, by and large we will find congruence across a wide variety of social characteristics. 'Like' will have paired with 'like' with regard to general social background, education, race, ethnic group, religion and so on. There will have been a typical sequence of events in the life course that led up to the forming of the partnership – completion of education, followed by employment and financial independence and, then *and only then*, falling in love and forming the permanent relationship. The women will tend to have fallen in love at the same age or a few years younger than their male partners. There will of course be many exceptions – people who remain single or break the sequence by having children while single or marry before attaining financial independence and so on – or people who cross the barriers of age, class or ethnicity to find a partner; but these will be 'exceptions that prove the rules' of endogamy and sequence. If love really is blind, we should not find these regularities: the choice of partner should have been more random with partnerships that cross barriers of race, ethnicity, social class or age as likely as those that do not. The age of falling in love should not be clustered in the 20s, but should be scattered equally from the early teens through to old age, and the pronounced sequence of falling in love shortly after obtaining secure employment should not exist.

Much of the explanation for these aggregate patterns in love and marriage can of course be found at quite mundane, commonsensical levels. Permanent relationships between couples, especially if they intend to have children, become much more practical once financial independence is attained. Patterns of social and residential endogamy mean that people of similar class and ethnic backgrounds are likely to interact with each other more often so that, by chance, they have more opportunities for pairing off. Nevertheless (assuming that most of these people are pairing off due to love rather than calculation or arranged marriages) events that are being experienced as intensely individual experiences *are* conforming to socially regular patterns. That increasing numbers of these partnerships may be dissolving later on in life does not constitute disproof. Instead, rises in divorce and/or single parent families are only complications – further intensely individually experienced phenomena that in fact also conform to predictable patterns at the aggregate level.

But the positivist perspective is more than simply an aggregate view. As well as noting that phenomena can display regular patterns at a group level, the positivist perspective goes further and posits a genuine level of reality *beyond* that of individuals or their aggregation. This hypothesized meta-reality is the core of the idea of the *social fact*. For instance, with regard to suicide, Durkheim proposed the idea of integration as a feature of a society as a whole, a feature that existed at the societal level but then worked downward to affect individuals. He suggested that variations in suicide rates could be related to the way in which individuals were integrated or not integrated within society and proposed a typology of three kinds of suicide:

- *altruistic* suicide, in which the individual is so integrated into society that the will to live can be overwhelmed by the social. For example, the cases of the Japanese samurai who commits ritual suicide or the soldier who throws himself/herself on a grenade in order to save the rest of the squad;

- *egoistic* suicide, in which individuals who lack day-to-day networks of social support and are less integrated into society are more likely to fall prey to psychological mood swings. The above-noted propensity for single people to be more likely to commit suicide is perhaps the clearest example;
- *anomic* suicide, in which societal integration drops during a time of social change when established mores of correct social behaviour become unclear. Durkheim predicted that suicide rates should rise during times of both economic depression *and* economic boom as an expression of *anomic* suicide.

The reliability and validity of Durkheim's analysis of suicide has been debated ever since it was proposed, but that is beside the point here. What is of relevance is that Durkheim deliberately chose an intensively individualistic act – suicide – and then used his analysis of suicide to present the idea of social facts and an approach to quantitative analysis.

Similarly, with regard to love, one can suggest that there are features of the whole society that can affect the individual's likelihood to fall in love. Concerning the uncannily regular timing of the point at which one forms a permanent relationship with a member of the opposite sex, societies develop a set of conventional institutionalized age-related behaviours as a common organizing principle that can be termed the life course. Love and forming a partnership is a set point on this general life course that is determined by the social milestones such as securing employment that precede it and those that follow, such as beginning to produce the next generation. Marital endogamy can be seen as a special case of general principles of inclusion and exclusion on the basis of ethnic identity and religion that translate into individual differences in choices of life partners. Similarly, general principles of stratification – social class – also translate into patterns of endogamy in the individual choice of life partners. From the positivist point of view, these constraints and propensities are operating meta-socially, independently of individual reality. It is this meta-social level, which has its full expression only at a level beyond that of individual consciousness and motivation, that constitutes what Durkheim meant by social facts.

The Positivist Paradigm in statistical analysis

This idea of the social fact forms the deep background that is the rationale underpinning hypothesis-testing statistical analysis. If group regularities in social behaviour are just the simple amalgamation of individuals, description – the empirical approach – would be sufficient. Hypothesis-based statistical testing goes a step further. All probability-based statistics, no matter how basic, are assuming that there are regularities in the data that exist at a level beyond that of the individual. The collection of information from groups causes the idiosyncratic differences between single individuals to be mutually cancelled out, allowing the meta-level relationships to emerge. In effect, the 'trees' blur together, allowing us to see 'the forest'. To propose that there is a link between two features of a group of people and then to test for the reality of that proposed link means that one is assuming that the link exists in a way that transcends any single individual – one is positing that a social fact exists.

The positivist approach to social science data analysis can be depicted in a diagram. In the 'Positivist Paradigm', the researcher begins with a general theory or set of abstract concepts. 'A *theory* is defined here as a set of interrelated propositions, some of which can be empirically tested. Thus, a theory has three important characteristics: (1) it consists of a set of propositions; (2) these propositions are interrelated; and (3) some of them are empirically testable' (Lin, 1976, p. 17). These general propositions can be applied to a specific situation in order to *deduce* a likely relationship or set of concrete phenomena in the real world. (In *deduction*, one moves from general, abstract principles to specific, concrete situations.) The conceptual ideas of the theory are applied to specific instances in the real world through a process called *operationalization*. A *hypothesis* is constructed, which is a statement of association or difference between concrete phenomena. The hypothesis is tested in the real world to see whether the expected association or difference actually occurs in the manner which has been predicted. If the predicted association or difference does occur as expected, the hypothesis is considered to have been supported (or at least not disproven) and, through a process called *generalization*, the researcher is led to *induce* that the general theory that he/she began with seems to have been confirmed in the real world. (In *induction*, one moves from specific, concrete observations to general, abstract principles.) If the predicted association or relationship is *not* found, the researcher is led to induce the opposite, that the general theory appears not to have been confirmed when tested against real facts.

The Positivist Paradigm

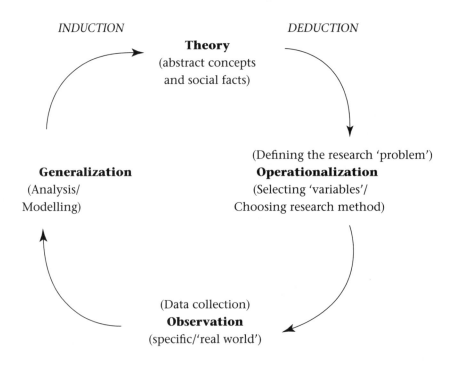

In Module 4, on *t*-tests, specific examples of this hypothesis-testing approach will be introduced. Here, using 'the causes of high educational attainment', let us present a general example in order to illustrate the positivist approach to data analysis. There are a large variety of competing explanations of educational attainment. One type of explanation is that the educational attainment of individuals can be attributed in part to the level of educationally relevant cultural knowledge present in a child's home. This fund of cultural knowledge is sometimes termed *cultural capital*. The concepts of cultural capital and educational attainment could be operationalized by developing specific measures for each – say, the number of 'quality' periodical or magazine subscriptions that a home takes as an operationalization of cultural capital and final secondary school exam results as a measure of educational attainment. At the same time, there are a myriad of other competing explanations for educational attainment. These also could be operationalized – say, a child's IQ score to indicate innate academic ability, household income to indicate the material capital of the family, a government-assessed rating of the child's secondary school to indicate the effect of good versus bad teaching and so on. Information on all these factors could be taken for a large number of children and the analysis would attempt to establish whether the measures of cultural capital exert positive effects upon the children's educational attainment that are independent of all the other potential factors that might also affect educational attainment. If this proves indeed to be the case, one induces that the original theory of cultural capital promoting educational attainment is supported. If the opposite proves to be the case, that once the effects of competing explanations are taken into account, there seems to be no independent effect of cultural capital upon educational attainment, the original theory is not supported. (This hypothetical example is solely for illustrative purposes. A real study of this nature obviously would be extremely complex and require more than a paragraph to summarize.)

In contrast, if the empirical approach had to be imposed upon the above figure, it would fall on the left-hand side of the chart only. In the empirical approach, one works straight from direct observation and, by a process of induction, moves toward generalization and, perhaps, to a set of abstract concepts or a proto-theory.

Critiques of the Positivist Paradigm

The Positivist Paradigm of social research is subscribed to by many researchers, is presented in many research textbooks as *the* correct way of carrying out social research, and certainly acts as a model for reporting much research. Nevertheless it has been subjected to critiques.

The 'scientific revolution' critique

Critiques of the Positivist Paradigm fall into two broad types. The first of these was laid out initially in Thomas Kuhn's *The Structure of Scientific Revolutions* (1962). The theory-testing approach of positivist social science research purports to have its origins in natural science practice. Kuhn, however, pointed out that the cycle of operationalization, testing hypotheses against data, and then using the results to confirm or disconfirm theory was, at best, an 'after the fact' logic. If a set of observations are found to disconfirm theory, rather than the theory being rejected as the paradigm would indicate, the most likely event in the real world of social researchers is that the research results will be questioned. That is, instead of the theory being rejected, the operationalization of the concepts or the accuracy of the data generation, collection or analysis or even the competence or veracity of the researcher may be questioned. This reluctance to reject theory out of hand stems partly from the inherent complexity of social science research. Ensuring complete control of a social process conflicts directly with the need to maintain a natural context. In fact, a controlled experiment is usually impossible, not feasible due to expense or time span, or unethical. Researchers have to work in natural situations and impose statistical controls that at best only mimic a true experimental design. So many parameters are left uncontrolled or fluid that a single negative result cannot be taken as grounds for the definitive rejection of a whole theory or body of concepts. To put it another way, in the event of a negative result, the researcher is more likely in the first instance to question the data and analysis rather than the theory being tested.

The reluctance to reject existing theory is, however, only partly based in methodological considerations. Existing theories are not neutral constructs. They are soundly based in scientific establishments and in the careers of the dominant academics in a given discipline. To cast doubt upon an existing theory is to threaten the academic status quo of a discipline. The result, Kuhn argues, is that *political* considerations affect the dissemination and take-up of contrary research results. For example, problematic results may not appear in the mainstream journals of a discipline and their proponents may be less likely to obtain secure professional appointments. Change in dominant theoretical perspectives does take place eventually, but more by demographic attrition than by impartial academic debate. The proponents of a new theoretical viewpoint gradually gain adherents and work into the centre from the periphery of academic respectability. With time, the 'old guard' quite literally will die out and be supplanted by a new generation whose careers are not dependent upon outmoded conceptual views.

A concrete example of this process could be the impact of feminism upon social stratification research. Up until the beginning of the 1970s, the study of social stratification concentrated solely upon the positions of men. The situation was not so much that women were relegated to a position of secondary importance in stratification studies, but rather that the position of women was completely absent from debates on stratification and that this was not even seen as an issue or problem. At that point, feminist social scientists began to develop a critique of this male bias, making points that seem obvious now: for instance, that women make up slightly more than half of the population; that most adults live as part of a couple in which their social position in a system of social stratification is determined by both partners; that both the father *and* the mother have profound effects upon an individual's social mobility; and so on. The issue was bitterly debated from the mid-1970s, beginning in peripheral, radical publications and only gradually penetrating into mainstream outlets. The conclusion that one would draw from the literature that was published is that proponents of the 'male only' view of social stratification were able to defend their position quite effectively. Based upon a review of the published literature of that time, one would have to conclude that at best the outcome was that women were incorporated into social stratification literature, but that both their position within that literature and their perceived significance in systems of social stratification are secondary relative to men. Despite this, a generation has turned over during the interim so that, aside from a few retrograde chauvinistic pockets of resistance, no serious student of social stratification working today would fail to treat women as having significance equal to men.

Hence, from this viewpoint, while positivist methods of concept-testing may serve to refine or secure minor modifications to existing theories, they cannot secure a profound shift in scientific paradigms. Instead, such shifts occur through social mechanisms that are essentially political in which the assessment of the scientific validity of competing arguments plays only an oblique role – changing the opinions of a younger, replacement generation.

The 'interpretive' critique

The 'scientific revolution' critique centres upon questioning the mechanisms of proof and disproof that are used to generate and refine social science conceptual systems. In contrast, the 'interpretive' critique centres upon the nature of social data, questioning whether social phenomena actually are stable and replicable. The 'interpretive' critique has its origin in qualitative social science. Its core is the assertion that social phenomena are qualitatively different in their nature from the types of phenomena studied by other scientific disciplines. Social phenomena are produced by conscious actors – human beings – and what is observed can only be the outward manifestations of inner meaningful intentions. The problems arise because we may observe *what* people do, but we can never be totally sure of the reasons *why* they do what they do. Even if we question them directly and they are willing to answer, we can be neither sure that they are capable of giving us a complete and accurate explanation of their reasoning and motivation, nor can we even assume that the reasons they do provide are truthful. Any explanations that the researcher attaches to explain phenomena are in fact the researcher's own constructs and can never be considered definitive.

Furthermore, unlike inanimate objects, human beings are conscious social actors. People who are the objects of research can react to the experience; for example, altering their behaviour once they realize they are being observed, reacting emotionally to the person carrying out an intensive in-depth interview, or modifying their answers to a questionnaire in order to provide answers they feel are socially acceptable (or, alternatively, giving deliberately provocative responses). Hence, social phenomena must be considered inherently unreliable. This social version of the Heisenburg Uncertainty Principle means that almost all social data must be considered potentially 'contaminated' in some way by a human's subjective reactions to being the object of research.

The implication of the 'interpretive' critique is to call into question the assumption of the positivist approach that there are stable regularities existing at a level beyond that of the individual – social facts – that can be measured. While regularities may appear to have a stable existence, this may be a chimera. The phenomena being recorded may be in part solely an artefact of the research itself. The subject's reaction to being researched may be so unpredictable as to be for all intents and purposes random. What appears to be a generalizable regularity could break down at any moment.

Parallels between this general view of social research phenomena as being inherently malleable and unstable can be found with two other perspectives that provide essentially the same criticisms of a positivist approach to social research – a postmodernist view and a 'chaotic' view.

Postmodernism argues that any social situation can be depicted by multiple explanations. Each participant can hold one, or several, different views of what is going on. Any or all of these stances may be equally correct and there is no valid means of choosing between them – nor need there be. The 'interpretive' critique of social research can be seen as a special case of this general 'postmodern' view of social reality.

Chaos theory asserts that apparently trivial events can have profound effects upon large, apparently stable, complex systems and that identifying which trivial event will have an effect or what the nature of that effect will be is beyond calculation. In practical terms, chaos theory implies that a complex system can exist for a long time in an apparent state of equilibrium, but that this equilibrium can break down unexpectedly at any time. Predictable relationships that appear to be stable do exist, but their permanence is an illusion. Since social systems are complex systems, the seemingly stable relationships that the researcher is observing and then using to validate sets of concepts statistically can break down at any moment in a manner that cannot be anticipated by a social theory.

Assessment

We presented these critiques of the positivist perspective with some trepidation in case students would be put off quantitative analysis before ever beginning. However we concluded that it would have been remiss if we had set out quantification as a totally accepted and unchallenged viewpoint in the social sciences. The existence of criticisms of the quantitative perspective do not in themselves automatically invalidate that perspective. Many quantitative researchers would take exception to at least some of the criticisms and assert the alternative, that quantification has a legitimate and valued role to play in the social sciences that cannot be neglected. Others who work with quantitative data do take the criticisms seriously, but regard them as cautions about how to make the best and most valid use of quantified information. A keen awareness of the potential effects of researchers upon the nature of the data they are collecting, instead of pointing to rejection, can lead to a more valid and realistic assessment of the findings of a quantitative analysis. As you turn to the very specific and detailed modules that follow, we hope that this brief introduction will help to set your efforts in context.

Orientation

As stated in the Preface, our approach to statistical analysis is very much based in practice and this is reflected in the design of this textbook. Our philosophy of teaching statistical analysis is that the best way for students to learn is through practice that utilizes real data with all its intricacy and 'messiness'. All worked examples in the following modules are based upon analyses of full-size national datasets drawn from the International Social Survey Program. In turn, the text is linked to an extensive selection of these national datasets that are freely available to students on the Internet and supported by extensive documentation both online and within this book.

THE INTERNATIONAL SOCIAL SURVEY PROGRAM

The International Social Survey Program (ISSP) was established in 1983 originally as a collaboration between four survey organizations: the General Social Survey (GSS) conducted by the National Opinion and Research Center (NORC) in the United States; the British Social Attitudes Survey (BSA) conducted by Social and Community Planning Research (SCPR, now the National Centre for Social Research); the Allgemeine Bevölkerungsumfrage der Sozialwissenschaften (ALLBUS) conducted by German Social Science Infrastructure Services (GESIS)–Zentrum für Umfragen, Methoden und Analysen (ZUMA); and the National Social Science Survey (NSSS) conducted by the Australian National University. Since 1985, the ISSP has been carrying out the development and operationalization of a centrally designed module of survey questions with a different topic being selected for each year (although the ISSP does repeat topics over the years). Research organizations from 44 different countries presently are members of the ISSP. A subset of ISSP members develops a central module of questions on the chosen topic for each year. These questions are piloted and then each participating organization carries out the fieldwork within their own country during the same year. The translated questions are usually a module within a larger national survey within the country. The resulting data are merged into a single international dataset by GESIS at the University of Cologne supported by the Spanish ISSP partner, ASEP, Madrid. Typically, over 30 countries will participate in the survey in any given year. The ISSP datasets constitute a unique resource for international comparative work.

The datasets

Data from the ISSP 2005 module on Work Orientations constitutes an integral part of this textbook. As well as coming from the most recent available year at the time of writing, the coverage of topics under the general heading of work orientations is a broad one that gives scope for students from a variety of disciplines to find material that is both relevant and of personal interest. The data also contain a comprehensive set of background information on the respondents, including basic demographic details such as: age; educational qualifications; social class, social standing and income; marital status and household characteristics; religion and ethnicity; and political orientation. The 2005 module was the third time that the ISSP had investigated orientations to work (previous Work Orientations modules having been in the field in 1989 and 1997). The module was drafted by a team from Israel, Germany, Hungary, Japan, South Africa and Venezuela. Thirty-one countries and provinces carried out the survey, generating datasets for: Australia; Germany; Great Britain; the United States; Hungary; Ireland; Norway; Sweden; the Czech Republic; Slovenia; Bulgaria; Russia; New Zealand; Canada; the Philippines; Israel; Japan; Spain; Latvia; France; Cyprus; Portugal; Denmark; Switzerland; Flanders; Finland; Mexico; Taiwan; South Africa; South Korea; the Dominican Republic.

You should note that the datasets have been adapted from the ISSP for teaching purposes and changes have been made to make them suitable for student use. To make the data more easily accessible for the novice, we have simplified some of the codings, particularly the missing values codes. In addition, in order to widen the scope of potential analyses that can be carried out, we generated a significant number of attitude scales and indices of social standing that are not in the original ISSP datasets. Information about the meanings of these additional variables and how to interpret them can be found in Appendix 1 at the back of the textbook. We must reiterate that while these data are of high quality and are taken from the complete surveys that generated them, these datasets, particularly the new scalar variables, have been generated solely for teaching purposes. Academics wishing to make use of the ISSP data for research purposes *must* access the original ISSP datasets.

Obtaining the practice datasets

As you can see, the practice ISSP Work Orientation datasets are an important feature of this book. We have exploited the global spread of the ISSP and created practice datasets for each of the 31 countries that participated in the 2005 survey. Each country has two versions of the dataset: (1) a full version that contains all the variables and all the respondents to the survey in that nation, and (2) an abridged version that contains approximately 45 variables and information on no more than 1500 respondents. (The reason for the abridged version is that SPSS has a special 'student version' of the package that is available at a much reduced price. It contains all the essential features of SPSS but is limited to no more than 50 variables and no more than 1500 cases and will cease to work four years after the purchase date. We are aware that many students and institutions will be operating with reduced resources and may only be able to use SPSS's student version and we wanted to maximize access to the data.)

Additionally, it is also possible to obtain a teaching version of the complete ISSP international dataset for all 31 countries. This will be particularly useful if your main interest is in comparative analyses between nations. However, please note that as this is a very large dataset containing more than 350 variables and over 43,000 cases, not all computers will be able to cope.

Either way, you will need to have a dataset on your computer before you can begin to work your way through the modules and exercises in this textbook. You obtain the datasets by downloading them directly from the Palgrave/Macmillan website located at: www.palgrave.com/sociology/miller2e. Detailed instructions for selecting a dataset and downloading it are given on this website. Alternatively, the instructor on your course may have obtained the datasets in advance and set them up for student use. If so, your instructor will tell you how to access the datasets at your institution. Instructors wishing to download the datasets and install them for teaching purposes on systems within their institutions have our permission to do so. This may be the most practical way of providing the datasets when student access to computing facilities and SPSS is through a central server.

INTRODUCTION TO THE WORKBOOK

This workbook has been designed as a step-by-step guide to data analysis using SPSS. It comprises 2 introductory chapters and 11 substantive modules which together serve to acquaint the reader with the key aspects of statistical analysis and data modification using SPSS. We began by examining the main features of the 'quantitative perspective' and considered some of the strengths (and weaknesses) of this approach to social research. The current chapter adopts a much sharper focus and its main purpose is to provide a brief introduction to some of the basic features of SPSS and the Windows environment within which this version of SPSS operates.

Subsequent chapters fit into a modular structure and take the reader through the various stages of quantitative analysis using SPSS, including data input, data modification, data exploration and statistical testing. The general pattern is for each module to focus on a single statistical procedure, beginning with an explanation of its underlying logic. This is followed by step-by-step instructions for the successful execution of the procedure using SPSS, and the resulting SPSS output is reproduced in the form of tables or charts and carefully analysed and explained. This structure should enable students to complete the modules successfully with minimum supervision and the exercises at the end of each chapter will help to consolidate learning.

INTRODUCTION TO SPSS FOR WINDOWS

This workbook is based upon the personal computer version of SPSS, and has been written specifically for users of Version 16 and 17. SPSS is a computer software program that is designed to perform statistical operations and facilitate data analysis and is by far the most popular statistical package used by social scientists today. It is worth pointing out at this stage that one of the best sources of information and help about SPSS and its various functions is literally at your fingertips, and can be accessed through the comprehensive **Help** menu within the SPSS program. Some of the important features of this Help Menu include the following.

The online tutorial

This is an excellent resource for novices as it adopts a clear step-by-step approach and provides a hands-on introduction to the most important features of SPSS. It is also a good idea to return to these tutorials when you become more familiar with the package as they are a useful tool for the consolidation of learning.

Case studies

The Case Studies section on the Help facility provides realistic hands-on examples of the various forms of statistical analysis available in SPSS. There is a strong emphasis on analysis and interpretation and the case studies are designed to allow students to work through statistical problems at their own pace.

The statistics coach

The Statistics Coach section on the Help facility provides some basic assistance with many of the statistical procedures available in SPSS. For more detailed statistical explanations you are advised to consult the SPSS applications guide or any good introductory statistics text.

The contextual help system

Available on earlier versions of SPSS until 16.0, this provides information on specific features. Pointing the mouse at the feature or control you want to know more about and clicking the right mouse key activates this help facility.

GETTING STARTED ON SPSS

The SPSS program (assuming, of course, that it is installed on your computer) is accessed by clicking on the **Start** button situated on the bottom left-hand side of the computer screen and selecting **SPSS** from the **Programs** menu.

(You should note that the menu system may be configured slightly differently on the computer you are using and therefore the location of SPSS may not be identical to that illustrated in Figure O.1a.)

Start button   Task bar

Figure O.1a *Starting SPSS*

This will start SPSS (the SPSS icon will appear in the Windows Task bar at the bottom of the screen) and the Data Editor window will open up automatically.

Once opened, there are a number of ways to begin using the SPSS package. The opening dialog box (shown in Figure O.1b) offers six options and you can proceed by clicking on the required option button and then on OK.

It is worth pointing out that this dialog box may not always appear when you open SPSS (for example, if the previous user has clicked on the **'Don't show this dialog box in the future'** option). However, all of the options available in the opening dialog box can be accessed through the SPSS menu system.

The opening dialog box can also be removed by clicking on **Cancel** and, as we want to take a closer look at the data editor window, you can do this now.

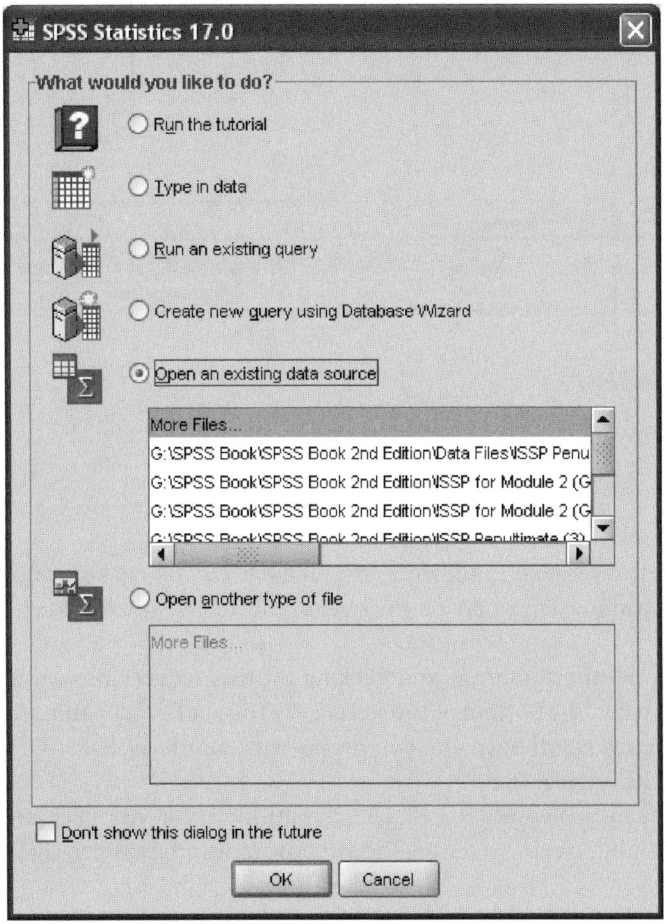

Figure O.1b   *SPSS for Windows 'opening dialog box'*

The Data Editor window is blank at this stage and contains no data (see Figure O.2). You will need to become familiar with the window in Figure O.2 if you are to navigate around SPSS successfully and some of its main features are explained below.

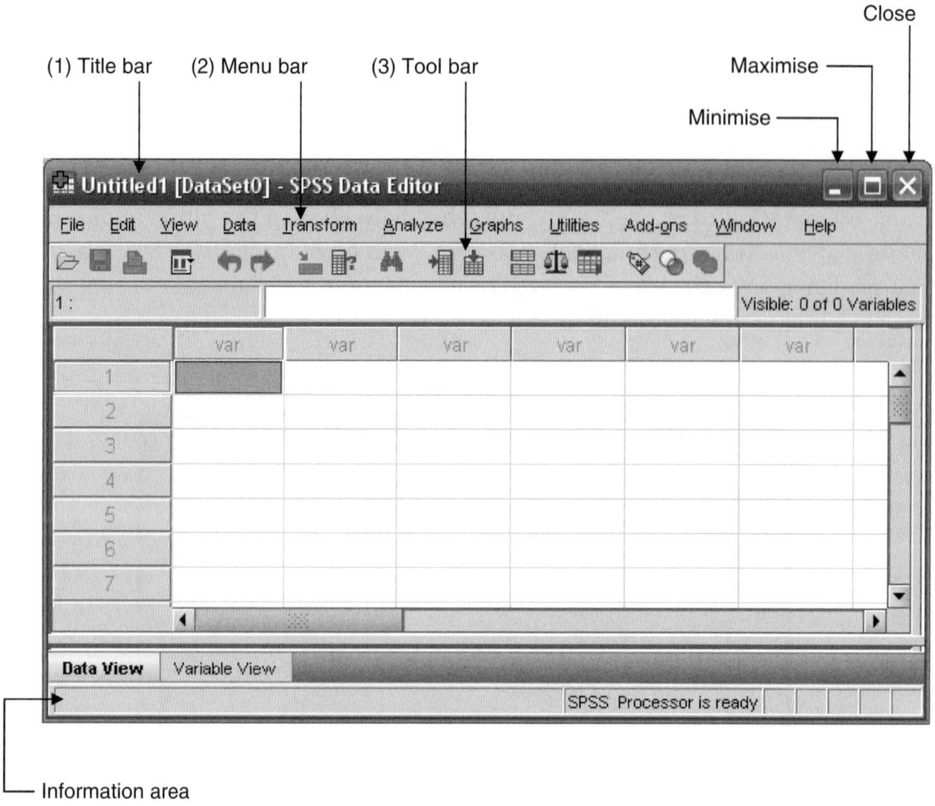

Figure 0.2   *Blank Data Editor window (data view)*

(1) The Title bar

The top section of the window is known as the title bar and by clicking and dragging on this you can reposition the window anywhere on the screen. On the right-hand side of the title bar are three small squares.

■ The first is the Minimize button and clicking on this reduces the window to an icon in the Windows Task bar at the bottom of the screen. Try this, but don't panic when the window disappears. This window is still open and you simply click on the SPSS icon in the Windows Task bar to restore it to its original size.

■ The second square represents the Maximize button and if you click on this the Data Editor window will fill the screen. To restore the window to its original size click on the second square again.

■ Clicking on the third square in the top right-hand corner of the Data Editor window closes the SPSS program down altogether. If you have made any changes to the dataset or produced any output you will be asked if you want to save them (more on saving SPSS files later in this chapter).

You can also resize the Data Editor window by clicking and dragging the sides or the corners of the window.

(2) **The Menu bar**

Underneath the Title bar you will find the Menu bar, which is the primary means of getting SPSS to carry out the tasks and procedures you require.

As can be seen from Figure O.2, the Menu bar contains 11 broad menu headings, beginning with **File** and ending with **Help**. If you click the mouse on any of these headings a variety of options relating to this topic will appear in a drop-down menu. Figure O.3, for instance, displays the **Edit** drop-down menu. To hide the drop-down menu again, simply click anywhere outside it.

A brief synopsis of some of the main functions associated with each of these menus is appropriate at this stage.

File – This menu includes facilities for creating, opening, closing, saving and printing files.

Edit – This menu is used if you want to cut, copy or paste items, either within SPSS or from SPSS to other programs such as Word. It also allows you to change some of the default settings in SPSS and provides a facility for locating particular cases or variables.

View – The View menu allows you to alter various features of what you see in the window. For example, in the Data editor window you are given the option of displaying value labels rather than number codes or removing grid lines.

Data – This menu allows you to manipulate the dataset in various ways. You can weight the dataset, insert additional variables or merge two datasets together via this menu. Also available in this menu is the facility for selecting out a subset of the data.

Transform – This menu contains facilities for transforming and modifying the dataset, including **Recode**, **Compute** and **Count** (these data modification procedures are explained in detail in Module 3).

Analyze – The Analyze menu is where the various forms of statistical analysis available in SPSS are located. We will be examining many of these statistical procedures in the course of this book.

Graphs – The Graphs menu provides a range of facilities to enable you to create various charts and graphs.

Utilities – The Utilities menu includes a number of useful tools, including facilities for creating smaller subsets of the data. Complete information about all the variables in the dataset can also be accessed through the Utilities menu.

Window – This menu allows you to switch between different windows (for example, between the Data Editor window and the Viewer window).

Add-ons – This relates to a variety of additional modules, applications and services. These include Predictive Service Enterprises, Neural Networks, Amos and Clementine.

Help – The Help menu provides a comprehensive range of information and help on various aspects of the SPSS package (see above for a brief summary of some of the main features of the Help menu).

(3) The Toolbar

The Toolbar in SPSS is located just below the Menu bar and, like the Toolbar in other Windows-based applications, provides a number of shortcuts for commonly used procedures or tasks. For instance, the first three icons in the Data Editor Toolbar perform the functions of opening a file, saving a file and printing a file. If you roll the mouse pointer over any of the icons in the toolbar a brief description of the function it performs will appear directly underneath the icon (and also in the information area at the bottom left-hand side of the screen). Do not click the mouse unless you want to carry out the procedure in question!

SOME MINOR ADJUSTMENTS TO SPSS

Before we proceed any further there are a couple of changes that we recommend you make to the default options in SPSS. You will find that resetting these options has two main advantages: (a) variables will be much easier to locate; (b) the results of your analysis will be labelled more fully. Moreover, you should find this book easier to follow if your SPSS settings are identical to ours.

1. **Resetting Variable Lists**

Before you carry out any kind of analysis in SPSS you need to select the variables you are interested in from a list of all the variables in your dataset. This selection process is much easier if the variables are displayed **alphabetically**, using **variable names** rather than variable labels. However, in order to achieve this we need to change the '**Variable Lists**' default options.

Click on **Edit** to open up the Edit drop-down menu (see Figure O.3) and select **Options** by clicking on it.

This will open up the Options dialog box shown in Figure O.4. Click on the **General** tab to ensure that the '**Variable Lists**' options are displayed and then select **Alphabetical** and **Display names** by clicking on them. Finally click on **OK**.

The effect of these changes can be observed in Figure O.9 and you will notice that variable *names*, rather than variable labels, appear in the variable list and these are ordered *alphabetically* (see Module 1 for more details on the distinction between variable names and variable labels).

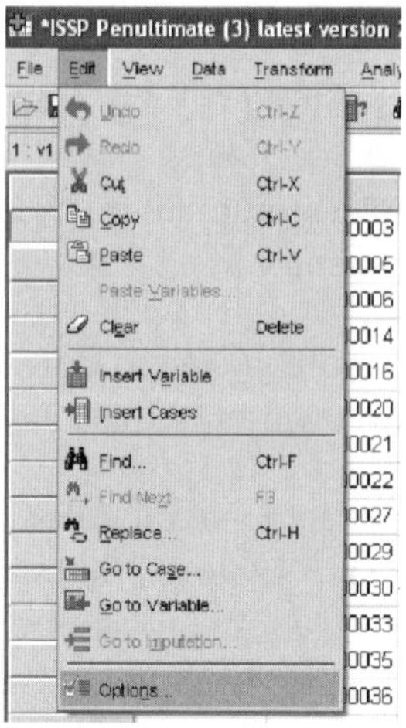

Figure O.3   *Edit: Options*

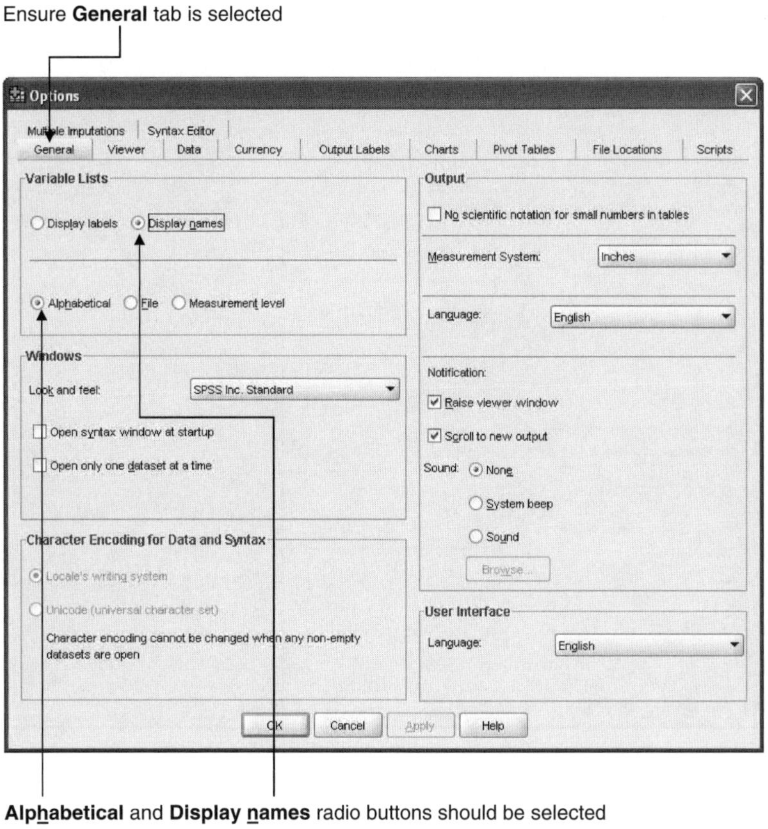

Ensure **General** tab is selected

Alpha**betical** and **Display names** radio buttons should be selected

Figure O.4 *Edit: Options dialog box*

2. Resetting Output Labels

The second change we want to make to the SPSS default settings relates to the output or results of our analysis. In general, we want our results to contain as much information as possible about the variables used. We therefore need to change the output settings in SPSS so that our output includes the variable names and labels as well as the category codes (values) and their labels.

Click on **Edit** to open up the Edit drop-down menu (see Figure O.3 again) and select **Options** as before.

This time, however, we need to click on the **Output Labels** tab in the Options dialog box and then change the settings in the four boxes to either **Names and Labels** or **Values and Labels** (see Figure O.5).

These adjustments to the output labels will take effect immediately and when you come to produce your first frequency table (see Module 2) your output should contain not just the variable names and category codes, but also a description of what these represent (i.e. variable and value labels).

LOADING A DATA FILE

So far we have been looking at a Data Editor window which contains no data. There are two main ways of rectifying this situation. The first is to create a data file by inputting your own data (this process will

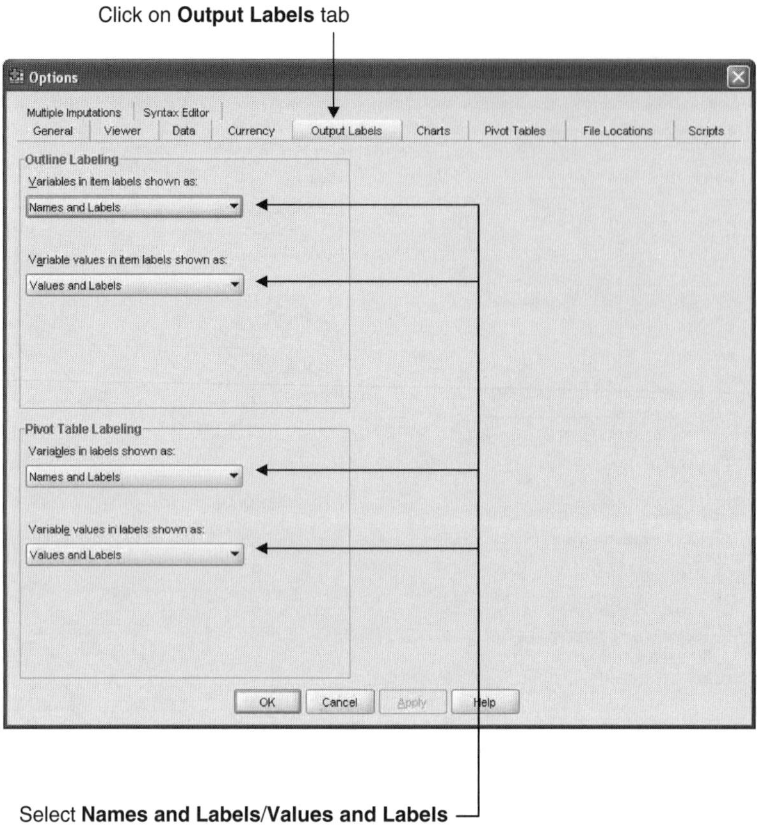

Click on **Output Labels** tab

Select **Names and Labels/Values and Labels**

Figure O.5   *Edit: Options: Output Labels dialog box*

be examined in detail in Module 1), while the alternative option is to open a previously created SPSS data file. Here we will go through the steps for opening an already existing SPSS data file, the ISSP dataset. (NOTE: Detailed instructions for selecting a dataset and downloading it are given on the Palgrave/Macmillan website located at: www.palgrave.com/sociology/miller2e).

First, click on **File** from the Menu bar and then select **Open** from the drop-down menu (see Figure O.6). This will give you the option of opening different types of files. As we want to open a data file, click on **Data**.

This will bring up the Open File dialog box (see Figure O.7). You now need to select the appropriate location of the SPSS file you wish to open (i.e. the relevant directory and folder).

For example, I have saved the **ISSP** dataset in a folder entitled SPSS Data Files. To open this dataset I simply locate the SPSS folder and double click on the icon next to the ISSP dataset, as illustrated in Figure O.7.

After a few moments the Data Editor window will reappear, but this time complete with the ISSP data (see Figure O.8). It is important to note that the data editor provides two different views of the data: the *data view* and the *variable view*. The data view displays the actual data values (or value labels) in a spreadsheet format, while the variable view displays variable information including variable and value labels, level of measurement and missing values (see Module 1 for more details on these). You can switch between these two views by clicking the data view and variable view buttons at the bottom left-hand corner of the screen (see Figure O.8).

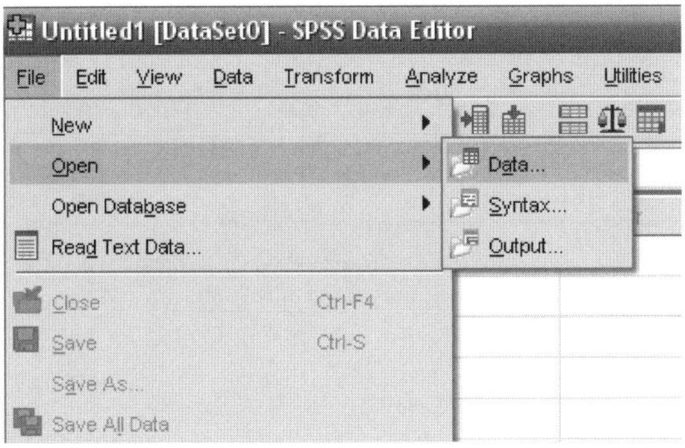

Figure O.6 *Opening a data file*

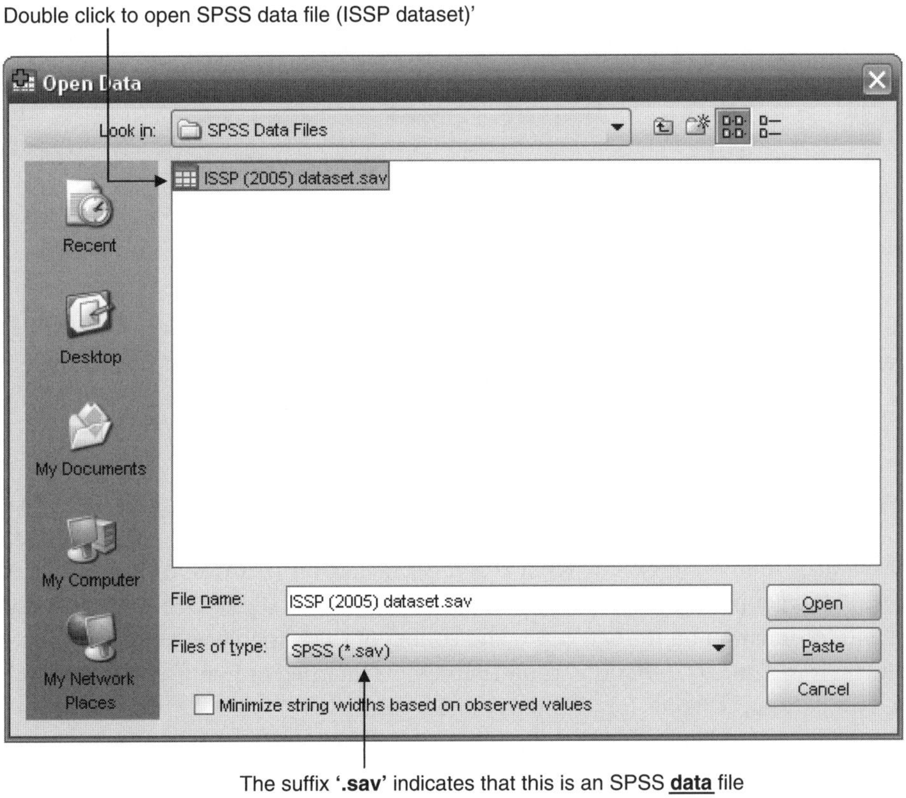

Double click to open SPSS data file (ISSP dataset)'

The suffix '**.sav**' indicates that this is an SPSS **data** file

Figure O.7 *Open File dialog box*

If you are not currently in the data view, click on the data view button now. You will see that the data grid is now full of numbers (referred to as values) which represent the various responses to the survey questions. A different column is allocated to each variable and a separate row for each case (respondent). As there is far too much information for it all to fit on the screen, we can use the vertical scroll arrows to scroll up or down through the cases and the horizontal scroll arrows to scroll back and forward through the different variables (note that if the image on your screen is not identical to the one in Figure O.8, this may be the reason why).

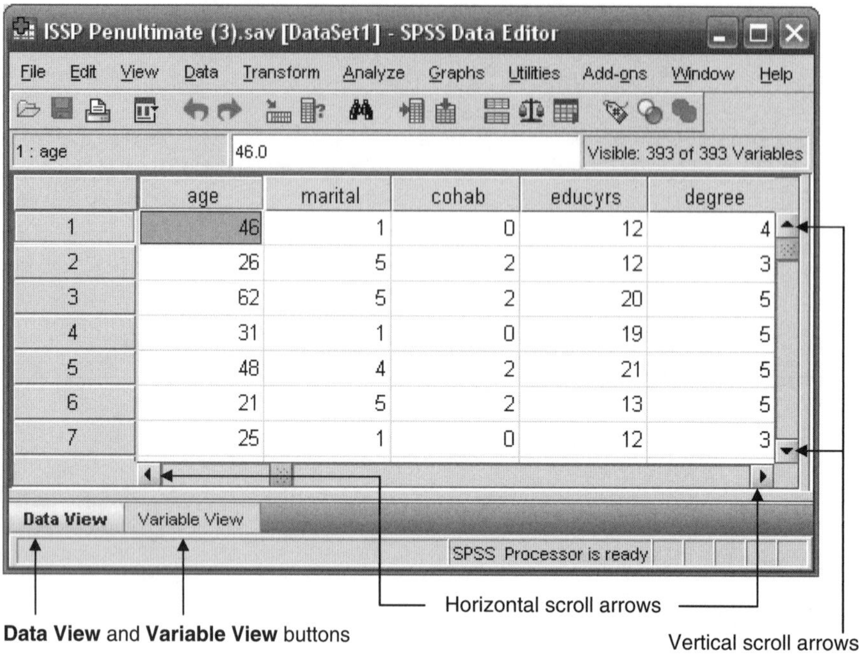

Figure O.8 *Data Editor window*

If we look at the first column in Figure O.8, for instance, we can see that it is labelled **age** (this is a variable that provides us with information on the respondent's age). The first cell in the grid (i.e. the highlighted cell where the first row and the first column intersect) contains the number 46, which informs us that the first respondent is 46 years old. Moving down the first column, we can see that the second respondent is 26, the third 62, the fourth 31 and so on.

However, if we look at the cell immediately to the right of the highlighted cell we see the number 1, which tells us that the first respondent has been allocated a value of 1 on the variable **marital** (respondent's marital status). To find out exactly what this means, click on **Utilities** in the Menu bar and then on **Variables**. This will open up the Variables dialog box, shown in Figure O.9. Click on **marital** in the variable list and information on the categories and coding of this variable will appear in the right hand box. We can see from Figure O.9 that the value 1 represents 'married or living as married', value 2 is the code for 'widowed', value 3 stands for 'divorced', and so on.

Returning to the Data Editor window in Figure O.8, we now know that the first respondent is 46 years old and is married or living as married and the second respondent is 26 years old and single. More importantly, we have drawn attention to a point that needs to be borne in mind as you proceed through this book. That is, for some variables the number values are meaningful in themselves (for instance 46 really does mean 46 years of age), but for others, the values are merely codes for different categories. This issue will be developed in more detail in Module 2 when we look at the concept of 'levels of measurement'.

It is worth noting at this point, however, that SPSS provides a facility for displaying value labels (rather than the actual values themselves) in the Data Editor Window:

Click on **View** in the Menu bar and then click on **Value Labels** in the drop-down menu. As you can see from Figure O.10, the values have now been replaced by labels. You will also notice that some

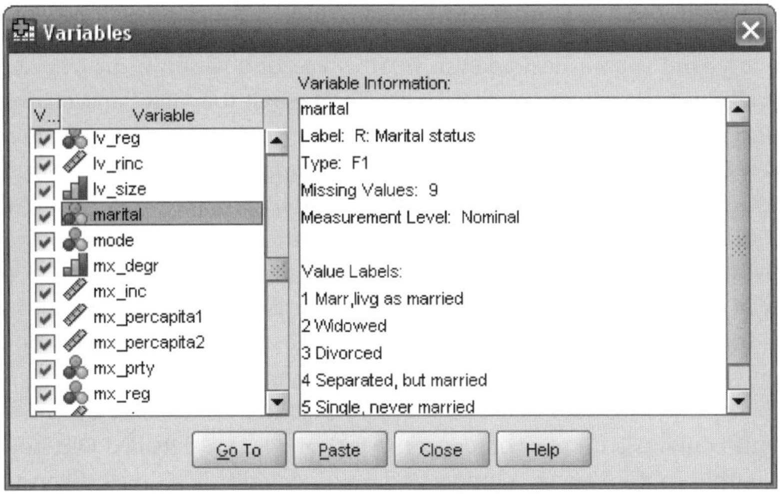

Figure O.9   *Variables dialog box*

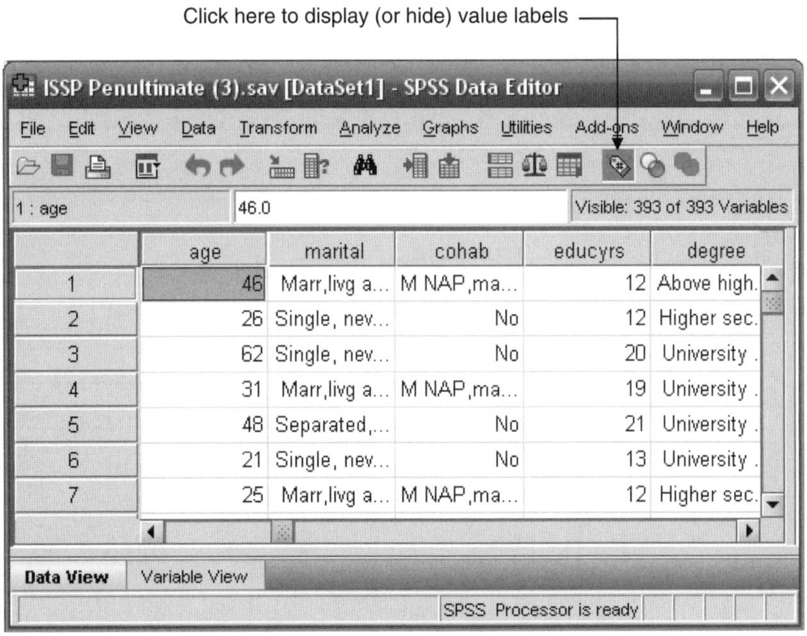

Figure O.10   *Data Editor Window with Value Labels displayed*

variables such as **age** and **educyrs** remain unchanged. Because the values for these 'quantitative' variables are meaningful in themselves there is no need for value labels.

You can also 'switch' the value labels 'on' or 'off' by clicking on the value labels icon in the tool bar.

The viewer window

When you begin any kind of statistical analysis in SPSS a second window, the Viewer Window, opens up. This is where all the output from your analysis is located (all the tables and charts you ask SPSS to produce). The information in the Viewer Window reproduced in Figure O.11 is the outcome of a request that SPSS produce a frequency table and a bar chart for the variable **sex** (detailed instructions on how to get SPSS to produce frequency tables and various charts will be provided in Module 2). As you can see from Figure O.11, the top part of this window is almost identical to the Data Editor window, while the bottom part is divided into two sections or **panes**. The pane on the left is known as the outline pane and this contains an outline view or summary of all the items that are included in the viewer. The right-hand pane is the display pane (sometimes referred to as the contents pane) and contains the output itself, although only part of this output is visible at any one time. To gain a better understanding of how the Viewer window operates we need to examine Figure O.11 in a bit more detail.

The outline pane contains a number of icons, the first of which is labelled Output. This is the container for all the output in the Viewer Window and if you double click on this icon the entire output disappears (double click on it again and it returns).

The third icon in the outline pane in Figure O.11 is labelled Frequencies and this refers to the statistical procedure we requested SPSS to carry out. All the other icons in the outline pane are represented by book symbols and relate to the different parts of the output which appear in the display pane.

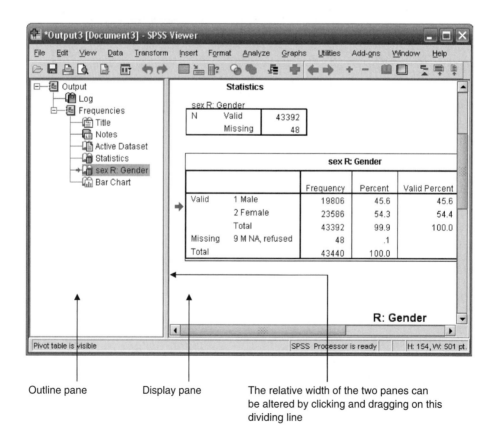

Figure O.11   *Viewer window*

The first of these book symbols is the log file which contains syntax commands relating to the Frequencies procedure (for a detailed discussion of SPSS syntax see Appendix 1). The icon labelled 'Title' simply refers to the title of the output. This is not visible in the Display pane in Figure O.11 because the output has been scrolled down to the middle of the table. The icon below this is entitled Notes and refers to technical information associated with the procedure. Such information is usually hidden from view and the closed book symbol confirms this. Double clicking on a closed book symbol reveals the information (the output appears in the display pane) and double clicking on an open book symbol conceals it. The next icon is labelled Statistics and refers to a table which reports the number of cases produced by the Frequency procedure we carried out on the **sex** variable. We can see from the display pane that there are 43,392 valid responses, 48 missing values and 43,440 cases in sum.

The penultimate icon in the outline pane relates to the frequency table for the sex variable. The arrow to the side of this icon (and the fact it is highlighted) indicates that the output associated with it is currently the focus of the display pane. Clicking on any of the other book icons will shift the focus of the display screen to their associated output. The different elements of a frequency table will be examined in detail in Module 2. The final icon in the outline pane represents the bar chart for **sex** and the title of this chart is just visible in the display window shown in Figure O.11.

SAVING TO A DISK

One of the most important things you will need to know before you begin analysing data is how to save SPSS files. While there are many different types of SPSS files, the two you are most likely to want to save are data files and output files. If you are using SPSS in a centralized computer facility you may not be able to save onto the hard drive or server and should therefore ensure that you have an alternative method of storage (e.g. a USB device) before you begin.

Saving your SPSS files

Under normal circumstances you will not need to save the data file. This is automatically saved in its original form when you exit from SPSS. However, if you have made any modifications to the data file you may want to save these for later use (see Module 3 for examples of the kinds of modifications that SPSS allows you to perform on the data).

To protect the original version of the data you should save the modified version under a different name. The procedures for saving a **data** file are as follows:

Ensure that the Data Editor window is the active window (that is, it should be the front window on the screen and you should be able to see the data grid unobstructed). Then click on **File** in the Menu bar and on **Save As** in the drop-down menu (see Figure O.12).

This will open up the **Save Data As** dialog box shown in Figure O.13. Select the appropriate drive, give the output file a name (different from the original name in order to prevent the old version from being overwritten), and click on **Save**. Saving your SPSS data file in this way means that your current working version of the data file will be preserved.

Saving your output file

Saving output when you exit SPSS

In addition to saving the SPSS data file you may also want to save the results of your SPSS analysis (the various tables and charts that you produce during a session). If you have created any output at all

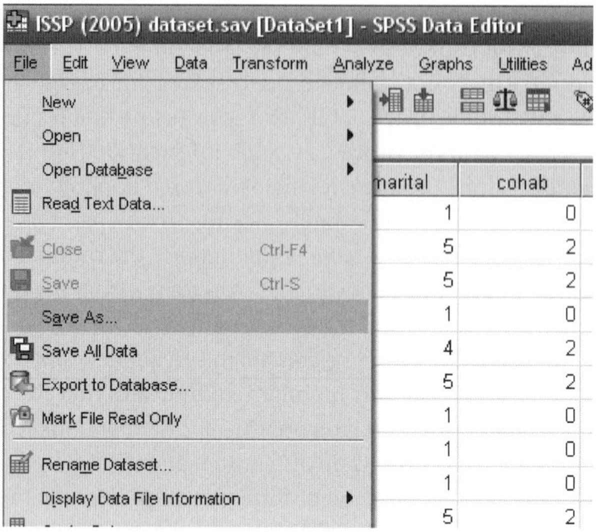

Figure O.12 *Saving a data file*

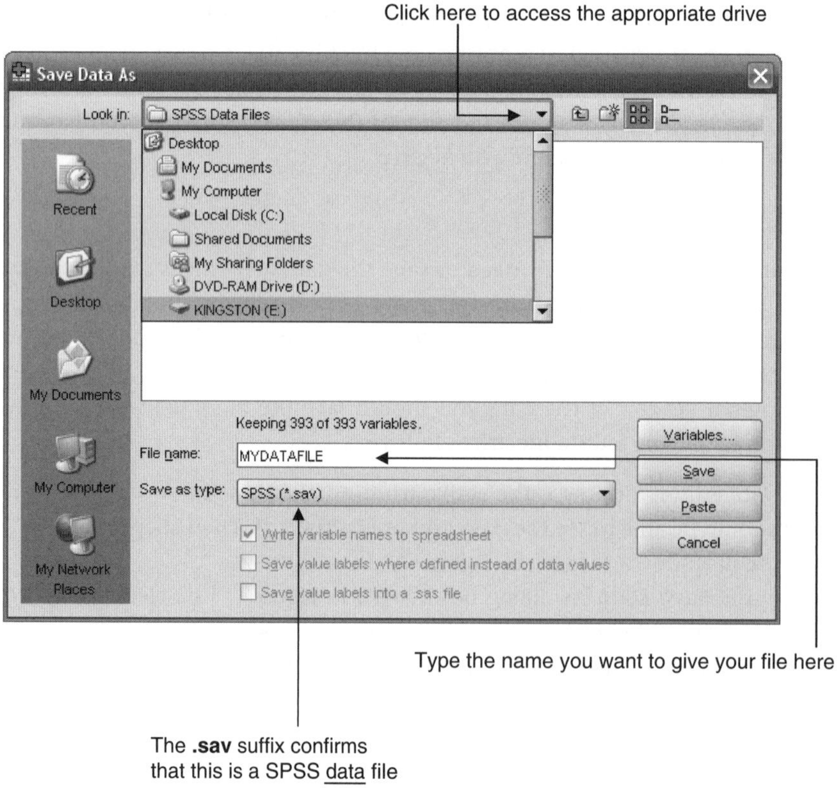

Click here to access the appropriate drive

Figure O.13 *Save Data As dialog box*

Type the name you want to give your file here

The **.sav** suffix confirms
that this is a SPSS <u>data</u> file

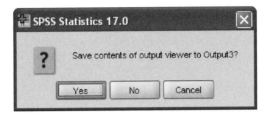

Figure O.14 *Save output prompt*

during a session, SPSS will produce the following prompt (see Figure O.14) when you go to close down the program:

Click **Yes** to open up the **Save As** dialog box. This is almost identical to the Save Data As dialog box (see Figure O.13) and the same procedures are followed to save the output file. So you need to select the appropriate drive, give the output file a name, and click on **Save**. Saving your output in this way means that all the output that appears in the Viewer Window will be saved.

If you want to be more selective you can edit out the unwanted tables or charts in the Viewer Window and save directly from there. The easiest way to delete tables and charts from your output is via the outline pane (see Figure O.11 again). Simply click on the relevant icons (those relating to the unwanted output) in the outline pane to highlight them and press the delete key on your keyboard. Note that by clicking on the appropriate icons in the outline pane you can highlight whole sections of output or even the complete contents of the output window in one go. For example, by clicking on the icon labelled 'Output' at the top of the outline pane (see Figure O.11) you can select all your output at once. When you have edited the output to your satisfaction, click on **File** in the menu bar of the Viewer window (make sure it is the Viewer window and *not* the Data Editor window) and then **Save As** from the File drop-down menu. This will bring you to the Save As dialog box and the remaining steps are the same as above.

PRINTING YOUR SPSS OUTPUT

Before you print it is vitally important to check that the **Viewer window** is the active window and *not* the Data Editor Window. **DO NOT PRINT** if the Data Editor window is to the front of your screen, otherwise you will print the complete dataset with serious repercussions for the world's rainforests, not to mention your printing costs!

You should edit your output before printing to ensure that you do not print out unwanted charts or tables. Alternatively, you can use the outline pane of the Viewer window to select only those parts of the output that you want to print.

To print, click on **File** in the menu bar of the Viewer window and then select **Print** from the File drop-down menu. The Print dialog box (shown in Figure O.15) will then open up.

If you have used the outline pane to select only part of the total output, the **Selected output** button will be highlighted (as in Figure O.15). If you click **OK** now, only that part of the output that you selected will be printed. However, if you didn't make a selection the **All visible output** button will be highlighted and clicking **OK** will result in all the output in the display pane being printed.

Finally, if you are using a centralized computing facility a 'queue' may develop as print jobs 'stack up' (especially if several users are trying to print their SPSS output at once). Print jobs can also 'stack up' if

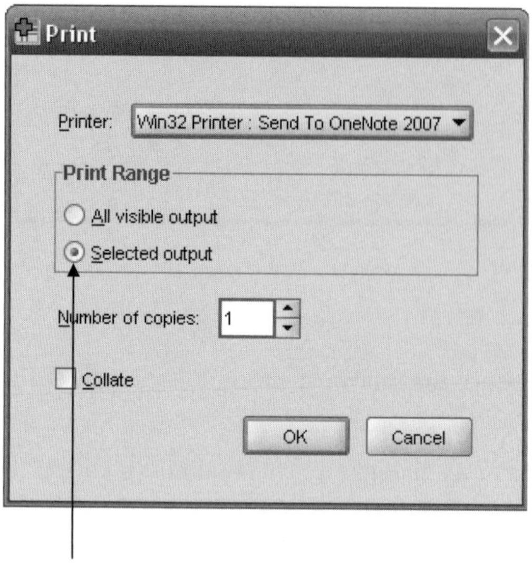

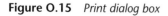

Click here to print selected output only

Figure O.15   *Print dialog box*

the printer is temporarily off-line or if it runs out of paper. If your output does not appear immediately, check to see if your output is waiting to be printed *before* resubmitting a Print command, as every time you do this you are requesting another copy of the output!

Now that you are familiar with some of the basic features of SPSS you should be in a position to begin the first module of this book which deals with the important task of inputting data.

1 Data Input

Raw data can come from a variety of sources. One of the most common data collection methods is the social survey which can be administered using formal interview schedules or self-completion questionnaires, such as the example reproduced at the end of this module. Other forms of data collection include *proforma* (for example, job or college applications) and *personal records*, such as academic transcripts, academic records or a company's personnel records. The possible sources of data can be almost infinite, depending upon circumstances and the ability of the researcher to recognize a source of good data when it presents itself.

In data input to SPSS, the task is to take the information which has been collected (raw data), organize it and move it to a working SPSS data file.

The process of inputting data can be broken into three stages:

- coding,
- the mechanics of transferring coded information into an SPSS file,
- configuring the data within SPSS.

CASES AND VARIABLES

For a computer package to be able to receive information in the form of data, these data must be put into a regular, predictable format.

A complete individual record is usually called a *case*. A short questionnaire is provided as an example at the end of this module and you should fill this in *now*, as it forms the basis of much of the explanation that will follow. Once you have completed it, *you* become a **case** and your responses to this questionnaire make up a single complete **record**. Anyone else who answers the questionnaire would also become a case in the data. (You may find in some manuals that the words 'record' or 'observation' are sometimes used in the place of 'case'.)

Cases, such as survey respondents, personnel records or medical files, often correspond to individual people. Cases, however, can also refer to *organizations* or *timespans*. For instance, in a household survey, the information obtained relates to the entire household rather than to individuals within the house. In these circumstances the case would be the household not the individual. It is also possible to have, for example, a database of hospitals (where each case is the information held on a complete hospital) or a geographically based dataset (where information on complete cities constitutes the cases). A historian might have a database where the cases are timespans – say, decades. The key point here is that, in each instance, the case is the information recorded on a single unit of analysis.

For each *Case*, the specific bits of information recorded for the case are called **Variables**. In the 'Drinking Questionnaire' (located at the end of this module), each separate answer you gave is a response to a variable in the dataset. For instance, **age**, where you said you are *X* years old, is a variable; and your response to Question 5 where you said you **never drink alcohol/drink rarely/drink moderately/drink frequently/drink heavily**, is another variable. Your particular answers to the various questions are the *values* that these variables have for you. A different person answering the questionnaire would give responses to the same questions/variables but their values for those variables could be different. For instance their name, age, faculty and drinking habits are unlikely to be the same as yours.

Some additional examples could be:

- A medical admission being the **case**, with **variables** being things like the cause of admission, the GP who attended, etc.
- If a household was the **case**, **variables** could be things like the number of people living in the house, tenure of housing, household income, the type of heating in the house, etc.

To recap, then, the questions you ask and the information you obtain represent **variables**, the specific answers become **values**, and the people or things you are investigating represent **cases**. It is important that you understand these concepts and appreciate how they relate to one another.

'RECTANGULAR' FORMAT

Computers keep track of the bits of information on cases by always having a variable's information (**codings**) appear in the same location. For most datasets, the data usually appear in what we can call a 'grid' of cases by variables. Each case (or record), makes up one complete row (or line) of data and the variables appear as columns. We can show how this would look for the answers some other respondents gave to the 'Drinking questionnnaire' (Figure 1.1).

Robert's responses to the questionnaire are presented in a row format. Each respondent is given a unique **identifier**. Robert for example has been allocated 001, and Margaret has been allocated 002. The third column contains details of the respondent's gender. The first case, Robert, is male which has the value 1, and the second respondent, Margaret, is female which has the value 2.

All cases reserve 'space' for each variable. In responding to the questionnaire, respondents may not answer all the questions; thus some information may be missing for some variables. For example, someone answering the Drinking questionnaire may not be able to remember how much they spent on alcohol last weekend or might refuse to tell how much they drank. It is important to record these data as **missing**. In some instances it may be that the question is not relevant (*not applicable*). For example, if the respondent did not drink alcohol during the previous weekend (Question 6) they did not need to

001	Robert	1	45	1	3	1	8	3	3	2	30.33
002	Margaret	2	23	2	2	1	2	2	0	0	0.00
003	Fred	1	52	3	2	1	2	0	2	1	4.55
004	Paddy	1	36	5	3	1	26	6	10	0	15.45

Figure 1.1 *Responses to the Drinking Questionnaire in Grid Format*

complete Questions 7 and 8 about types of alcohol consumed and the amount spent. In this instance a '*not applicable*' code might be used for Questions 7 and 8. (We will return to this below.)

> ■ **Exercise:** As an exercise, try transferring *your* responses to the questionnaire on to 'line 5' of the grid in Figure 1.1.

INPUTTING DATA INTO SPSS

It is possible to input data to SPSS in a number of ways. Since the SPSS 'data grid' is in the form of a spreadsheet, the normal conventions for using a spreadsheet apply. This means that data can be brought into SPSS in one of four ways.

1. Imported from SPSS on another computer as an SPSS Portable file (*.por)
2. Imported from *database spreadsheets* (for example, Excel, dBase, Foxpro, Access)
3. Imported from *text files* (ascii files)
4. Entered directly onto the *SPSS Data Editor Window*

Option 1: Importing an SPSS portable file

Often we will want to transfer an SPSS data file from one computer to another. This is accomplished by putting the data file that is to be transferred into a special form – an SPSS **portable file**. The data are read from the portable file and immediately saved as a normal SPSS data file. The reason we do this is that the 'internal architecture' of computers can differ and there is no guarantee that an SPSS data file that works fine on one computer will always work automatically on another. Below we have an example of importing the ISSP dataset. (Note that before you begin, you should have already downloaded the SPSS portable file from the Palgrave website onto the hard disk of your computer. Instructions on how to do this are provided on the Palgrave website: www.palgrave.com/sociology/miller2e)

Click on the **File** menu and select **Open** and then **Data** to obtain the **Open File** dialog box (shown in Figure 1.2a). Go to the '**Look in**' box and locate the ISSP portable file (i.e. whatever drive and folder you saved it to). In the example shown in Figure 1.2a the ISSP portable file has been saved in a folder entitled SPSS Data Files. Open the 'pull-down' menu for **Files of type** and scroll down to select **Portable (*.por)**. Now, highlight the appropriate SPSS portable file (for example, in Figure 1.2a the file is called *ISSP dataset.por*) and when the name appears in the **File name** box, click **Open**.

The imported ISSP data should now fill the grid, but you still need to save it as a standard SPSS data file. You can do this by selecting the **File** menu again and then clicking on **Save As** to open the **Save Data As** dialog box (shown in Figure 1.2b). You need to ensure that the **SPSS (*.sav)** option has been selected in the **Save as type** box and then give the file a name and click **Save**. From now on, whenever you want to analyse the ISSP dataset you will call up this SPSS *.sav file.

Option 2: Importing data from spreadsheets

Those of you that have used a spreadsheet package probably will have noticed that the SPSS 'grid', which consists rows of 'cases' and 'columns' of variables, corresponds to the way a spreadsheet configures data.

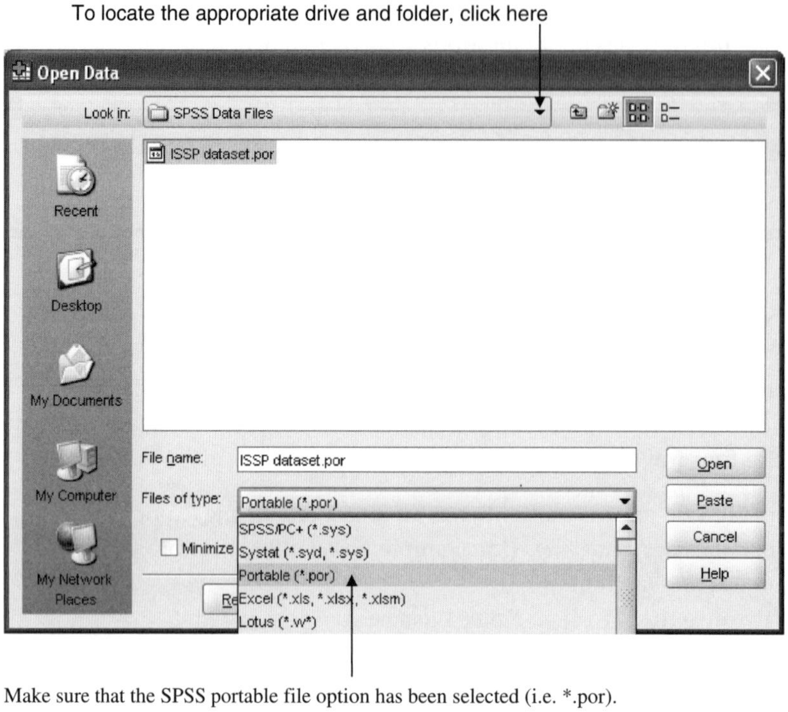

To locate the appropriate drive and folder, click here

Make sure that the SPSS portable file option has been selected (i.e. *.por).

Figure 1.2a *Importing a SPSS portable file **(ISSP dataset)** using **File Open Data***

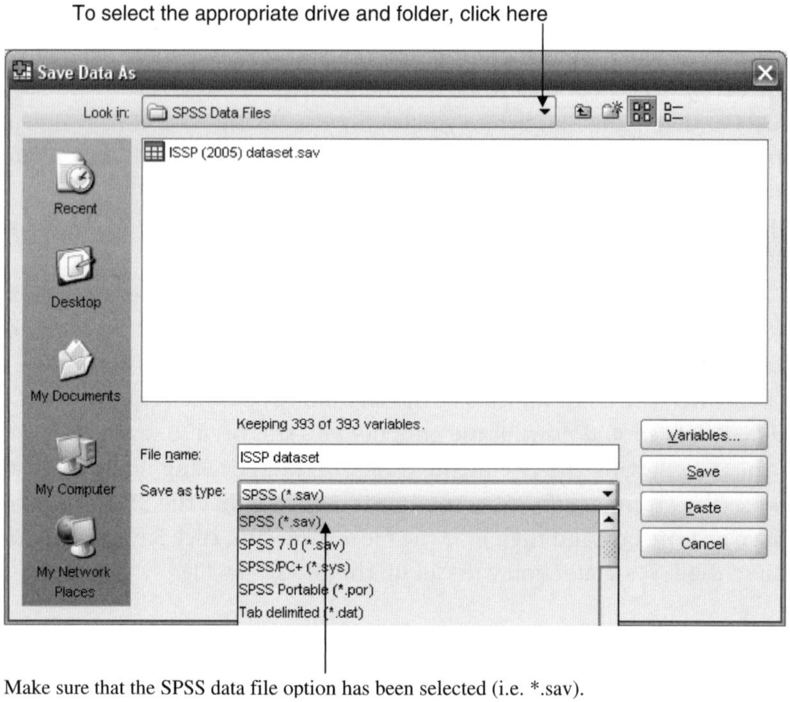

To select the appropriate drive and folder, click here

Make sure that the SPSS data file option has been selected (i.e. *.sav).

Figure 1.2b *Saving an imported SPSS portable file as an SPSS *.sav file*

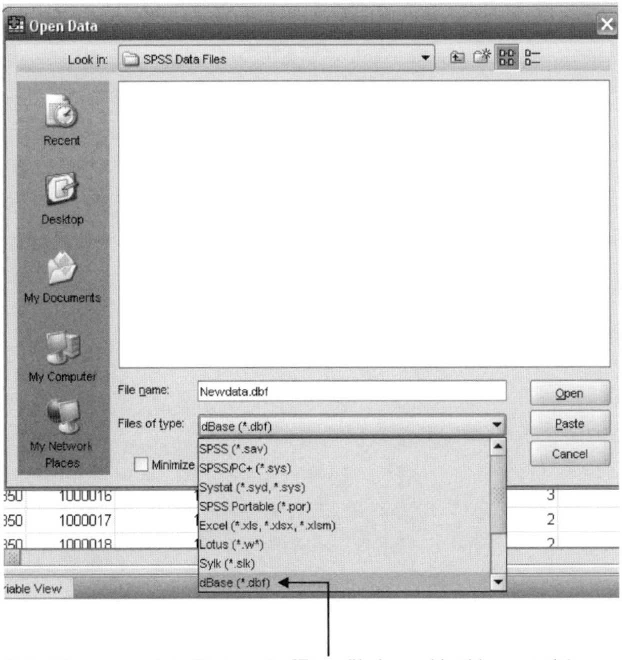

Select the appropriate file type (a **dBase** file is used in this example).

Figure 1.2c   *Importing files **from** other spreadsheets using File Open Data*

Spreadsheet users sometimes find that a convenient way to input data into SPSS is to type the data into your favourite spreadsheet program and then import the data to SPSS. SPSS has facilities for handling data from the more commonly used spreadsheets. It is possible to use the File Open option to import a spreadsheet file. Click on the **File** menu and select **Open** and then **Data** to obtain the **Open File** dialog box (shown in Figure 1.2c). Select the location of the file and the appropriate file type (e.g. here we have selected a **dBase** file called *'Newdata.dbf'*. Finally click **OK**.

Some caution is needed when importing files from different applications. Check if the SPSS version you are using can read the latest version of the database application you want to import. If SPSS cannot read the latest version, save the spreadsheet data using a version which can be read by the SPSS program you are using.

SPSS also provides the option to import database files using the **Database Wizard**. From the **File** menu, select **Open Database** and then **New Query.** This will open the **Database Wizard** (shown in Figure 1.2d) and you can follow a set of step-by-step instructions to introduce a database file into SPSS.

It is also possible to use **Copy** and **Paste** commands to import to and export from SPSS and other spreadsheet applications. To bring a distinct block of data from a spreadsheet into SPSS, simply open the spreadsheet application and, using the cursor to highlight the data block (excluding any headings), click on **Copy** from the **Edit** menu to copy the complete data block. Once you have copied the data, go to the **Data View** window in SPSS (the SPSS data grid), 'drag' your mouse from the upper-left hand corner of the data grid to highlight a block of cells in the grid and **Paste** the data onto the grid. NOTE: for this 'copy and paste' to work, the number of rows and columns highlighted on the data grid must match the number of rows and columns of data that are being taken from the spreadsheet. Once the

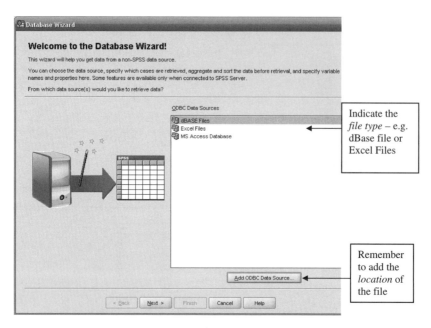

Figure 1.2d *Importing spreadsheet files using the Database Wizard*

data values are safely imported, the variables are labelled using **Variable View** (a detailed explanation of labelling is provided below).

Option 3: Importing text files

Others may have data coming from a non-spreadsheet source. These sources probably will be put into the form of an ASCII file. Basically, here an ASCII file is a grid of rows and columns of raw numbers laid out in a similar manner to a spreadsheet, but without any of the labelling that a spreadsheet grid would have. ASCII files are a form of data that is basic to many different types of computer programs and hence is used as a common means of transferring information between them. SPSS can handle data from an ASCII file quite happily.

Open the main **File** menu and select **Read Text Data**. When you locate your text file the **Text Import Wizard** (shown in Figure 1.2e) will open up automatically and you can follow a set of step-by-step instructions to introduce the data into SPSS.

Option 4: Creating a new SPSS data file

We have looked at a number of ways of importing data into SPSS, but many researchers prefer to enter their data directly to the program's **Data Editor**. In this section we are going to go through the process of creating a new SPSS data file, using the 'Drinking questionnaire' data from Figure 1.1. There are two key stages to this process – entering the data and defining the data. Data entry is relatively straightforward and merely involves typing the coded responses obtained during the data collection process into SPSS. In general these values are numeric, but SPSS is also able to cope with 'string' (non-numeric) variables. Defining the data involves specifying the name, type and other characteristics of each variable and this

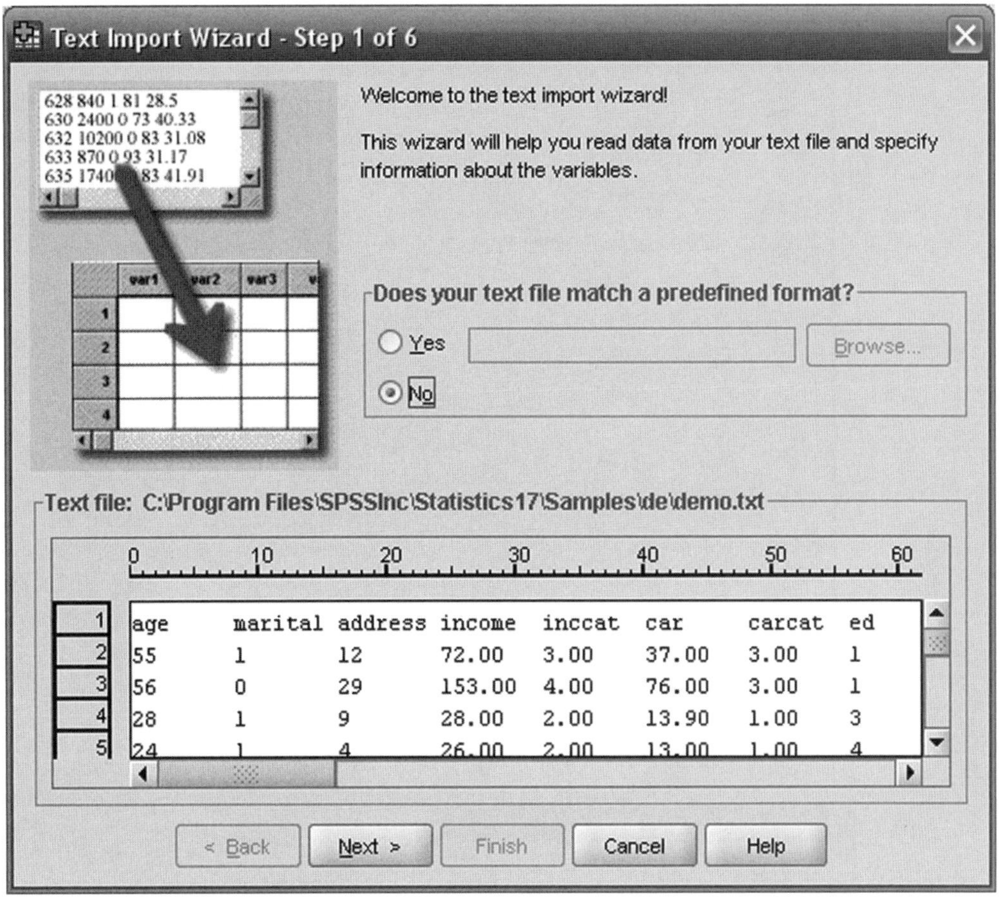

Figure 1.2e   *Text Import Wizard*

process requires a little more thought and preparation. It is a matter of personal preference which stage to carry out first but for the purposes of this exercise we will begin with data entry.

Entering the data

When you start up SPSS the Opening Dialog Box offers a range of options (see Figure1.2f). A new file can be opened by selecting the '**Type in data**' option and clicking OK.

Alternatively, a new data file can be opened by selecting the pull-down **File** menu and clicking on **New** and then **Data**. Both of these alternatives will open an empty file in the **Data Editor** and, as we saw in the Orientation Chapter, this Window offers two alternative views:

■ **Data View** which is the spreadsheet for entering the data (the default format)
■ **Variable View** for naming and specifying the characteristics of variables

To change between the Data View and Variable View formats, click on the tab label on the bottom left hand side of the window.

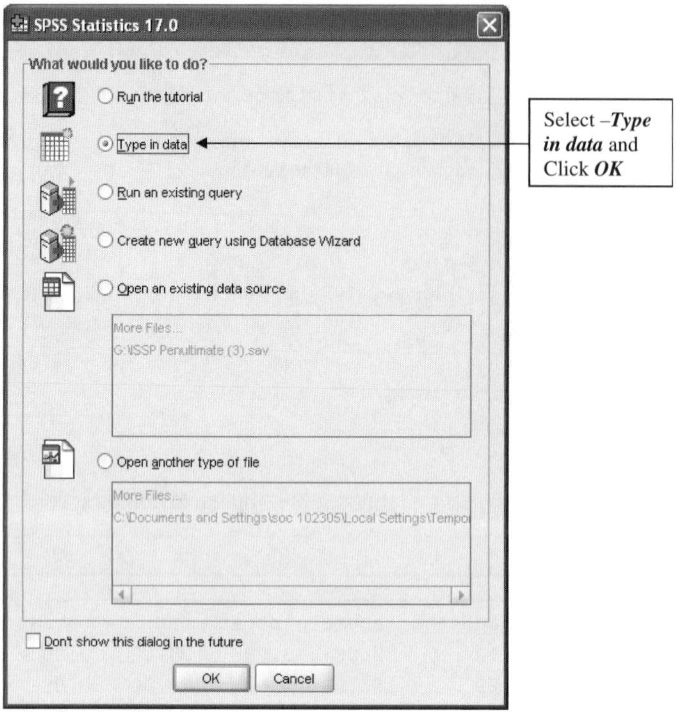

Figure 1.2f   *SPSS Opening Dialog Box*

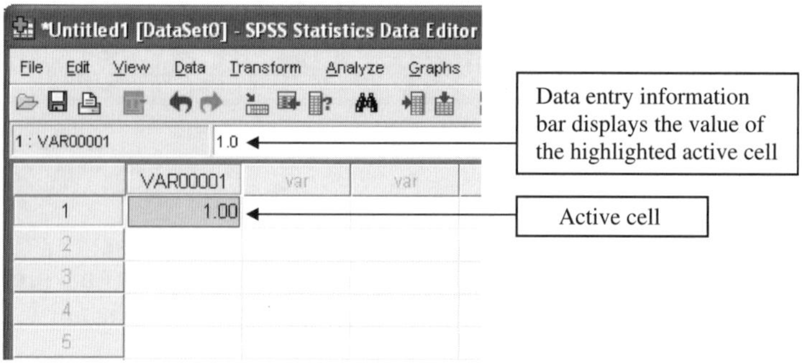

Figure 1.2g   *Data entry directly to Data View Window of the Data Editor*

To enter data using the **Data View** format in the Data Editor window, bring the cursor to the upper left-hand corner of the grid (row 1, column 1). Clicking here will make this the active cell and you can now begin the proces of entering the data from Figure 1.1. Type in the first value (i.e. 001 or 1) and then press the **Enter** key (to move down the column) or the **Tab** key (to move across the row), and the next cell will be highlighted. As you enter data into the cells the value will appear in the data entry information bar above the column headings (see Figure 1.2g).

Enter all of the data from Figure 1.1, including your own responses to the questionnaire, bearing in mind that each **row** represents a case (i.e. an individual respondent) and each **column** represents a variable (i.e. a response to a particular question). If you have entered all of the data corrrectly, the grid in the Data View of your Data Editor Window should now look something like Figure 1.2h.

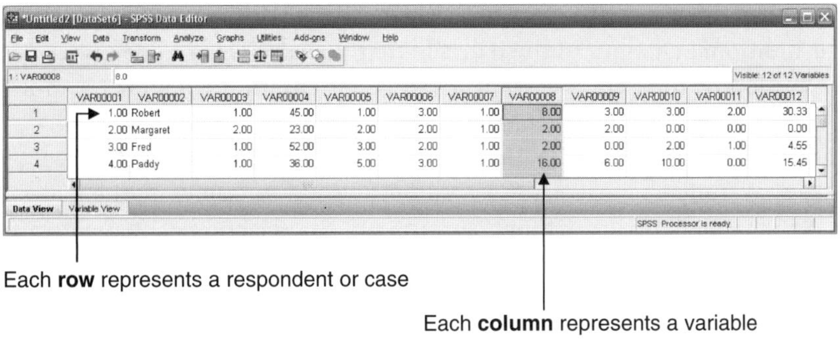

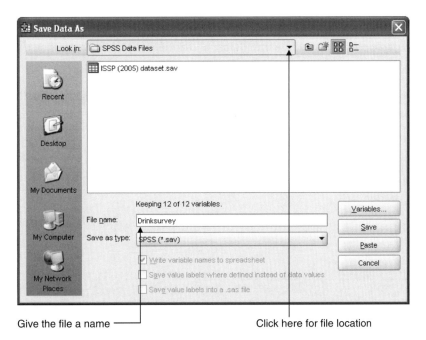

Each **row** represents a respondent or case

Each **column** represents a variable

Figure 1.2h   *Data Entry using the Data View Window of the Data Editor*

Saving the new data file

It is important to **name and save** the new data file you have just created. If you are working with a large amount of material do not wait until you have entered all the data, as computer malfunctions or power cuts can result in lost work. To save the file you must assign a unique name to it, preferably one which clearly identifies the data contained in the file. For example, we might assign the name *drinksurvey* to the file which contains the data from the Student Drinking Questionnaire.

To save this data file, select the **File** menu and click on **Save As**. Then use the Save Data As dialog box to select the drive and the folder that you are going to save the data to. Enter the new name of the file in the **File name** box (see Figure 1.3), and click **OK**.

Give the file a name ——

Click here for file location

Figure 1.3   *Save Data As dialog box*

SPSS will save the data as an SPSS data file (*.sav) as it is at that particular point in time. Later on, if you make additional changes to the data file that you also want to be saved, you will want to save the newer version of the data file again. (See the Orientation Chapter for more details about saving files.)

Be careful that the version of the data file you save is the version you want to keep! For instance, a common mistake that students make is to select a subset of cases (say, only the males in the sample) and then save the data file later on without 'turning off' the selection. The next time they come to analyse the data file, they discover to their consternation that only the selected cases are left! A 'safety net' is to save your later version under a slightly different file name (e.g. VERS2). Then, if you realize you have made a mistake, you can always go back and resurrect the earlier version of the data file; VERS1.

Defining the data

Even though all the data have been entered into SPSS there is still a considerable amount of work to be done before we can analyse the dataset successfully. For instance, it is important to give the variables meaningful names, to assign the appropriate levels of measurement, to allocate variable and value labels, and to declare missing values. We will consider each of these procedures now in the context of the drinking dataset that we have just created.

The first thing we need to do is change the Data Editor to **Variable View**. This allows us to amend information relating to the different variables and, as can be seen from Figure 1.4, the 12 variables (VAR00001 to VAR00012) are now allocated to the rows of the grid and there are ten new columns ranging from 'Name' to 'Measure'. We will go through each of these in turn.

1. Name

SPSS requires that each variable has a unique 'name' that distinguishes it from the other variables in the dataset. These variable names should be intelligible and adhere to the SPSS rules for naming variables.

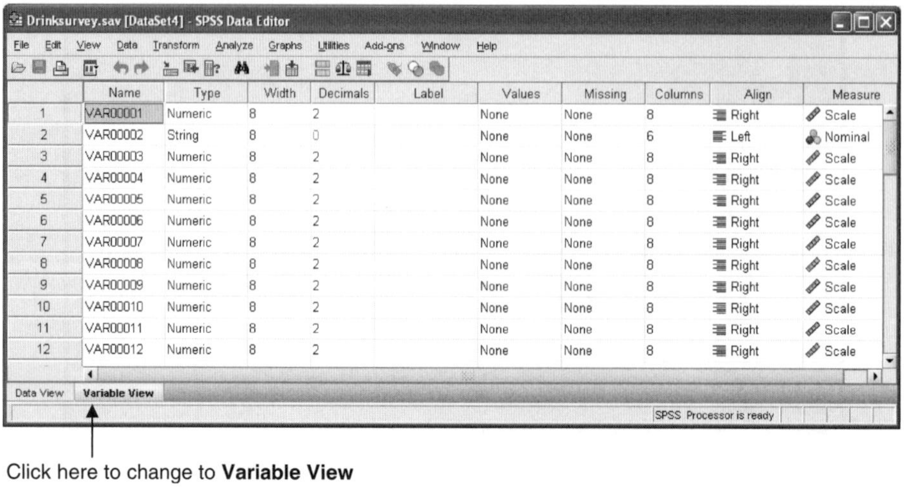

Click here to change to **Variable View**

Figure 1.4   *Data Editor: Variable View*

It is good practice for these **Variable Names** to be one of three types:

- *Self-explanatory* terms stating what information the variable signifies (for example, **Sex, Age, Faculty**)
- *An acronym* that helps jog the researcher's memory about what the variable is (for example, HOH for 'Head Of Household' or DENOM for religious denomination)
- Just a list of letters and numbers in sequence (for example, V1, V2, V3, V4, . . . Vn)

Which is best largely depends upon personal preference and convenience. Some researchers use the question numbers as variable names, for example, **ques1** as a variable name for the first question in a survey.

However, there are some conventions that *must* be followed when assigning variable names in SPSS:

- the variable names must begin with a letter (not a number);
- they cannot have a blank space within the name (for example **DOG DAY** would *not* be acceptable but **DOG_DAY** would);
- a variable name cannot contain special characters (with the exception of $, #, and @);
- a variable name cannot be one of the words SPSS uses as keywords (for example, ALL, AND, BY, EQ, GE, GT, LE, LT, NE, NOT, OR, TO, and WITH);
- a variable name cannot end with a full stop.

SPSS automatically assigns names to variables whenever data are entered but it is advisable to change these to something more meaningful. This is achieved by simply typing over the existing variable name while in Variable View. Do this now for the drink survey data (to make things easier just replicate the names listed in the first column of the SPSS grid shown in Figure 1.5).

2. Type

The second column of the grid in Variable View relates to variable type and the default option in SPSS is 'numeric'. While numbers are normally used to record information, it is possible to enter letters or, more exactly, alphanumeric codes. Sometimes an interview schedule may contain 'open-ended' questions where you might want to record exactly what a person said in response to a question *verbatim* instead of converting this into a number code. There may also be good reason to record respondents' names, and an example of this is provided in the Drinksurvey dataset with the variable '*Name*'. These alphanumeric codes, referred to as string variables in SPSS, cannot be subjected to statistical analysis and for this reason they are fairly rare. They have been mentioned here since you may encounter them, but we recommend that you avoid using string variables if possible.

To change the variable type settings, click on the appropriate cell in the **Type** column and then on the ellipsis (...) when it appears. This will open up the Variable Type dialog box (Figure 1.6) and you can then choose the appropriate variable type.

The number of digits and decimal places (or characters when using string variables) can also be adjusted here. While the default width of 8 is likely to be sufficient for most variables, you should change the decimal places setting to zero for variables that contain only whole numbers. This applies to most of the data in the Drinking questionnaire, with the exception of the final variable (**Money**) where 2 decimal places are required. For instance, Fred answered on the Drinking questionnaire that he spent £4.55 on alcohol last weekend. If we set the decimal places to zero for this variable Fred's answer

Assign **variable names** by typing in the first column, while in Variable View.

	Name	Type	Width	Decimals	Label	
1	ID	Numeric	8	0	Identification number	N
2	Name	String	8	0	Respondent's name	N
3	Sex	Numeric	8	0	Sex of respondent	{
4	Age	Numeric	8	0	Respondent's age	N
5	Faculty	Numeric	8	0	University faculty	{
6	Drink	Numeric	8	0	Type of drinker	{
7	Weekend	Numeric	8	0	Weekend drinker	{
8	Total	Numeric	8	0	Total alcohol consumed at w/end	N
9	Beer	Numeric	8	0	Amount of beer consumed at w/end	N
10	Wine	Numeric	8	0	Amount of wine consumed at w/end	N
11	Spirits	Numeric	8	0	Amount of spirits consumed at w/end	N
12	Money	Numeric	8	2	Expenditure on alcohol at w/end	N
13						
14						

Data View **Variable View**

SPSS Processor is ready

Click here to open **variable type** dialog box

Add **variable labels** by typing in the relevant cell

Figure 1.5 *Data Editor: Variable View ('Name' to 'Label')*

The number of digits and decimal places can be adjusted here

Figure 1.6 *Variable Type dialog box*

would be rounded up to £5 and we would lose important information. It is always better to retain as much detail as possible at the data input stage and leave any recategorization or aggregating until later on in the process. This provides greater flexibiliy and ensures that we can return to the original, more detailed data if required.

3. Width

This column sets limits on the number of digits or characters that a variable's values can contain. The default setting in SPSS is 8 and although this is sufficient for most variables it can be adjusted quite easily by clicking on the appropriate cell in the width column. As we saw in the previous section, width can also be adjusted through the Variable Type dialog box (Figure 1.6).

4. Decimals

Decimals were dealt with earlier, but if you did not make adjustments through the Variable Type dialog box, please do so now. For all the variables in the Drinksurvey dataset (except '**Money**'), set the decimal place to zero by highlighting the appropriate cell in the Decimals column and clicking the down arrow twice. When you have finished the decimals column should be identical to that in Figure 1.5.

5. Labels

The fifth column in Variable View enables us to include fuller details for each variable name by attaching a longer label to it. While some variable names are self-explanatory, others may require more detailed descriptions to help users identify them, particulary with large datasets. For example, we might want to give the variable **Total** (i.e. the survey question which asks respondents *how many alcoholic drinks they had last weekend between 12 noon on Friday and last Saturday night*) a longer label to help us remember what it relates to. To add a variable label, just type it into the appropriate cell of the **Label** column. Do this now for the variables in the Drinksurvey, using the labels shown in Figure 1.5.

6. Values

It is also important to *label each of the number codes* for categorical variables and the **Values** column in Variable View allows you to do this. To illustrate this we will use the **Faculty** variable which relates to Question 4 of the Drinking questionnaire. We can see that this pre-coded question contains six categories – 1 = 'Social Sciences'; 2 = 'Arts'; 3 = 'Science'; 4 = 'Engineering'; 5 = 'Other'; and 9 = 'Not applicable' – and it is important that these labels are produced in any SPSS output.

To add these labels, click on the appropriate cell of the **Values** column (see Figure 1.7) and then on the ellipsis (...). This will open up the Value Labels dialog box (Figure 1.8) where you can add the labels for each of the values. Type in the first number code (i.e. '1') in the **Val**u**e** box, then click on the **L**abel box and type in the relevant label (i.e. 'Social sciences'). Click on the **A**dd button, and the value and its label are entered into the 'work box'. Repeat this for each value (as shown in Figure 1.8), and then click on **OK** to save the labels.

Value labels are not usually applied to quantitative or scale variables (see Chapter 2 for an explanation of the different levels of measurement) as the values here are meaningful in themselves (e.g. if we think of a variable like 'Age', the value 22 is not a code for anything but actually represents 22 years of age). However, it is often necessary to include labels for 'missing values' on these variables (i.e. respondents who have not answered the question for some reason). For example, Questions 7 and 8 of the Student

Values	Missing	Columns	Align	Measure
None	None	8	≣ Right	🖉 Scale
None	None	8	≣ Left	🟤 Nominal
{1, Male}...	None	8	≣ Right	🟤 Nominal
None	-1	8	≣ Right	🖉 Scale
{1, Social ⎸...⎸	9	8	≣ Right	🟤 Nominal
{1, Never dri⬆.	None	8	≣ Right	⣠ Ordinal
{1, Yes}...	None	8	≣ Right	🟤 Nominal
None	99	8	≣ Right	🖉 Scale
None	99	8	≣ Right	🖉 Scale
None	99	8	≣ Right	🖉 Scale
None	99	8	≣ Right	🖉 Scale
None	999.00	8	≣ Right	🖉 Scale

SPSS Processor is ready

Click **here** to open the Value Labels dialog box

Figure 1.7 *Data Editor: Variable View ('Values' to 'Measure')*

Value Labels

Value Labels

Value: 9

Label: Not applicable

Spelling...

Add
Change
Remove

1 = "Social sciences"
2 = "Arts"
3 = "Science"
4 = "Engineering"
5 = "Other"

OK   Cancel   Help

Enter appropriate **value** and **label** and then click **Add**

Click **OK** when all values and labels have been entered

Figure 1.8 *Value Labels dialog box*

Drinking Questionnaire are not applicable to those respondents who answered 'No' to Question 6. This was not the case for any of the four respondents highlighted in Figure 1.1, but it is a strong possibility if the questionnaire is completed by a larger sample that it would include non-drinkers and we should therefore allocate missing value codes (see below for a more detailed discussion of missing values).

Add Value Labels to the remainder of the variables in the Drinksurvey dataset now, using the following labels:

SEX: 1 = Male; 2 = Female

AGE: −1 = Refused

DRINK: 1 = Never drink alcohol; 2 = Drink rarely; 3 = Drink moderately; 4 = Drink frequently; 5 = Drink heavily

WEEKEND: 1 = Yes; 2 = No

TOTAL: 99 = Not applicable

BEER: 99 = Not applicable

WINE: 99 = Not applicable

SPIRITS: 99 = Not applicable

MONEY: 999 = Not applicable

It is important to point out that the longer descriptive labels attached to the short variable names (*Variable Labels*) or to the number codes of variables (*Value Labels*) have no effect whatever on any analysis that SPSS will carry out. The primary function of these labels is to make the output resulting from an analysis easier to interpret. Once these definitions have been added SPSS will automatically print the longer labels next to variable names and values, making the output much easier for you to read and understand.

7. Missing

Although you discovered how to include labels for missing values in the previous section, it is also necessary to 'declare' these codes so that SPSS will treat them as '**missing values**' (see below for a more detailed discussion on missing data). To allocate missing value codes click on the appropriate cell of the **Missing** column and then on the ellipsis (...). This will open up the Missing Values dialog box (Figure 1.9)

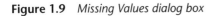

Click here to allocate up to three missing values

Figure 1.9 *Missing Values dialog box*

where you can allocate up to three missing value codes. Click on the **Discrete missing values** button and enter the value(s) that you want to declare as missing.

Very often the same missing values are used across a number of variables and, rather than entering all the individual details, you can copy a format from one variable to another using Copy and Paste. Highlight the cell in which missing values have been declared and copy the format using **Edit** and **Copy**. Move to the cell of the variable you want to copy the format to, and paste the format using **Edit** and **Paste**. This can also be used to copy value labels for variables with the same values and labels such as Likert scales (see Glossary).

8. Columns

This column relates to the width of the columns when data is displayed in the Data Editor. The default setting is 8 characters wide and the width can also be altered by clicking and dragging the column borders in Data View.

9. Align

The alignment column determines the display of data values and labels in Data View. As can be seen from Figure 1.7, *numeric* variables are aligned to the right and *string* variables to the left and it should not be necessary to alter these default settings.

10. Measure

The final column in Variable View allows us to specify a variable's level of measurement. This is dealt with in much more detail in Chapter 2, but it is important to know how to change the level of measurement in SPSS at this stage. 'Scale' is the default setting for all numeric variables. To change this, click on the relevant cell in the 'Measure' column. Then click on the down arrow (shown in Figure 1.10) to reveal the options and select the appropriate level of measurement (Scale, Ordinal or Nominal). Change these now for the variables in the Drinksurvey dataset (to correspond to Figure 1.7) and see Module 2 for an explanation of the different levels of measurement.

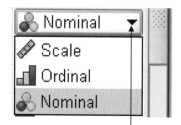

Click **here** to reveal the options for level of measurement

Figure 1.10 *Specifying level of measurement*

EDITING DATA

It is possible to **edit or change** data in an existing data file by locating the data you wish to edit, clicking once on the cell, and replacing the old value in the cell by typing in a new value. You might want to edit data if you discover errors or mistakes in the existing data. Data editing can be done at any time, not just when a new dataset is first being created.

Adding new variables or cases

It is possible to add new variables or cases to a data file. To insert a new case (for instance, a new respondent to a survey) while in Variable View, simply select a cell in the row above which you want to insert the new row. Select the **Edit** menu and click on **Insert Cases** (or simply click on the **Insert Cases icon** on the toolbar). This creates a new row, into which the data can be entered. Altenatively, go to the empty rows at the bottom of the grid and enter the data onto the first empty row.

To insert a new variable (or column), select any cell in the column to the right of which you want the new column. Open the **Edit** menu and click on **Insert Variable** (or click on the **Insert Variable icon** on the toolbar). This creates a new variable, into which new data can be entered. Again, alternatively you can go to the empty columns at the far right-hand side of the grid and enter the data into the first empty column.

Deleting a variable or case

It is also possible to delete a variable or case. To delete a case or row click on the case number on the shaded column in the left-hand side of the file. This will highlight the entire row, then open the **Edit** menu and click **Clear** or press the **Del** key. In the example shown in Figure 1.11 we are deleting Margaret.

To delete a variable or column click on the variable name on the shaded row. This will highlight the entire column, open the **Edit** main menu and delete the column by clicking **Clear** or press the **Del** key. In the example shown in Figure 1.12 we are deleting the variable **Age**.

Validating the dataset

Validation of a dataset is conducted using consistency checks to remove or control errors and missing information in the dataset. It is easy for errors in codings to creep into a dataset from a variety of sources. Before commencing the first real analyses, it is good practice to try to remove as many errors

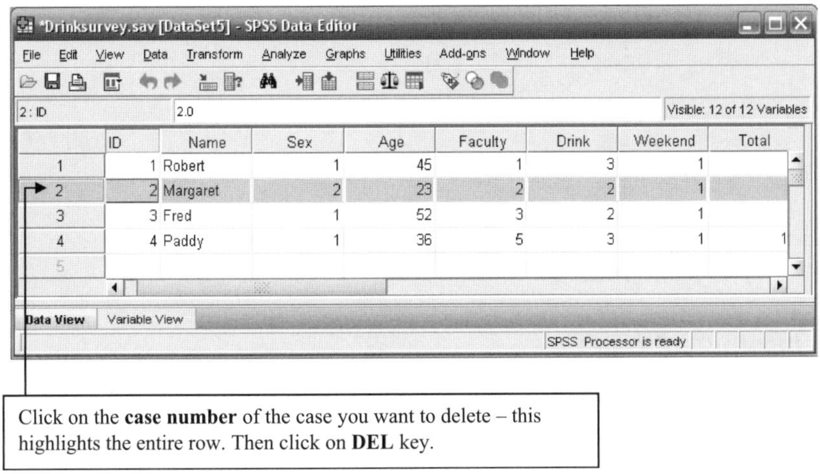

Click on the **case number** of the case you want to delete – this highlights the entire row. Then click on **DEL** key.

Figure 1.11 *Deleting a case*

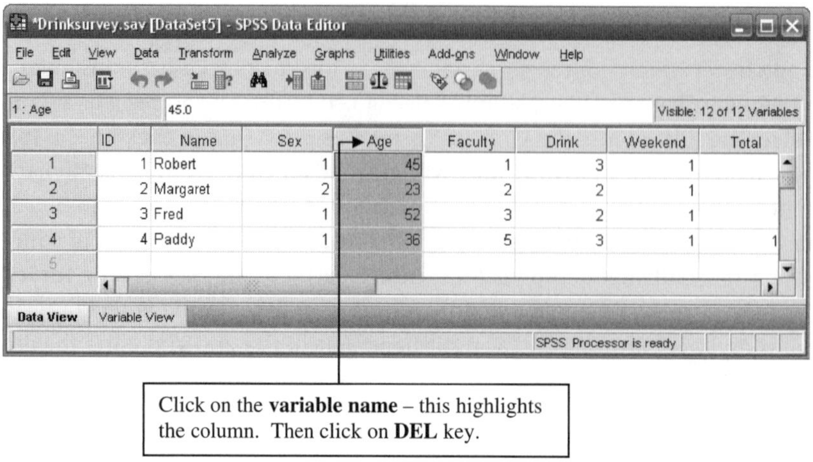

Click on the **variable name** – this highlights the column. Then click on **DEL** key.

Figure 1.12 *Deleting a variable*

as practicable. One efficient means of removing errors is to use the computer package itself to check for errors. Errors can be identified by checking for invalid or inconsistent codes.

Checking for invalid codes

The most obvious validation is to check for incorrect codes by seeking out impossible or invalid values. All possible *correct* code values for a variable are specified. Then, if any codes exist other than the possible values, they must be errors. For instance, if we look at the **Faculty** variable from the Drinking questionnaire we see that the only possible values are within the range 1 to 5 and 9. So, if you found a zero or a 6, 7 or 8 (or any other invalid value), it must be a coding error. These coding errors would have to be kept out of any analysis.

Variable: Faculty, University faculty		
0	*3*	*X*
1	*Social sciences*	55
2	*Arts*	186
3	*Science*	97
4	*Engineering*	131
5	*Other*	4
6	*1*	*X*
9	*Not applicable*	23
Total		500

Checking for inconsistent codes

Sometimes, a particular code or codes for one variable will mean that the codes for another variable must, or must not, fall within a certain range of values – that is, the codings of the two variables, while both are within the range of possible codes, may be *inconsistent* with each other.

For instance, you might do a consistency check with the Drinking questionnaire data to see whether everyone coded as a 1 on the variable **Drink** (that is, everyone who said they *'never drink alcohol'*) *also* has the appropriate codings for the remaining variables. In other words, non-drinkers should not have consumed any alcohol over the previous weekend or spent any money on alcohol. If it appears that a claimed non-drinker has consumed alcohol, an inconsistency exists which should be resolved. This might require going back to the original source of the information in order to trace the reason for the apparent error. If the correct code can be established, the data grid can be edited to replace the error. If a correct code cannot be established, it may be necessary to declare the inconsistent or incorrect code as a missing value.

Software checks on invalid codes

You will note that tracking down the original sources of invalid codings or inconsistencies and then correcting them within the dataset can be a tedious and time-consuming operation, perhaps requiring going all the way back to the original source of the data. It is possible to get around this by using a specialist data entry package which is capable of performing checks for valid values and for inconsistencies between variables *at the point of coding the data*. The data are coded directly and the package is continually checking for out-of-range and/or inconsistent values as they are keyed in. If an invalid or inconsistent value is entered, the error is highlighted on the spot. This allows the coder to check the error against the original source while that original source is in front of them and to repair the damage immediately.

Dealing with missing values

The expression 'missing values' may sound a bit odd to you, but there are many instances where, for only some variables or cases, data may be missing. For instance, our Drinking questionnaire might have a second page where people are asked to tell us about the ill effects they suffer from drinking (hangovers). People who do not drink would not need to answer that section. That is, often a variable will not be coded for some cases because the variable is *'not applicable'* to those cases. Another example could be where only people who live in rented accommodation would answer the question about *'How much rent do you pay?'* or where questions about a person's children would not apply to childless respondents.

Information can of course be missing for other reasons. The information may not be available simply because it is **not known**. A person may **refuse** to answer some questions on a questionnaire or in an interview. Respondents sometimes write illegible answers on a questionnaire or make simple mistakes like inadvertently skipping over some questions or even circling two answers when only one is required. **Errors** may have occurred in the coding or transcription of data so that you know the code is incorrect but you cannot find the correct one.

Regardless of cause, all types of missing data are normally dealt with in the same manner; a special code is applied to each instance of missing information. For example, with the **Faculty** variable on the Drinking questionnaire, the code 9 was used to indicate those cases where the information on 'Faculty or division' was not applicable for some reason.

While any codes can be used to signify missing values, there are some rules of good practice with missing values which are advisable to follow.

Strategies for coding missing values

It is tempting to avoid the problem of missing values by leaving blank the space where the code should go. After all, one does not know the code, so why not just put nothing? However, this is not advisable. A blank space can easily end up being converted into a zero by accident. If zero can be a genuine code for the variable, the result is an error in the dataset.

Second, blanks can occur for other reasons, such as someone accidentally skipping a space when typing in the data. Therefore, one could not be sure if the blank space is a genuine missing value or just a mistake.

Similarly, people often choose to use zero as a missing value code. While better than blanks, this is still not advisable. As before, an accidentally entered blank space can end up being read as zero, introducing an error. Also, often the value zero can be a genuine code. For example, if people are asked to state how many children they have; many will legitimately say '0'.

The best practice is to use a value that is completely out of the range of real possible values as a missing value code. For instance, with **Faculty** above, the genuine code values were 1 to 5 and 9 is used as a missing value code. It is completely out of the range of possible values and, being an actual number, has to be entered in as a deliberate code (so it cannot appear by accident as a zero or blank could).

Sometimes people use more than one missing value code so that they can keep track of *why* the value is missing. For instance, one might use different missing value codes to distinguish between: *'refused to answer'*; *'not applicable'*; *'answer not known'*, etc. Whether one chooses to use more than one missing value code depends upon whether knowing the reason for data being missing is of importance. For instance, it may be important to know if people refuse to answer a certain question.

One convention many people follow with missing values is to use the highest possible values available. For instance, with our example of **Faculty** where all the values are single digit numbers (i.e. 1, 2, 3, 4 or 5) one might use: 9 to mean *'Refused'*; 8 to mean *'Not applicable'*; and 7 to mean *'Missing for some other reason'*.

	Variable: Faculty, University faculty	
1	Social sciences	55
2	Arts	186
3	Science	97
4	Engineering	131
5	Other	4
7	**Missing, other reason**	3
8	**Not applicable**	1
9	**Refused**	23
Total		500

If a variable contains values with two digits say, 'Number of children', you could maintain this practice of using the highest values (double-digit values in this instance) to signify missing values; for example, 97, 98 and 99 or 77, 88 and 99. People might have 0, 1, 2, 3, 4 ... maybe even some with 10, 11, 12+ children; but no one would have 77, 88, 97, 98 or 99 children!

For variables with values that contain three digits, one could use 777, 888, 997, 998 or 999; 7777, 8888, 9997, 9998, 9999 for variables with four digit values, and so on.

Another conventional way of handling missing values is to assign them negative numbers. For instance, in our example, the missing value code for Age is −1. People obviously cannot have a minus value for their age, so there is no chance of confusing the missing value code with a legitimate value for someone's age.

The importance of missing values

The importance of specifying missing value codes goes beyond just the cosmetic reasons of having them clearly displayed as missing values in tabulations. When certain codes for a variable are identified for SPSS as 'missing values', these codes will be excluded automatically from any mathematical calculations that are carried out on the variables. If this was not the case, completely misleading results would occur. For instance, take the example of a code for '*number of children*' where the missing values codes of 97, 98 and 99 have been used. If the average number of children was calculated for the dataset with even a *small* proportion of missing value codes 97, 98 and 99 being averaged in with the true codes of 0, 1, 2, 3, etc., the overall average would be grossly inflated. Once these missing values have been specified or 'declared' to SPSS, however, they will play no part in the calculation and a misleading result will be avoided. A similar example of how SPSS would exclude missing values can be seen if we look at the tabulation of our variable **Faculty** with the numbers in each legitimate category being given as a percentage of the whole:

	Variable: Faculty, University faculty	N	%
1	Social sciences	55	11.6
2	Arts	186	39.3
3	Science	97	20.5
4	Engineering	131	27.7
5	Other	4	0.1
7	Missing, other reason	3	—
8	Not applicable	1	—
9	Refused	23	—
Total		500	100.0

27 cases are missing values

CONCLUSION

In the end, once:

- ▪ the data have been entered
- ▪ variables and their values have been 'labelled' and defined fully
- ▪ missing values are specified fully
- ▪ and the data have been 'cleaned' by checking for valid ranges of values and internal consistency

you have a fully operational and self-supporting dataset, ready for analysis.

Some tips

▦ *Save your file frequently* as you enter the data. Do not wait until you have entered all of the data – save your file every 15 minutes. That way, you'll have a permanent copy of most of your data even if something goes wrong while you're working.

▦ Make a *backup copy* (an extra copy) of the data to use in case your original data file is somehow lost or destroyed. Since disks and flash drives can be damaged, store the backup copy in a different physical location.

▦ Use the pull-down **Help** menu on the toolbar and the tutorial for *further advice and help*.

SPSS EXERCISE FOR DATA INPUT

If you have not done so already, try creating your own 'Drinker' SPSS data file:

▦ Write *your* responses to the questionnaire onto the grid in Figure 1.1.

▦ Enter the data for the five cases into a new data file in the Data View window. Remember you will need to define the variables in the Variable View window.

▦ Open the Variable View window, enter a short variable name for each question (variable), indicate the width and type of the variable, set up the variable labels, declare missing values where appropriate, and set the level of measurement.

▦ Using **Save As**, name and save the resulting SPSS data file to a disk or flash drive.

SUPPLEMENT 1   STUDENT 'DRINKING' QUESTIONNAIRE

Serial number: _____

1. What is your first name? (write in) _____
2. What is your sex?   1 Male   2 Female
3. What is your age in years? _____
4. What faculty/division are you in at your University/College
    1. Social Sciences
    2. Arts
    3. Science
    4. Engineering
    5. Other
    9. Not applicable
5. Do you:
    1. never drink alcohol
    2. drink rarely
    3. drink moderately
    4. drink frequently
    5. drink heavily
6. Did you drink last weekend between 12 noon on Friday and last Sunday night?
                        1. Yes   2. No
    If **YES** please answer question 7,
    If **NO** thank you for completing the questionnaire.
7. Please write down how many alcoholic drinks you had last weekend between 12 noon on Friday and late Sunday night.
    [*Write in the number*] _____
    How many pints of beer or cider in total did you have? _____
                        [*If none, write in* 0]
    How many glasses of wine in total did you have? _____
                        [*If none, write in* 0]
    How many measures of spirits/mixed cocktails did you have? _____
                        [*If none, write in* 0]
8. As close as possible, to the exact pound and pence, how much money did you spend on alcoholic drinks during the same time period?
    [*Write in the amount with the decimal point; for example,* 5.25]
        £_____ [*If you spent nothing, write in* 0.00]

Thank you for your cooperation.

2

Listing and Exploring Data

INTRODUCTION

The process of data analysis should always begin with a close examination of the data you are working with. This is an important prerequisite to formal statistical testing and in this module we are going to examine some of the more common ways of exploring and summarizing data using the dataset for **Great Britain (GB)**. We have already looked at the SPSS menu system and identified the main features of each of the eleven drop-down menus. The procedures we are going to focus on in this chapter can be accessed through either the *Analyze* or the *Graphs* menu. However, before we proceed to the practical application of SPSS we need to consider some important conceptual issues.

LEVELS OF MEASUREMENT

The concept of levels or scales of measurement is central to statistical analysis and helps to determine the types of procedure that may be carried out on particular variables. We can identify four broad levels of measurement according to the amount of information we have about a variable.

Nominal/Categorical

This is the lowest level of measurement. The most we can do with nominal variables is to differentiate between the categories. We cannot place these categories in any meaningful order. Examples of variables measured on the nominal scale in the ISSP dataset include **religgrp** (Religious main group), and **marital** (marital status). Although numbers have been assigned to the categories of these variables they are merely labels and have no intrinsic meaning. For instance, if we look at the frequency table for **marital** (Figure 2.3) we can see that the numbering of the categories from 1 to 5 is purely arbitrary as no meaningful order exists for them.

Ordinal

Ordinal variables differ from nominal variables in that the different categories *can* be arranged into some kind of meaningful order (for example, from highest to lowest). In this respect assigning numbers to ordinal variables takes on a greater significance. However, we cannot determine the degree of difference between the categories. For example, we can say that the response 'strongly disagree' is more extreme than 'disagree', but we cannot measure the precise difference between these two responses. There are numerous examples of ordinal level variables in the ISSP dataset, including **degree** (highest education level) and **attend** (attendance of religious services). A frequency table for **degree** is reproduced in Figure 2.4 and we can see there is a meaningful order to the categories (ranging from 'no formal qualification' to 'university degree completed').

Interval

Variables measured at the interval level share all the qualities of nominal and ordinal variables and, in addition, it is possible to measure the precise distance between each of the categories. However, the interval scale does not have an absolute zero point and it is therefore inappropriate to compute ratios between two values measured on this scale. True interval variables are extremely rare, but one oft-cited example is temperature on the Fahrenheit scale.

Ratio

This is the highest level of measurement as it possesses all the features of the other three and, in addition has an absolute zero. Ratio statements can be meaningfully made about such variables (for example, £20 is twice as much as £10). An obvious example of a ratio-level variable from the ISSP dataset is **age**.

We should point out that for all practical purposes the distinction between interval and ratio scales has little significance in terms of the statistical procedures covered in this book and the two categories are generally grouped together as interval/ratio or simply ratio. In SPSS these are known as **scalar** variables, but you may also see them referred to as quantitative, metric or continuous data.

It is also important to be aware that a variable's level of measurement can be altered, but generally only in a downward direction. So, while a ratio variable such as age has the information contained in it that would allow you to recode it into an ordinal scale by creating a series of age categories or groups, it would not be possible to do this in reverse (see Module 3 for details on how to recode variables using SPSS).

An ability to distinguish between the different levels of measurement (nominal, ordinal, and interval/ratio) is a *fundamental* prerequisite to even the most basic forms of statistical analysis. This issue will be examined in more detail later in the chapter when we consider the various descriptive statistics available in SPSS.

FREQUENCY TABLES

Frequency tables allow you to summarize the data by counting the number of times each value or category of a particular variable occurs. For instance, if we wanted to find out how many of the respondents in the ISSP dataset for Great Britain were married, single, divorced, and so on, we would ask SPSS to produce a frequency table for the variable **marital** (marital status). We can illustrate how this is done by requesting SPSS to produce frequency tables for **marital** (marital status) and **degree** (highest education level). Step-by-step instructions are as follows.

1. Access the **Analyze** menu (by clicking on Analyze in the menu bar) and click on **Descriptive Statistics** and then **Frequencies...** (see Figure 2.1).

    This will open up the Frequencies dialog box shown in Figure 2.2.
2. The next step is to transfer the required variable(s) from the source variable list (the left-hand box) to the target variable list (the right-hand box), either by using the variable transfer arrow or simply

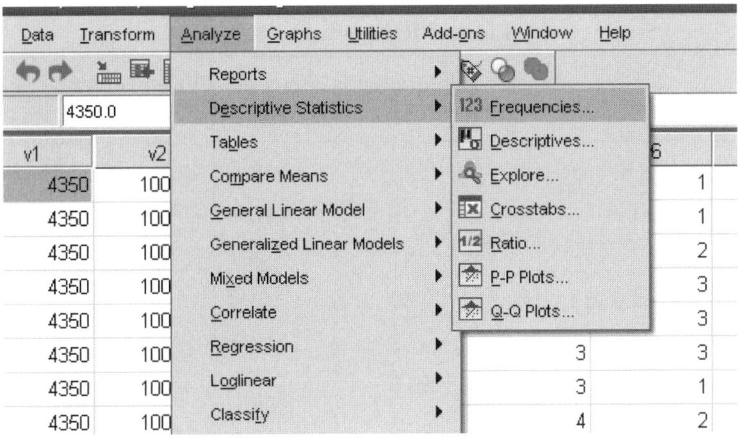

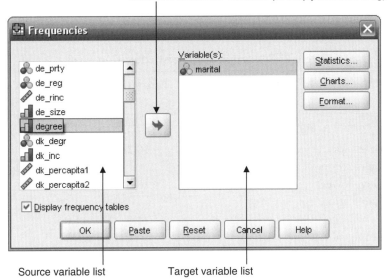

Figure 2.1   *Descriptive statistics and frequencies*

Click here to transfer variables (or simply click and drag)

Source variable list   Target variable list

Figure 2.2   *Frequencies dialog box*

clicking and dragging the variable(s) across. So we need to click on **marital** in the source variable list and drag it across to the target variable list (as shown in Figure 2.2). Repeat this process for the **degree** variable.

You can put as many variables into this target variable list as you wish, but for the purposes of this exercise we just want to produce frequency tables for **marital** and **degree.**

3. Finally, make sure the 'Display frequency tables' checkbox is 'on' and click **OK** (we will discuss the Statistics, Charts and Format options later).

The Viewer window should now open up and frequency tables for **marital** and **degree** should appear in the display pane (the right-hand section of the window). These tables have been reproduced in Figures 2.3 and 2.4 and their main features are described below. You should examine these frequency tables carefully and familiarize yourself with the information they provide.

marital R: Marital status

		Frequency	Percent	Valid Percent	Cumulative Percent
Valid	1 Marr,livg as married	535	58.6	58.7	58.7
	2 Widowed	98	10.7	10.8	69.5
	3 Divorced	81	8.9	8.9	78.4
	4 Separated, but married	30	3.3	3.3	81.7
	5 Single, never married	167	18.3	18.3	100.0
	Total	911	99.8	100.0	
Missing	9 M NA, refused	2	.2		
Total		913	100.0		

Figure 2.3   *Frequency table for* ***marital***

degree R: Education II-highest education level

		Frequency	Percent	Valid Percent	Cumulative Percent
Valid	0 No formal qualification	234	25.6	25.7	25.7
	1 Lowest formal qualification	93	10.2	10.2	35.9
	2 Above lowest qualification	188	20.6	20.6	56.5
	3 Higher secondary completed	128	14.0	14.0	70.5
	4 Above higher secondary level	117	12.8	12.8	83.3
	5 University degree completed	152	16.6	16.7	100.0
	Total	912	99.9	100.0	
Missing	9 M NA	1	.1		
Total		913	100.0		

Figure 2.4   *Frequency table for* ***degree***

This first column lists the different categories of the variables complete with number codes (e.g. 1, Married, living as married; 2, Widowed; 3, Divorced, and so on). Column two provides a frequency count for each of these categories and we can see from Figure 2.3, for instance, that 535 respondents are married, 98 respondents are widowed, and so on. Similarly, Figure 2.4 informs us that 234 respondents had no formal qualifications while 152 had completed a university degree.

The third column transfers these raw figures into percentages so we can say, for example, that 58.6 per cent of all respondents are married or living as married, 10.7 per cent are widowed and 8.9 per cent are divorced.

The next column, 'Valid Percent', excludes 'missing values' (if there are any) and provides a percentage breakdown of only those respondents who gave a valid answer to the question (see Module 1 for a more detailed discussion on missing values).

The final column (cumulative per cent) only really becomes relevant when the variables are ordinal or scale (in other words, where there is some sense of increase or decrease as we proceed through the categories). This column totals the percentages cumulatively, so we can say, for example, that 56.5 per cent of respondents have not completed higher secondary level of education.

While frequency tables represent a useful first step in data analysis they are fairly limited in terms of the information they provide. To summarize the data further we would need to access some of the many descriptive or summary statistics available within SPSS. However, before showing you how to obtain these through SPSS it is necessary to consider briefly a number of important statistical concepts such as central tendency and dispersion.

MEASURES OF CENTRAL TENDENCY

The concept of central tendency refers to the 'average' or 'most typical' value of a distribution and, while the overall aim is to produce a figure that best represents the 'middle point' in the data, there are a number of different ways of doing this. We will examine the three most common measures of central tendency – the mean, the median and the mode.

The mean

The arithmetic mean is the most familiar of all the measures of central tendency and corresponds with most people's notion of what an average is. The mean possesses a number of important mathematical properties and should only be calculated for interval/ratio data.

To calculate the mean you add together all the values in a batch and divide the total by the number of values. For example, if a tutorial group consisted of 7 students with the following ages: 17, 18, 18, 19, 20, 20, 21, – the average age would be 19 (133 divided by 7). However, one of the main weaknesses of the mean as a measure of central tendency is that it is not 'resistant'. That is, it is disproportionately affected by extreme values in a distribution. So if we replaced our 21-year-old student with a 56-year-old mature student, the average age now becomes 24 (168 divided by 7). We can see, then, that one student has dragged up the average age of the class considerably, even though the other 6 students are all under 21. If there are extreme values in your batch the mean could be misleading. In such circumstances it may be preferable to use an alternative measure of central tendency such as the trimmed mean or the median. The trimmed mean is available in SPSS and involves removing the top and bottom 5 per cent of values before calculating the mean.

The median

The median is the most suitable measure of central tendency for ordinal data, although it is also widely used with interval/ratio variables. It is simply the middle value in a distribution when the scores are ranked in order of size. To return to the tutorial example used above, the median age of our original 7 students (17, 18, 18, 19, 20, 20, 21) would be 19. This is the value that splits the batch in two with three scores above it and three scores below it. So the median is the same as the mean for these seven students.

However, unlike the mean, the median is resistant to extreme values and the introduction of our mature student in place of the 21-year-old does not have any effect on the result. The middle value in the batch is still 19 (17, 18, 18, 19, 20, 20, 56). (Note that if there is an even number of scores (for example: 17, 18, 18, 19, 20, 20, 56, 60) we will have two middle values (19 and 20). In this case we simply calculate the average of these two values (19 + 20 divided by 2 = 19.5).)

The mode

The mode is the simplest measure of central tendency to calculate and is the only measure that is appropriate for nominal data. The mode is the value that occurs most frequently in a distribution. So, for example, we can see clearly from Figure 2.3 that the modal value for the variable **marital** (marital status) is 1 (the code for married or living as married). In other words, more people (535 or 58.6 per cent) fall into the married category than any of the other categories. One of the drawbacks of using this as a measure of central tendency is that a distribution may have two or more modal values (these are referred to as bimodal and multimodal distributions, respectively).

MEASURES OF DISPERSION

In the tutorial example above we saw that both the mean and the median of our original 7 students (aged 17, 18, 18, 19, 20, 20, and 21) was 19. If we consider the following 7 family members (aged 2, 2, 8, 19, 20, 40 and 42) we see that the mean and median ages also turn out to be 19. However, the figures in the first batch are tightly concentrated around the central value while the second set of figures is much more dispersed. Clearly we need to measure more than just central tendency if we are to describe these two very different datasets adequately. Consequently this section will look at a number of measures which provide us with information on how dispersed or spread out the values in a distribution are. When dealing with ordinal data we are restricted to the range and interquartile range, while the variance and standard deviation are usually only calculated for interval/ratio variables. There are no appropriate measures of dispersion for nominal variables.

The range

The range is the most straightforward measure of dispersion and is calculated by subtracting the smallest value from the largest. However, this is a rather crude measure as it is totally dependent on the two most extreme values in the distribution. We need to treat the range with caution if either of these values differs substantially from the rest of the values in the batch.

The interquartile range

The interquartile range is designed to overcome the main flaw of the range by eliminating the most extreme scores in the distribution. It is obtained by ordering the batch from lowest to highest, then dividing the batch into four equal parts (quartiles) and concentrating on the middle 50 per cent of the distribution. The interquartile range is therefore the range of the middle half of observations, the difference between the first quartile and the third quartile. If you are using the median as a measure of central tendency then the interquartile range would be the appropriate measure of dispersion to accompany it.

The variance

The variance and standard deviation tell us how widely dispersed the values in a distribution are around the mean. Like the mean they require variables to be measured on the interval/ratio scale. If the values are closely concentrated around the mean the variance will be small, while a large variance suggests a batch of values which are much more dispersed.

There are three basic steps in calculating the variance:

1. subtract the mean from each of the scores
2. square each of these 'differences from the mean'
3. add all the 'squared differences' together and divide by the total number of observations minus 1.

In general terms, then, the variance represents the average squared deviation from the mean. However, the main problem with the variance is that because the individual differences from the mean have been squared it is not measured in the same units as the original variable (you should be aware that there are sound statistical reasons for squaring the deviations in the first place). To remove the effect of squaring we need to obtain the square root of the variance, more commonly referred to as the **standard deviation**.

The standard deviation

The standard deviation is the most widely used measure of dispersion and is obtained by simply calculating the square root of the variance. As this returns us to the original unit of measurement the standard deviation is much more meaningful than the variance. If the mean is being used as the measure of central tendency it is usually accompanied by the standard deviation. It is important to be aware that because the standard deviation, like the mean, is calculated using all the observations it can be distorted by a small number of extreme values. As a general rule, therefore, *it is advisable to check your data for any unusually high or low values before employing these kinds of statistics.*

DESCRIPTIVE STATISTICS AND CHARTS IN SPSS

Armed with an understanding of the concepts of central tendency, dispersion and levels of measurement, and an appreciation of the relationship between them, you should now be in a position to select the appropriate descriptive statistics and charts for the different types of variables. These procedures can be accessed from within the Frequencies dialog box. To emphasize some of the points raised above we will select two variables at different levels of measurement (one nominal and one interval/ratio).

Example 1 We will begin with a variable you should be familiar with by now, **marital**. Descriptive statistics are located within the Frequencies command, so proceed as before until you obtain the Frequencies dialog box shown in Figure 2.2. In other words, select **Analyse, Descriptive Statistics**, and **Frequencies.** Then transfer **marital** into the target variable list. You will see the Statistics and Charts and Format options (Figure 2.5) at the right-hand side of this dialog box. We will examine each of these options in turn.

Figure 2.5   *Statistics, charts and format options*

If we click on the **Statistics** button, the Frequencies: Statistics dialog box (Figure 2.6) will open up. This dialog box offers a number of different options including measures of central tendency, dispersion, distribution and percentiles. As **marital** is a nominal variable the most informative and appropriate

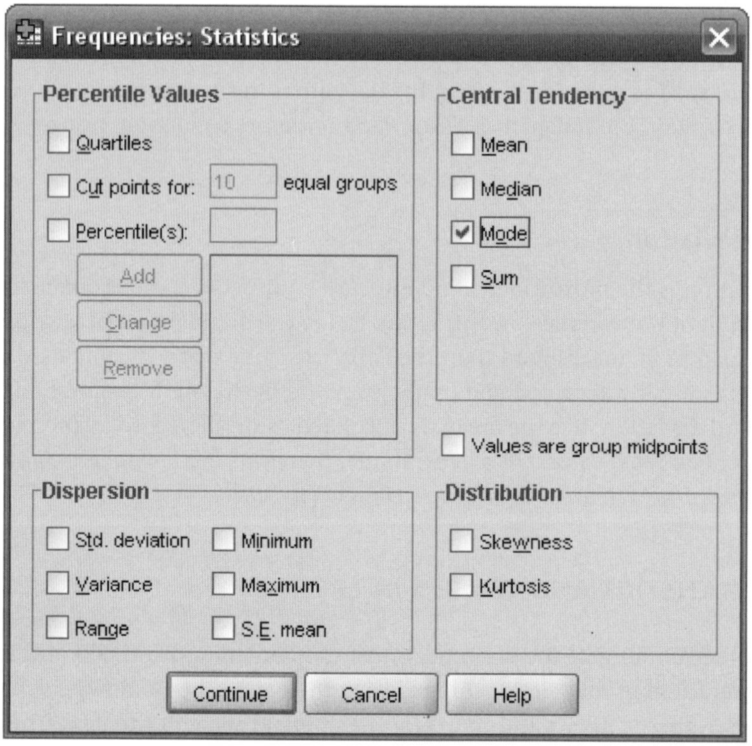

Figure 2.6   *Frequencies: Statistics dialog box*

statistic available to us here is the **mode**. Select this by clicking in the Mode check box. Then click on **Continue**.

You will now be returned to the Frequencies dialog box. As we also want to select the appropriate chart for **marital**, simply click on the **Charts** button:

This will open up the Frequencies: Charts dialog box (Figure 2.7). The options here include bar charts, pie charts and histograms (with bar charts you can choose whether to have frequencies or percentages displayed).

A bar chart is an appropriate graphical display for nominal or ordinal level variables and the length of the bars is proportional to the value of the items. Click on the radio button next to **Bar charts and if you want to** obtain percentages rather than frequencies you need to select the **Percentages** button. Click on **Continue** to return to the Frequencies dialog box and finally click on **OK**.

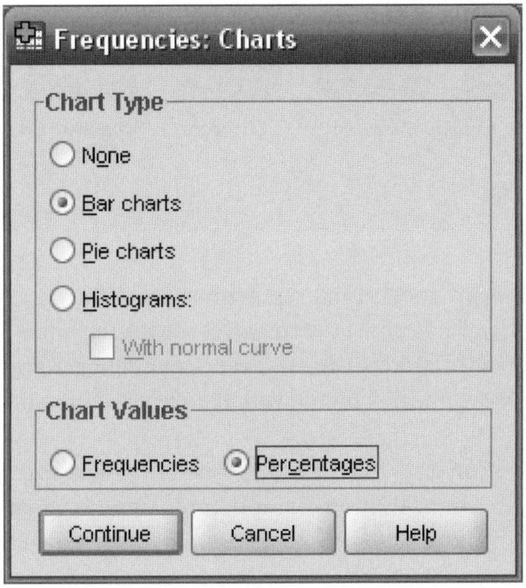

Figure 2.7 *Frequencies: Charts dialog box*

The resultant output is shown below and we can see from Figure 2.8a that there are 911 valid responses, 2 missing values and the mode is 1 (the value code for 'Married or living as married'). However, the bar chart in Figure 2.8b highlights the modal value much more vividly and we can see immediately that almost 60 per cent of respondents fall into the 'Married/living as married' category.

Statistics

marital R: Marital status

N	Valid	911
	Missing	2
	Mode	1

Figure 2.8a *Statistics output for **marital***

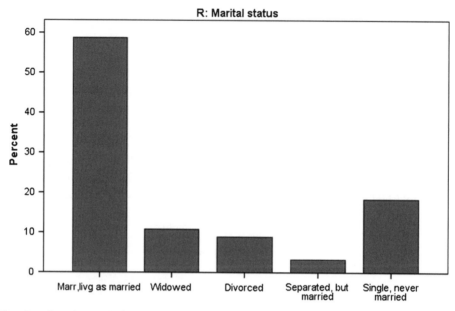

Figure 2.8b *Bar chart for* **marital**

The bar chart, then, provides a good visual representation of the data, as the height of each bar is proportional to the frequency or percentage (percentage in this example) of each category. However, bar charts are not always the most appropriate way to present data graphically and, as with descriptive statistics, our choice is largely determined by the variable's level of measurement.

Example 2 For our second example, we will use **age**, one of the few true quantitative variables in the ISSP dataset. As our earlier discussion showed, because interval/ratio variables are measured on a more sophisticated scale than nominal variables, it is appropriate to use a much broader range of summary statistics.

We access the Frequencies dialog box in the usual way (**A**nalyse, **D**escriptive Statistics, and **F**requencies) and then click and drag the variable **age** over to the target variable list. With interval/ratio variables, however, we do not always want a frequency table to be produced, especially if the variable contains a large number of values. For instance, if the sample size is large, a frequency table for a variable like income may constitute several pages of output. To 'switch off' the frequency table, simply click on the **Display frequency tables** check box at the bottom of the Frequencies dialog box to remove the 'tick' (Figure 2.9).

When this check box is blank, frequency tables will be suppressed.

Figure 2.9 *Display frequency tables check box*

An alternative method of curtailing lengthy frequency tables can be accessed via the **Format** option. Click on the Format button on the right-hand side of the main Frequencies dialog box (see Figure 2.2) to open the Format dialog box (Figure 2.10).

Click on the **Suppress tables** check box and adjust the number of categories as required. This option is particularly useful if you are carrying out analysis on both quantitative and categorical variables simultaneously. However, you need to be careful not to set the number of categories too low, otherwise you will suppress frequency tables for some of the larger categorical variables. For instance, the variable **relig** (religious denomination) in the ISSP dataset contains more than 60 different categories.

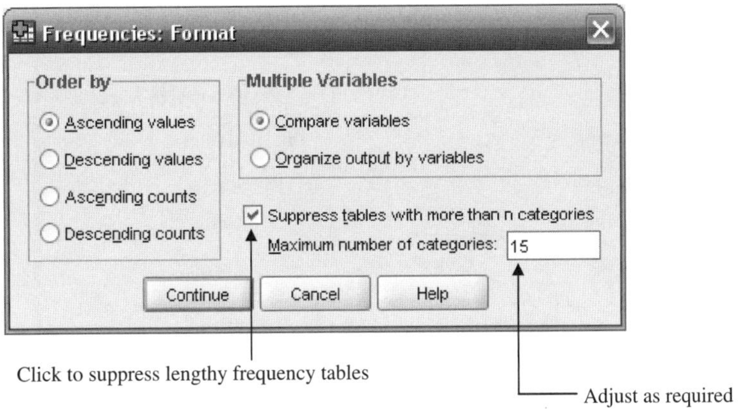

Click to suppress lengthy frequency tables

Adjust as required

Figure 2.10 *Format dialog box*

We want to access the statistics option again (see Figure 2.2) but as we are working with a scale variable this time we can request a much broader range of statistics (as shown in Figure 2.11): three measures of central tendency (mean, median and mode); three measures of dispersion (standard deviation, variance, and range); minimum and maximum values; and the quartiles (the 25th, 50th and 75th percentiles).

These are obtained by clicking the appropriate boxes in the Frequencies: Statistics dialog box as shown in Figure 2.11. Of course, when using the Frequencies procedure for your own examples, you are free to select any of the available statistical options so long as these are appropriate for the particular variables you are working with.

(A NOTE OF CAUTION: Be aware that SPSS will carry out statistical procedures even if what you request is incorrect. For instance, if we had asked SPSS to produce all of these statistics for our earlier example, **marital**, it would have done so even though the results would not have made much sense.)

Click on **Continue** to return to the Frequencies dialog box and then select the **Charts** option. As **age** is measured on the ratio scale, we need to select **Histograms** this time. Make sure that there is a tick in the 'With normal curve' checkbox (see Figure 2.12) as this will help us determine visually the extent to which the data are normally distributed.

Finally click on **Continue** and then **OK**. The results of our efforts are displayed in Figures 2.13a and 2.13b.

Figure 2.13a informs us that there were 913 valid responses with no missing values and then reports the various summary statistics we requested. You should try to relate these results to our earlier discussion of central tendency and dispersion. For example, we can see that the mean (the average age) is 51.03. The median (the middle value in the batch) is almost identical to the mean at 51 years of age. The fact

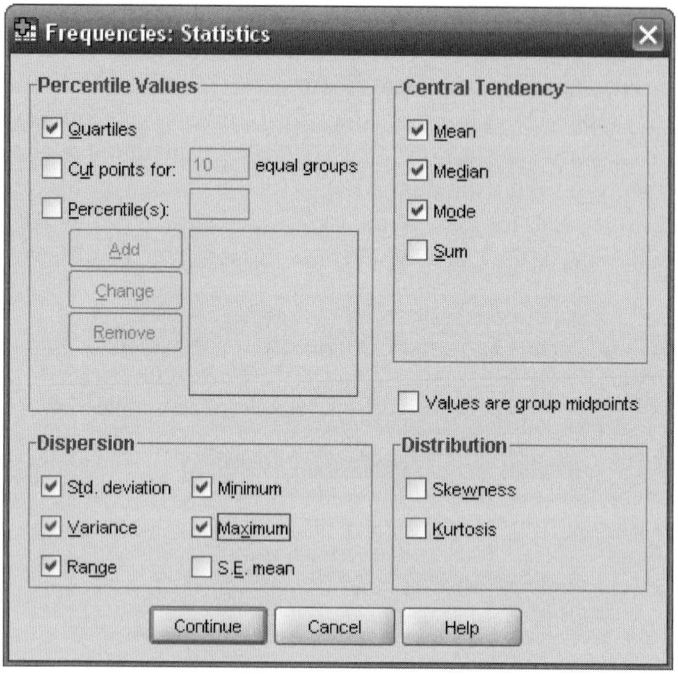

Figure 2.11   *Frequencies: Statistics dialog box*

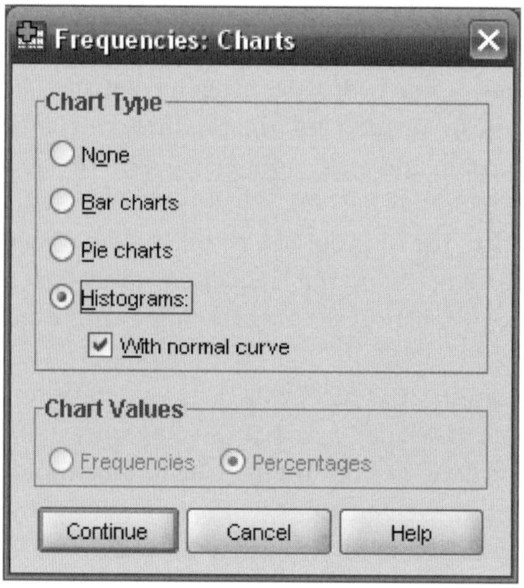

Figure 2.12   *Charts dialog box*

that the median and mean are very similar implies that the data are not skewed. The modal value (the one that occurs most frequently) is a bit higher at 58 years of age.

In terms of dispersion, we can see there is a standard deviation of approximately 18 years and a variance of 319 (remember that the standard deviation is the more meaningful of these two figures and represents the square root of the variance). There is a range of 78 years of age (96 minus 18). The table also

Statistics

age R: Age

N	Valid	913
	Missing	0
Mean		51.03
Median		51.00
Mode		58
Std. Deviation		17.866
Variance		319.190
Range		78
Minimum		18
Maximum		96
Percentiles	25	36.00
	50	51.00
	75	65.00

Figure 2.13a   *Descriptive statistics for the variable **age***

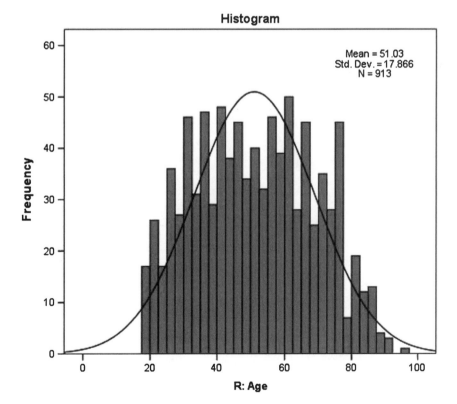

Figure 2.13b   *Histogram for the variable **age***

reports the quartiles and, as we saw earlier, we can calculate the interquartile range by subtracting the lower quartile (or 25th percentile) from the upper quartile (75th percentile) (65 minus 36 = 29). Finally, we also know from our earlier discussion that the 50th percentile represents the median value (51).

Figure 2.13b shows the histogram for **age**. Each bar of the histogram covers a 2.5-year age range. So, the first bar represents respondents between aged between 17.5 and 20 years of age, the second relates to those between 20 and 22.5 years of age, and so on. We can determine how many respondents fall into each age category by looking at the vertical axis (frequency). As you can see from the graph below, the histogram also includes the mean and standard deviation of the distribution. Note that the chart starts abruptly with 18-year-olds since children were not sampled in this survey. There is also a slight 'upward skew' to the data with decreasing proportions of respondents in the oldest age bands.

Explore

The facilities available under the Explore procedure in SPSS allow us to bring our exploration of the data a stage further. This section will focus on two techniques which fall under the rubric of Exploratory Data Analysis (EDA; see Tukey, 1977): the **boxplot** and the **stem and leaf display**. The Explore procedure is particularly useful because it provides a visual representation of some of the statistics we have just been considering. Locating these summary statistics within a graphical framework makes them more vivid and facilitates comparison between subgroups. In addition, Explore enables us to identify easily any values which are very different from the rest of the distribution.

To access the Explore option go to the **Analyze** menu and select **Descriptive Statistics** and then **Explore** (see Figure 2.14).

This will open the Explore dialog box shown in Figure 2.15. Let's continue looking at age, only this time separately for men and women. Transfer the variable **age** into the **Dependent List** box Explore

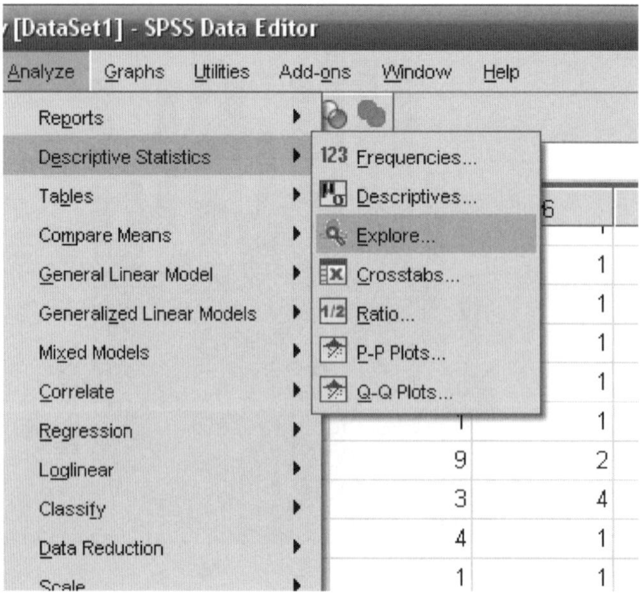

Figure 2.14 *Descriptive Statistics and Explore*

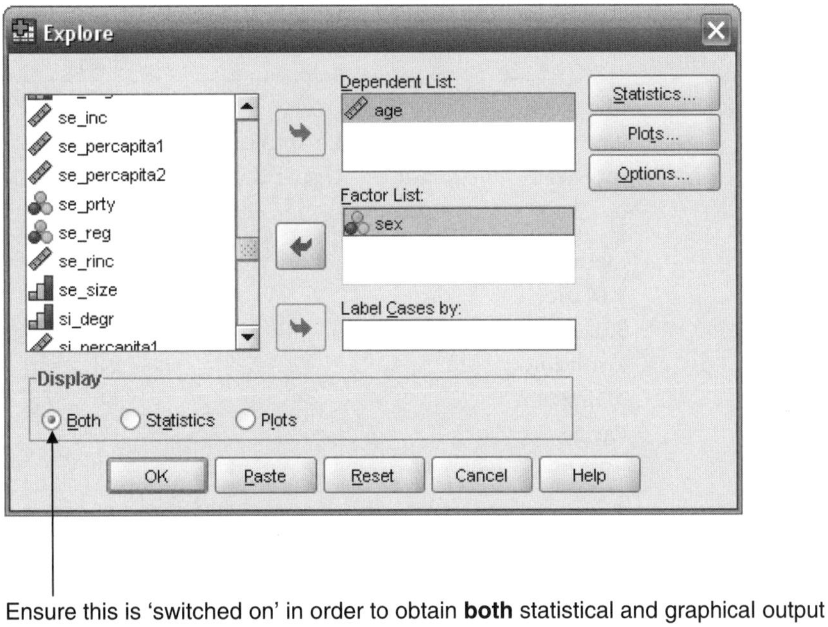

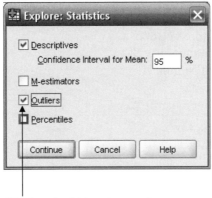

Ensure this is 'switched on' in order to obtain **both** statistical and graphical output

Figure 2.15 *Explore dialog box*

Click here to obtain extreme values

Figure 2.16 *Explore: Statistics dialog box*

will calculate a variety of descriptive statistics for this variable, including the mean, the trimmed mean, the median and the standard deviation. As we want to calculate these statistics for males and females separately we need to put the variable **sex** into the **Factor List** box.

Then Click on the **Statistics** button to open the Explore: Statistics dialog box (Figure 2.16). You will see that the **Descriptives** check box is already 'switched on' (the Explore procedure produces a variety of descriptive statistics by default). However, you may want to identify 'outliers', the most extreme cases in the distribution. These can be obtained by clicking the **Outliers** check box.

Descriptives

sexR: Gender				Statistic	Std. Error
age R: Age	1 Male	Mean		52.46	.853
		95% Confidence Interval for Mean	Lower Bound	50.78	
			Upper Bound	54.14	
		5% Trimmed Mean		52.44	
		Median		52.50	
		Variance		284.079	
		Std. Deviation		16.855	
		Minimum		18	
		Maximum		88	
		Range		70	
		Interquartile Range		27	
		Skewness		.018	.124
		Kurtosis		−.907	.247
	2 Female	Mean		49.97	.810
		95% Confidence Interval for Mean	Lower Bound	48.38	
			Upper Bound	51.56	
		5% Trimmed Mean		49.69	
		Median		49.00	
		Variance		343.304	
		Std. Deviation		18.528	
		Minimum		18	
		Maximum		96	
		Range		78	
		Interquartile Range		30	
		Skewness		.165	.107
		Kurtosis		−.951	.213

Figure 2.17a   *Descriptive statistics from Explore procedure*

Then click on **Continue** to return to the Explore dialog box and finally click on **OK**. The output from this procedure is shown in Figures 2.17a–2.17d and is discussed under four broad headings:

1. *Descriptive Statistics*
   Figure 2.17a includes a wide variety of descriptive statistics and we have already discussed the key features of most of these. Now, however, is an appropriate point to introduce two additional statistics that indicate how well the distribution of the data conform to a Normal distribution: skewness and kurtosis. 'Skewness' is a measure of the extent to which the distribution of the data is symmetrical around its midpoint, the mean. A value of zero indicates exact symmetry. A negative value indicates a 'negative' skew – that there are some values that are unusually low that are not matched by equivalent high values. To put it another way, the distribution will have a long 'tail' running towards low values on its left. A positive value indicates a 'positive' skew – some unusually high values that are

Extreme Values

sex R: Gender				Case Number	Value
age R: Age	1 Male	Highest	1	4150	88
			2	4142	87
			3	3935	86
			4	4095	86
			5	4291	86[a]
		Lowest	1	4187	18
			2	4259	19
			3	3762	19
			4	4280	20
			5	4021	20[b]
	2 Female	Highest	1	3986	96
			2	4058	91
			3	3869	90
			4	4256	90
			5	4241	89
		Lowest	1	4256	18
			2	4429	18
			3	4243	18
			4	4169	18
			5	4081	18[c]

[a.] Only a partial list of cases with the value 86 are shown in the table of upper extremes.
[b.] Only a partial list of cases with the value 20 are shown in the table of lower extremes.
[c.] Only a partial list of cases with the value 18 are shown in the table of lower extremes.

Figure 2.17b   *Extreme values from Explore procedure*

not matched by low values. Here, we see that the skewness value for men is very close to zero, .018; so the male distribution is almost perfectly symmetric. The skewness value for women is higher, at .165, indicating a moderate upward skew among the women. (As we will see immediately below, this is caused by there being a few more elderly women in the sample.) As general rules of thumb, the smaller the absolute value of skewness, the better, as this indicates a more symmetrical batch of data. Also, if the absolute value of skew is below two, this is generally regarded as acceptable.

'Kurtosis' refers to the extent to which the shape of the distribution of a batch of data conforms precisely to the 'bell-shaped curve' of a Normal distribution. If kurtosis is zero, the shape is exactly normal. If kurtosis is a positive number, the shape is more 'humped' than a Normal distribution, with values tending to pile up or cluster in the middle. If kurtosis is negative, the shape tends towards being more 'flat' than a classic Normal distribution. Here, the values of kurtosis for men and women are both quite similar and negative, –.907 and –.951, respectively. If you glance back at Figure 2.13b, the histogram for **age**, you will see that the distribution indeed is a bit 'flatter' than the Normal curve that is superimposed on it.

```
R: Age Stem-and-Leaf Plot for
Sex = Male

 Frequency    Stem &  Leaf
      3.00       1 .  899
     15.00       2 .  000222222233444
     19.00       2 .  5667777788899999999
     33.00       3 .  000011111222222222223333333444444
     31.00       3 .  5555555666667777788888888899999
     38.00       4 .  00000001111122222222223334444444444444444
     32.00       4 .  55555666666666666667778888888899999
     36.00       5 .  000000000111111122222222333333444444
     39.00       5 .  555555556666666666677777777888888888888999
     38.00       6 .  000000000000111111111222222333333344444
     30.00       6 .  555555556666666666677777777788899
     31.00       7 .  000001111122222222223333333444444
     24.00       7 .  5555556666666666667777779
     14.00       8 .  00001111233444
      7.00       8 .  5666678

Stem width:   10
Each leaf:         1 case(s)
```

Figure 2.17c *Stem and leaf plots from Explore procedure*

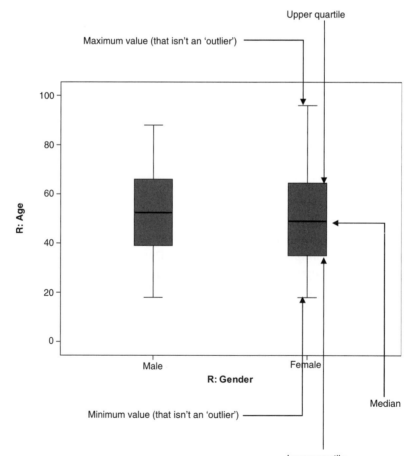

Figure 2.17d *Boxplots from Explore procedure*

As the statistics for age are broken down by gender we are able to make comparisons between the men and women who make up our sample. For instance, if we focus on the mean we can see that the males (52.46) in our sample are, on average, slightly older than the females (49.97). We should be careful, however, not to draw any firm conclusions from this regarding the differences between men and women in the population as a whole (see Module 4 for an introduction to issues such as inferential statistics and significance testing).

Have a look at the other statistics in Figure 2.17a and try to get a grasp of what they are telling us about the data. For example, is there a substantial difference between the trimmed mean and the mean? What do the standard deviations tell us about the spread of the data (e.g. are females less closely concentrated around the mean than males)?

2. *Extreme values*

The second part of the output from Explore is shown in Figure 2.17b and relates to the **Outliers** option in the Explore: Statistics dialog box.

Selecting the **Outliers** option instructs SPSS to report the most extreme values in the distribution (that is, the five highest and five lowest values for each category of the **sex** variable) and their respective case numbers. So we can see from Figure 2.17b that the five oldest males are 88, 87, 86, 86, and 86 and the five youngest males are 18, 19, 19, 20 and 20. The five oldest females are 96, 91, 90, 90 and 89 and the five youngest are all 18. Identifying the most extreme values in this way helps us to become more familiar with the data and allows us to examine those cases to see if they are genuine values (and not due to an error at the data input stage, for example).

We should point out here that there is no way of telling from this table whether any of these values are 'outliers' or 'extreme values' in the technical sense. They are merely the most extreme values in the distribution, which may or may not be all that different from the other values in the batch (for a statistical definition of 'outliers' and 'extreme values' see the discussion on boxplots below).

3. *Stem and Leaf Plots*

Stem and leaf plots constitute the next section of the Explore output and, as you can see from Figure 2.17c, in graphical terms they resemble histograms quite closely. However, one of the main advantages of the stem and leaf plot is its ability to retain a considerable amount of information about the data. We can illustrate this by focusing on the main features of the plot shown in Figure 2.17c. (Please note that although SPSS did produce separate stem and leaf plots for males and females, the two plots are very similar and for reasons of space we have only included the plot for males here.)

The figures in the middle of the diagram represent the 'stem' and the figures to the right represent the 'leaves'. In this example, the 'stem' represents 'tens' and the 'leaves' are units, so, to transfer the information into actual values you need to multiply the 'stem' by 10 (stem width = 10) and add it to the value of the 'leaf'. In this example each leaf represents one case (i.e. survey respondent), so if we look at the first set of figures in the plot we can see that there are three male respondents in their teens (aged 18, 19 and 19). The second row of figures informs us that there are 15 respondents aged 20–24 (three aged 20, seven aged 22, two aged 23 and three aged 24). Finally, the last row of figures indicates that there are seven males 85 or above (one 85-year-old, four 86-year-olds, one 87-year-old and one 88-year-old).

4. *Boxplots*

The boxplot is an extremely efficient means of describing a number of important features of the data visually. You can quickly identify the median, the range and the quartiles as well as any 'outliers' or 'extreme values' and the graphical nature of this information makes the impact all the more powerful. Moreover, by producing individual boxplots for each category of a particular variable, SPSS allows you to make quick comparisons between the different groups.

Figure 2.17d shows the boxplots for age by gender. As the top of the box represents the upper quartile (75th percentile) and the bottom of the box the lower quartile (25th percentile) we can see the interquartile range at a glance (the length of the box). We know from our earlier discussion that 50 per cent of cases lie within this range. The median value can also be identified quite easily and is represented by the line inside the box.

The outer lines of the boxplot represent the maximum and minimum values in the batch that don't qualify as '**outliers**' or '**extreme values**' (no cases qualify as 'outliers' or 'extreme values' for the age variable). (NOTE: 'Outliers', which are defined as those values that lie between 1.5 and 3 box lengths from the upper or lower quartiles, are represented in SPSS by the symbol O. 'Extreme values' are cases which are more than 3 box lengths from the upper or lower quartiles and are designated in SPSS by an asterisk (*).)

The overall conclusion to be drawn from Figure 2.17d is that the boxplots for males and females are remarkably similar, reflecting the similar age distribution for male and female respondents. However, although the median for males is slightly higher, we can detect a slight positive skew in the female data, caused by the existence of a small number of older females.

OTHER GRAPHS AND CHARTS

The **Graphs** menu in SPSS contains a wide variety of techniques for presenting data in graphical form. Not only is this menu an alternative means of obtaining the charts and plots we have already looked at (i.e. bar charts, histograms, stem and leaf displays, boxplots), but a variety of other options including line, area and pie charts are also available. In the remainder of this module we will consider some of the most widely used graphical procedures. However, it is important to stress that this is only an introduction and you should consult the online help menu or the SPSS User's Guide (SPSS Inc., 2008) to obtain a more comprehensive picture of the wide range of graphs and charts available in SPSS.

The easiest way to produce charts in SPSS is to employ the **Chart Builder**. This can be accessed through the **Graphs** menu and we will use the Chart Builder to create a number of different charts beginning with the Pie Chart.

Pie charts

A pie chart provides a pictorial display of the frequency distribution for nominal or ordinal variables and can be used as an alternative to a bar chart. Although these constitute one of the chart options in the frequencies procedure we will use the Chart Builder to produce one here in order to highlight its simplicity.

Select **Chart Builder** from the **Graphs** menu (see Figure 2.18) and click on the Gallery tab in the Chart Builder dialog box (Figure 2.19). Click on the **Pie/Polar** option from the list of charts and click and drag the pie chart icon from the gallery (located in the bottom right-hand panel) to the 'canvas' (the area located in the top right-hand section of the dialog box).

As we want to examine the different types of community our respondents live in, select **urbrural** (type of community) from the list of variables and click and drag it to the panel just below the pie chart on the canvas (see Figure 2.19) and click **OK**. The pie chart (reproduced in Figure 2.20) clearly shows that, reflecting the urban character of Great Britain, the majority of respondents described their area of residence as a 'town or small city', with the smallest number claiming to live in a 'farm or home in the country'. Although this pie chart is quite basic, it can be amended in a variety of ways through the Chart Editor (see the online Help facility in SPSS for more detail on this).

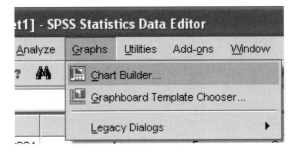

Figure 2.18 *Graphs menu: Chart Builder*

Canvas

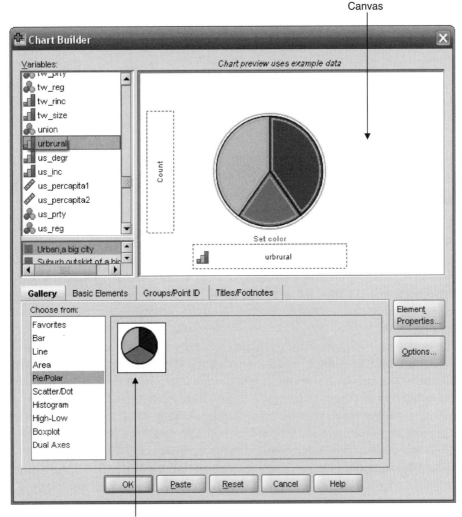

Click and drag the pie chart onto the canvas (i.e. to the top right-hand panel)

Figure 2.19 *Chart Builder dialog box: pie chart*

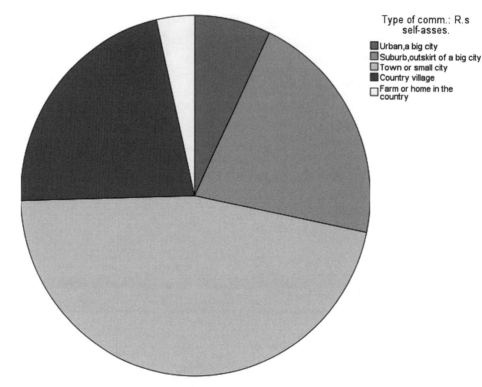

Type of comm.: R.s
self-asses.

■ Urban,a big city
■ Suburb,outskirt of a big city
□ Town or small city
■ Country village
□ Farm or home in the
country

Figure 2.20   *Pie chart for **urbrural***

Scatterplots

While we have looked at pie charts, bar charts and histograms in the context of single variables, the scatterplot is a graphical display that allows us to examine the relationship between two quantitative variables. As this type of display will be considered in more detail in the chapter on correlation and regression, we will confine ourselves here to the mechanics of using the Chart Builder to produce a scatterplot. The process is similar to the one described above except this time we need to select the **Scatter/ Dot** option from the list of charts. Then click on the **Simple Scatter** icon in the gallery and drag it onto the canvas (see Figure 2.21).

We now need to select two quantitative variables from the variable list and transfer one to the Y axis and one to the X axis. In this example we have selected the variables **wrkhrs** (hours worked per week) and **jobhard** (the extent to which working conditions are difficult) in the expectation that there is a positive relationship between them. In other words, the assumption is that those who work longer hours are more likely to experience their working conditions as difficult. Click and drag **wrkhrs** from the list of variables to the X axis drop zone and **jobhard** to the Y axis drop zone (as shown in Figure 2.21) and click **OK**. (There is a general convention to place the more independent, 'causal' variable on the horizontal X axis and the more dependent, 'caused' variable on the Y axis.)

The resulting scatterplot is shown in Figure 2.22 and the pattern, although not totally clear, appears to suggest a positive relationship between the two variables. In general, low scores on the **wrkhrs** variable correspond with low scores on the **jobhard** variable, while those who work longer hours (high scores on **wrkhrs**) are more likely to report difficult working conditions (high scores on **jobhard**). It

Y Axis Drop Zone   X Axis Drop Zone

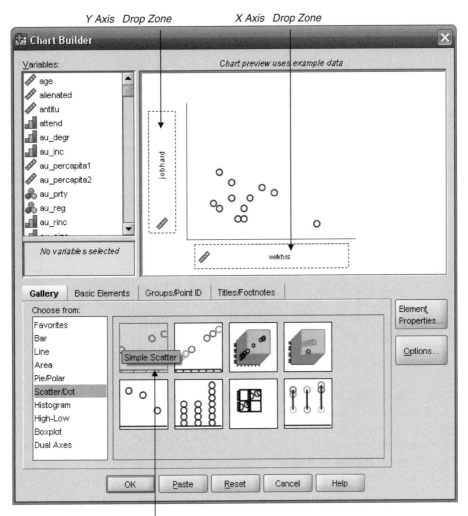

Click and drag the Simple Scatter plot onto the canvas (i.e. to the top right-hand panel)

Figure 2.21   *Chart Builder dialog box: scatterplot*

is important to point out, however, that in order to determine whether this relationship is statistically significant we would need to carry out a correlation on these two variables. A more detailed examination of scatterplots in the context of correlation and regression can be found in Module 8.

Line charts

Line charts bear a much closer visual resemblance to bar charts and histograms than the pie chart we considered earlier. However the use of a straight line to describe the data means the line graph often has a much more immediate impact, particularly comparing the distribution of a variable across two or more categories of a second variable. Line charts are particularly suitable for charting the distribution of quantitative variables that have been recoded into distinct ranked categories (see Module 3 for details on how to recode variables).

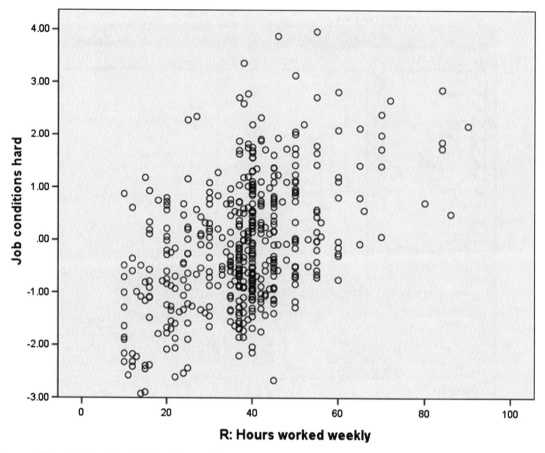

Figure 2.22   *Scatterplot of jobhard by wrkhrs*

In the following examples we will use an income variable, **gb_rinc** (respondent's earnings) and as this is already coded as income categories it is an ordinal rather than an interval/ratio variable. We will first produce a line chart for **gb_rinc** on its own and then compare the distribution of this variable for males and females.

To obtain line graphs in SPSS, select **Legacy Dialogs** and then **Line** from the **Graphs** drop-down menu (see Figure 2.23). This will open up the Line Charts dialog box, shown in Figure 2.24, where we have the option of choosing Simple, Multiple or Drop-line charts. We will begin with a Simple Line Chart for **gb_rinc** and as 'Simple' and 'Summaries for groups of cases' are the default options we only need to click on **Define**.

This will open up the *Define Simple Line* dialog box shown in Figure 2.25. Move the variable **gb_rinc** over to the Category Axis box in the usual way and then click on % **of cases** to obtain percentages rather than the number of cases. Then click on **Continue** and finally on **OK**.

The results are displayed in Figure 2.26 and we can see from the line chart that there is a steep increase until the modal value of £12, 000 to £14,999 is reached and thereafter there is a steady decline with two notable exceptions (a peak at £22,000 to £22, 999 and another at the very end, the £50,000 or more category). This chart indicates that the majority of respondents fall into the low to middle income categories with relatively few respondents in the high income groups. While this line graph provides

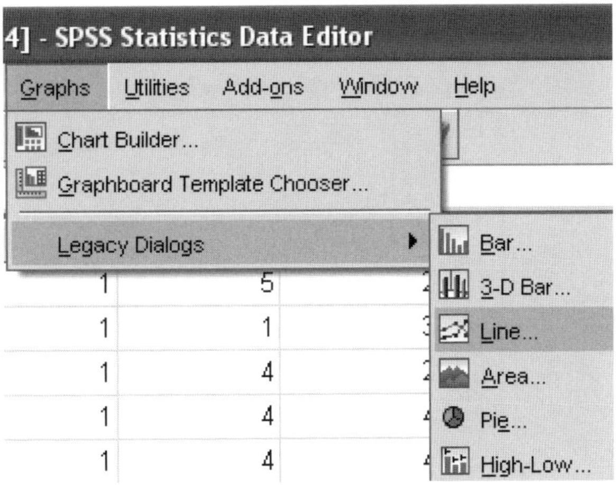

Figure 2.23   *Accessing Line charts from Graphs Menu*

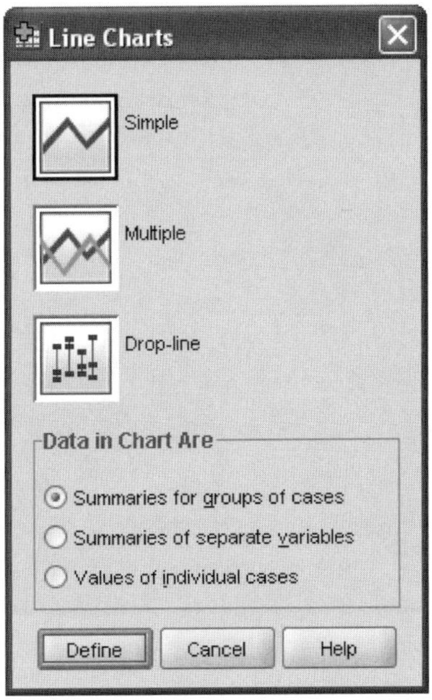

Figure 2.24   *Line Charts dialog box*

a vivid picture of the income distribution of our sample, it would be interesting to break this down according to gender. To compare males and females we need to produce a Multiple Line Chart.

Choose **Line** from the **Graphs** menu as before, only this time select **Multiple** in the Line Charts dialog box (see Figure 2.24). This will open the Define Multiple Line dialog box shown in Figure 2.27 below. Transfer the variable **gb_rinc** to the Category Axis box and **rsex** to the Define Lines by box and select **% of cases** as before. Then click on **Continue** and finally on **OK**.

The results are reproduced in Figure 2.28 and clearly illustrate the disparity between the income distributions of males and females. The is most evident at either end of the chart. For example,

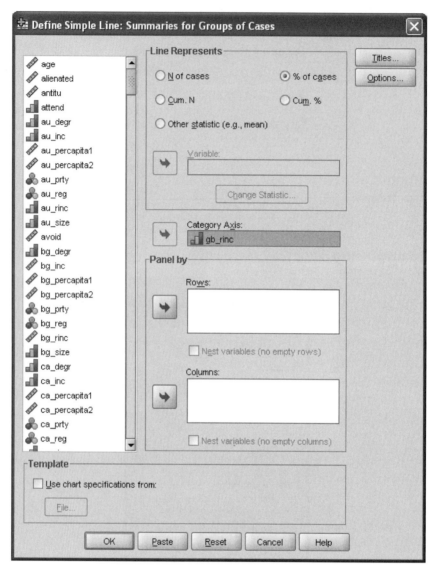

Figure 2.25 *Define Simple Line: Summaries for Groups of Cases*

we can see that there is a very small percentage of males in the four lowest income categories (less than 2 per cent as opposed to approximately 7.5 per cent of females). By contrast there are very few females in the higher income category and the sharp peak at the end (representing respondents who fall into the the highest income category of £56,000 or more) is almost exclusively accounted for by males.

Bar charts

In this example, we will see how the bar chart can be employed to examine the relationship between two variables. This might be carried out as a precursor to more formal statistical analyses or it may serve

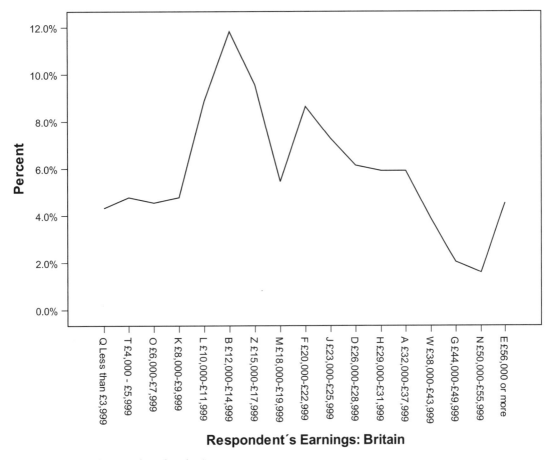

Figure 2.26   *Simple Line Chart for gb_rinc*

to illustrate the results of a statistical test. We are going to look at the relationship between income and level of education and use the bar chart to highlight the differences in average income between the various educational categories.

Open the **Chart Builder** through the **Graphs** menu and select **Bar** option from the list of charts. Click and drag the **Simple Bar** chart icon from the gallery (located in the bottom right-hand panel) to the 'canvas' (the area located in the top right-hand section of the dialog box). Then click and drag **degree** (education level) from the list of variables to the X axis drop zone and **gb_percapita2** (income per adult in the household) to the Y axis drop zone (as shown in Figure 2.29) and click **OK**.

As you can see from Figure 2.30 there is a clear relationship between income and level of education to the extent that those with greater educational attainment have a higher average income. So, it appears that the sacrifices you are making to obtain additional qualifications will be worth it after all! However, we cannot know from the chart if the relationship between income and education is statistically significant. To ascertain this you would need to carry out an appropriate statistical test and you might want to use these variables for your ANOVA exercise at the end of Module 7.

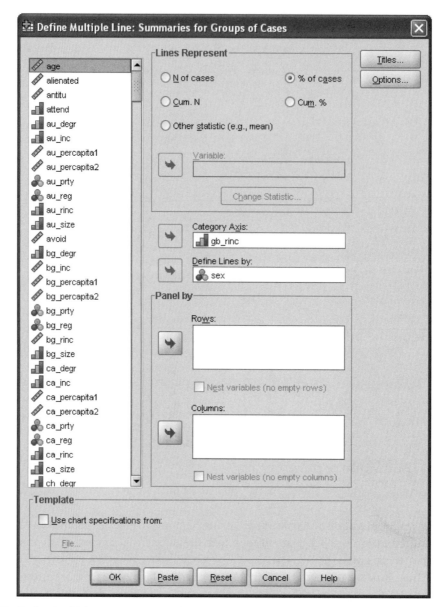

Figure 2.27 *Define Multiple Line: Summaries for Groups of Cases*

The chart editor

It is important to point out that SPSS allows you the freedom to modify your graphs and charts once you have created them. This is done through the Chart Editor, which is activated by double-clicking on any of the charts in the display pane of your Viewer window. The Chart Editor window (see Figure 2.31) contains its own menu bar and tool bar which offer a variety of options for modifying charts and graphs. Most chart types contain their own unique set of options (the Scatterplot Chart Editor, for example, provides the very useful facility for placing a regression line onto the plot) and details about these can be accessed through the Help menu.

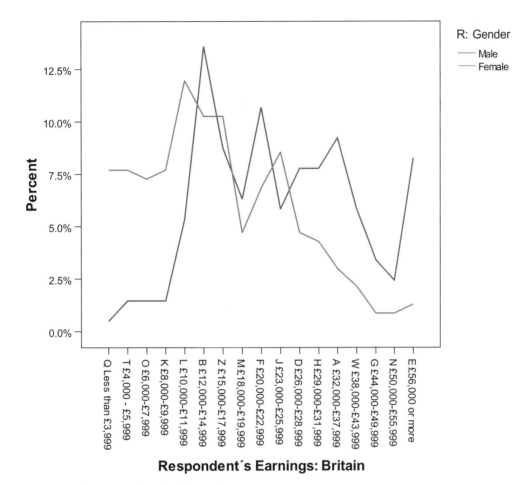

Figure 2.28 *Multiple Line Chart for gb_rinc by sex*

While it is not possible to cover all aspects of the Chart Editor here, the following discussion provides an indication of its potential by focusing on a few of the more commonly used features. To make things easier we will stick with the example we have just been working on and use the Chart Editor to modify the Bar Chart of Income by Education Level.

1. **Inserting data value labels**
   While the bar chart provides a good visual representation of the relative differences in income between the different levels of education, it would be helpful to know the precise amount for each of these. One way of achieving this is to superimpose the data value labels onto the bar chart.
   First we need to activate the Chart Editor by double-clicking on the bar chart in the Viewer Window. Then click on **Show Data Labels** in the **Elements** menu (Figure 2.31). The average income for each category of the **degree** variable should now appear on the bar chart and this can be transferred to a percentage should you wish.

2. **Adding titles and footnotes**
   You may want to insert additional information into your chart from time to time (e.g. a title or the source of your data) and the Chart Editor provides an easy way to do this. If the Chart Editor isn't open, activate it by double-clicking on the chart in the Viewer Window. Click on **Options** and then **Title**

Y Axis Drop Zone   X Axis Drop Zone

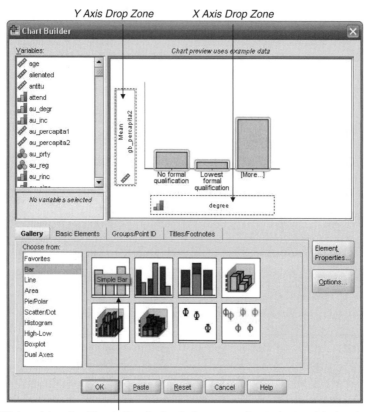

Click and drag the **Simple Bar** chart onto the canvas (i.e. to the top right-hand panel)

Figure 2.29 *Chart Builder dialog box: bar chart*

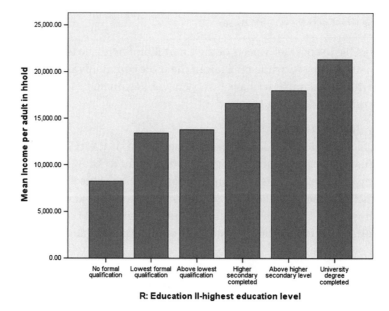

Figure 2.30 *Bar chart of Income by education level*

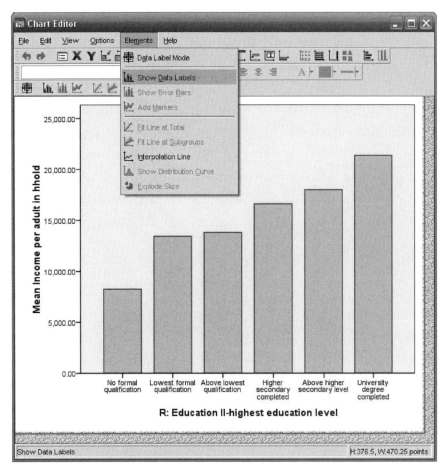

Figure 2.31 *Chart Editor: show data labels*

(Figure 2.32) and type in 'Income by Education Level' as the chart title. We also want to include details of the source of the data, so select **Options** again and then **Footnote** and type in the following: 'Source: ISSP (2005) Module on Work Orientations'.

3. **Altering the colour scheme**
   The Chart Editor also allows you to alter the colour scheme of your chart and this can enhance its impact significantly. There are various ways of achieving this, but in this example we are only going to focus on changing the colour of the bars. Open the Chart Editor and select **Properties** from the **Edit** menu to open the Properties dialog box (see Figure 2.33).

   Making sure the **Fill & Border** tab is selected, click in the box labelled **Fill** and then select one of the colours (e.g. blue) by clicking on it. Close the Chart Editor and return to the SPSS Viewer Window.

   If you have carried out these modifications correctly your bar chart should now resemble the one in Figure 2.34.

   Finally, it is necessary to stress that while the graphical procedures covered in this module represent the most widely used techniques for presenting survey data visually, they account for only a small proportion of the data display options available within SPSS. You are encouraged to try out the procedures we have not covered and different variations on those we have.

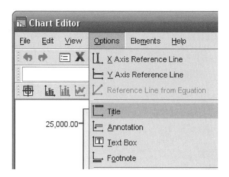

Figure 2.32 *Chart Editor: title and footnotes*

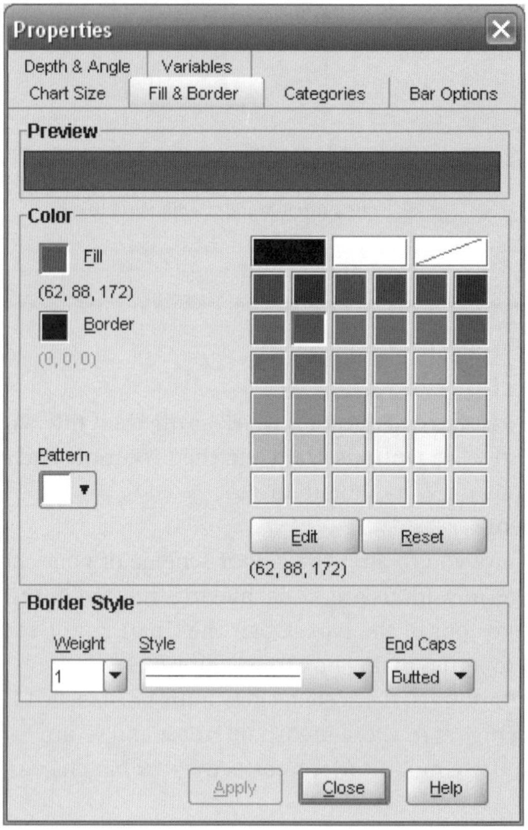

Figure 2.33 *Chart Editor: properties*

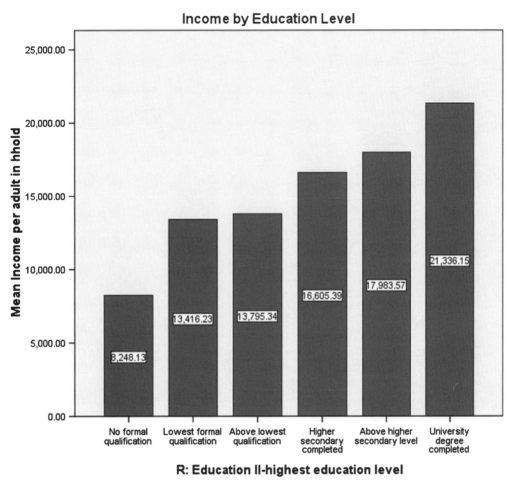

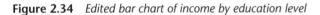

R: Education II-highest education level

Source: ISSP (2005) Module on Work Orientations

Figure 2.34 *Edited bar chart of income by education level*

SPSS EXERCISE FOR LISTING AND EXPLORING DATA

Using the ISSP dataset from the country of your choice, carry out the following procedures:

1. Select a number of variables from one of the datasets and produce appropriate statistics and charts using the Frequencies procedure in SPSS. Remember to take into account the level of measurement of each variable.
2. Using the Explore procedure in SPSS, examine the distribution of a scale variable across the categories of a nominal or ordinal variable. Focus in particular on the median, interquartile range and the most extreme values for each category.
3. Use the Chart Builder to create some pie charts, scattergrams and bar charts, selecting variables at the appropriate level of measurement.

3 Data Selection and Manipulation

INTRODUCTION

Often a researcher carrying out an analysis of a dataset may want to alter or change the makeup of the dataset in some way. This could particularly be the case if the researcher is analysing a dataset that was originally collected by others for different purposes. This is the situation here where you are analysing datasets that were collected, not for students to 'practice' on, but as part of the ISSP members' ongoing research into work orientations. This analysis of an already-existing dataset is called *secondary analysis*.

Even if researchers have collected the data themselves, they may want to alter the form of the data in some way in order to carry out a particular analysis. These alterations to the 'core' dataset may even have been anticipated or planned from the outset of a project. The alterations are of two basic types: *data selection* or *data manipulation*. Practically all social science data analysis packages will have at least rudimentary facilities for data selection and data manipulation. The facilities that SPSS offers are quite advanced.

Since the goals of data selection and manipulation are similar – to 'recast' a dataset into a form more amenable to analysis – and much of the logic of the two processes are also similar, we will consider both processes in this module.

DATA SELECTION

Sometimes researchers know that they will not need all of the information contained within a dataset for a certain analysis or course of analyses that they intend to carry out. Hence, either the *cases* of interest or the *variables* of interest for the given analysis may be selected. This is done for two main reasons.

- *Efficiency*. If the analysis is restricted to less than the whole dataset, the technical demands on memory space, time to read the data and so forth will be lessened.
- *Safety*. By restricting the analysis to only the cases and variables of interest, one can ensure that unwanted cases and variables do not inadvertently get included in an analysis by mistake.

Researchers usually consider the gains in efficiency that can be made through wise data selection but often fail to recognize those *safety* aspect – the utility of data selection as an important safeguard for a valid analysis of only those cases of interest.

There are two generally recognized methods of data selection: **choosing subsets of cases**; and **choosing subsets of variables**. We will consider each in turn.

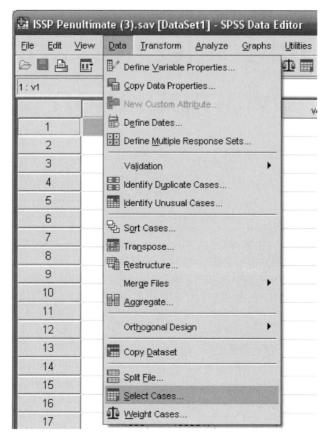

Figure 3.1 *Data menu: Select Cases*

Subsets of cases

Often, the analyst may only be interested in a portion of the cases within the dataset. Which portion or portions will depend upon the dataset and the interests of the particular analysis in question. For instance, when we were preparing this chapter we made a decision to use Germany for our examples. However, since the ISSP provided separate datasets for East and West Germany, we needed to create one ourselves. This involved selecting out the data for East Germany and West Germany from the complete ISSP dataset for all countries and then saving this permanently as a new 'all Germany' dataset. The following section provides a step-by-step guide to this process.

Using Select Cases to create a new dataset

This section shows you how to create a new dataset by permanently selecting a subset of cases from a larger dataset. As the discussion below relates to the creation of the German dataset (which is available to you through the website) it is for illustrative purposes only.[1] Our first step was to open the complete ISSP dataset (i.e. for all countries) and then click on the **Select Cases** option from the **Data** menu (see Figure 3.1).

[1] If you really wish to carry out these steps you will need to download the complete ISSP dataset for all 31 countries.

*Click the '**If condition is satisfied**'button and '**If**' (after naming the dataset)*

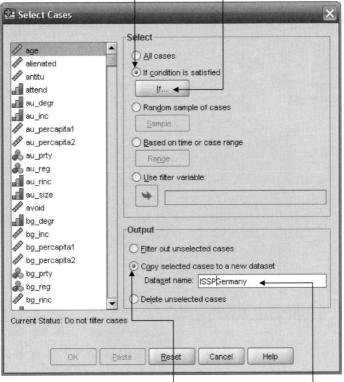

To make the selection permanent click **here** and type a new name in the **box**

Figure 3.2   *Select Cases dialog box*

This opens up the **Select Cases** dialog box with the '**All Cases**' Button selected by default. However, as we wanted to select a subset of cases from the dataset (i.e. only respondents from East Germany and West Germany), we needed to change this and 'switch on' the '**If condition is satisfied**' button (as in Figure 3.2).

The **Output** section of the Select Cases Dialog box provides us with three options and it worth looking at each of these in turn.

1. Filter out unselected cases

   This is the option that you are likely to use most frequently as it filters out unselected cases *temporarily*, allowing you to return to the complete dataset with ease. An example is provided later in the chapter.

2. Copy selected cases to a new dataset

   The second option creates a completely new dataset based upon the selection of cases you have made and this is the one we are going to focus on in the current example. In other words, in order to select out respondents from Germany (East and West) we needed to ask SPSS to create a new dataset that only contained those cases.

3. Delete unselected cases

   You need to be *extremely* careful about using this final option as it permanently deletes unselected cases from the dataset. If you do need to use this option it is recommended that you have a back-up version of the original dataset.

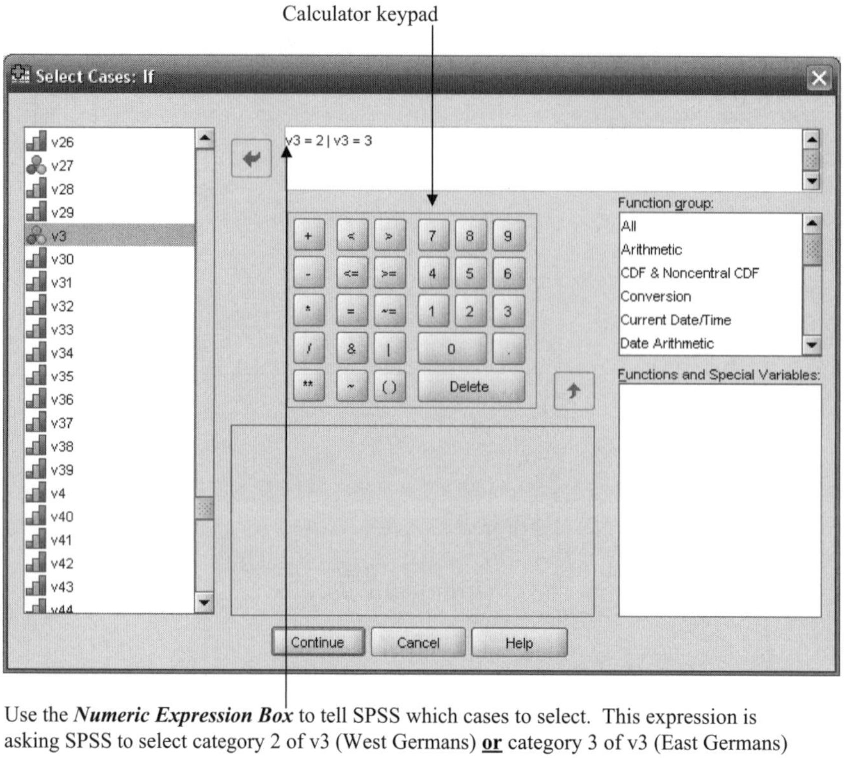

Calculator keypad

Use the *Numeric Expression Box* to tell SPSS which cases to select. This expression is asking SPSS to select category 2 of v3 (West Germans) **or** category 3 of v3 (East Germans)

Figure 3.3 *Select Cases If dialog box*

v3 Country

		Frequency	Percent	Valid Percent	Cumulative Percent
Valid	1 AU-Australia	1988	4.6	4.6	4.6
	2 DE-W-Germany-West	1114	2.6	2.6	7.1
	3 DE-E-Germany-East	587	1.4	1.4	8.5
	4 GB-Great Britain	913	2.1	2.1	10.6
	6 US-United States	1518	3.5	3.5	14.1
	8 HU-Hungary	1012	2.3	2.3	16.4
	10 IE-Ireland	1001	2.3	2.3	18.7

Figure 3.4 *Frequency table for 'v3 Country' (partial view)*

After selecting the second option in the **Output** section of the **Select Cases** dialog box (Figure 3.2) we needed to type in the name we were going to give the new dataset (i.e. ISSPGermany). Finally, we clicked on 'If...' to open the **Select Cases: If** dialog box (shown in Figure 3.3).

The next step is to enter the expression that identifies the cases that are to be selected by SPSS. For the purposes of this chapter we wanted to select only respondents from Germany (East and West). We can see from the frequency table in Figure 3.4 that West Germany and East Germany are represented by categories 2 and 3 of the variable '**v3 Country**'. We therefore needed to tell SPSS to select either category 2 or category 3 of the variable 'v3 Country'.

The relevant expression is shown in Figure 3.3 and while this could be typed in directly, it is probably safer to use the variable list and calculator keypad until you become more familiar with SPSS (see below for a brief explanation of some of the most frequently used functions on the keypad). We scrolled down through the list of variables until reaching **v3** (the variable for country) and then clicked and dragged it across to the Numeric Expression Box. Then we used the calculator keypad to enter the 'equals' symbol (=) and the number **2**. At this point the Numeric Expression Box should contain the first part of the expression relating to West German respondents (i.e. **v3 = 2**). Next we used the keypad to select '|' (the symbol for 'or') and clicked and dragged **v3** over to the Numeric Expression box again. Finally, we used the keypad to enter = and **3**.

The Numeric Expression Box then contained the complete expression requesting SPSS to select only West Germans or East Germans: v3 = 2 | v3 =3 (In English: '*v3 equals 2 or v3 equals 3*'). To generate the German dataset, we clicked on **Continue** to return to the Select Cases dialog box and clicked **OK**.

In carrying out this procedure we created a new dataset containing only German respondents and we will be working with this subset of respondents for the remainder of the current chapter. The goal of *efficiency* is met since the new dataset is only a fraction of the size (1701 respondents compared to over 43,000 in the original dataset). The goal of *safety* is also met since, after selection, it is impossible for non-German respondents to become inadvertently mixed up in the analysis. The researcher will know for sure that any results obtained relate only to Germany.

The calculator keypad in SPSS

Before continuing, you may want to take a good look at the functions available on the 'calculator keypad':

- Some, like **+**, **−** , and **=** are obvious;
- ***** means '*multiply*', **/** is '*divide*', ****** is '*square*';
- Others include: **>** for '*greater than*'; **>=** for '*greater than or equal to*'; **&** for '*and*'; **|** for '*or*'; and **[ ]** to enclose part of a statement in *brackets*;
- **~=** means '*not equal to*';
- As you might guess, **<** means '*less than*' and **<=** is '*less than or equal to*'.

You can also scroll up and down to the right of the 'keypad' to see some more obscure functions.

Temporarily filtering out unwanted cases

Researchers often need to carry out different types of analysis on specific subsets of the data and the Select Cases option can be used to *temporarily* filter out unwanted cases. To illustrate this we will work through two examples using the full German dataset.

A simple example

The ISSP datasets are made up of individuals drawn from the general population who are respondents to a sample survey. Let us say the researcher wishes to carry out a certain analysis on only women in the sample. Since the survey respondents have their sex coded as a variable, the data selection procedure in SPSS can be employed to ensure that only the data from the females is used.

*Click the '**If condition is satisfied**' button and 'If'*

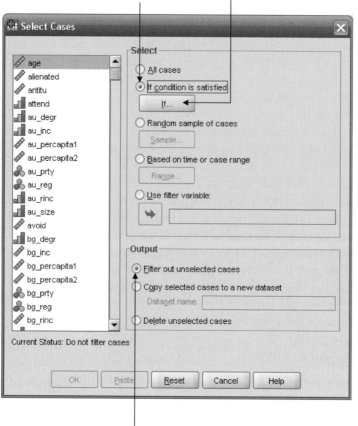

Click **here** to <u>temporarily</u> filter out unselected cases

Figure 3.5   *Select Cases dialog box*

To temporarily select a subset of the data, open the **Data** menu and click on the **Select Cases** option (as shown in Figure 3.1). This will open up the **Select Cases** dialog box and, as we want to select a subset of cases from the dataset (i.e. only females), click on the 'If **condition is satisfied**' button (see Figure 3.5). However, we only want to make a *temporary* selection this time, so click on the '**Filter out unselected cases**' button.

Finally click on 'If...' to open the **Select Cases: If** dialog box (shown in Figure 3.6). We now need to tell SPSS to select out only females from the dataset (i.e. category **2** of the **sex** variable). Scroll down through the list of variables until you come to **sex** and then click and drag it across to the Numeric Expression Box. Use the calculator keypad (or your computer keyboard) to enter the remainder of the expression (i.e. = **2**). When you have entered the full expression (sex = 2), click on **Continue** to return to the Select Cases dialog box and then click **OK**.

After this procedure, all the unselected cases (i.e. males) will be marked with an oblique bar on the grid in Data View (see Figure 3.7). Any statistical analysis carried out from now on will only apply to females.

After the special analysis of this subset of cases is complete, the researcher can restore the dataset to its original full form if desired. The way to do this is to go back through the **Data** menu to the **Select Cases** dialog box and click on the '**All cases**' button and then **OK**. (NOTE: Make sure you do this before moving on to the next section, otherwise you will be operating with an incomplete dataset!)

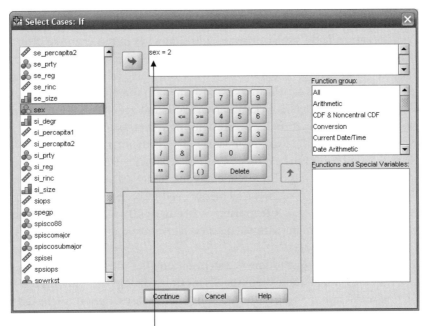

Use the **Numeric Expression Box** to tell SPSS which cases to select. This expression is asking SPSS to select category **2** of the **sex** variable (i.e. females).

Figure 3.6   *Select Cases If dialog box*

	v1	v2	v3	v4	v5	v6	
1	4350	2001105	2	2	3	3	
2	4350	2001106	2	2	3	2	
3	4350	2001111	2	5	3	3	
4	4350	2001202	2	2	3	3	
5	4350	2001209	2	2	5	4	
6	4350	2001306	2	1	3	3	
7	4350	2001311	2	2	3	3	
8	4350	2001404	2	5	3	3	
9	4350	2001406	2	2	2	8	
10	4350	2001501	2	3	4	1	
11	4350	2001503	2	4	3	2	
12	4350	2001506	2	3	3	3	

Figure 3.7   *Example of selected cases on the Data View window*

A more complex example

The selection of cases can be fairly straightforward and simple, as in our example of picking people of one sex, or the criteria used for selection of cases can be quite complex. A researcher might be interested in exploring 'a subset of a subset'. For example, we may be interested in examining the attitudes to work of young single males. The process of selecting cases is similar to the previous example except this time we need to take three factors into account (sex, marital status and age). You should run frequency tables for these three variables to help you formulate the appropriate expression. As we want to select males for the variable sex we need to enter the expression '**sex = 1**'. For the marital status variable, the category for single is 5, so the second part of the expression will be '**marital = 5**'. Finally we are going to be quite generous in our definition of 'young' and include anyone under 40, so the final part of our numeric expression will be '**age < 40**'. These different elements need to be joined together with & symbols so the final expression should read '**sex = 1 & marital = 5 & age < 40**' (see Figure 3.8). Note that since we linked the three parts of the statement with '&' *all these parts* must apply; i.e. *only* males that are single and under 40 will be selected.

To carry out this procedure we just follow the steps outlined in the previous example. Click on the **Select Cases** option in the **Data** menu to open the **Select Cases** dialog box. Click on the '**If condition is satisfied**' button and make sure that the '**Filter out unselected cases**' option is selected before clicking on '**If...**'. This will open the **Select Cases: If** dialog box where you can enter the appropriate numeric expression (sex = 1 & marital = 5 & age < 40), either by typing it in or using the variable list and calculator keypad. When you have entered the full expression (as shown in Figure 3.8), click on **Continue** to return to the Select Cases dialog box and then **OK**.

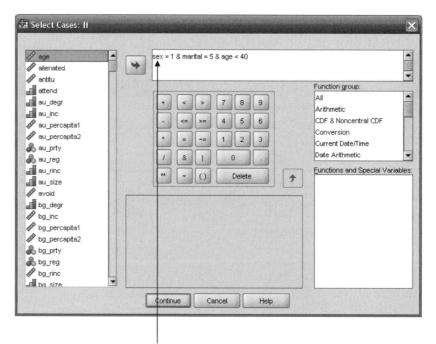

Use the *Numeric Expression Box* to tell SPSS which cases to select. This expression is asking SPSS to select single males less than 40 years of age

Figure 3.8 *Example of a more complex selection using Select Cases: If*

Again, you will see that the unselected cases are marked with an oblique bar and any analysis carried out now will only apply to single males under 40. It is therefore **very important** that you undo this temporary selection, restoring the dataset to its original form, before moving on to the next section. To do this, return to the Select Cases dialog box (by clicking on **S**elect Cases in the **D**ata Menu) and click on the '**A**ll cases' button and then **OK**.

SPSS EXERCISES FOR SELECTING CASES

Now, try out the **Select Cases** procedure for yourself. You can use any of the ISSP datasets but think carefully about the subset of respondents you want to select before carrying out the procedure. Try a simple selection first and then perhaps a more complicated statement. (**Remember**, to make a temporary selection you should use the '**Filter out unselected cases**' option. This way you can always get back to the original unselected dataset by 'pushing' the '**A**ll cases' button on the Select Cases dialog box.)

Subsets of variables

As well as choosing subsets of cases, the researcher can select a subset of **variables** from a complete dataset. As with case selection, this could be done either for reasons of efficiency or for reasons of safety. For example, the authors of this textbook created a special smaller-sized version of each country-specific ISSP dataset by selecting a subset of variables from the overall ISSP dataset. This was done to enable readers to use the inexpensive 'student version' of SPSS which only works on datasets with 55 or fewer variables.

Efficiency

As with taking a smaller number of cases, reducing the number of variables within a dataset will decrease its gross size which can lead to reductions in the amount of computing resources required and to significant increases in the speed of computations.

Safety Reasons

While it is not as often realized, greater safety can also be attained through selecting subsets of variables.

Contamination

Sometimes a data analyst will discover that a variable or variables in a dataset are inaccurate or 'contaminated' in some way. For instance, there could have been an error in coding that cannot be fixed. If the 'contaminated' variable(s) was left in the dataset, it could cause problems for subsequent analysts who might use it without realizing that the variable was unreliable. Hence, the 'data manager' might conclude that the safest course is to 'purge' the variable from the dataset altogether.

Restrict Access

The 'owner' or 'data manager' of a dataset may want to give access to the data to someone else so that person can carry out a specific analysis. The 'data manager', however, may not want to give the person *full* access to all the information in the dataset.

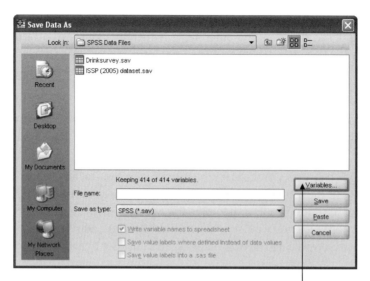

Click on Variables button

Figure 3.9 *Save Data As* dialog box

For instance, some variables may contain information that would make it possible to identify individual respondents. The 'data manager' may want to 'mask' these variables in order to preserve confidentiality. One way to do this is to release a partial dataset that contains only those variables necessary to attain the goals of a specific analysis. Scrupulous secondary analysts are in no way inconvenienced by possessing only a partial dataset – for their purposes it is as if the data were complete.

The procedure for selecting a subset of variables is also very straightforward. Select **Save As** from the **File** menu to open the **Save Data As** dialog box (see Figure 3.9) and click on the '**Variables**' button. You now need to select the specific variables you want to include in the new version of the dataset by clicking in the appropriate boxes in the **Keep** column (as shown in Figure 3.10). Then select **Continue** and don't forget to give the file a new name before saving. One can of course combine variable selection and case selection in order to produce a doubly truncated partial dataset.

Splitting files

It is sometimes helpful to split a file by the levels of a categorical variable so that data analysis is conducted automatically at each level separately. For example, this could be done according to the sex of respondent whereby each analysis is carried out separately for males and females. To split a file, open the **Data** pull-down menu and select **Split File**. Scroll down through the variables in the source list in the Split File dialog box to locate the variable 'sex' and click and drag it over to the target box (as shown in Figure 3.11).

Click on the **Compare Groups** (or **Organize Output by Groups**) button, and then on **OK**. Once the file has been split, any subsequent analysis will be run for each group in turn and then SPSS will present separate results for each group. Figure 3.12 shows a frequency table for the variable **union** (Trade union membership) after the Split File (Compare Groups) procedure has been applied (i.e. split by the variable **sex**).

The **Compare Groups** option produces separate results for males and females presented in a single table, whereas if we had selected **Organize Output by Groups** SPSS would have presented two

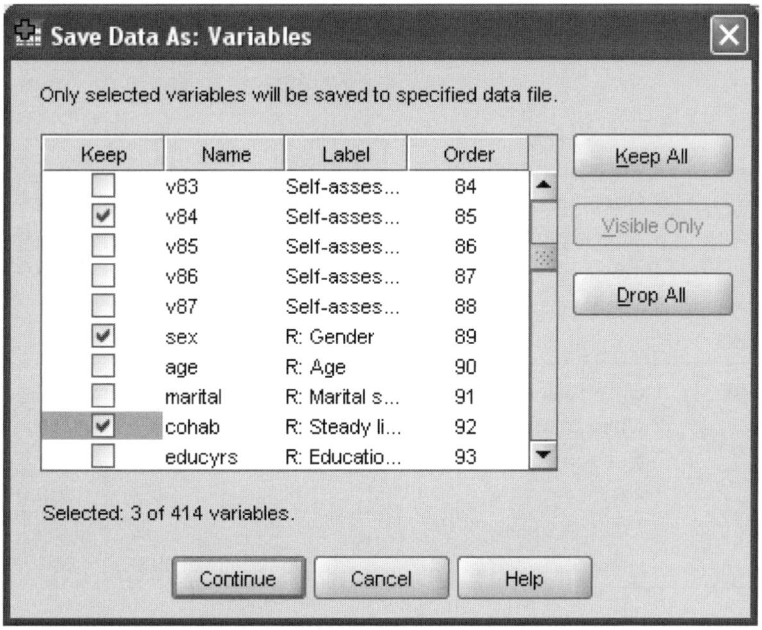

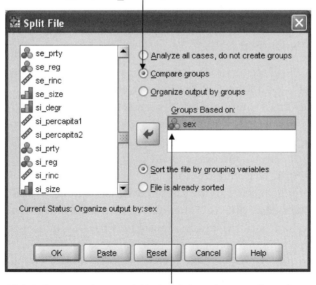

Figure 3.10 *Selecting a subset of variables*

Select the **Compare groups** option

Figure 3.11 *An example of splitting a file by **sex***

union R: Trade union membership

sexR: Gender			Frequency	Percent	Valid Percent	Cumulative Percent
1 Male	Valid	1 Currently member	181	17.6	17.7	17.7
		2 Once member, not now	218	21.2	21.3	39.0
		3 Never member	624	60.9	61.0	100.0
		Total	1022	99.8	100.0	
	Missing	9 MNA, refuced	2	.2		
	Total		1024	100.0		
2 Female	Valid	1 Currently member	85	7.8	7.8	7.8
		2 Once member, not now	181	16.6	16.7	24.5
		3 Never member	819	75.4	75.5	100.0
		Total	1084	99.8	100.0	
	Missing	9 MNA, refuced	2	.2		
	Total		1087	100.0		

Figure 3.12   *Frequency table for **union** after application of Split File by **sex***

completely separate frequency tables. To cancel the split and return to the original settings, select the 'Analyze all cases, do not create groups' option in the Split File dialog box and then click on OK (you will need to do this before you move on to the next section of the book).

WEIGHTING

Note: The dataset for Germany provided with this book comes with a 'weighting variable': wtdeutsch. If you are using the German dataset to duplicate our examples, make sure the weight is 'switched on'.

While not strictly selection, the procedure for weighting the cases in a dataset – that is, counting some cases more or less than others – does follow on from case selection.

The need to **weight** usually arises when a probability sample has been taken and the researcher knows or discovers that some categories of cases in the sample have been over- or under-selected. That is, some groups of cases have had a better chance of being selected in the sample than others. (Weighting is quite a normal procedure. Sample designs for surveys often are deliberately designed to over- or under-sample some groups.) If researchers want to generalize from the sample results to the target population, they will want to equalize the representation of all the cases in their sample. If the over- or under-represented groups can be identified in the dataset (that is, if there are variables in the dataset that allow the over- or under-represented groups to be identified) and the researchers have an idea of how much the groups have been over- or under-represented, a corrective weight can be applied.

For example, the German ISSP dataset actually comes from two survey samples, one carried out in former East Germany and one carried out in former West Germany. While the West German sample is about twice as large as that for East Germany, the actual population size of former West Germany, at 63.25 million, is almost 4 times larger than the 16.1 million population size of former East Germany. If we were to combine the two samples without weighting, the net effect would be that the East German respondents would be over-represented by a factor of two. Since the topic of the ISSP survey is 'orientations to work' and we can anticipate that people who grew up in the formerly socialist GDR are likely to have quite different views about work than those who grew up in the *'übercapitalist'* Federal Republic of (West) Germany, this would undermine the validity of any analysis. We need to apply a corrective weight, wtdeutsch.

Approaches to weighting

A normal convention is never to weight any individual case by more than a factor of 2. The reason for this is that, if individual cases are counted more than twice, the possibility of a distortion in the results due solely to weighting increases. If a case is weighted more than 2, and the case happens to be 'peculiar' in some way, the researcher may end up erroneously concluding that an odd characteristic is really quite common. Hence, it is generally better practice to weight the *over*-represented groups by a weight *less than* one and to weight the *under*-represented groups by a weight *more than* one. In this way, the chance of anomalous results resulting from some cases receiving too large a weight are minimized. For instance, in our example instead of weighting the West Germans by 2 it is better to give the under-represented West German group a weight of 1.5 and the over-represented East German group a weight of 0.75, producing a balanced unified sample in which the proportions from both groups match the proportionate sizes of the populations from which they were drawn. (Note that even though the East Germans now will be weighted less than 1.0, none of the East Germans respondents actually have been removed from the data. Each East German person is still there, only they count a bit less.)

An example of weighting

Here is an example of using SPSS to apply a weight to the German dataset. Go to the **Data** list on the main Data View window of the Data Editor and select **Weight Cases...** (as in Figure 3.13) A Weight Cases window as in Figure 3.14 will open. Activate the **'Weight cases by'** button and move the variable **wtdeutsch** (which is a variable we have computed to give the East and West German weights) into the **Frequency** variable box and apply the weight by clicking **OK**. Once the weight has been applied a **WEIGHT ON** note appears on the bottom right-hand row of the Data Editor. Ensure that the weight remains on while working with the German dataset.

DATA MANIPULATION

As well as employing data selection to 'recast' a dataset into a smaller dataset made up of fewer cases or fewer variables or to weight the cases in a dataset, an analyst can also 'recast' a dataset by employing one or more techniques of *data manipulation*. In data manipulation, the number of cases usually remains the same and the number of variables is not reduced (in fact, the number of variables is often *increased*).

Data manipulation involves taking existing variables and either:

1. *altering* the values/codes of the variables in some way;
   or
2. *combining* the codes/values of two or more variables with some sort of logical statement to create a new variable.

Data manipulation is a powerful tool. No one, no matter how well organized they are or how clear a preconception they have of their analysis plans, can anticipate every eventuality. At least some of the variables in a dataset will almost inevitably need to be modified or changed during the course of an

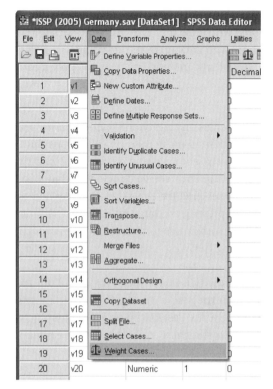

Figure 3.13   *Choosing the Weight Cases window*

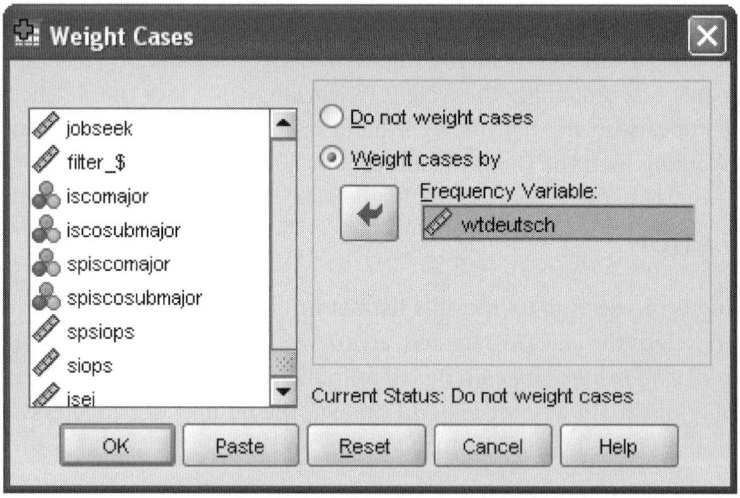

Figure 3.14   *An example of the variable, **wtdeutsch**, being used to weight a dataset*

analysis program in order to satisfy the changing requirements of the analysis. (Indeed there is an expectation that the researcher's own ideas and plans will (*should!*) change as a result of early findings.)

These considerations of course will apply doubly to *secondary analysts* who are adapting a dataset collected by others to goals of their own. In fact, data manipulation is so normal a practice that people setting up datasets will expect to do some data manipulation. In many cases data manipulation forms an essential preliminary step in the overall process of data analysis. Rather than trying to create a dataset that will cater for every conceivable type of statistical analysis, researchers will set up the variables in a form that is *most readily amenable* for *later* data manipulation.

This means that those setting up a dataset will opt for the maximum practical amount of detail at the stages of coding and data input. Due to the modern technologies of data input and the possibilities available with data manipulation, coding a set of information using codes based upon many detailed categories rather than codes made up of a few large, aggregate, categories is *always* a better practice in the long run.

SPSS has excellent facilities for data manipulation.

There are some fairly esoteric data manipulation procedures but, thankfully, there are four main basic types of data manipulation techniques that are the most useful and that are employed 95 per cent of the time.

The four main data manipulation techniques are as follows.

1. Altering individual codes or groups of codes of variables by either changing the actual individual values of the codes or combining blocks of codes together into larger aggregates (**R**ecode and **A**utomatic **Recode**).
2. Manipulating a variable's codes by carrying out simple or complex arithmetic operations on variables (**C**ompute).
3. Carrying out logical manipulations on variables by combining the codes/values of two or more variables with some sort of logical statement to create a new variable (**If**).
4. Creating new variables by counting the occurrences of a value or a range of values across a number of variables (**C**o**unt**).

We will consider each of these in turn.

ALTERING INDIVIDUAL CODES OR GROUPS OF CODES (**R**ECODE)

Altering a variable's individual codes or groups of codes by changing either the individual values of the codes or combining blocks of codes together into larger aggregates is one form of data manipulation. Perhaps the best way to explain this is to provide some examples.

Combining codes
Combining blocks of codes together into larger aggregates

Often a variable will have a large number of highly detailed codes. An analyst may wish to merge these detailed codes into a smaller number of aggregate categories.

Example 1   In the simplest cases, the original detailed codes are a series of numbers where the numbers represent real quantities (integers). For instance, the respondents to the ISSP all have their age recorded in years (the variable '**age**'); the analyst may wish to lump these values into three categories:

1. young adults (those aged between 18 and 29)
2. adults (those aged between 30 and 64)
3. elderly (those aged 65 or more)

Visually, one wants to do something that would look like Figure 3.15.

Age-Years	Age-Category
18 19 ⇑ ⇓ 29	**(1) Young adults**
30 31 ⇑ ⇓ 64	**(2) Adults**
65 ⇑ ⇓ 92	**(3) Elderly**

Figure 3.15 *Recoding age in years to age category*

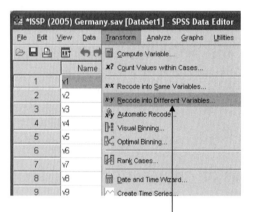

Select the 'Recode into **Different** Variables' option

Figure 3.16a *Transform: Recode into Different Variables*

It is important to point out that there are two recode commands: **Recode into Same Variables** and **Recode into Different Variables**. The first of these commands alters the codes of the existing variable, whereas the second creates a completely new variable which contains the modified codes. It is generally advisable to select the second option so that, as well as creating a new, recoded, variable, the original variable with its codes is retained intact.

To recode '**age**', open the **Transform** pull-down menu and select the **Recode into Different Variables** option (see Figure 3.16a).

This will open the '**Recode into Different Values**' dialog window (see Figure 3.16b). From the source variable list, select '**age**' and click and drag it across into the 'target box'. We choose the **Recode into Different Variables** option because we want to retain a variable with the original year-by-year age values as well as having one with the new age categories. Go to the **Output Variable** box and type in the **Name** of the new variable, **agecats**. **Label** this new variable as **age recoded**, and click on the **Change** button to replace the '?' for the new variable with its name, **agecats**.

To collapse age in years into categories, we click on the **Old and New Values** box which opens a sub-window for us to create the categories (Figure 3.16c).

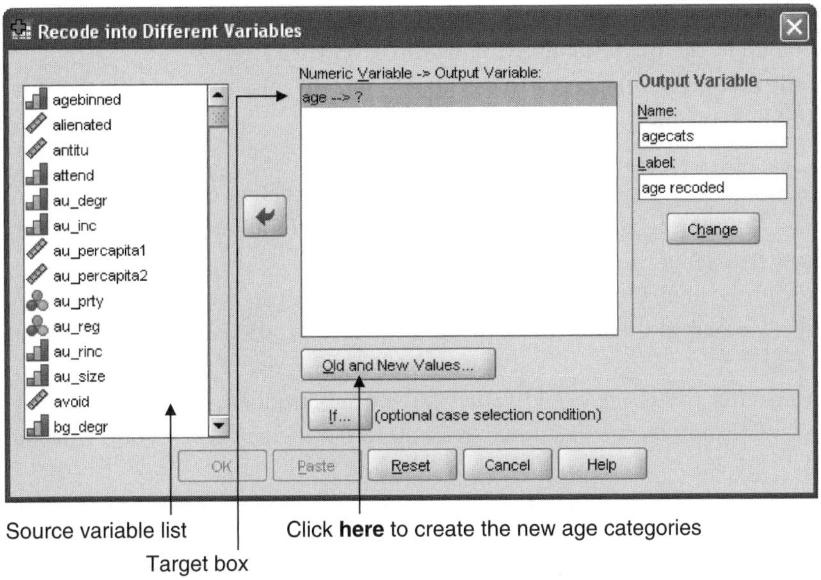

Figure 3.16b   *Recode into Different Variables (**age** → **agecats**)*

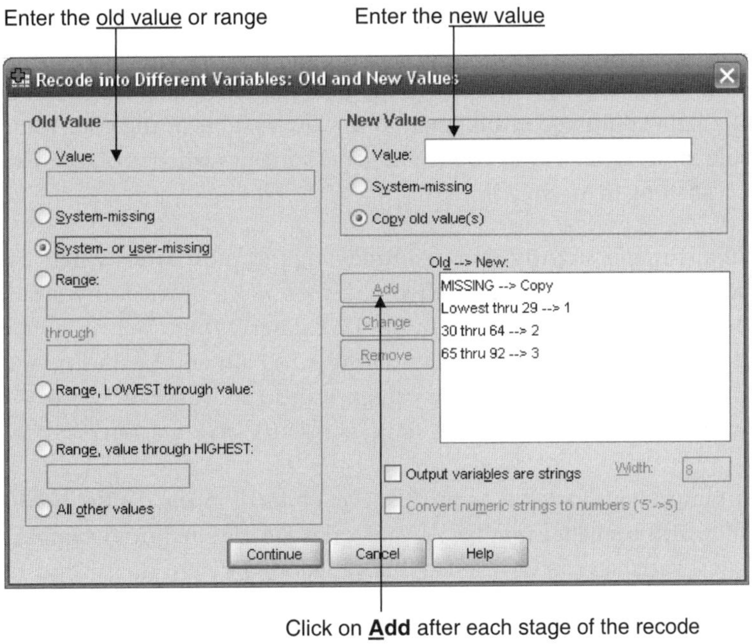

Figure 3.16c   *Identifying old and new values for **agecats***

Here you work between the **Old Value** and **New Value** boxes to fill in the commands in the '**work box**' on the mid right-hand side of the window. There is a variety of ways you can specify the 'old values' that are to be converted into 'new values'. It is possible to:

■ specify individual values
■ specify a range of values (for example, **30 thru 64**)

- specify the lowest value up to a limit (for example, **Lowest thru 29**)
- specify a value up to the highest value (for example, **65 thru highest**)
- ensure that the missing values in the 'old' variable remain missing values in the 'new' variable (for example, **MISSING →Copy**)

The keywords 'lowest' and 'highest' are used to avoid the problem of our not being sure of the exact code of the lowest or highest value. Here, 'Lowest thru 29' includes everyone aged 29 or younger, even if we do not know the age of the youngest person.

Note how since the value '99' in the original variable, **age**, was a missing value ('NA, refused') and not an actual age, we had to use '**65 thru 92** $->$ **3**' instead of '65 thru highest' to create the 'Elderly' category in **agecats**.

In all instances, after the range of old values have been specified, the new value for each category must be entered. For example, the age range from 30 to 64, inclusive, is recoded into age category '2'; **30 thru 64 -> 2**.

After each recode has been entered, it is added to the 'work box' by clicking the **Add** button. The best way to ensure that all missing values are dealt with is to finish off by clicking on '**System or user-missing**' (under Old Value) and '**Copy old value(s)**' in the New Value section. When all the recode from 'old' to 'new' values are set, click on the **Continue** button, and **OK** to run the re-code.

A new variable, **agecats**, will come into existence. You can verify this by scanning to the far right-hand side of the Data Editor grid. There you will find a new column in the data grid which contains the values for the variable **agecats**.

The next stage is to label each of the values of the new variable. To label agecats, open the **Variable View** window of the Data Editor and scroll down to the last variable in the grid. You can now label the new recoded variable in the same way as you would label variables when you are creating a new dataset (see the section on Labelling in Module 1).

Example 2 A similar, though slightly more complex, aggregation arises when we have a variable with a series of detailed codes, but the detailed codes do *not* represent any steadily increasing or decreasing 'run' of quantities. For example, in the ISSP dataset there is a variable which provides a detailed list of reasons why the respondent is no longer in paid employment (**v66**). As can be seen from the table in Figure 3.17, there are nine categories in this variable, some of which have very low frequency counts (e.g. only 2.2 per cent of respondents gave marriage as the main reason for leaving their job).

While it is important to have variables with this level of detail in the dataset there will also be occasions where variables with a smaller number of categories are required (for example, see Module 5 on Crosstabulation). Most variables can be recoded in a variety of different ways, depending on the nature of the analysis one intends to carry out, and it is important to remember that the example below provides just one possible solution. Here the intention is to aggregate the data from the nine valid categories (and two missing value categories) in the original variable (v66) into a smaller number of larger categories. The old and new categories with codes are presented in Figure 3.18.

The step-by-step procedures required for recoding the variable **v66** into a new variable, **whyjobend**, are described below and highlighted in Figures 3.19a and 3.19b. As before, choose the **Recode into Different Variables** option from the **Transform** pull-down menu. This opens the **Recode into Different Variables** dialog box (Figure 3.19a) where you need to specify the original variable and provide a name and label for the new variable.

v66 Not currently working: main reason for job end

		Frequency	Percent	Valid Percent	Cumulative Percent
Valid	1 Retired by age	230	10.9	29.4	29.4
	2 Retired by choice	91	4.3	11.6	41.0
	3 Retired not by choice	47	2.2	6.0	47.0
	4 Became disabled	112	5.3	14.4	61.3
	5 Workplace shut down	47	2.2	6.0	67.4
	6 Dismissed	76	3.6	9.7	77.0
	7 Contract ended	31	1.5	3.9	81.0
	8 Family responsibilities	132	6.3	16.8	97.8
	9 Got married	17	.8	2.2	100.0
	Total	784	37.1	100.0	
Missing	0 Not applicable (code 1 in V27 or code 2 in V64)	1297	61.4		
	99 NA, refused	31	1.5		
	Total	1328	62.9		
Total		2111	100.0		

Figure 3.17 *Frequency table for variable* ***v66***

Old CODE	Current Categories	New Categories	New CODE
1 2 3	Retired by age Retired by choice Retired not by choice	→ RETIRED	1
4	Became disabled	→ BECAME DISABLED	2
5 6 7	Workplace shut down Dismissed Contract ended	→ EMPLOYER-RELATED	3
8 9	Family responsibilities Got married	→ FAMILY REASONS	4
0	Not applicable (code 1 in V27 or code 2 in V64)	→ NOT APPLICABLE	0
99	NA, refused	→ REFUSED	99

Figure 3.18 *Recoding* ***v66*** *into a new variable,* ***whyjobend***

Click and drag **v66** from the source variable list to the target box. Then give the new variable a name (e.g. **whyjobend**) and a label (e.g. **v66 recoded [reasons why last job ended]**) and click on the **Change** button to confirm this. Finally click on **Old and New Values** to open up the dialog box shown in Figure 3.19b.

This is where we need to inform SPSS of the old and new category codes. We know from Figure 3.18 that the first three categories of v66 are going to be grouped together to form the first category of our new recoded variable. So the first step is to select **Range 1 through 3** in the Old Value section and enter

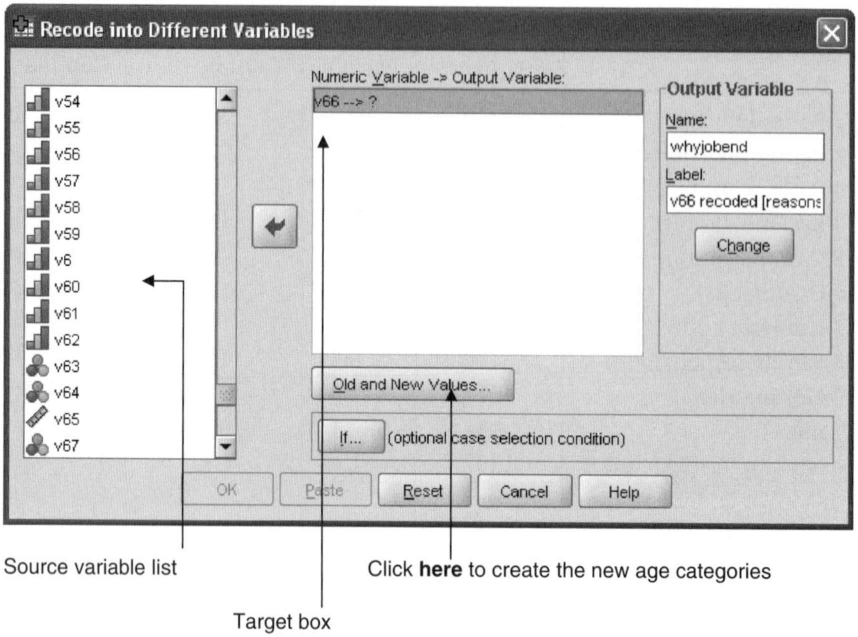

Figure 3.19a   *Collapsing the **v66** categories into a new variable, **whyjobend***

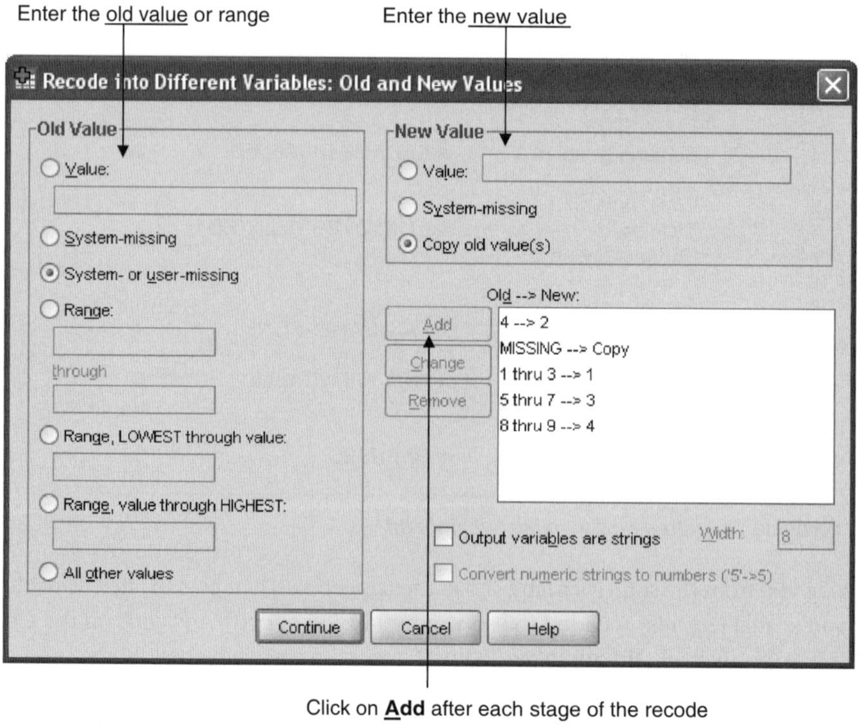

Figure 3.19b   *Identifying Old and New Values*

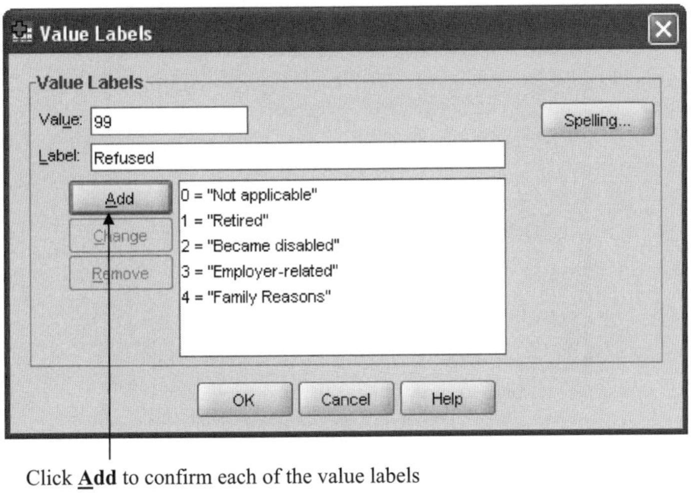

Click **Add** to confirm each of the value labels

Figure 3.20 *Defining Value Labels for the new variable* **whyjobend**

the value **1** under New Value. Then click **Add** to confirm this. As the fourth category of v66 (Became disabled) is going to become the second category of our new variable, enter the number **4** in the Old Value box and **2** in the New Value box and click **Add**. For the third step select **Range 5 through 7** in the Old Value section and enter the value **3** under New Value and click **Add**. Then allocate the final categories of v66 (values 8 and 9) to category 4. The final step in this part of the process is to allocate 'missing values' and as we want to be able to distinguish between those for whom the question was not applicable and those who refused to answer the question it is best to copy the original missing value codes. To do this, select '**System or user-missing**' in the Old Value section and '**Copy old value(s)**' in the New Value section. When all the values of the original variable have been recoded (your dialog box should be identical to Figure 3.19b), click on the **Continue** button and then **OK**.

Although the new variable, **whyjobend**, has been created there are still a few further refinements to be made. The next stage is to label each of the values of the new variable. You do this in the same way as you would label variables when you are creating a new dataset. Scroll down to the last variable in the **Variable View** window of the Data Editor and click on the appropriate cell of the **Values** column to open up the Value Labels dialog box (see the section on Labelling in Module 1 and Figure 3.20).

To complete the process we need to 'declare' missing values and set the level of measurement (see Module 1 for more detailed descriptions of these procedures). Click on the ellipsis in the appropriate cell of the **Missing** column in Variable View to open the Missing Values dialog box (shown in Figure 3.21) and enter the missing values for **whyjobend** (i.e. **0** and **99**).

Finally, click on the appropriate cell in the **Measure** column and set the level of measurement to nominal (see Module 2 for an explanation of the different levels of measurement). You can now run a frequency table of the new recoded variable which should resemble Figure 3.22, complete with variable and value labels and 'declared' missing values.

Altering variable codes

Sometimes, we might want to alter the codes of a variable without aggregating. For instance, we might want to change the numerical order of a series of codes for a variable in order to improve its presentation. We may also want to alter a variable's codes for more mundane reasons. For instance, when cleaning

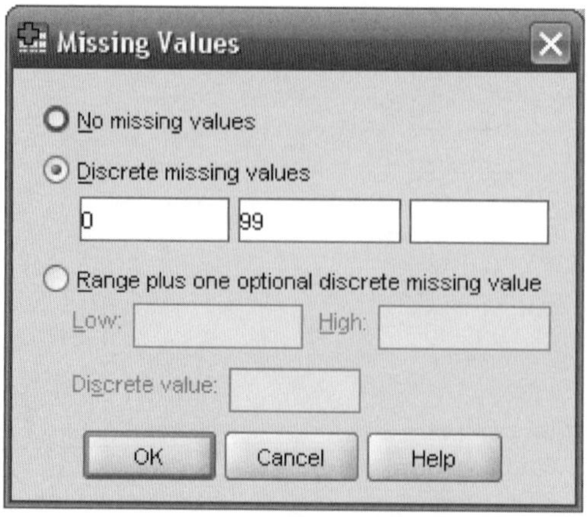

Figure 3.21   *Missing Values dialog box*

whyjobend v66 recoded (reasons why last job ended)

		Frequency	Percent	Valid Percent	Cumulative Percent
Valid	1 Retired	368	17.4	47.0	47.0
	2 Became disabled	112	5.3	14.4	61.3
	3 Employer-related	154	7.3	19.6	81.0
	4 Family Reasons	149	7.1	19.0	100.0
	Total	784	37.1	100.0	
Missing	0 Not applicable	1297	61.4		
	99 Refused	31	1.5		
	Total	1328	62.9		
Total		2111	100.0		

Figure 3.22   *Frequency table for new variable* **whyjobend** *(v66 recoded)*

data, we might discover some invalid codes in a variable. We might want to simplify matters by 'sweeping' all these invalid codes together into a single 'missing value' code, or, if we check back and establish what the correct code should be, we will want to change the invalid code to its correct value. For example, we might find that some error has been made in entering information into the **sex** variable (which should have only two values, 1 = Male and 2 = Female), and that some codes 6 and 7 have been entered erroneously. Using **Transform → Recode → Into the Same Variable**, the codes 6 and 7 can be recoded to a third category 3 = Don't Know.

Recoding a list of variables

SPSS provides a way of specifying a range of variables without having to put in the recoding commands for each variable separately. For instance, in the original ISSP dataset there are four questions concerning things that respondents would be willing to do to avoid unemployment (v59 to v62). These are ordinal level variables with 8 categories (1 = Strongly agree, 2 = Agree, 3 = Neither agree nor disagree, 4 = Disagree, 5 = Strongly disagree, 0= Not applicable, 8 = Can't choose, 9 = Refused). The last three categories have been coded as missing but there is a strong argument for changing the 'Can't choose' category to a valid value (i.e. recoding the value 8 ('Can't choose') to 3 ('Neither agree nor disagree'). Figure 3.23a shows the new values and labels alongside the original coding.

Within the **Recode into Different Variables** dialog box, more than one 'old' variable can be selected, with each 'old' variable having a different 'new' variable name and label specified (see Figure 3.23b).

It is important to bear in mind that the settings in the **Recode into Different Variables: Old and New Values** dialog box window (shown in Figure 3.23c) apply to all the selected variables. Change the old code 8 to 3 by typing 8 in the Old Value section <u>V</u>alue box and 3 in the New Value section <u>V</u>alue box, and then click on **Add**. To keep the remaining codes click on **All <u>o</u>ther values** in the old value section, and click on **Copy old value(s)** and then **Add**. Once all changes have been completed click on the '**Continue**' button and then **OK**.

Original Values & Categories			New Values & Categories	
1	Strongly Agree		1	Strongly Agree
2	Agree		2	Agree
3	Neither Agree nor Disagree		3	Neither Agree nor Disagree
4	Disagree		4	Disagree
5	Strongly Disagree		5	Strongly Disagree
0	Not Applicable		0	Not Applicable
8	Can't Choose	⟶	3	Neither Agree nor Disagree
9	Refused		9	Refused

Figure 3.23a   *Chart of recoding values – v59, v60, v61 & v62*

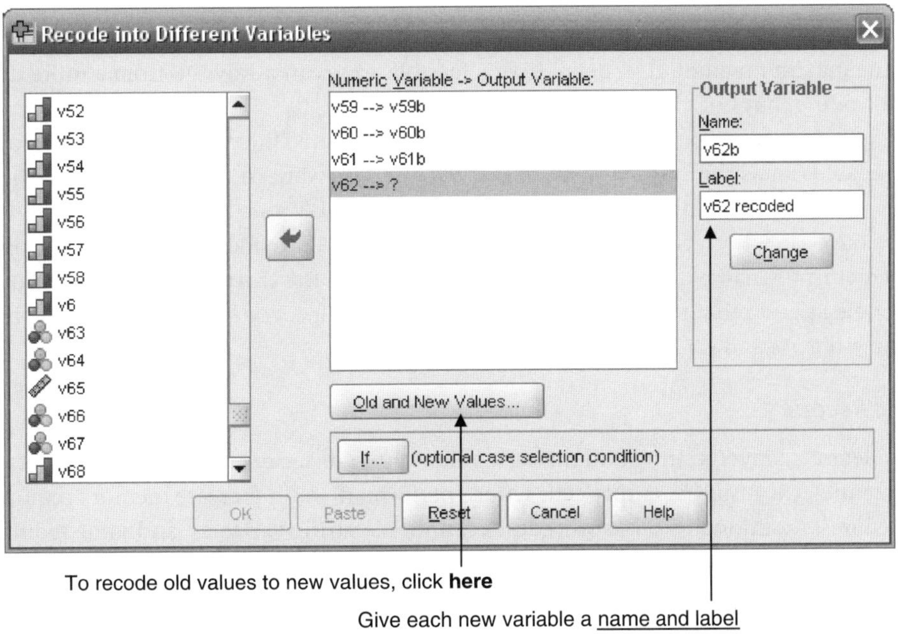

To recode old values to new values, click **here**

Give each new variable a <u>name and label</u>

Figure 3.23b   *Recoding four variables (v59 to v62) into new variables*

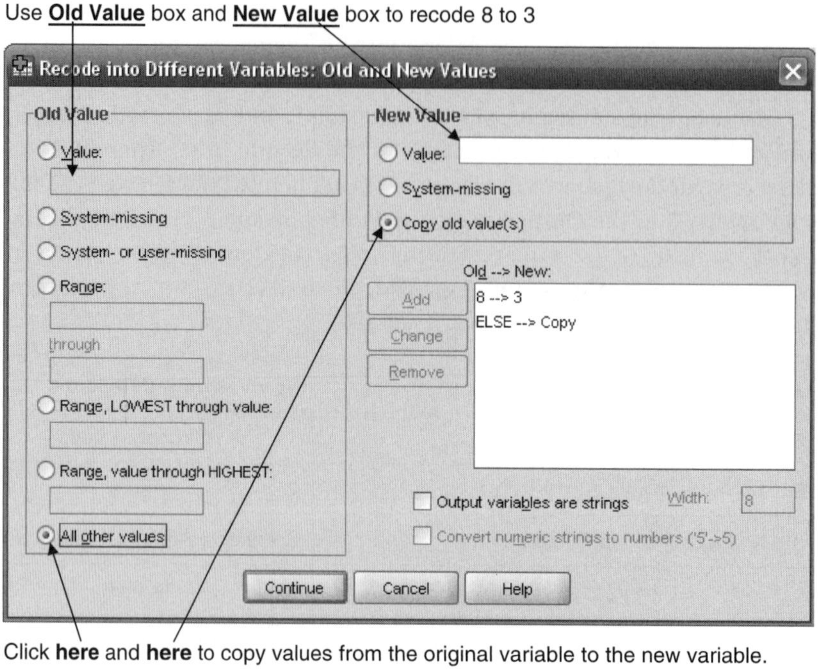

Use **Old Value** box and **New Value** box to recode 8 to 3

Click **here** and **here** to copy values from the original variable to the new variable.

Figure 3.23c   *Recoding new variables – v59 to v62*

You have now created four new variables (v59b, v60b, v61b & v62b), but still need to attach labels, declare missing values and set the level of measurement for each of these (see the examples above and Module 1 for more details).

Good practice

From these examples of 'recodes', it should be clearer now why it is good practice to code variables initially into the maximum amount of detail that is feasible. One can always go from a more detailed to a less detailed coding, but not vice versa.

Note how SPSS is set up so that when you use the 'Recode into Different Variables' window, you create a new variable that is the *exact duplicate* of the variable you want to alter. The codes of the new 'mirror' variable are altered, leaving the original variable untouched (Figure 3.24 shows some of the recoded variables we have already created, alongside the originals). SPSS provides this 'mirroring' automatically when you enter in the name of the new (recoded) variable into the **Output Variable** box. So, if you discover sometime later on that you need the original, more detailed, codes, you still have them. (*In effect, you* can *have your cake* and *eat it too!*).

Automatic Recode

Automatic Recode converts string and numeric values into consecutive integers. When category codes are not sequential, the resulting empty cells reduce performance and increase memory requirements for many procedures. Additionally, some procedures cannot use string variables, and some require consecutive integer values for factor levels.

In this example we are going to use Automatic Recode to alter the coding of six variables in the ISSP dataset (v70 to v75). All of these relate to job-seeking and the different steps that the respondent may have taken to help them gain employment. The variables currently use geometric codes (see Glossary)

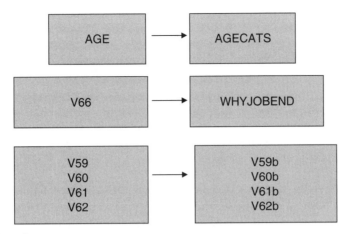

Figure 3.24   *Recoding chart*

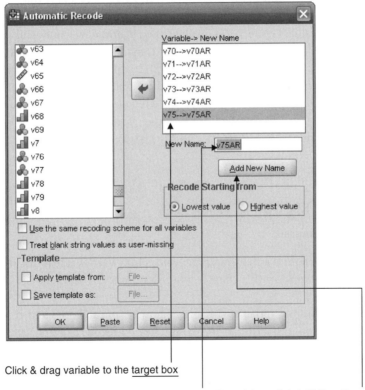

Click & drag variable to the target box

Give the variable a new name (e.g. v75AR) and then click **Add New Name**

Figure 3.25a   *An example of using Automatic Recode to create a new variable*

and while this has advantages it would also be beneficial to have the option of using a more conventional form of coding (as we will see later in the Module when we discuss the Count procedure). The Automatic Recode procedure will convert the codes for each variable into consecutive integers, thereby ensuring that a negative response receives a value of 1 and a positive response receives a value of 2.

Select **Automatic Recode** from the **Transform** menu to open up the **Automatic Recode** dialog box (shown in Figure 3.25a). Click and drag the first variable you want to recode ('**v70**' in this example) from

```
  V74          v74AR       Not working: applied directly to employers

Old Value   New Value       Value Label

     0           1          Didn't do this activity
    16           2          Applied to employers directly
    -3           3          Refused
    -1           4          Not applicable (code 1 in v27)
```

Figure 3.25b *Table displaying new and old values of v74AR*

the list of variables over to the target variable box. Give the variable a new name (e.g. v70AR) and click on **Add New Name**. Click and drag the second variable (v71) to the target variable box and, give it a new name (v71AR) and click on **Add New Name** again. Do this for the other four variables (as shown in Figure 3.25a) and then click on **OK** to run the procedure.

The new variables created by Automatic Recode (v70AR to v75AR) retain the defined variable and value labels from the old variable. For any values without a defined value label, the original value is used as the label for the recoded value. Figure 3.25b displays the old and new values and value labels for one of the variables used in this example (v74/v74AR). Run frequency tables for v70AR to v75AR now to check that the values 1 and 2 have been applied to the valid responses for each of these variables.

If a variable contains string values these are recoded in alphabetical order, with uppercase letters preceding their lowercase counterparts. Missing values are recoded into missing values higher than any non-missing values, with their order preserved. For example, if the original variable has 10 non-missing values, the lowest missing value would be recoded to 11, and the value 11 would be a missing value for the new variable.

SPSS EXERCISE FOR RECODING VARIABLES

Now, try some recodes yourself.

■ Choose a 'scale' variable and amalgamate the values into a set of categories, in a similar way to the first recode example in this chapter where a number of different age categories were created.

■ Chose a nominal or ordinal variable with a large number of categories and create a new variable with fewer categories in a similar way to the second recode example above.

ARITHMETICAL OPERATIONS ON A VARIABLE'S CODES (COMPUTE)

Carrying out simple or complex arithmetical operations on a variable's codes is a second basic form of data manipulation. If the number codes of one or more variables truly represent quantities and not just labels of categories, these codes can be subjected to arithmetical operations.

These arithmetical commands are algebraic in form and can be quite simple. For example, we have a variable in the ISSP dataset indicating the number of hours a respondent works per week (**wrkhrs**). Multiplying wrkhrs by 52 would produce a variable that represents an estimate of the number of hours worked by respondents in a year. We can carry this out using the **Compute** procedure as outlined below.

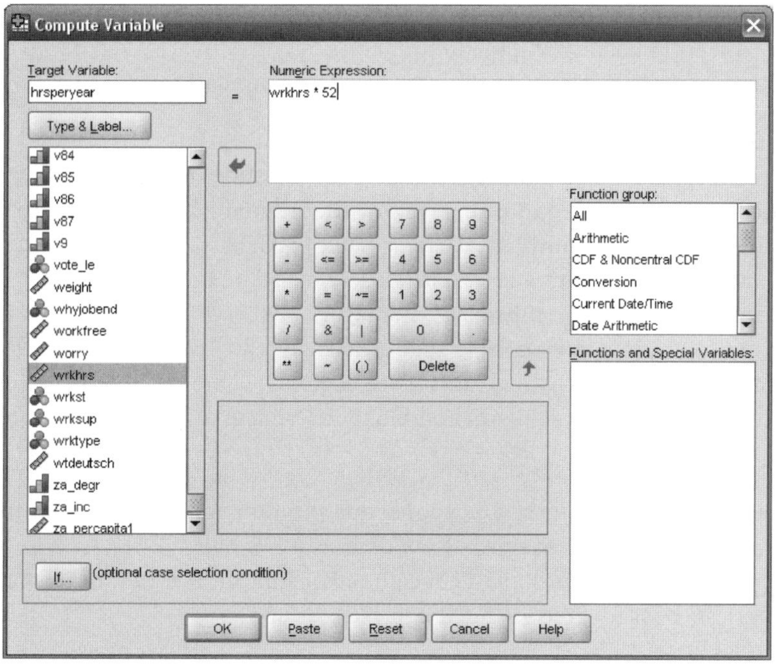

Figure 3.26   *An example of using Compute to create a new variable*

Select **Compute Variable** from the **Transform** menu to open the **Compute Variable** dialog box (shown in Figure 3.26). Then give the new variable a name (e.g. **hrsperyear**) and enter it in 'Target Variable' box. The next step is to enter the calculation you want SPSS to perform into the Numeric Expression box: locate the variable **wrkhrs** from the source list and click and drag it over to the Numeric Expression box and use the calculator keypad to enter * (the multiply symbol) and **52** (see Figure 3.26). Finally click **OK** to run the procedure. A new variable called **hrsperyear** should appear at the end of the grid in Variable View. As this is a scale variable it is not necessary to add value labels or alter the level of measurement (scale is the default level of measurement in SPSS).

Compute can of course be used to perform more complex arithmetical operations, but it is necessary to use brackets to ensure that the steps of the computation are carried out in the correct order. SPSS will carry out the expression inside the innermost brackets first, and then work its way out to the outmost brackets.

SPSS EXERCISES FOR COMPUTE

Now, try to do some computing yourself. Using quantitative variables in the dataset (variables whose codes represent true numerical values), carry out some arithmetical computations.

IF – USING LOGICAL STATEMENTS TO CREATE A NEW VARIABLE

So far, we have demonstrated the use of **Recode** to manipulate data by altering or combining the codes of a variable and the use of **Compute** to carry out the arithmetical manipulation of variables.

Using a *logical statement* to create a new variable by combining the codes/values of two or more variables is the third basic sort of data manipulation that one can do with SPSS. Again, we will use examples drawn from the data to explain the use of this sort of data manipulation.

An example of using logical statements

In the ISSP survey the level of educational qualification of respondents was coded in the variable called **degree**. Respondents could be coded into six levels of educational qualification, with the highest level being Code 5 '**University degree completed**'. The variable **egp** deals with the social class of respondents and the top two categories (higher service and lower service) relate to the most prestigious occupations (including professionals, senior administrators, managers, higher-grade technicians and supervisors). Let us say you want to create a new variable that creates an 'elite' category, those who have *both* the highest level of educational qualification (university degree) *and* are in one of the two highest social class codes (i.e. service class). We use logical combinations of **degree** and **egp** to create a new variable, **elite**, which will have the codes:

Code 1: Possessing both the highest educational qualification and having one of the top two social class codes (**degree** = 5 & **egp** = 1 OR **degree** = 5 & **egp** = 2);

Code 2: *Either* not possessing the highest educational qualification and/or not having one of the top social class codes (**degree** ~= 5 OR **egp** > 2).

We create the new variable **elite** by selecting **Compute** from the **Transform** menu. In the **Compute Variable** dialog window type in 'elite' as the **Target variable** (a variable label can also be entered at this point using the Type and Label box). Then enter the first numeric value of the new variable in the **Numeric Expression** box, code '1' in this example (see Figure 3.27a).

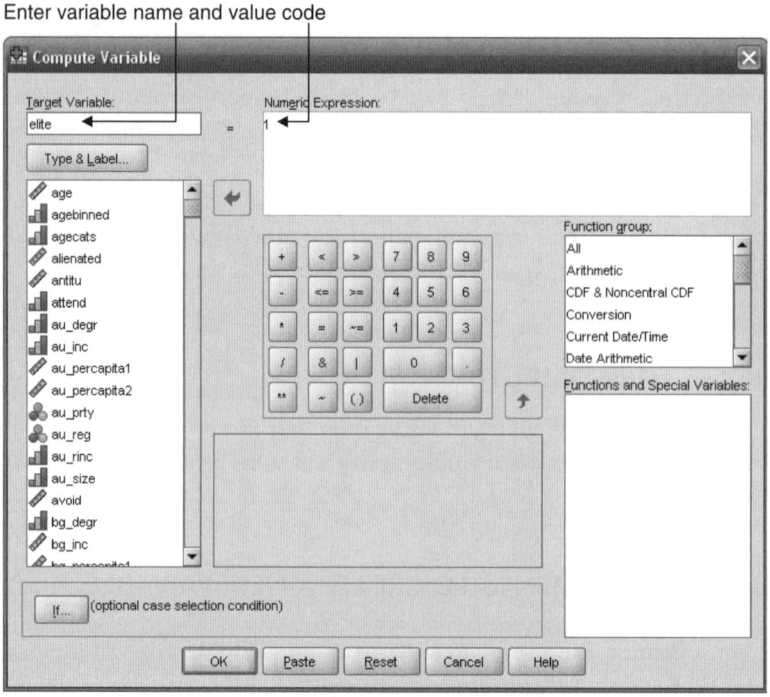

Figure 3.27a   *Creating a new variable using Compute and If (first code)*

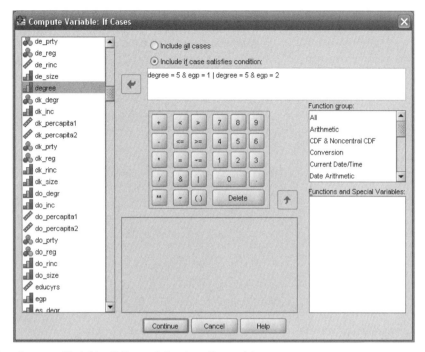

Figure 3.27b   *Compute Variable: If Cases dialog box (1st code)*

Once the target variable and code have been entered click on the **If** button to bring up the **Compute Variable: If Cases** window and click on the **Include if case satisfies condition** button (Figure 3.27b). Then type in the condition required to create the first category of the new variable into the workbox: in this example: **degree = 5 & egp = 1 | degree = 5 & egp = 2**. (In English, *'IF degree is university AND class is higher service OR degree is university AND class is lower service.'*) Then, click on **Continue** to go back to the **Compute Variable** window and run it by clicking on **OK**. The new variable **elite** will appear on the far right-hand side of the Data Editor grid in Data View with a code '1' for every case in which the condition in the IF statement is satisfied.

Since in this example there are two logical possibilities (being in the top 'elite' category or not) the two possibilities need to be set up individually in order to obtain the codes 1 and 2 for the new variable, **elite**. This means repeating the above process for code 2. Return to the **Compute Variable** dialog box and change the value in the Numeric Expression box from '1' to '2' (see Figure 3.27c).

As before, click on the **If** button to bring up the **Compute Variable If Cases** window (Figure 3.27d), click on the **Include if case satisfies condition** button and type the 'condition' into the work box. This time the condition will represent all those respondents who EITHER are NOT university graduates OR are not in the service class: **degree ~= 5 | egp > 2** (in English, *'degree is NOT university OR class is NOT service class'*). Then, click on **Continue** to go back to the **Compute Variable** window and run it by clicking on **OK**. When you make the second change, SPSS will advise you that this procedure will change the existing variable, don't worry, just click **OK**.

The new variable **elite** will now have values 1 *and* 2 (in fact, since most respondents do not fall into the exclusive 'elite' combination, most values will be 2). You can label these two categories now in the same way as you did in previous examples (see Module 1). Note that the creation of **elite** was not complete until you went through the procedure of using IF to create new categories *twice* (see Figure 3.27e for a Frequency table of **elite**).

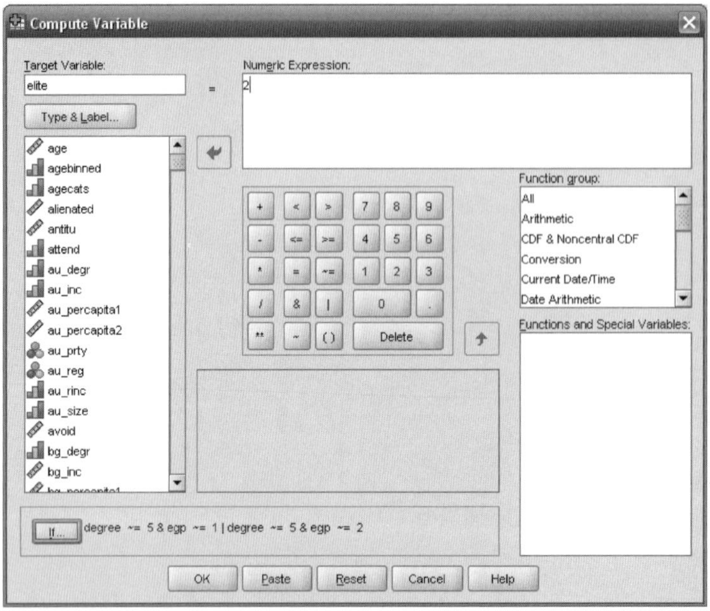

Figure 3.27c *Creating a new variable using Compute and If (2nd code)*

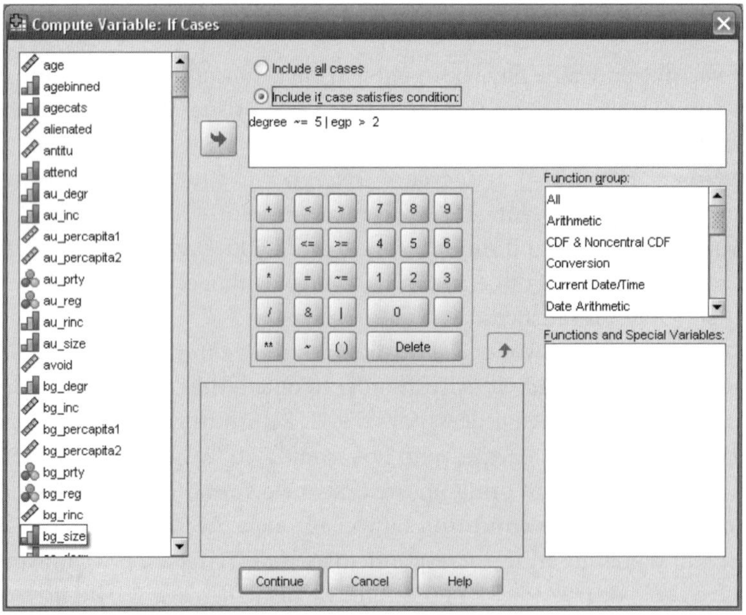

Figure 3.27d *Compute Variable: If Cases dialog box (2nd code)*

Logical operators

There are a number of conventional operators appearing on the 'calculator keypads' of the 'Recode Variable: If Cases' and the 'Compute Variable: If Cases' windows that are used to make up these logical statements. These have been mentioned before, but each is presented below.

elite

		Frequency	Percent	Valid Percent	Cumulative Percent
Valid	1 Degree and Service Class	153	7.2	7.3	7.3
	2 All Others	1937	91.8	92.7	100.0
	Total	2090	99.0	100.0	
Missing	System	21	1.0		
Total		2111	100.0		

Figure 3.27e   *Frequency count of the new variable, elite*

Comparisons

■ the codes of two variables can be compared to see if they are the same (equal (=)) or different (*not equal* (~=));

■ the codes of two variables can be compared to see if the codes of one variable are more than (greater than (>) or less than (<) another variable.

And the 'equals to' and the 'greater than'/'less than' operators are often combined to give:

greater than <u>or</u> equal to (=>) and
less than <u>or</u> equal to (<=);

Summarizing:

■ for the same (equal) (=);
■ for different (not equal) (¯=);
■ for more than (greater than) (>);
■ for less than (<);
■ for greater than <u>or</u> equal to (>=);
■ for less than <u>or</u> equal to (<=).

Booleans

A second type of operator, the so-called 'Boolean' operators, are used to link different portions of a logical statement together. There are two 'Boolean' operators, 'AND' (&) and 'OR' (|) where:

■ AND means that a statement holds *only* if *both* 'halves' of the statement are 'true'; and
■ OR means that a statement holds if *either* 'half' of the statement is 'true'.

For instance, going back to our example, respondents only fell into the 'elite' category if they had *both* the highest educational qualification code *and* the highest social class code OR *both* the highest educational qualification code *and* the second highest social class code:

degree = 5 & egp = 1 | degree = 5 & egp = 2

Complex statements

All of these operators for logical statements can, as you would expect, be combined to produce quite involved, complex statements. As a hint, however, once you learn how to use the SPSS CROSSTABS statistical procedure (see Module 5), you can produce a crosstabulation table of two variables that you want to combine in a series of IF statements. Looking at the crosstabulation table will help you remember all of the possible combinations of categories of two variables and will show you how many cases you can expect to fall into each combination of categories. For example, Figure 3.28 shows the crosstabulation of **epg** and **degree**. We can see that there are 154 cases (71 + 83) in the two top right-hand cells of the crosstabulation table, the same number as appear in category 1 of the variable **elite**, confirming that the logic of our IF statements is correct. (Note that the slight discrepancy of one unit between these two figures is the result of using weighted data. You should also be aware that the totals are different because the **elite** variable includes respondents that were 'missing' from the **egp** and **degree** variables.)

We have presented a fairly simple version of an IF statement where we used the procedure to generate a new variable with only two categories. IF statements can be very complex, involving combinations of more than two original variables and generating new variables with more than two categories. In general, if you can think of a logical combination of variables that could create a new variable, it is possible (*with care!*) to generate a series of IF statements that will create it. You really are only limited by your imagination!

EXERCISES FOR IF

Now, look over the variables in the dataset and think up some interesting logical manipulations that can be performed on them.

- As before, start out with something fairly simple, say, a logical manipulation involving only two variables where neither of them has too many *codes*.
- Then, try moving on to something more complicated, perhaps using more than two variables and/or an imaginative combination.

Try to have some statements that make (sensible) use of both the 'Boolean' operatives, AND and OR. Remember that you must go through the procedure of setting up a logical IF statement for *each* category of the new variable you are creating.

TRANSFORMATIONS USING COUNT

Sometimes you may want to find out how often a certain code or range of codes occurs across a number of different variables. SPSS has a special procedure called **Count** that allows this to be done easily.

In the ISSP dataset there are a number of variables that relate specifically to the characteristics of a person's job. For the variables v29 to v36, respondents were asked whether they agreed or disagreed with a series of positive statements about their main job and we can employ the **Count** procedure to aggregate this information. Our aim here is to use these eight variables to create a scale that represents the degree to which respondents see their job in a positive light.

egp EGP class categories * degree R: Education II-highest education level Crosstabulation

Count

		degree R: Education II-highest education level						
		0 No formal qualification	1 Lowest formal qualification	2 Above lowest qualification	3 Higher secondary completed	4 above higher secondary level	5 University degree completed	Total
egp EGP class categories	1.00 I Higher Service	2	14	16	5	29	71	137
	2.00 II Lower Service	0	74	137	35	47	83	376
	3.00 III Routine Clerical, Sales	0	185	295	39	17	2	538
	4.00 IVa Small Employers	1	4	5	0	1	0	11
	5.00 Ivb Own account workers	0	13	14	5	3	4	39
	7.00 V Manual Forepersons	2	65	74	5	5	6	157
	8.00 VI Skilled Manual	5	126	70	5	2	1	209
	9.00 VIIa Semi & Unskilled Manual	16	214	90	5	4	0	329
	10.00 VIIb Agricultural workers	5	29	5	0	0	0	39
	Total	31	724	706	99	108	167	1835

Figure 3.28   Crosstabulation of *egp* by *degree* as a check on IF statements

Count will scan across the eight variables, and count the number of times the values 1 or 2 (i.e. strongly agree or agree) appear for each respondent. A score of 8 would indicate that the respondent agreed with all of the statements and thus viewed their job in an extremely positive light, while scores at the lower end of the scale represent respondents who believe their job has very few redeeming features.

To carry out the count procedure, go to the **Transform** menu and click on **Count**. This opens the main Count dialog box (Figure 3.29a), where the new **Target Variable** and **Target Label** must be specified, and the variables to be counted must be selected and entered in the **Numeric Variables** box.

Here, our new variable will be called **PerfectJob** with the label 'Positive characteristics of job' and the variables v29 to v36 go into the Numeric Variables box. Once the variables have been selected and moved across, click on the **Define Values** box to bring up Figure 3.29b. To define the **Value** (or values) to be counted, enter the number in the value box and click on the **Add** button to bring it across to the **Values to Count** box. In this example we need to do this for the values 1 and 2 (i.e. representing 'Strongly agree' and 'Agree'), and then click on **Continue** to return to the main Count window. Finally click on OK to create the new variable, **PerfectJob**.

Looking at a table of frequencies of the new variable (**PerfectJob**) we can see that almost 50 per cent of respondents did not feel that *any* of the positive statement applied to their job. At the other end of the scale, only 64 respondents (3 per cent of the total sample) agreed with all eight statements (Figure 3.29c).

NEW VARIABLES

By now you will have noted that data manipulation, unlike data selection, does not reduce the total number of variables held in a dataset. In fact, the opposite is likely to happen: after data manipulation it

Figure 3.29a *Main Count dialog box*

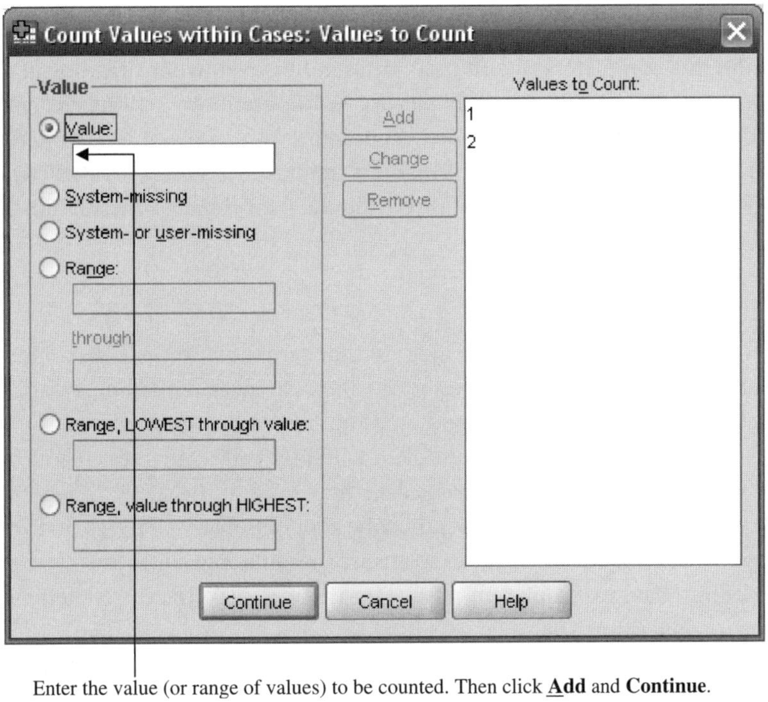

Enter the value (or range of values) to be counted. Then click **Add** and **Continue**.

Figure 3.29b   *Example of setting values to COUNT*

Perfect Job Positive characteristics of job

		Frequency	Percent	Valid Percent	Cumulative Percent
Valid	0	1001	47.4	47.4	47.4
	1	39	1.8	1.8	49.3
	2	76	3.6	3.6	52.9
	3	128	6.1	6.1	59.0
	4	171	8.1	8.1	67.1
	5	249	11.8	11.8	78.9
	6	255	12.1	12.1	90.9
	7	128	6.0	6.0	97.0
	8	64	3.0	3.0	100.0
	Total	2111	100.0	100.0	

Figure 3.29c   *Frequency table for **PerfectJob***

is quite possible that there will be some 'new' variables existing in the dataset (e.g. **agecats**, **whyjobend**, **PerfectJob**, etc.).

These 'new' variables can be considered to be similar to the variables in a dataset immediately after the data have been 'read into' a data analysis package. The 'new' variables are part of the dataset – they are formatted and possess 'variable names'.

Labelling

As with the variables in a completely 'brand new' dataset, however, what they do *not* possess are *labels*. So, in order to document the dataset correctly and to avoid potentially serious errors in interpretation, these 'new' variables must have labels assigned. You define the labels of a variable created by a data transformation in the same way as you would label variables in a newly created dataset: by going to the Data Editor grid in Variable View format. See Module 1 for detailed instructions on how to label variables.

Missing values

You may also remember from the Data Input module that care must be taken to declare as 'missing values' any codings that have been used to represent invalid responses. This is necessary in order to avoid these invalid codes being inadvertently incorporated into any statistical analyses.

As you might guess, this is also a potential problem with any 'new' variables created by data manipulation. Being 'new', it is possible that one or more codes may exist in the 'new' variable that in fact represent invalid cases. As before, these invalid codes must be kept out of any analyses that will assume that all codings are genuine. Hence, care must be taken to ensure that missing values are established for the 'new' variables that result from data manipulation, just as for the variables in a completely new dataset.

SPSS does have a convention that acts as a partial 'fail safe' to ensure the correct declaration of missing values for 'new' variables arising from data manipulation. During data manipulation, if SPSS encounters a missing value code for the variables that go into making up a 'new' variable *and* the analyst has not used that variable in his/her recoding, that case's coding for the 'new' variable will be set to a 'system missing' code.

Note, however, that this is only a partial 'fail safe'; the safest practice is for the analyst to declare missing values for a new variable. (Module 1 explains how to declare missing values by going to the 'Missing' column in the Variable View window of the Data Editor.)

A final bit of advice about data manipulation

Whenever you have created new variables with data manipulation, you are *strongly* advised to 'check' them with a quick **Frequencies** run to ensure that the data manipulation actually did what you intended. You may discover that you have fooled yourself and the manipulation did not turn out quite like you expected.

While data manipulation requires care on the part of the analyst, the ability to 'customize' datasets and create or modify variables to suit the needs of your own analysis is one of the most useful features of SPSS.

4 Hypothesis Testing and *t*-Tests

CONFIRMATORY STATISTICS

This module covers hypothesis testing using *t*-tests and we will be using the data set for **Japan**. Modules 1 to 3 have covered the preliminary stages in data entry and analysis. Module 2 provided examples of data exploration and description. Exploring and describing the data using descriptive statistics (means, medians, frequency counts, etc.) and charts has provided us with the opportunity to become more familiar with the data, and may generate questions for further analysis and testing.

Such questions may be concerned with the testing of *relationships* between variables in the data – for example, the gender of the respondent and the amount of their attendance at religious services or respondents' social class and the extent of their alienation from work. You may have ideas (called **hypotheses**) about the relationships between variables, and may want to *test* these ideas to see if they really hold true. To do so you need to use confirmatory statistics. Confirmatory statistics allow you to test or evaluate the validity of results. Hence, confirmatory statistics are sometimes called *hypothesis-testing statistics*.

The data set contains a variable called **compat** – a scale of the respondent's view of whether work and private life (family, friends and leisure) can be compatible; the higher the score, the more compatible the respondent considers work and private life to be. It might be interesting to explore, for those who work, whether women or men consider the two facets of life to be more compatible. We could start exploring by using *descriptive statistics* such as the mean compatibility score for each gender or generating boxplots of the relative distributions of 'compatibility' (see Module 2 for details about how to generate these and other descriptive statistics). Figure 4.1a and Figure 4.1b present the descriptive statistics and boxplots of 'compatibilty' by gender (**sex**) for those who work.

Inspection of Figure 4.1a and 4.1b *suggests* a gender differences in 'compatibility', as the mean score for men is higher than the mean for women. However, we must test this observation using confirmatory statistics. In this case our research question might be: '*Among those who work, do the two genders differ in their assessment of the compatibility between work and private life?*'

Hypothesis testing

Before proceeding with our research question, we must specify the comparisons to be completed by translating our research question into a **hypothesis**. A hypothesis is a statement of a relationship between population parameters or variables – a statement or prediction of what you expect to find. This statement typically takes the form of predicting *differences* between groups or of *relationships* between variables.

Gender	Mean	N	Std. Deviation
1 Male	.6670	303	1.17027
2 Female	.0167	255	1.31315

Figure 4.1a *Descriptive statistics for Compatibility scale (compat) by gender (sex)*

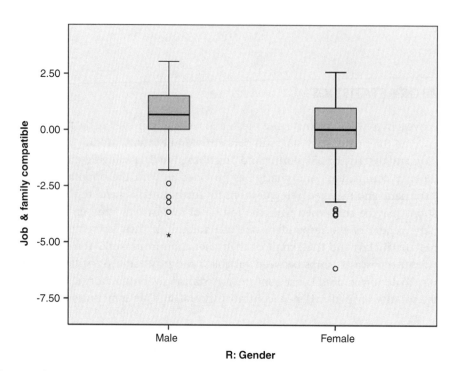

Figure 4.1b *Boxplot of Compatibility scale (compat) by gender (sex)*

Erickson and Nosanchuk (1992) deploy a useful analogy to distinguish between exploratory, descriptive statistics like those we have covered so far in this book and the confirmatory, hypothesis-testing statistical procedures that we are introducing now. An analyst employing descriptive statistics in order to get a feel for their data and what might be fruitful avenues of enquiry to pursue is a bit like a police detective who investigates a crime by sifting through evidence and looking at things that past experience have been shown to be likely to produce results quickly but also using their intuition to follow up hunches and leads. An arrest and the formal charge is a bit like a hypothesis – a formal statement accusing the assumed perpetuator of the crime. To take the analogy further, the ensuing trial is, as you will see, remarkably like performing a confirmatory statistical test. Instead of the rough and ready rules of thumb of a criminal investigation, the courtroom trial is a very formal process with strict rules of procedure and what constitutes valid evidence and how it can be evaluated. Confirmatory statistical testing is the same – there are set rules about what constitutes proof or disproof of your hypothesis and you can hardly alter the statistical formulae to produce the result you want.

Using our example, the hypothesis might be: *Among those who work, the mean compatibility scale score for males will be higher than the mean compatibility scale score for females.* Thus, we are hypothesizing a difference, *and* giving a direction to the difference – men differ from women by having on average a higher compatibility score.

For every hypothesis in research, there is a **Null hypothesis**, which is a statement of no or opposite relationship between the two variables. The Null hypothesis is the logical opposite of the hypothesis. Once we have generated the hypothesis, we must prove it by *disproving* its logical opposite. Using our example, the Null hypothesis would be: *Among those who work, the mean compatibility scale score for males will be* **the same or less than** *the mean compatibility scale score for females.*

However, it is also important to remember that these data come from a survey and it is possible that, by chance, we might have sampled respondents who are not typical of the population. If this is the case, any observed difference may be a product of chance and may not be a real reflection of the two genders' feelings about the compatibility between work and private life. That is, even with a correctly designed sample survey, it is possible that we may have been unlucky and just happened to have picked up a set of men in the sample who feel more than the rest of the male population that their work and private life is compatible and a set of women who feel less than the rest of the female population that their work and private life is compatible. To put it in jargon, our *sample estimates* might not match the true *population parameters.*

In our example here, in order to test whether the difference between the sexes in their compatibility scores is real, we must conduct a confirmatory statistical test on the data. The *t*-test, which we will introduce below, is just such a confirmatory statistic. The *t*-test is explicitly designed to test whether the differences between the means of two groups are real, or *statistically significant.*

Before we can look directly at the *t*-test statistic and how to use SPSS to carry out a *t*-test, however, we need to consider more closely the logic that underlies confirmatory statistical testing.

Statistical tests are not infallible and we can make mistakes. There are two types of errors possible with confirmatory statistical testing:

- ■ **Type I Error**: Occurs if you accept a hypothesis as being *correct* when it is *really false*. A Type I Error is the worst type of error to make.
- ■ **Type II Error**: Occurs if you *reject* a hypothesis as being wrong when it is actually *true.*

Figure 4.2 summarizes the different errors.

	Hypothesis is really. . .	
Researer decides to	FALSE	TRUE
Accept hypothesis	**TYPE I ERROR –** accepting a false hypothesis as true (the worst!)	You *accepted* an hypothesis that is True – a correct decision
Reject hypothesis	You *rejected* an hypothesis that is False – a correct decision	**TYPE II ERROR –** rejecting a true hypothesis

Figure 4.2   *Errors in confirmatory statistics*

Statistical significance

The results of all statistical tests are expressed in these terms of probability or risk (for example, $p < 0.001$). This is the odds that a Type I Error has been made. So, the *smaller* the size of the level of significance, the *less likely* it is that a Type I Error has been made and the *more likely* it is that our hypothesis really is true. There are 'standard' cut-off points for accepting hypotheses:

- $p < 0.05$ means less than a 5 in 100 (1 in 20) chance of a Type I Error
- $p < 0.01$ means less than a 1 in 100 chance that a Type I Error has been made
- $p < 0.001$ means less than a 1 in 1000 chance of a Type I Error

Note that these cut-offs are conventions, there is nothing essential about choosing these values over any others except that each, even the least strict 0.05 level, gives odds that are very unlikely to result in the analyst making a Type I Error.

To test the significance, you need to set a risk level (called the alpha level). In most social research, the 'rule of thumb' is to set the alpha level at 0.05 (which means that 5 times out of every 100 you would find a statistically significant difference even if there was none). Usually, levels of significance (or risk) greater than 0.05 are not considered good enough to reject the Null hypothesis. For instance, even though $p < 0.10$ means only a 1 in 10 chance of a Type I Error, we usually would not accept the hypothesis. The reason for this is that it is much less of a calamity to make a Type II Error (rejecting a true hypothesis) than it is to make a Type I Error (accepting a false hypothesis). So, the odds of probability testing are highly skewed against making Type I Errors.

It is worth saying a bit more about this important point. One can make an analogy between a traveller trying to make his or her way down an unfamiliar road and a researcher embarking on a flawed course of research. The traveller may come to a fork in the road where he/she has an idea (a hypothesis!) that the left-hand fork is the correct way. In fact, however, the right-hand fork is the way they should go. If they decide that the left-hand way is the correct way and proceed down that road, they have made what amounts to a Type I Error. As they go further and further down the wrong way, they will become more and more confused and ever more hopelessly lost. Eventually, they will realize that a mistake must have been made some time ago and then will have to painfully retrace their steps back to the point of the original mistake. On the other hand, if they stay at the fork, unable to establish which is the correct way, they are making what amounts to a Type II Error. They are stuck at a crossroads, but at least they know they are stuck and are not rushing down the wrong route. In our 'compatibility' example, a researcher could make a Type I Error and wrongly conclude that one gender more than the other considers work and private life to be compatible. If the researcher then acted on their wrong conclusion and implemented a large-scale research project founded on an incorrect assumption, a considerable amount of money and effort would be wasted. Because a Type I Error means that a researcher will act on erroneous premises, it is more serious than a Type II Error.

Type I Errors can have serious consequences. The classic example is that of the treatment for stomach ulcers. For decades, doctors made a Type I Error, assuming that stomach ulcers resulted from excess stomach acid, brought on by 'stress' and exacerbated by spicy foods. The standard treatment was a lengthy course of antacid drugs combined with a diet of bland foods and milk. However, two Australian doctors, Robin Warren and Barry Marshall, established after a 20-year battle against the medical establishment that the real cause of 80% of stomach ulcers is *Helicobacter pylori*, a bacterium that lives in the lining of the stomach. *H. pylori* survives by reducing the amount of stomach acid in its immediate area. So, the accepted treatment had the *opposite* of its intended effect, prolonging the infection, leading to lengthy disability and, often, death from massive haemorrhage. Nowadays, patients are given a combination therapy of antibiotics followed by antacid drugs and a quick cure rate of up to 85% is the result. (Marshall and Warren's struggle to get their results accepted also is an excellent example of Kuhn's observation reported in the Introduction chapter that scientific discoveries that challenge established views win out more through political processes of attrition than rational scientific debate. Warren and Marshall had early papers rejected by the American Medical Society and the Australian Society of Gastroenterology and at one point Marshall took the drastic step of infecting himself by drinking a glass of *H. pylori* to demonstrate that the bacterium was the vector of the disease. Drs Marshall and Warren were awarded the Nobel Prize in 2005. *'He who laughs last.'*)

Hence, 'really important research' (for instance, research in which the consequences of reaching a wrong decision would entail high financial costs or in a case like *H. pylori* perhaps even the loss of life) often adopts a stricter level of confidence cut-off than the 0.05 level, usually the 0.001 level.

CONFIRMATORY STATISTICS: *t*-TESTS

The descriptive statistics in Figures 4.1a and 4.1b reveal that the mean compatibility score for women is 0.0167, and for men is 0.6670. There appears to be a difference between the two, with men on average finding work and private life more compatible. However, we must remember that there is a chance of a Type I Error. The mean (average) is calculated by dividing the sum of the total score by the number of respondents. The mean score provides an average score for this variable, but does not provide details of the range of scores – the variability. Extreme values at either end of the scale can distort the overall mean. As the boxplots in Figure 4.1b show, while the mean for men is higher, there is considerable overlap between individual female and male scores with many women having higher scores than most men and many men having lower scores than most women. In addition there are a number of outliers with extremely low values, and the person with the lowest outlying score is a woman. Thus, relying solely on the observed differences in mean scores between two groups could be misleading. When comparing the scores of the two groups, it is important to examine the difference between their mean scores relative to the spread or variability of their scores. The *t*-test statistic does this.

t-tests are most commonly used to examine whether the means of *two* groups of data are significantly different from one another. Hence with a *t*-test the independent variable is nominal or categorical and the dependent variable is measured at *interval* or *ratio* scale of measurement. The populations from which the two groups are drawn can be independent (or unrelated) or matched (related). *t*-Tests indicate the sample differences by using means and the distribution of sample scores around the mean. The underlying logic of the *t*-test is quite straightforward. Basically, the distribution of values of two groups are compared to see whether they come from the same population – that is, whether any differences in the average values of the two groups or their distributions are due just to chance or, alternatively, whether in fact the two groups come from truly different populations. If this latter case is true, then the observed differences between the two groups reflect the real differences between the larger populations from which they come. Figure 4.3 shows the problem. The distributions of the compatibility scores of the women and men look fairly similar, but there are noticeable differences. Are these differences enough that we could conclude these apparent differences are real?

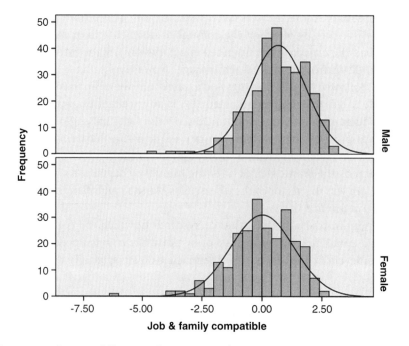

Figure 4.3 *Histograms of compatibility score for women and men*

You may have noticed in the above paragraph that we have slipped in (yet another) bit of statistical jargon: 'independent variable' and 'dependent variable'. When a relationship, association or difference between two variables is hypothesized, where a Variable X can be said to precede, affect or 'cause' another Variable Y, one uses the words 'independent' and 'dependent'. The 'caused' Variable Y is hypothetically considered to result from or to be affected in some way by the 'causal' Variable X, so the values of Variable Y logically to some extent are considered to depend upon Variable X; hence Variable Y is called a *dependent variable*. Variable X, being the 'affector' rather than the affected, logically is not considered to depend on Variable Y; hence Variable X is termed an *independent* variable. As a convention, independent variables will appear in statistical notation represented by 'x' and dependent variables will be represented by 'y'. Note that this terminology of independence and dependence is only relevant where one variable is hypothesized to cause or affect another. It is quite possible to have hypotheses or research questions where causality is not asserted, instead only that two things are related or associated in some way with no 'direction' of effect or link. Two of the examples that follow in this module are examples of hypotheses with no causal direction implied.

We will look at three versions of *t*-test within SPSS. The first type of *t*-test we will examine is used with unmatched data and is known under a number of names including '**independent samples *t*-test**', '*t*-test for two independent means', 'independent *t*-test', and '*t*-test for unrelated samples'. Regardless of the exact title, with this type of *t*-test there are *two distinct categories* for the independent variable (such as women and men) and one 'scalar' dependent variable measured at the interval or ratio level (here, the 'compatibility' score). The 'independent samples *t*-test' will be testing whether the means of the dependent variable for each group defined by the independent variable are significantly different.

The second type of *t*-test we will show is a '**one-sample *t*-test**', which investigates whether the mean of a specified variable (in our case, the 'compatibility' score) differs from some set value. We will show circumstances in which this could be a relevant question.

The third type of *t*-test we will demonstrate is used with matched data and is also known under a number of names, these include '**paired samples *t*-test**', '*t*-test for related measures', 'related *t*-test', or 'correlated *t*-test'. This test can be used in a number of circumstances where the question calls for the repeated measurement of responses from the *same respondent*. Data might be collected on a single occasion where individuals are asked to respond to the same or similar questions twice (for example, where a researcher decides to repeat a question later on in an interview in order to see if respondents will give the same answer if asked a second time). The same or similar data may also be collected on more than one occasion (where individuals are followed over a period of time, for example, repeated measures). Longitudinal surveys and 'before and after' studies or experiments are examples of designs where respondents may be required to provide an answer to the same question on different occasions. The 'paired samples *t*-test' will be testing whether the means of each of the 'paired' or 'before/after' variables are significantly different or not.

Independent samples *t*-test – example 1

Now (finally!) we will test the hypothesis in our 'compatibility' example. Remember the hypothesis is: *Among workers, men have a higher 'compatibility' score than women.* In order to disprove the Null hypothesis, we must carry out an **independent samples *t*-test**. It will tell us the odds (or probability) that the difference we see in the raw figures really *is* genuine. If it is real (or statistically significant), we accept our hypothesis and reject the Null hypothesis. (Remember the variable **sex** (independent variable) is categorical with two categories: Male and Female. **compat** (the dependent variable) is a scalar (interval/ratio) variable.)

The independent samples *t*-test establishes whether the means of two unrelated samples differ by comparing the difference between the two means with the standard error in the means of the different samples:

$$t = \frac{\text{Sample one mean} - \text{Sample two mean}}{\text{Standard error of the difference in mean}}$$

Figure 4.4a indicates the steps required to run the independent-samples *t*-test. Pull down the **Analyze** main menu, point to **Compare Means**, and click on **Independent-Samples T Test**.

The window in Figure 4.4b will appear. Transfer the variable **compat** to the **Test Variable(s) box** by using the cursor to highlight it, and clicking on the > button to move the required dependent variable to the Test Variable(s) box. Similarly highlight the grouping variable **sex** and transfer it to the **Grouping Variable** box.

You have to define the two values of the grouping variable. Define the values of the groups by clicking on the **Define Groups** button. The sub-window in Figure 4.4c will appear.

In the example used here we wish to compare males and females. The **sex** variable has two values: 1 = Male, 2 = Female. We specify males as Group 1 by typing the value '1' in the Group 1 box and similarly '2' for females in the Group 2 box; then click on 'Continue' to return to the main window. The values 1, 2 will appear in the brackets after **sex**. Now click on OK to run the *t*-test. (As well as defining groups by using specified values, it is possible to select cut-points in order to define the groups by splitting a variable into two categories.)

Once SPSS has completed running the *t*-test procedure the viewer window opens displaying the output. Figure 4.5 provides an example of the output from an independent-sample *t*-test.

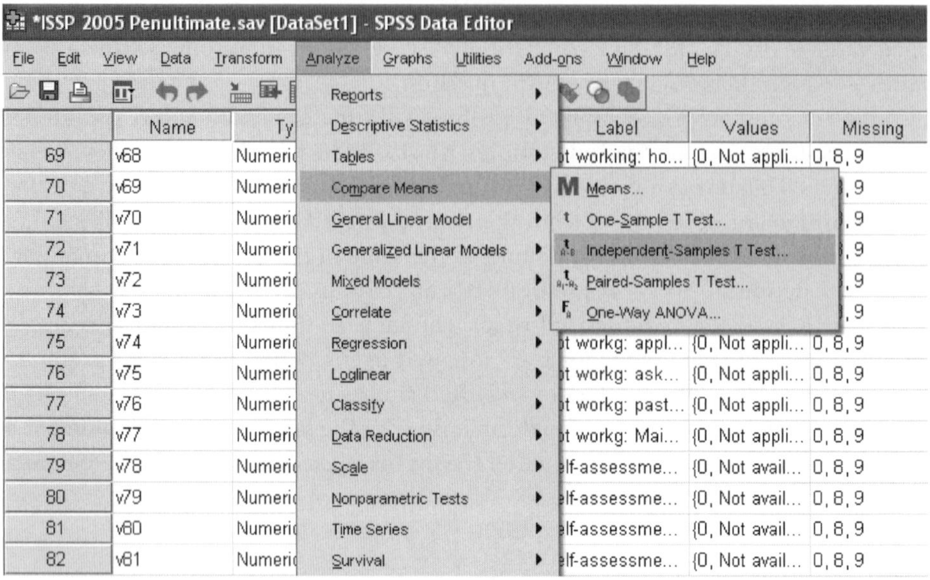

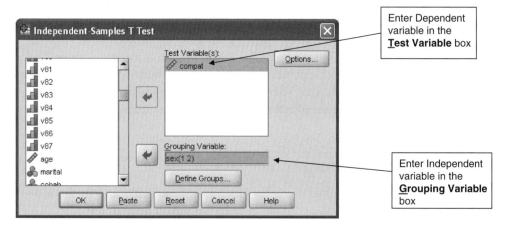

Figure 4.4a   *Example of independent* t-*test procedures*

Figure 4.4b   *Running the independent* t-*test*

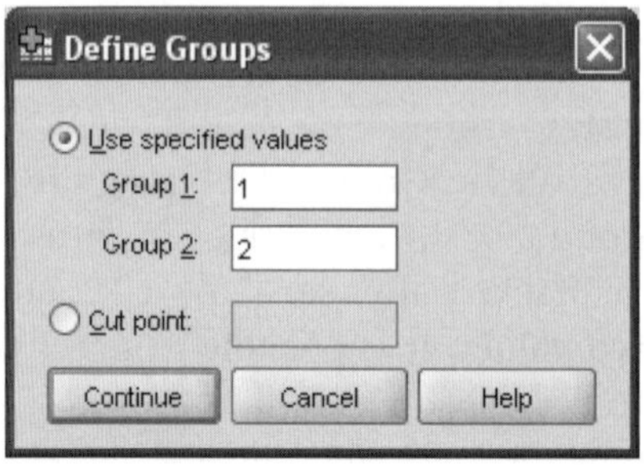

Figure 4.4c   *Defining values of grouping variable*

Group Statistics

	sex R: Gender	N	Mean	Std. Deviation	Std. Error Mean
compat Job & family compatible	1 Male	303	.6670	1.17027	.06723
	2 Female	255	.0167	1.31315	.08223

Independent Samples Test

		Levene's Test for Equality of Variances		t-test for Equality of Means					95% Confidence Interval of the Difference	
		F	Sig.	t	df	Sig. (2-tailed)	Mean Difference	Std. Error Difference	Lower	Upper
compat Job & family compatible	Equal variances assumed	3.223	.073	6.183	556	.000	.65030	.10517	.44372	.85689
	Equal variances not assumed			6.122	513.920	.000	.65030	.10622	.44163	.85898

Figure 4.5 *Independent t-test output: 'Compatibility' score (compat) by gender (sex)*

Interpreting the output

The *t*-test output on the Output Viewer window starts with descriptive statistics for the two groups. We can see that for 303 men the mean compatibility score was 0.6670 (standard deviation = 1.17), while for 255 women the mean score was 0.0167 (standard deviation = 1.31). We now want to see if there is a significant difference between the mean scores for the two independent groups.

Interpretation of the independent *t*-test output is a two-stage process. The first stage involves examining the homogeneity of the variance between the two groups. In order to test your hypotheses, a number of assumptions about the populations being compared must be made. Firstly, the researcher assumes that the variance in the populations being compared is the same. The independent-samples *t*-test analysis tests this assumption using **Levene's Test for Equality of Variances.** This test is based on the *F* statistic (which will be covered in the next modules). SPSS computes both the *F* statistic and *p* value (Sig.). If 'Sig.' is less than 0.05 ($p < 0.05$), the Levene's test indicates that the variances between the two populations are not equal. If 'Sig.' is greater than 0.05 ($p > 0.05$), the Levene's test indicates that equal variances can be assumed. In this instance $F = 3.223$ and Sig. (p) = 0.073, which indicates that $p < 0.05$, thus *equal* variances can be assumed and we test the hypothesis using the *t*-test row of results labelled *Equal variances assumed*. This provides the *t* value ($t = 6.183$) and the degrees of freedom (df = 556). SPSS calculates a Sig. (2-tailed) value, which is the actual probability of making a Type 1 Error. From the table, we find a two-tailed significance (*p*-value) of .000. ('.000' means a *p* that is 'off the scale', *less than 0.0005*.) Hence the difference between means is significant at $p < 0.001$. Therefore, we can reject the Null hypothesis and conclude that a statistically significant difference exists between the two groups in their compatibility scores. The research hypothesis that men really do have a higher average compatibility score than women is upheld, and the Null hypothesis is rejected. The chances of a Type I Error being made is less than 1 in 1000 ($p < 0.001$). You could report this result by saying: '*a* t *of 6.183 with 556 degrees of freedom indicates that the difference between genders in their mean compatibility scores is statistically significant at the 0.001 level*'.

Independent samples *t*-test – example 2

Let's take another example from the data set for Japan. One might anticipate that people who live in small towns would have incomes different from those who live in villages. Similar to the last example, we must specify the comparison to be completed by translating our research idea into a hypothesis. For this example the hypothesis could be: *The mean individual income of respondents living in small towns will be different in comparison to those living in villages.* The Null hypothesis would be: *The mean individual income of respondents living in small towns will **not** be different in comparison to those living in villages.*

For this example, we follow the same pathway as in Example 1: **Analyze** >**Compare Means** > **Independent**-Samples **T** **Test.** Transfer the variable **jp_rinc** to the **Test** Variable(s) box by using the cursor to highlight it, and clicking on the > button. Similarly, highlight the grouping variable **jp_size** and transfer it to the **Grouping Variable** box, clicking on the **Define Groups** button to define its values as before. Note that in this case the two groups being compared for the independent variable **jp_size** are code **4**, those living in towns with a population less than 100,000, and code **5**, those living in villages. (*t*-test can only compare two groups at a time. By selecting categories 4 and 5 of **jp_size** to compare, we in effect have excluded all those living in larger town and cities (codes 1, 2 and 3 of **jp_size**) from this analysis.) Figure 4.6 below provides the resulting output from our second example of an independent-sample *t*-test.

Group Statistics

	jp_size Size of community: Japan	N	Mean	Std. Deviation	Std. Error Mean
jp_rinc Respondent's Earnings: Japan	4 Less than 100.000	138	2619.57	2601.624	221.465
	5 Village	149	2748.32	2572.348	210.735

Independent Samples Test

		Levene's Test for Equality of Variances		t-test for Equality of Means					95% Confidence Interval of the Difference	
		F	Sig.	t	df	Sig. (2-tailed)	Mean Difference	Std. Error Difference	Lower	Upper
jp_rinc Respondent's Earnings: Japan	Equal variances assumed	.460	.498	-.421	285	.674	-128.757	305.573	-730.222	472.709
	Equal variances not assumed			-.421	282.796	.674	-128.757	305.706	-730.504	472.990

Figure 4.6 *Independent t-test output: Respondent's income (jp_rinc) by size of smaller communities (jp_size)*

Interpreting the output

We see that for the 138 respondents who live in small towns the mean individual income is ¥ 2619.57 yen (sd = ¥ 2601), while for the 149 village dwellers the mean income is ¥ 2748.32 yen (sd = ¥ 2548). The difference between the means for the two groups is ¥ 128.75 yen, with the villagers earning more on average. There appears to be not much difference between the two groups, but we can confirm this using the independent t-test.

As with the last example, interpretation of the independent t-test output is a two-stage process. This time when we examine the homogeneity of the variance between the two groups using **Levene's Test for Equality of Variances**, the F value is 0.460, and the 'Sig.' (p value) for this test is 0.498. This is considerably greater than 0.05 (thus not significant), indicating that equal variances can be assumed, so we go to the row of results labelled *Equal variances assumed* in order to test the hypothesis. This provides the t value ($t = -0.421$) and the degrees of freedom (df = 285). From the table, we find that 'Sig. (2-tailed)' is 0.674; considerably greater than the 5% cut-off level ($p > 0.05$). Thus, the result is not significant. Therefore, we reject the hypothesis, and accept the Null hypothesis.

This is expressed as $t = -0.421$, df = 285, $p = 0.674$ (ns).

There is not a significant difference in the average individual income between those living in smaller towns and those living in villages.

Note that the value of t in the first example was positive, while the value of t in the second example was negative. This is solely an artefact of the order in which the difference of the two means is compared. In the first example, since men appeared as Group 1, the difference subtracting the mean of Group 1 from the mean of Group 2 (the women) was positive and the value of t was positive. In the second example, those living in small towns were designated as Group 1 and those living in villages as Group 2. Here, subtracting the mean income of Group 2 from the mean of Group 1 produced a negative difference and consequently t was negative. If we had reversed the ordering of the groups, the same absolute values of t would have appeared, only with the signs reversed.

Note also that, while we used Levene's Test for Equality of Variances to choose which row of the t-test output was appropriate, the differences between the rows were negligible, and we would have reached the same conclusions if we had used the other row. This is the case for our two examples, but it is not always the case. The two rows may differ substantially, particularly when the F of the Levene's Test is significant. In such instances, which row is selected can make a substantial difference; sometimes the result of the t-test will be significant in one row but not the other.

A digression into some statistical principles

Before proceeding further with t-test, there are a few things that you may have noticed about the presentations of these t-test results that we should clear up.

Degrees of freedom (df)

You may wonder what is meant by the curious phrase *degrees of freedom* (df). Basically, df is the amount of sources of variation in the data being examined. For instance, in Example 2, there are a total of 287 respondents being analysed, 138 living in smaller towns and 149 in villages. Once you know the total income of all the people in towns or in villages, you do not need to know the individual income of every person because you can infer the income amount of the last person in each category. That is, the last person's income is not *free* to vary. So, in this case, the total degrees of freedom is the total number of individual respondents, minus one person in each of the two categories (df = 285 = 287 − 2). Similar considerations apply for determining the degrees of freedom in the statistics that will be covered in later modules.

The effect of number of cases on statistical significance

Note that the size of *t* does not in itself determine whether a result is statistically significant or not. The larger the value of *t*, the more likely a difference is to be statistically significant, but the size of *t* needed to reach a given level of significance depends upon the number of degrees of freedom. In general, the larger the number of degrees of freedom, the smaller *t* needs to be to attain statistical significance. For instance, a value of *t* of 1.70 would not be significant at the 0.05 level if df = 20; however, the same *t* of 1.70 would be significant at the 0.05 level if df = 285. This effect gradually wears off as the number of cases rises. After degrees of freedom exceeds about 120, the effect of increasing the number cases become negligible.

This effect of a larger number of cases applies to virtually all confirmatory statistical tests: *holding everything else equal, an observed relationship or difference in a batch of data is more likely to* be *statistically significant if the number of cases in the data is large.* The implication of this is that whenever one is analysing a batch of data based upon a sample, there must be a reasonably large number of cases in order for even quite strong relationships or pronounced differences to attain statistical significance. (This also leads to a caution: note that if a data set with a very large number of cases is being analysed (say a national census with millions of individual cases), a very minute difference or a very weak relationship can be returned as being statistically significant; even a tiny difference can involve tens of thousands of people. That is, with a very large number of cases, a very unimportant, inconsequential difference or relationship of no real substantive importance can appear as *statistically* significant.)

The Central Limit Theorem

This effect, that it is easier to attain statistical significance with a larger number of cases, can be considered to follow on from the Central Limit Theorem, which states: '*If repeated random samples of size* N *are drawn from any population, with mean (a certain value)* μ *and standard deviation* σ*, then, as* N *becomes large, the sampling distribution of sampling means will approach normality (take the form of a Normal distribution), with mean* μ *and standard deviation of* σ /√N. As sample sizes, and numbers of cases, become larger, the chances that the values of any given batch of data will diverge widely from the total population figures become smaller; that is, a larger number of cases is more likely to be truly representative. The odds of a sample result varying from 'truth' is calculable. The Central Limit Theorem is the principle that is the foundation underlying all confirmatory statistical testing and the expression of statistical results in terms of '*p*', the *probability* that the result does not mirror the true population difference or relationship.

Another important effect of the principles in the Central Limit Theorem is that a statistical test that has an assumption that the data being tested have a normal distribution can have that assumption violated (or at least considerably bent) if the number of cases in the data is large.

At the risk of confusing you, we are going to interject one additional observation here. Note that the Central Limit Theorem and its associated confirmatory statistical testing with results expressed in term of probability levels is only relevant when the data are a sample or subset of a larger population. Taking the logic of confirmatory statistical testing literally at face value, if one has a batch of data that covers *all* cases (for instance, an administrative data file kept by a large corporation of 100% of its employees), strictly speaking there is no need for any confirmatory statistical analysis. Any observed differences or relationships must be by definition real since the analyst possesses the information from all the possible cases. There is no need to test to establish statistically whether an observed difference or relationship is a reliable reflection of a larger population – the data *are* the larger population. All that is really required is simply to report what is observed.

Analysts, however, still analyse population data sets as if they were samples. Sometimes, this is just a conditioned reflex – the analyst is so used to carrying out confirmatory analyses that he or she has forgotten the reason why they began statistical testing in the first place. In other instances, however, it is a bit less of a 'knee jerk' reaction. Even when carried out on populations where they are not strictly required, confirmatory statistical results do provide a means of systematically reporting the strength of an observed difference or relationship. Also, as you will discover when you move to some of the latter modules in this text, multivariate statistical techniques where the relationships between a number of variables can be depicted simultaneously provide a means for modelling reality – depicting it in a manner that simplifies and highlights the essential dynamics of whatever is going on.

One-sample *t*-test

The **one-sample *t*-test** is used when one wants to establish whether the mean value of some scalar variable is significantly different from a value set by the researcher. The external value that the researcher chooses could come from a variety of sources; for example, the theoretical literature may predict a certain value or research carried out at some other time or place may have generated a mean value different from that observed in the present data set.

Running the one-sample t-test: an example

Let us return to the 'compatibility' scale. We have established that the Japanese women and men in our sample differ significantly in their scores on 'compatibility' between their work and their private life. In general, however, does the average compatibility score for the Japanese data set differ significantly from the overall average compatibility score for all the countries in the ISSP data sets?

Lumping the data sets for all the countries together, the mean compatibility score is 0.0333. The mean score for Japan is 0.3698. So, Japan is higher; i.e. more compatible on average, but there is a wide variation in individual compatibility scores both for the Japanese and for the other nations in the ISSP data sets, so is this difference large enough for the difference to be statistically significant?

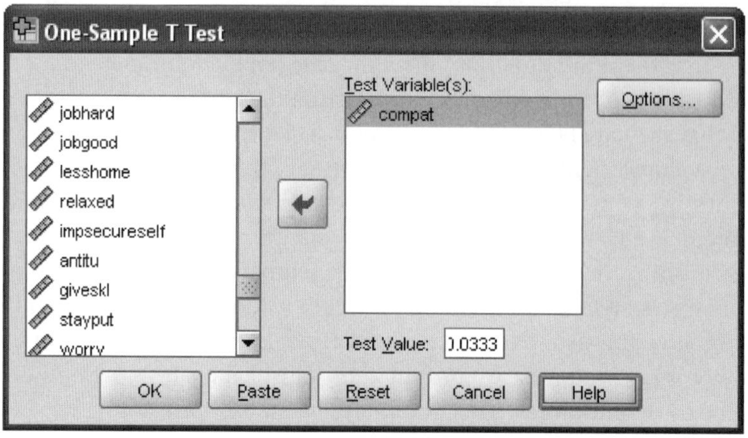

Figure 4.7 *Running the one-sample t-test*

One-Sample Statistics

	N	Mean	Std. Deviation	Std. Error Mean
compat Job & family compatible	558	.3698	1.27828	.05411

One-Sample Test

	Test Value = 0.0333					
					95% Confidence Interval of the Difference	
	t	df	Sig. (2-tailed)	Mean Difference	Lower	Upper
compat Job & family compatible	6.218	557	.000	.33648	.2302	.4428

Figure 4.8   *Output from the one-sample* t-*test*

In this instance, our hypothesis could be worded: *The mean compatibility score for Japan is significantly higher than the mean compatibility score for all the ISSP data sets combined.*

Our Null hypothesis could be worded: *The mean compatibility score for Japan is the same as or significantly lower than the mean compatibility score for all the ISSP data sets combined.*

The one-sample *t*-test is selected by opening the **Analyze** menu, selecting **Compare Means** and then **One-Sample T test.**

Enter the overall mean for the whole ISSP, **0.0333**, in the **Test Value** box. Select the variable **compat** and click on > to transfer it to the **Test Variable(s)** box, then click on **OK** to run the procedure (Figure 4.7).

Interpreting the output of a one-sample t-test

Figure 4.8 provides an example of output from a one-sample *t*-test.

The first box in Figure 4.8 presents descriptive statistics for **compat** for the whole of the Japanese sample (mean, standard deviation and standard error). As noted above, the mean is 0.3698 with a standard deviation of 1.27828 for 558 survey respondents.

The second box in Figure 4.8 presents the results of the one-sample *t*-test: $t = 6.218$, $df = 557$, $p < 0.001$. So, we reject our Null and accept the hypothesis; compared to the ISSP countries as a whole, the Japanese do score higher on average in their score of 'compatibility' between work and private life.

Paired-samples *t*-test (for dependent/matched groups)

The third *t*-test, the **paired-samples *t*-test**, is used with matched pair data, or is used in circumstances where the research question calls for the repeated measurement of responses from the same individual. Data might be collected on one occasion where individuals are asked to respond to similar questions two or more times. For example, a paired-sample *t*-test might be used to compare a person's responses to the same question administered by means of a self-completion questionnaire and a face-to-face interview. Alternatively, data may have been collected on more than one occasion where individuals are followed over a period of time and asked the same or similar questions at different times; for example, comparing before and after values in an experiment. This test is also used when a researcher wants to ensure that two subjects who had been allocated to matched groups are evenly matched before beginning an experiment or study.

Running the paired-sample t-test – an example

While a new ISSP data set appears each year, different samples are drawn each year, so the same people do not appear in subsequent years of the survey. Also, the ISSP module for 2005 does not have any examples of paired variables where the same people have been asked the same question twice during their interview. In order to provide an example of running the **paired-sample *t*-test** procedure, we have decided to use the two ratio-level questions on income. The first variable, **jp_percapita1**, has details of per-capita income based upon the total household income averaged out over all members of the household. The second variable, **jp_percapita2**, has per-capita income details averaged out for only the adults in the household. The same respondents have provided the responses to the two questions. Note that, technically, it is not appropriate to use the paired-sample *t*-test to examine the differences between these two variables, as the questions are slightly different and measure different per-capita incomes. We are using these variables because the ISSP data set does not contain any appropriate variables and it is important that we cover the use of this version of *t*-test. Our hypothesis is: *The average per-capita income based upon all household members is significantly different than the average per-capita income based upon adults only*; and our Null hypothesis is: *The average per-capita income based upon all household members is **not** significantly different than the average per-capita income based upon adults only*.

The paired-samples *t*-test is selected by opening the **Analyze** menu, selecting **Compare Means** and then **Paired-Sample T test**.

In order to select two variables for comparison, use the paired *t*-test dialog box to highlight the required variables, and click on > to transfer to the paired variables box. Here, we have chosen **jp_percapita1** and **jp_percapita2** to produce the *Paired-Samples t-Test* window in Figure 4.9. Click on OK to run the procedure.

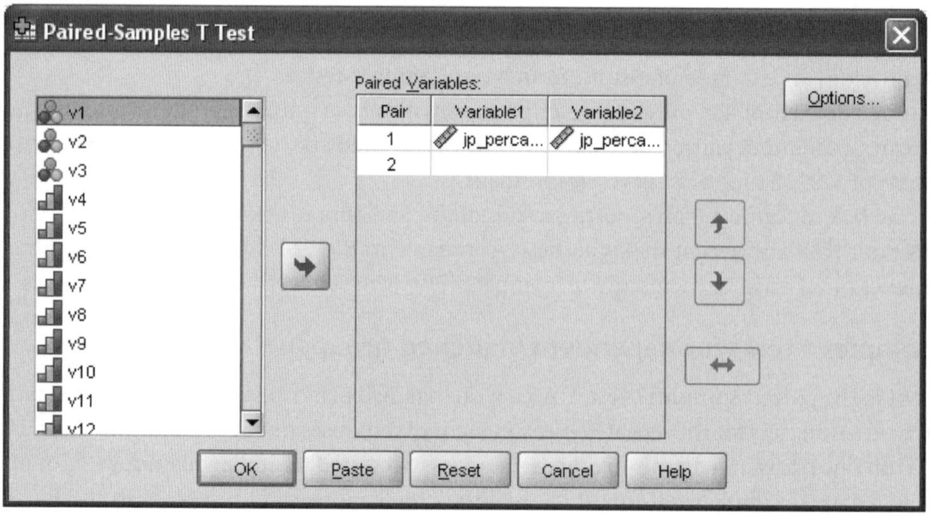

Figure 4.9 *Selecting the variables for the paired-sample t-test*

Paired Samples Statistics

		Mean	N	Std. Deviation	Std. Error Mean
Pair 1	jp_percapita1 Income per person in hhold	1909.3848	518	1339.48673	58.85367
	jp_percapita2 Income per adult in hhold	2186.2199	518	1398.98474	61.46786

Paired Samples Correlations

		N	Correlation	Sig.
Pair 1	jp_percapita1 Income per person in hhold & jp_percapita2 Income per adult in hhold	518	.916	.000

Paired Samples Test

	Paired Differences							
				95% Confidence Interval of the Difference				Sig. (2-tailed)
	Mean	Std. Deviation	Std. Error Mean	Lower	Upper	t	df	
Pair 1 jp_percapita1 Income per person in hhold - jp_percapita2 Income per adult in hhold	−276.83513	563.93769	24.77800	−325.51307	−228.15718	−11.173	517	.000

Figure 4.10   *Output from the paired-sample t-test*

Interpreting the output of paired-samples t-test

Figure 4.10 provides an example of the output from the paired-samples *t*-test.

The first box in Figure 4.10 presents the paired samples statistics (mean, standard deviation, and standard error) for both variables. For instance, the mean value of **jp_percapita1** is ¥ 1909.38 yen with a standard deviation of ¥ 11339.49 yen for 518 respondents.

The second box in Figure 4.10 presents information on the extent to which the two variables are similar or correlated. As one might expect there is a high correlation between the two variables ($r = 0.916$, significant at $p < 0.001$). This is not surprising as the variables are very similar, both concerned with a household's per-capita income.

The third box in Figure 4.10 presents the findings from the paired *t*-test: $t = -11.173$, df $=517$, $p < 0.001$. The mean difference between **jp_percapita1** and **jp_percapita2** is ¥ 276.84 and the *t*-test indicates that this difference is highly significant. Thus our hypothesis is confirmed: the average per-capita income based upon all household members is significantly different (it is less) than the average per-capita income based upon adults only.

EXERCISE

Using the ISSP data set from the country of your choice, test hypotheses using the independent samples *t*-test.

To complete the task you need to: (1) state your research question; (2) generate your research hypothesis and the Null hypothesis; (3) select the appropriate variables; and (4) describe and interpret the output.

You could also try a one-sample *t*-test. You can pick a scalar variable for which you might have conceptual reasons to indicate a certain average value different from the mean for that variable for your country. You could also repeat a one-sample *t*-test analysis for one of the other attitude scales in the data set, but of course you need to know the mean value of the attitude scale in question for the combined ISSP data sets. You do not know this; however, the attitude scales were constructed in such a way that their means across the summed ISSP data sets tend to be close to zero. If you want to try this latter approach to a one-sample *t*-test, set the **Test Value** equal to 0.000.

For practice, you may also want to try out the paired samples *t*-test, but recognize that, since the ISSP data sets do not contain appropriate variables for a paired samples *t*-test, you will have to choose two interval/ratio variables that do not strictly meet the 'repeated measurements' assumption of the test.

5 Crosstabulation

INTRODUCTION

Crosstabulation tables, or contingency tables, are frequently employed to examine the relationship between two variables (usually nominal or ordinal) that have a relatively small number of categories. However, as we saw in Module 3, quantitative variables such as age can be transformed into broad categories using the **Recode** procedure. Displaying the distribution of two or more variables jointly in the form of a crosstabulation table allows us to make some important observations about the relationship between them. Using the ISSP data from Mexico, this module will demonstrate the Crosstabs procedure in SPSS and explain some of the most frequently used measures of association.

Before proceeding to the ISSP data, we will use a more straightforward example to highlight the key features of a crosstabulation table and explain the logic underpinning the Chi-square statistic. The frequency tables below are taken from a hypothetical dataset of 200 respondents.

As you can see from Figures 5.1a and 5.1b, the gender breakdown of this sample is 100 males and 100 females, with 80 respondents (40 per cent) categorized as smokers and 120 (60 per cent) as non-smokers. However, looking at each variable in isolation provides a very limited amount of information and we need to produce a crosstabulation to find out more about the relationship between gender and smoking. Although the table in Figure 5.2a is quite basic in relation to some of the crosstabulations you will encounter later on in the chapter, it nevertheless contains important information and a closer examination will allow us to identify some of the key elements of a crosstabulation.

If it is possible to identify an independent or causal variable this, by convention, should be our column variable. In this example **Gender** is the column variable because we are hypothesizing that the respondent's gender is an important factor in determining whether or not they smoke. We will begin with the number in the bottom right hand corner of the table which is known as the grand total. This figure (200) represents the total number of people in the sample (or, more accurately, the total number who provided valid responses for both variables). The numbers around the edge of the table represent the individual row and column totals (or marginals) and provide frequency counts for each of the variables on their own. So, for example, if we look at the row marginals we can see that 80 of our 200 respondents (40 per cent) are smokers, while 120 (60 per cent) are non-smokers. Similarly, the column marginals tell us how many of the 200 respondents were male (100) and how many were female (100). In other words the row and column marginals replicate the information we already have from the individual frequency tables. It is important to point out that only column percentages are included in this table. This means that each column will add up to 100 per cent, facilitating comparison **across** the categories of the independent variable (gender in this example).

Gender

		Frequency	Percent	Valid Percent	Cumulative Percent
Valid	1 Male	100	50.0	50.0	50.0
	2 Female	100	50.0	50.0	100.0
	Total	200	100.0	100.0	

Figure 5.1a   *Frequency table of **Gender***

Smoke

		Frequency	Percent	Valid Percent	Cumulative Percent
Valid	1 Smoker	80	40.0	40.0	40.0
	2 Non-smoker	120	60.0	60.0	100.0
	Total	200	100.0	100.0	

Figure 5.1b   *Frequency table of **Smoke***

Smoke * Gender Crosstabulation

			Gender 1 Male	Gender 2 Female	Total
Smoke	1 Smoker	Count	20	60	80
		% within Gender	20.0%	60.0%	40.0%
	2 Non-smoker	Count	80	40	120
		% within Gender	80.0%	40.0%	60.0%
	Total	Count	100	100	200
		% within Gender	100.0%	100.0%	100.0%

Column Marginals

Row Marginals

Grand Total

Figure 5.2a   *Crosstabulation of **Smoke** by **Gender** with column percentages*

As **Gender** and **Smoke** are dichotomous variables (i.e. they each contain only two categories) the main body of the table takes the form of a basic two by two crosstabulation, containing just four cells. These cells represent the combination of categories of the two variables and contain both the frequencies and the corresponding column percentages. So, for example, the first cell informs us that 20 males (20 per cent of all males) are smokers. The cell below this tells us that 80 males (80 per cent) are non-smokers. In relation to females, 60 (60 per cent of all females) declared themselves to be smokers while 40 (40 per cent) were non-smokers. We can conclude that for this particular sample of 200 people there is an association between gender and smoking (if there was no association we would expect to find the same percentages of male and female smokers).

Smoke* Gender Crosstabulation

			Gender		
			1 Male	2 Female	Total
Smoke	1 Smoker	Count	20	60	80
		% within Smoke	25.0%	75.0%	100.0%
	2 Non-smoker	Count	80	40	120
		% within Smoke	66.7%	33.3%	100.0%
	Total	Count	100	100	200
		% within Smoke	50.0%	50.0%	100.0%

Figure 5.2b   *Crosstabulation of **Smoke** by **Gender** with row percentages*

Smoke* Gender Crosstabulation

			Gender		
			1 Male	2 Female	Total
Smoke	1 Smoker	Count	20	60	80
		% of Total	10.0%	30.0%	40.0%
	2 Non-smoker	Count	80	40	120
		% of Total	40.0%	20.0%	60.0%
	Total	Count	100	100	200
		% of Total	50.0%	50.0%	100.0%

Figure 5.2c   *Crosstabulation of **Smoke** by **Gender** with total percentages*

It is important to point out that our emphasis on the proportions of males and females that are either smokers or non-smokers is a result of the fact that we requested column percentages. If we had requested row percentages or total percentages the focus of our analysis would be rather different.

For example, the table in Figure 5.2b uses row percentages and this allows us to highlight the proportions of smokers and non-smokers that are male and female. By looking at the first row of this table we can see that 25% of smokers are male and 75% are female. You will also have noticed that the rows add up to 100% (as opposed to the columns in the previous table).

By contrast, requesting total percentages allows us to identify the proportions that each combination of **Smoke** and **Gender** contributes to the table. For example, the table in Figure 5.2c informs us that 10% of the total sample of 200 respondents are male smokers, 30% are female smokers, 40% are male non-smokers and 20% are female non-smokers. Although the additional information provided by row and total percentages is useful, it is difficult to interpret your results if the table is too cluttered. For this reason, in the remaining examples we will request only column percentages.

However, as we discussed in the previous chapter, with inferential statistics we are more interested in drawing conclusions about the 'population' that the sample was drawn from than in the sample itself. In other words, we want to find out whether the difference between males and females that we observed in the crosstabulation table above actually represents a real difference in the population as a whole. The Chi-square test enables us to make such a judgment and before proceeding to an SPSS example, it is worth examining the logic underpinning this procedure.

THE CHI-SQUARE (χ^2) TEST

The Chi-square test allows us to determine whether or not there is a *statistically significant association* between two variables. If the variables are not associated they are said to be *statistically independent* (hence Chi-square is often referred to as the 'Chi-square test of independence'). As an inferential statistic it allows us to draw conclusions about the population on the basis of our sample results. So, for example, we can calculate the probability that the differences between males and females observed in the crosstabulation above are the result of a real association between **Gender** and **Smoke** in the population as a whole. This can be put into more formal language by framing the Null (H_0) and alternative (H_1) hypotheses.

H_0: **Gender** and **Smoke** are independent (any observed association has occurred by chance).
H_1: **Gender** and **Smoke** are dependent (any observed association is the result of a real association).

As with the *t*-test (see Module 4), the Chi-square (χ^2) test allows us to choose between H_0 and H_1 and determine whether or not there is a statistical association between the two variables. In broad terms, Chi-square is a measure of the overall difference between the observed frequencies (the actual frequency counts in the cells of the crosstabulation) and the expected frequencies (the frequency counts we would expect to find if there was no association between the variables). This is represented by the formula, $(O - E)^2/E$, where O signifies the 'observed' frequencies and E the 'expected' frequencies. While this formula may appear complex at first sight, we can break it down into a number of simple steps as shown in Figure 5.3.

The first column in the table in Figure 5.3, headed **O**, contains the *observed frequencie*s from the **Gender** by **Smoke** crosstabulation (i.e. the actual values that are present in the tables above – Figures 5.2a to 5.2c). The second column, headed **E**, gives the frequencies we would expect to find in each of the cells of the crosstabulation if there was *no association* between the variables (the *expected frequencies*). For example, if **Gender** and **Smoke** were totally independent we would expect equal proportions, 40 per cent of both males and females, to smoke (i.e. a frequency count of 40 in both cases). The next step is to subtract the expected frequencies from the observed frequencies (column 3, O – E). Then, to get rid of the negative signs, we square this figure (column 4, $(O - E)^2$) and divide the result by the expected frequency (column 5, $(O - E)^2/E$). Adding these figures together will give us the final Chi-square result (33.34 in this example).

So, as alluded to above, the value of Chi-square provides a standard measure of the overall difference between the observed frequencies and the expected frequencies. In general, the greater the overall difference, the larger the value of Chi-square and the more confident we can be that there is a real association between these variables in the population. Taking degrees of freedom (df) into account

O	E	O-E	$(O-E)^2$	$(O-E)^2/E$
20	40	−20	400	10
80	60	20	400	6.67
60	40	20	400	10
40	60	−20	400	6.67
				33.34

Figure 5.3 *Calculating Chi-square (by hand)*

(For Chi-square, degrees of freedom (df) is determined by multiplying the numbers of rows (r) minus one times the number of columns (c) minus one (df = $(r - 1)(c - 1)$), SPSS will produce the significance values automatically. As we saw in Module 4, we need to decide just how confident we want to be (95 per cent, 99 per cent or 99.9 per cent).

MEASURES OF ASSOCIATION

Although a Chi-square result may confirm the existence of a statistically significant association we are also interested in finding out the strength of that association. However, because Chi-square is heavily dependent upon the size of the sample, it cannot provide us with this information. (For example, if you multiply the sample size by ten, the size of Chi-square will increase by a factor of ten also. Hence, with very large sample sizes, quite small, not very important differences in a crosstabulation table can produce a result that is *statistically* significant.) Fortunately, a number of statistics are available for the purposes of measuring the strength of an association.

As usual, our choice will be influenced by the level of measurement of the variables we are working with. Two such measures, phi and Cramer's V, are frequently used if one or more of the variables is nominal (phi for 2 by 2 tables and Cramer's V for tables larger than 2 by 2 (i.e. more than two rows or two columns)). Absolute values of phi and Cramers V range between 0 and 1, with 0 representing no association and 1 a perfect association. (The Crosstabs procedure in SPSS provides a variety of alternative measures of association and a number of these options are discussed briefly in the appendix at the end of this module.)

CROSSTABS IN SPSS

The remainder of the chapter will focus on the Crosstabs procedure in SPSS with illustrative examples from the ISSP data for Mexico. We will begin by looking at the relationship between educational qualifications (*degree*) and paid employment (*v27*), using Chi-square to test the following hypothesis:

H_0: **v27** and **degree** are *independent* (any observed association has occurred by chance).
H_1: **v27** and **degree** are dependent (any observed association is the result of a real association).

To access Crosstabs in SPSS, click on **D**escriptive **A**nalyze, **Statistics** and then **C**rosstabs (see Figure 5.4).

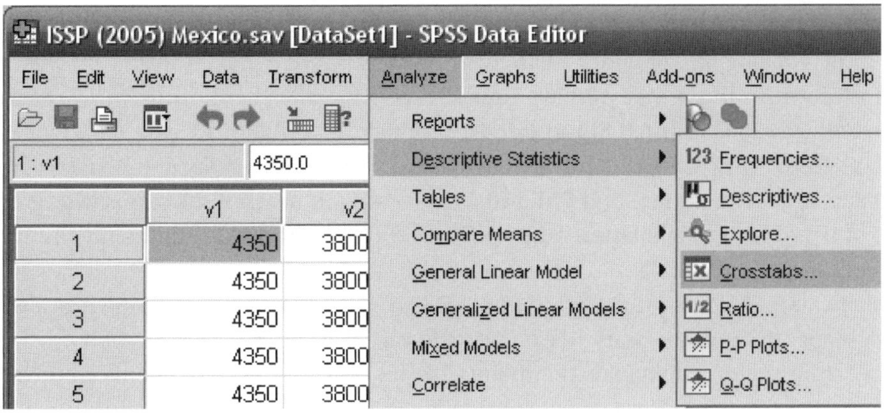

Figure 5.4 *Accessing the Crosstabs procedure*

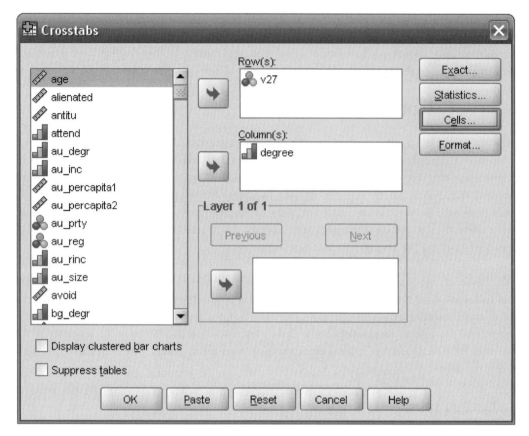

Figure 5.5   *Crosstabs dialog box*

This will open up the Crosstabs dialog box (Figure 5.5). As we want to examine the relationship between paid employment (**v27**) and level of education (**degree**) we simply transfer these variables from the source list to the *Row* and *Column* boxes, respectively. Since **degree** is the independent or causal variable in this example it should be located in the *Columns* box (i.e. we are hypothesizing that the respondents' level of education is an important factor in determining whether or not they are in paid employment).

Then Click on **Cells** to open up the Cell Display dialog box (Figure 5.6).

The cell display dialog box provides a variety of options but to avoid cluttering up the table we will restrict our selection to those that we have found to be generally the most useful: **O**bserved Counts, **C**olumn Percentages and **Adj**usted **Standardized** residuals (as shown in Figure 5.6). Once these three options are selected, click on **Continue**. Then click on **Statistics** to open the statistics dialog box (Figure 5.7) and select **Chi-square** and **Phi** and Cramer's **V** (all of these selections will be explained in the context of the SPSS crosstabulation output). Then click on **Continue** and finally on **OK** to run the Crosstabs procedure.

The resultant output is shown in Figures 5.8a, 5.8b and 5.8c. In order to gain an understanding of how Crosstabs operates it is necessary to examine the various elements of these tables.

We can see from the row marginals that half (49.8 per cent) of the respondents are in paid employment. However, the top row of cells shows considerable variation according to educational attainment.

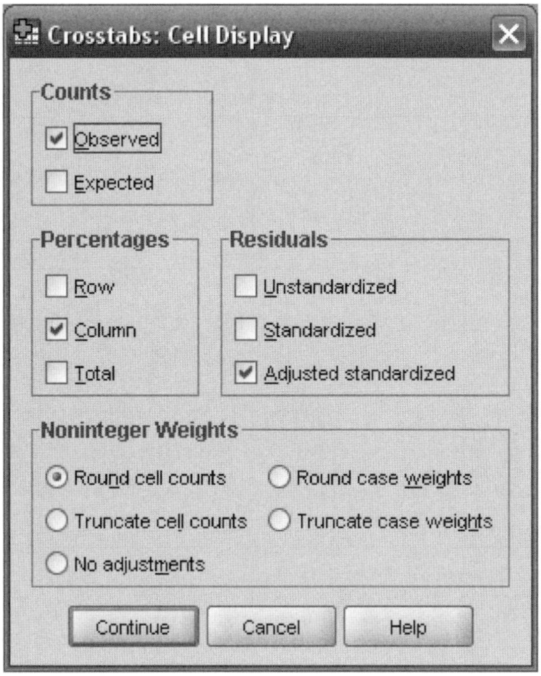

Figure 5.6   *Crosstabs: Cell Display dialog box*

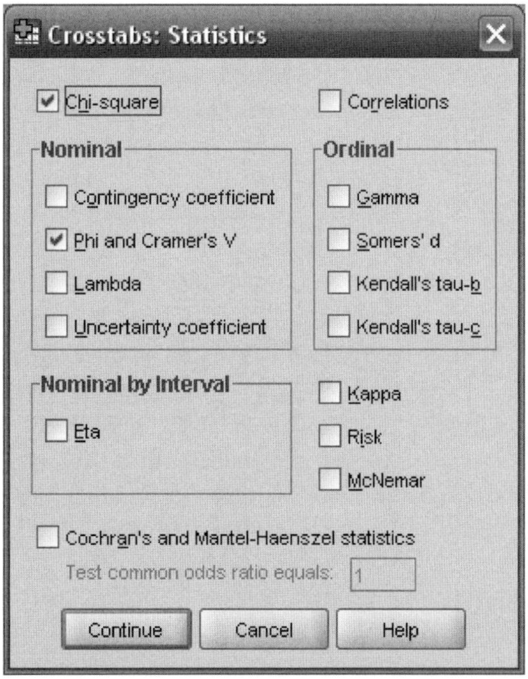

Figure 5.7   *Crosstabs: Statistics dialog box*

v27 Respondent currently working for pay * degree R: Education II-highest education level Crosstabulation

			degree R: Eucation II-highest education level						Total
			0 No formal qualification	1 Lowest formal Qualification	2 above Lowest Qualification	3 Higher secondary completed	4 Above Higher secondary level	5 University degree completed	
V27 Respondent currently working for pay	1 Yes	Count	86	112	199	124	31	137	689
		% within degree R: Education II-highest education level	35.7%	42.6%	50.9%	48.1%	60.8%	76.1%	49.8%
		Adjusted Residual	-4.8	-2.6	.5	.6	1.6	7.6	
	2 No	Count	155	151	192	134	20	43	695
		% within degree R: Education II-highest education level	64.3%	57.4%	49.1%	51.9%	39.2%	23.9%	50.2%
		Adjusted Residual	4.8	2.6	-.5	.6	-1.6	-7.6	
Total		Count	241	263	391	258	51	180	1384
		% within degree R: Education II-highest education level	100.0%	100.0%	100.0%	100.0%	100.0%	100.0%	100.0%

Figure 5.8a Crosstabulation of *v27* by *degree*

Chi-Square Tests

	Value	df	Asymp. Sig. (2-sided)
Pearson Chi-Square	77.488[a]	5	.000
Likelihood Ratio	80.324	5	.000
Linear-by-Linear Association	67.540	1	.000
N of Valid Cases	1384		

a. 0 cells (.0%) have expected count less than 5. The minimum expected count is 25.39

Figure 5.8b *Chi-square results for v27 by degree*

Symmetric Measures

		Value	Approx. Sig.
Nominal by Nominal	Phi	.237	.000
	Cramer's V	.237	.000
	N of Valid Cases	1384	

Figure 5.8c *Measures of association for v27 by degree*

Those with little or no qualifications appear least likely to be in paid employment (35.7 per cent) while those with the highest level of educational qualifications have the greatest percentage in work (76.1 per cent). To ascertain whether or not this association is statistically significant it is necessary to consult the Chi-square results.

From Figure 5.8b we can see that the Chi-square value (Pearson Chi-Square) is 77.488 with a significance level of .000. Remember that when SPSS records a significance level of .000 this should be read as .0005 or less, rather than zero. As this significance level is less than .001 we can be at least 99.9 per cent certain that there is an association between educational attainment and employment in the population. To put it another way, we would only expect to find an association of this strength and a Chi-square as large as 77.488 by chance in less than 5 out of every 10,000 samples. Therefore we can safely reject our Null hypothesis.

Once we have detected a significant association between two variables, the focus shifts to the strength and the nature of that association. Cramer's V is used to determine the strength of an association for tables larger than 2 by 2 with a potential range of absolute values between 0 and 1, with 0 representing no association and 1 a perfect association. So, while Figure 5.8c confirms that there is a significant association between v27 and gender, the Cramer's V value of .237 informs us that this association is relatively weak (although it is important to point out that this kind of social data is unlikely to produce many very strong associations).

Finally, it is important to recognize that a significant Chi-square result only tells us that the two variables in the table are associated. It does *not* tell us about the form of that association. A common mistake that many beginning students make is to assume that a significant result automatically confirms their hypothesis. However, it is quite possible that another form of link between the two variables in the table, perhaps *contrary to the expectation of the hypothesis*, has generated the significant Chi-square. In order to determine the form that the significant association in this table takes we need to return to the original table and examine the individual cells. This is where the adjusted standardized residuals come in handy (see Figure 5.8a). Any cells with adjusted residual values greater than 2 or less than −2 should be given special attention. For example, if we concentrate on two of the cells with high values (7.6 and 4.8) we can see that those with a degree are much more likely to be in paid employment than all other respondents (76.1 per cent compared to 49.8 per cent of the overall sample) and those with no formal qualifications are much more likely to be without a job (64.3 per cent compared to 50.2 per cent of respondents overall). The adjusted residuals of −7.6 and −4.8 indicate a similar pattern, albeit in reverse. As these are the four cells of the table that vary most from what we would expect to find by chance we can conclude that they have contributed most to the significant Chi-square result. In large tables with many cells, it can be very hard to identify which cells are the most important. The adjusted standardized residual gives you an impartial way of identifying them reliably.

A note of caution

Before moving on to a second Chi-square example and a consideration of the concept of a 'control' variable, it is necessary to draw attention to some of the restrictions that apply when using Chi-square.

(a) For a 2 by 2 table (2 rows and 2 columns) Chi-square should not be used if any of the expected frequencies are less than 5.
(b) For tables larger than 2 by 2, Chi-square should not be used if any of the expected frequencies are less than 1 or more than 20 per cent of the expected frequencies are less than 5.

It is not necessary to request expected frequencies in order to check this when running the Crosstabs procedure as SPSS automatically includes the relevant information in the output (note the bottom of Figure 5.8b).

In certain circumstances it may be possible to overcome the problem of low expected frequencies by combining some of the categories of the variables you are using. This will have the effect of reducing the number of categories and increasing the number of cases in the cells. (See Module 3 for details on how to combine categories using the Recode procedure.)

CHI-SQUARE: A SECOND EXAMPLE

As a precursor to a discussion of control variables we will carry out a second Crosstabs, this time using the variables **sex** (gender of respondent) and **v26b** (a recoded version of v26, preferred work situation). We can see from the frequency table of **v26b** (shown in Figure 5.9) that almost 50 per cent of respondents would prefer to work full-time (i.e. 30 hours or more), just over a third would like to work part-time (10–29 hours) and around a sixth have a preference for less than 10 hours or no work at all. (Note: This is an example of where some categories of the variables need to be combined in order to retain large enough numbers of cases in the cells. As there are very few respondents in category 4 of the original **v26** it is appropriate to combine categories 3 and 4 and you will need to do this (and create **v26b**) before proceeding any further. See Module 3 for more information on recoding variables.)

It would be interesting to produce a crosstabulation to see what impact, if any, gender has on people's work preferences. In this example, then, we want to see whether or not there is a significant association between **v26b** and **sex**.

H_0: **v26b** and **sex** are independent (any observed association has occurred by chance).
H_1: **v26b** and **sex** are dependent (any observed association is the result of a real association).

v26b v26 recoded (preferred work situation)

		Frequency	Percent	Valid Percent	Cumulative Percent
Valid	1 Full-time job (30 hrs or more)	633	45.2	47.0	47.0
	2 Part-time job (10 to 29 hrs)	481	34.3	35.7	82.7
	3 Less than 10 hrs or no job at all	233	16.6	17.3	100.0
	Total	1347	96.1	100.0	
Missing	8 Can't choose	20	1.4		
	9 NA, refused	34	2.4		
	Total	54	3.9		
Total		1401	100.0		

Figure 5.9 *Frequency table for v26b*

Open the Crosstabs dialog box as before (click on **Analyze**, **Descriptive Statistics** and then **Crosstabs**). This time transfer the variable **v26b** over to the row box and **sex** to the column box (**sex** is the independent or causal variable in this instance because we are hypothesizing that a person's gender has a determining influence on the number of hours they would prefer to work).

Then click on **Cells** to open the Cell Display dialog box. Select the **Observed** frequencies, **Column** percentages and **Adj. standardized** residuals (as we did in the previous example shown in Figure 5.6).

Click on **Continue** to return you to the Crosstabs dialog box and then click on **Statistics** to open the Crosstabs: Statistics dialog box. Select **Chi-square** and **Phi and Cramer's V** (see previous example, Figure 5.7) and then click on **Continue** and finally on **OK**.

The output is shown in Figures 5.10a, 5.10b and 5.10c below. We will consider these tables briefly before examining the impact of the introduction of a 'control' variable on the relationship between the two variables.

Figure 5.10a shows the crosstabulation table for **v26b** by **sex**. Again, the decision to select only frequency counts, column percentages and adjusted residuals ensures that the table is still relatively easy to interpret. Before commenting on the individual cells of the table, however, we need to consult the Chi-square results in Figure 10b.

We can see from Figure 5.10b that the Chi-square result of 46.666 has a significance level of .000. This should be read as $p<.0005$, so if the Null hypothesis was true we would expect to find a Chi-square as large as 46.666 in less than 5 out of every 10,000 samples. Consequently we can safely reject the Null and conclude that there is a significant association between gender and preferred work situation.

(Note that Figure 5.10b also informs us that there are no cells with an expected count lower than 5 and indeed that the minimum expected count is 114.68. Consequently we can be sure that the prerequisites, referred to earlier in relation to low expected frequencies, have been met.)

As the crosstabulation is larger than 2 by 2 we need to consult Cramer's V rather than phi for our measure of association. We have already determined that there is an highly significant association ($p<.0005$) between these two variables. However, the Cramer's V value of .186 indicates that this association is relatively weak (see Figure 5.10c).

The final stage in our analysis of these tables involves an examination of the form that this significant association takes. As it is possible for the same Chi-square value to be produced by *completely*

v26b v26 recoded (preferred work situation) * sex R: Gender Crosstabulation

			sex R: Gender		Total
			1 Male	2 Female	
v26b v26 recoded (preferred work situation)	1 Full-time job (30 hrs or more)	Count	374	259	633
		% within sex R: Gender	56.4%	37.9%	47.0%
		Adjusted Residual	6.8	−6.8	
	2Part-time job (10 to 29 hrs)	Count	192	289	481
		% within sex R: Gender	29.0%	42.3%	35.7%
		Adjusted Residual	−5.1	5.1	
	3 Less than 10 hrs or no job at all	Count	97	136	233
		% within sex R: Gender	14.6%	19.9%	17.3%
		Adjusted Residual	−2.5	2.5	
		Count	663	684	1347
		% within sex R: Gender	100.0%	100.0%	100.0%

Figure 5.10a *Crosstabulation table for v26b by sex*

Chi-Square Tests

	Value	df	Asymp. Sig. (2-sided)
Pearson Chi-Square	46.666[a]	2	.000
Likelihood Ratio	46.936	2	.000
Linear-by-Linear Association	34.344	1	.000
N of Valid Cases	1347		

a. 0 cells (.0%) have expected count less than 5. The minimum expected count is 114.68

Figure 5.10b *Chi-square results for v26b by sex*

Symmetric Measures

		Value	Approx. Sig.
Nominal by Nominal	Phi	.186	.000
	Cramer's V	.186	.000
	N of Valid Cases	1347	

Figure 5.10c *Measures of Association for v26b by sex*

different patterns of association it is essential that we look closely at the adjusted residuals. As already mentioned, by focusing on the cells with the most extreme adjusted residuals (those that have an absolute value greater than 2) we can identify the pattern of association that has produced a significant result. So, for example, the first cell in the table shown in Figure 5.10a contains an adjusted residual value of 6.8. This informs us that a proportionately much larger number of males (than we would expect if the variables were independent) prefer to be in a full-time job (56.4 per cent of males compared to 47 per cent of all respondents). By contrast, the adjusted residual of − 6.8 in the adjacent cell suggests a smaller percentage of females (38 per cent compared to 47 per cent overall) have a preference for full-time employment.

The cells relating to part-time work with adjusted residuals of −5.1 and 5.1 are also noteworthy and indicate a contrary position to the one described above and show women to be more favourably disposed to part-time work.

From these results, then, we can conclude that there is a significant association between gender and preferred work patterns, to the extent that males favour full-time work and females are more inclined towards part-time employment.

Introducing a control variable

Very often we will want to develop our crosstabulation analysis further and examine the relationship between two variables for each category of a third variable. Introducing a second independent or 'control' variable in this way represents a shift from bivariate to multivariate analysis. SPSS allows us to carry this out quite easily. We may suspect, for example, that the relationship between work patterns and gender that we observed above is somehow mediated by marital status. It may be that the relationship is different, or even non-existent, for certain marital categories.

(Note that it is often necessary to recode variables before using them in a crosstabulation. For this example three of the categories of the original marital status variable (**marital**) have been combined in the new recoded variable, **Marital2** (i.e. widowed, divorced and separated). Module 3 gives details on how to recode variables.) See Figure 5.11 for a frequency table of the new recoded variable, **Marital2**.

Marital2 marital recoded (marital status)

		Frequency	Percent	Valid Percent	Cumulative Percent
Valid	1 Marr, livg as married	730	52.1	52.7	52.7
	2 Widowed, divorced or separated	186	13.3	13.4	66.1
	3 Single, never married	470	33.5	33.9	100.0
	Total	1386	98.9	100.0	
Missing	9 M NA, refused	15	1.1		
Total		1401	100.0		

Figure 5.11 *Frequency table for **Marital2***

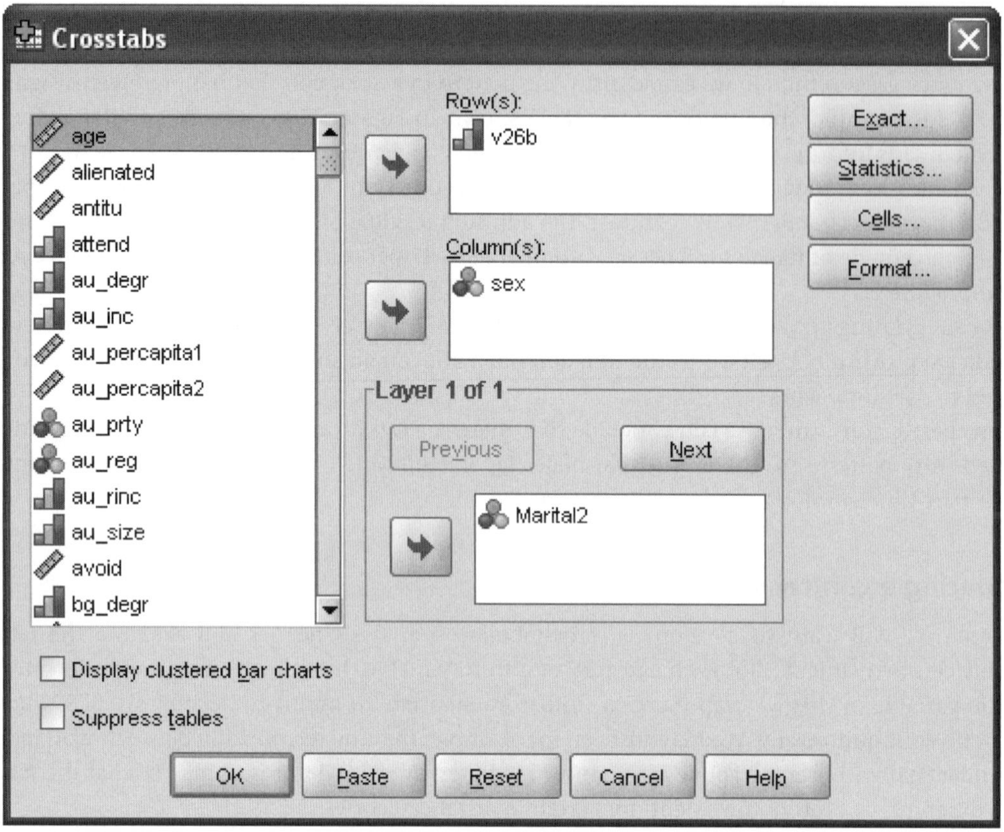

Figure 5.12 *Crosstabs dialog box*

The introduction of Marital2 as a control variable effectively holds marital status constant (that is, we are *controlling* for the effects of marital status). In practical terms, we are asking SPSS to produce three separate tables of **v26b** by **sex** (one for 'married/living as married', one for 'widowed/divorced/separated', and one for 'single, never married' respondents).

To obtain these tables simply open up the Crosstabs dialog box (Figure 5.12) as we did for the bivariate analysis (click on **Analyze**, **Descriptive Statistics** and then **Crosstabs**).

This time, however, in addition to the row and column variables we need to select our control variable (**Marital2**) and transfer it to the box labelled 'Layer 1 of 1' at the bottom of the dialog box (as shown in Figure 5.12). Select the same **Cells** (**Observed** frequencies, **Column** percentages and **Adj. standardized** residuals) and **Statistics** (**Chi-square** and **Phi and Cramer's V**) as before, and then click on **OK** to run the procedure.

The output from this multivariate analysis is shown in Figures 5.13a, 5.13b and 5.13c.

If we look at the Chi-square results in Figure 5.13b, we can see that there is a significant association between preferred work situation by gender for 'Married' people. The Chi-square statistic is 55.319 with a significance level of .0005 (remember that we read .000 as .0005). However, if we look at the Chi-square results for the other two marital status categories we can see that they are *not* significant.

v26b v26 recoded (preferred work situation) * sex R: Gender * Marital2 marital recoded (marital status) Crosstabulation

Marital2 marital recoded (marital status)				Sex R: Gender		
				1 Male	2 Female	Total
1 Marr, livg as married	v26b v26 recoded (preferred work situation)	1 Full-time job (30 hrs or more)	Count	209	120	329
			% within Sex R: Gender	60.9%	33.2%	46.7%
			Adjusted Residual	7.4	–7.4	
		2 Part-time job (10 to 29 hrs)	Count	83	163	246
			% within Sex R: Gender	24.2%	45.2%	34.9%
			Adjusted Residual	–5.8	5.8	
		3 Less than 10 hrs or no job at all	Count	51	78	129
			% within Sex R: Gender	14.9%	21.6%	18.3%
			Adjusted Residual	–2.3	2.3	
		Total	Count	343	361	704
			% within Sex R: Gender	100.0%	100.0%	100.0%
2 Widowed, divorced or separated	v26b v26 recoded (preferred work situation)	1 Full-time job (30 hrs or more)	Count	35	40	75
			% within Sex R: Gender	50.7%	38.1%	43.1%
			Adjusted Residual	1.6	–1.6	
		2 Part-time job (10 to 29 hrs)	Count	22	40	62
			% within Sex R: Gender	31.9%	38.1%	35.6%
			Adjusted Residual	–.8	.8	
		3 Less than 10 hrs or no job at all	Count	12	25	37
			% within Sex R: Gender	17.4%	23.8%	21.3%
			Adjusted Residual	–1.0	1.0	
		Total	Count	69	105	174
			% within Sex R: Gender	100.0%	100.0%	100.0%
3 Single, never married	v26b v26 recoded (preferred work situation)	1 Full-time job (30 hrs or more)	Count	128	97	225
			% within Sex R: Gender	52.2%	46.2%	49.5%
			Adjusted Residual	1.3	–1.3	
		2 Part-time job (10 to 29 hrs)	Count	84	82	166
			% within Sex R: Gender	34.3%	39.0%	36.5%
			Adjusted Residual	–1.1	1.1	
		3 Less than 10 hrs or no job at all	Count	33	31	64
			% within Sex R: Gender	13.5%	14.8%	14.1%
			Adjusted Residual	–.4	.4	
		Total	Count	245	210	455
			% within Sex R: Gender	100.0%	100.0%	00.0%

Figure 5.13a Crosstabulation table for *v26b* by *sex* by *Marital2*

Chi-Square Tests

Marital2 marital recoded (marital status)		Value	df	Asymp. Sig. (2-sided)
1 Marr, livg as married	Pearson Chi-Square	55.319[a]	2	.000
	Likelihood Ratio	56.107	2	.000
	Linear-by-Linear Association	36.535	1	.000
	N of Valid Cases	704		
2 Widowed, divorced or separated	Pearson Chi-Square	2.798[b]	2	.247
	likelihood Ratio	2.800	2	.247
	Linear-by-Linear Association	2.520	1	.112
	N of Valid Cases	174		
3 Single, never married	Pearson Chi-Square	1.675[c]	2	.433
	Likelihood Ratio	1.676	2	.432
	Linear-by-Linear Association	1.194	1	.274
	N of Valid Cases	455		

a. 0 cells (.0%) have expected count less than 5. The minimum expected count is 62.85.
b. 0 cells (.0%) have expected count less than 5. The minimum expected count is 14.67.
c. 0 cells (.0%) have expected count less than 5. The minimum expected count is 29.54.

Figure 5.13b   *Chi-square results for **v26b** by **sex** by **Marital2***

Symmetric Measures

Marital2 marital recoded (marital status)			Value	Approx. Sig.
1 Marr, livg as married	Nominal by Nominal	Phi	.280	.000
		Cramer's V	.280	.000
		N of Valid Cases	704	
2 Widowed, divorced or separated	Nominal by Nominal	Phi	.127	.247
		Cramer's V	.127	.247
		N of Valid Cases	174	
3 Single, never married	Nominal by Nominal	Phi	.061	.433
		Cramer's V	.061	.433
		N of Valid Cases	455	

Figure 5.13c   *Measures of association for **v26b** by **sex** by **Marital2***

For instance there is *not* a significant association between **v26b** and **sex** for those who are widowed/divorced/separated (Chi-square = 2.798, significance level = .247). Similarly, the bottom section of Figure 5.13b informs us that there is *not* a significant association between preferred working hours and gender for 'single' people either (Chi-square = 1.675, significance level = .433).

A closer examination of the individual cells in the crosstabulation table (Figure 5.13a) will provide us with more detailed information on these results. We will begin with the table for 'Married' people and focus on those cells with high (positive or negative) adjusted residual values. We can see that married men and married women have very different preferences regarding working patterns. The adjusted residual values are very similar to those in the table displayed in Figure 5.10a and highlight the impact of gender on one's preference for full-time employment (60.9 per cent of married men compared to 33.2 per cent of married women). By contrast, married women had a disproportionate preference for part-time work in comparison to married men (45.2 per cent of married women expressed a preference for part-time work compared to only 24.2 per cent of married men).

As the Chi-square results for the other two marital status categories ('widowed/divorced/separated' and 'single') are not significant we would not expect to find any noteworthy adjusted residuals (they all lie between 2 and -2). Indeed, if we look at the column percentages we can see that although there are differences between males and females these are smaller than the ones encountered in the top section of the table (i.e. in relation to married respondents) and involve fewer people.

Finally, Figure 5.13c provides information on the strength of the association between **v26** and **sex** for each of the categories of the control variable, **Marital2**. We can see from the table that the value of Cramer's V for the 'Married' category is .280, indicating a slightly stronger association than our previous example (as we already know, the results are not significant for the other two age groups).

From these results, then, we can conclude that there is a significant association between gender and preferred working hours, but for married people only, to the extent that married men favour full-time hours in contrast to married women who prefer part-time employment.

SPSS EXERCISES FOR CROSSTABULATION

You should now produce some crosstabulation tables yourself.

1. Select some pairs of nominal or ordinal variables and produce crosstabulation tables for these.
   Get SPSS to carry out chi-square tests for these tables and determine whether or not a statistically significant association exists between the variables.
   If a significant association does exist, look at the adjusted residuals in the cells of the table to see which cells have produced the significant association by having significantly more or significantly fewer cases in them than would be expected by chance.
2. Choose one or more of the pairs of variables that produced interesting results and carry out the exercise again, only this time introducing a third variable as a 'control' variable. Is the relationship between the two variables in the tables different for different layers of the control variable? What information can we glean from the adjusted residuals?

*Note that the total number of cells in a crosstabulation table is the product of the number of rows times the number of columns times the number of 'layers'. For this reason you should take care that you do not request a table with so many cells that it becomes nonsensical. For instance, if you had 3 variables with 9 categories each crosstabulating two of these with a third as a control would produce 729 cells (9 multiplied by 9 multiplied by 9)! Even if all of the 1401 cases in the ISSP dataset for Mexico appear in the tables, there would be fewer than 2 people, on average, in each cell.

MODULE 5 APPENDIX: MEASURES OF ASSOCIATION

When selecting an appropriate measure of association to accompany a crosstabulation our choice is influenced by a variety of factors and, as with most of the statistics covered in this book, the level of measurement of the variables we are using is a key determinant. In this appendix we will consider some of the most commonly used measures.

Measures of Association for Nominal Variables

As we have already seen, **Phi** is an appropriate measure of association when the variables in a crosstabulation table are categorical. It is closely related to Chi-square and is easily calculated by dividing the Chi-square result by the sample size and obtaining the square root of the result. Values are bounded between 0 and 1, with 0 representing no association and 1 signifying a perfect association. Phi is suitable for 2 by 2 tables only as with larger tables it may produce values greater than 1. **Cramer's V** should be used for tables exceeding 2 rows or 2 columns.

An alternative measure of association for nominal variables is **Lambda**. This is one of a family of measures based upon the principle of proportional reduction in error (PRE). In basic terms, PRE measures calculate the degree to which you can predict values of the dependent variable when you know the values of the independent variable. Where the independent variable allows you to accurately predict all values of the dependent variable, lambda will achieve a value of 1 (a perfect association). On the other hand, where our knowledge of the independent variable provides no help in predicting the dependent variable Lambda will equal zero. SPSS produces both symmetric and asymmetric versions of Lambda and you should use the symmetric value if you are unable to make a decision as to which of your variables is dependent/independent. Finally, we should point out that **Goodman and Kruskall's tau**, another PRE-based measure for nominal variables, is automatically produced by SPSS when Lambda is requested.

Measures of Association for Ordinal Variables

Gamma is the most popular measure of association when both variables are ordinal. Like Lambda, it is a PRE measure, although Gamma takes advantage of the fact that ordinal data can be ranked. The calculation of Gamma is based upon the difference between the number of concordant pairs (two cases that are ranked the same on both variables) and the number of discordant pairs (two cases that are ranked differently on both variables). Moreover, because we are dealing with ordinal data it is possible to achieve negative values for Gamma. A negative Gamma score indicates that there are more discordant than concordant pairs, whereas a greater proportion of concordant pairs will produce a positive result (-1 represents a perfect negative association, whereas $+1$ indicates a perfect positive association). Finally, as Gamma is a symmetric measure of association the result will be the same regardless of which variable you deem to be dependent/independent.

One of the problems with Gamma is that it ignores all pairs that are tied so it may over-estimate the strength of an association if there is a high percentage of tied cases.

Somer's d is an alternative measure of association for ordinal variables and differs from Gamma in that it is asymmetric and also takes into account cases tied on the dependent variable. As with Gamma, SPSS also calculates a symmetric version of this statistic.

Kendall's tau-b takes account of tied pairs on both variables (separately) and is therefore a good alternative to Gamma when there is a high proportion of tied ranks. One limitation of Kendall's tau-b is that it can only obtain the values of $+1$ or -1 if the crosstabulation table has the same number of rows and columns. Kendall's tau-b is also a symmetric measure of association.

Making a decision regarding the most appropriate measure of association to use can sometimes be a complex process and many of the issues involved are beyond the remit of this text. There are a variety of additional measures that have not been considered here, some of which are specifically designed for tables that have combinations of levels of measurement. For further details on these procedures, including discussions on when and under what conditions they should be employed, you should consult a statistical text dedicated to the statistical measures associated with crosstabulation tables or the relevant sections of some of the suggested readings below.

FURTHER READING

De Vaus, D. (1991) *Surveys in Social Research* London: Allen and Unwin.
Loether, H.J. and McTavish, D.G. (1974) *Descriptive Statistics for Sociologists* Boston: Allyn and Bacon.
Norusis, M.J. (2008) *SPSS 16.0 Guide to Data Analysis* New Jersey: Prentice-Hall.

6 Multiple Response Sets

INTRODUCTION

Module 6, 'Multiple Response Sets', uses data from the Philippines survey.

Occasionally, the categorical responses to what is essentially a single question can be spread across a series of variables and the analyst may wish to combine these responses together. The ISSP dataset contains examples of these types of variables.

1. **Sets of 'dichotomous' variables.** Questions all relating to the same core topic may be asked across a spread of categories with the answer for each category being a dichotomy, either positive or negative. For instance, respondents who were not currently working were asked a number of questions for which the response options were a straight 'Yes' or 'No':

   Have you ever had a paid job for one year or more?
   Would you like to have a paid job, either now or in the future?
   Are you currently looking for a job?
   Over the past 12 months, have you had any training to improve your job skills?

   Respondents could answer either *YES* or *NO* to each question. Four variables result, **v64**, **v67**, **v69** and **v76**, each of which was coded '1' for 'Yes' and '2' for 'No'. These variables can each be analysed in their own right, such as in the four *Frequencies* counts that appear in Figure 6.1a, but a researcher might wish to combine the responses across all four items into a single item.

2. **Sets of categorical variables with each variable having a unique code.** A single basic question may be asked across a spread of categories with the answer for each category being given a unique code. For instance, respondents to the ISSP Work Orientation survey were asked:

   '*Thinking about the last 12 months, have you done any of the following in order to find a job?*' Respondents were shown a list of six job-seeking activities:

   - *Registered at a public employment agency;*
   - *Registered at a private employment agency;*
   - *Answered advertisements for jobs;*
   - *Advertised for a job in newspaper or journals;*
   - *Applied directly to employers;*
   - *Asked relatives, friends, or colleagues to help find a job.*

v64 Not currently working: had paid job for 1 year or more

		Frequency	Percent	Valid Percent	Cumulative Percent
Valid	1 Yes	222	18.5	39.4	39.4
	2 No	342	28.5	60.6	100.0
	Total	564	47.0	100.0	
Missing	0 Not applicable (code 1 in V27)	636	53.0		
Total		1200	100.0		

v67 Not working:like to have a paid job now or in future

		Frequency	Percent	Valid Percent	Cumulative Percent
Valid	1 Yes	156	13.0	70.3	70.3
	2 No	66	5.5	29.7	100.0
	Total	222	18.5	100.0	
Missing	0 Not applicable	978	81.5		
Total		1200	100.0		

v69 Not working: Resp currently looking for a job?

		Frequency	Percent	Valid Percent	Cumulative Percent
Valid	1 Yes	145	12.1	25.7	25.7
	2 No	419	34.9	74.3	100.0
	Total	564	47.0	100.0	
Missing	0 Not applicable	636	53.0		
Total		1200	100.0		

v76 Not working: past 12 months training to improve job skills

		Frequency	Percent	Valid Percent	Cumulative Percent
Valid	1 Yes	98	8.2	17.9	17.9
	2 No	448	37.3	82.1	100.0
	Total	546	45.5	100.0	
Missing	0 Not applicable	636	53.0		
	8 Cant choose	18	1.5		
	Total	654	54.5		
Total		1200	100.0		

Figure 6.1a *Normal Frequencies counts of the four dichotomous 'not working' variables, **v64; v67; v69; v76***

A person could report having done one job-seeking activity, some combination of activities, or none. Six variables result, **v70** to **v75**, one for each of the six job-seeking activities. Instead of dichotomous YES/NO codes, however, the variable for each activity has a unique code for the 'presence' of that job-seeking activity. For example, as shown in Figure 6.1b, respondents who said they '*answered advertisements for jobs*' are coded as '4' in the variable **v72** and respondents who '*applied directly to employers*' are coded as '16' in the variable **v74**. While each variable can be analysed in its own right, again, the researcher might wish to combine the responses across all six job-seeking variables into a single item in order to see the aggregate pattern of membership.

3. **Sets of categorical variables with a set of codes that is the same across all the variables.** Thirdly, a series of questions may all have the same set of response categories and the analyst may wish to

v70 Not working: registered at a public agency

		Frequency	Percent	Valid Percent	Cumulative Percent
Valid	0 Didn't do this activity	517	43.1	91.7	91.7
	1 Registered at public emp agency	47	3.9	8.3	100.0
	Total	564	47.0	100.0	
Missing	-1 Not applic - Code 1 in v27	636	53.0		
Total		1200	100.0		

v71 Not working: registered at a private agency

		Frequency	Percent	Valid Percent	Cumulative Percent
Valid	0 Didn't do this activity	526	43.8	93.3	93.3
	2 Registered at private emp agency	38	3.2	6.7	100.0
	Total	564	47.0	100.0	
Missing	-1 Not applic - Code 1 in v27	636	53.0		
Total		1200	100.0		

v72 Not working: answered advertisements

		Frequency	Percent	Valid Percent	Cumulative Percent
Valid	0 Didn't do this activity	512	42.7	90.8	90.8
	4 Answered job advertisements	52	4.3	9.2	100.0
	Total	564	47.0	100.0	
Missing	-1 Not applic - Code 1 in v27	636	53.0		
Total		1200	100.0		

Figure 6.1b   *Normal Frequencies counts of the 'job seeking activities' variables, **v70** to **v75***

v73 Not working: advertised in newspapers

		Frequency	Percent	Valid Percent	Cumulative Percent
Valid	0 Didn't do this activity	538	44.8	95.4	95.4
	8 Advertised in newspapers	26	2.2	4.6	100.0
	Total	564	47.0	100.0	
Missing	-1 Not applic - Code 1 in v27	636	53.0		
Total		1200	100.0		

v74 Not working: applied directly to employers

		Frequency	Percent	Valid Percent	Cumulative Percent
Valid	0 Didn't do this activity	453	37.8	80.3	80.3
	16 Applied to employers directly	111	9.2	19.7	100.0
	Total	564	47.0	100.0	
Missing	-1 Not applic - Code 1 in v27	636	53.0		
Total		1200	100.0		

v75 Not working: asked relatives, friends

		Frequency	Percent	Valid Percent	Cumulative Percent
Valid	0 Didn't do this activity	428	35.7	75.9	75.9
	32 Asked relative, friends	136	11.3	24.1	100.0
	Total	564	47.0	100.0	
Missing	-1 Not applic - Code 1 in v27	636	53.0		
Total		1200	100.0		

Figure 6.1b *Continued*

combine the responses to all the questions. For instance, respondents were asked to tick boxes for four items that related to how often negative working conditions applied to their work:

How often

1. *do you come home from work exhausted?*
2. *do you have to do hard physical work?*
3. *do you find your work stressful?*
4. *do you work in dangerous conditions?*

Respondents could say whether each condition applied to their work 'Always', 'Often', 'Sometime', 'Hardly ever' or 'Never'.

Normal Frequencies counts of the four resulting variables, **v37** to **v40**, are shown in Figure 6.1c. Instead of knowing how a respondent responded to each individual item on its own, an analyst may want to find out how frequently respondents gave each response: *Always / Often / Sometime / Hardly ever / Never*.

v37 How often: come home from work exhausted

		Frequency	Percent	Valid Percent	Cumulative Percent
Valid	1 Always	142	11.8	22.6	22.6
	2 Often	161	13.4	25.6	48.2
	3 Sometimes	229	19.1	36.5	84.7
	4 Hardly ever	63	5.2	10.0	94.7
	5 Never	33	2.8	5.3	100.0
	Total	628	52.3	100.0	
Missing	0 Not applicable	564	47.0		
	8 Cant choose	8	.7		
	Total	572	47.7		
Total		1200	100.0		

v38 How often: do hard physical work

		Frequency	Percent	Valid Percent	Cumulative Percent
Valid	1 Always	103	8.6	16.4	16.4
	2 Often	140	11.7	22.3	38.7
	3 Sometimes	213	17.8	33.9	72.6
	4 Hardly ever	126	10.5	20.1	92.7
	5 Never	46	3.8	7.3	100.0
	Total	628	52.3	100.0	
Missing	0 Not applicable	564	47.0		
	8 Cant choose	8	.7		
	Total	572	47.7		
Total		1200	100.0		

v39 How often: finds work stressful

		Frequency	Percent	Valid Percent	Cumulative Percent
Valid	1 Always	74	6.2	11.8	11.8
	2 Often	139	11.6	22.2	34.0
	3 Sometimes	210	17.5	33.5	67.5
	4 Hardly ever	147	12.2	23.4	90.9
	5 Never	57	4.8	9.1	100.0
	Total	627	52.2	100.0	
Missing	0 Not applicable	564	47.0		
	8 Cant choose	9	.8		
	Total	573	47.8		
Total		1200	100.0		

Figure 6.1c   *Normal Frequencies counts of the 'adverse working conditions' variables, **v37** to **v40***

v40 How often: work in dangerous conditions

		Frequency	Percent	Valid Percent	Cumulative Percent
Valid	1 Always	69	5.8	11.0	11.0
	2 Often	87	7.2	13.9	24.9
	3 Sometimes	150	12.5	24.0	48.9
	4 Hardly ever	186	15.5	29.7	78.6
	5 Never	134	11.2	21.4	100.0
	Total	626	52.2	100.0	
Missing	0 Not applicable	564	47.0		
	8 Cant choose	10	.8		
	Total	574	47.8		
Total		1200	100.0		

Figure 6.1c   *Continued*

Each of these situations is basically the same, in each instance the analyst has a range of variables that are all codings of a single core item, and in each instance the analyst may wish to combine the responses across the range of variables. SPSS has a procedure, **Multiple Response**, that caters for this specific problem.

USING MULTIPLE RESPONSE

Multiple Response is a procedure for combining the responses across a range of related variables and then displaying the result in the format of a frequency distribution and/or a crosstabulation table.

As shown in Figure 6.2, Multiple Response is selected by going to the **Analyze** menu, choosing **Multiple Response** and then **Define Variable Sets....** A **Define Multiple Response Sets** window will open up (Figure 6.3a).

The analyst must define the variables that will go into making up a 'multiple response set'. The set of variables can be either a group of dichotomous variables or a group of variables with a range of categories for codes. First, we will look at an example of a multiple response set that is defined by dichotomous variables.

Creating a multiple response set from a group of dichotomous variables

Figure 6.3a, '**Define Multiple Response Sets window for a group of dichotomous variables**', shows how this is done. Here, the four dichotomous variables that resulted from questions asked of those not currently working are used to create a multiple response set called **$mrnotwork**. This is done by selecting the variables **v64**, **v67**, **v69** and **v75** from the list of variables in the 'Set definition' column on the left-hand side of the window and bringing them into the **Variables in Set** box in the centre of the window. SPSS has to be told which value to count as the dichotomous variable. This is done by ticking the '**Dichotomies**' option and entering in '1' (the code for 'Yes' in each of the variables) as the '**Counted value**'. 'mrnotwork' is typed into the '**Name**' box and the multiple response set is given the '**Label**' *'Multiple responses of the not working'*. Then, when the '**Add**' button is clicked, '**$mrnotwork**' appears in the '**Mult Response Sets**' box on the right-hand side of the window. (The names of multiple response sets always have a '$' inserted at the beginning of their name.)

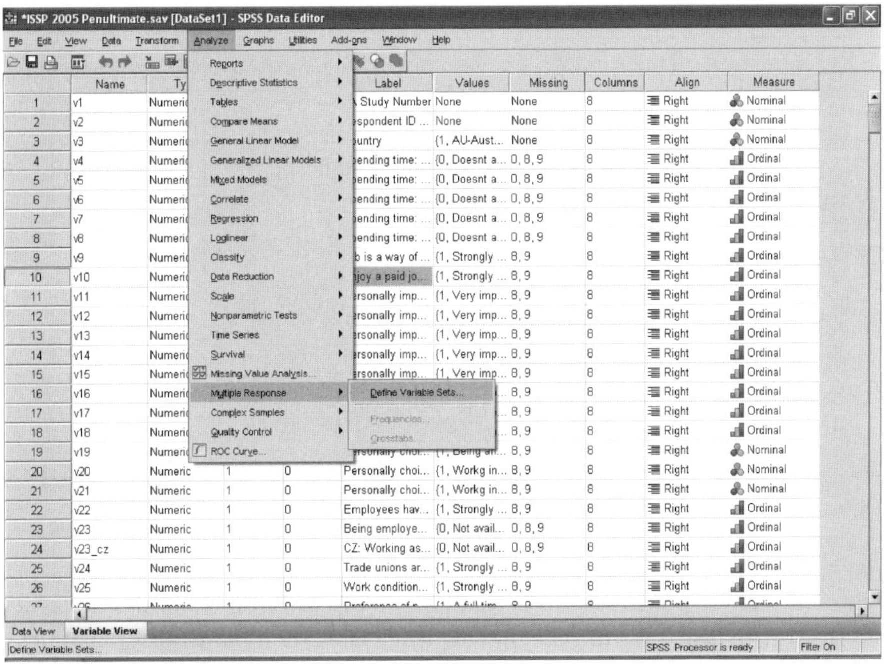

Figure 6.2 *Selecting Multiple Response from the Analyze menu*

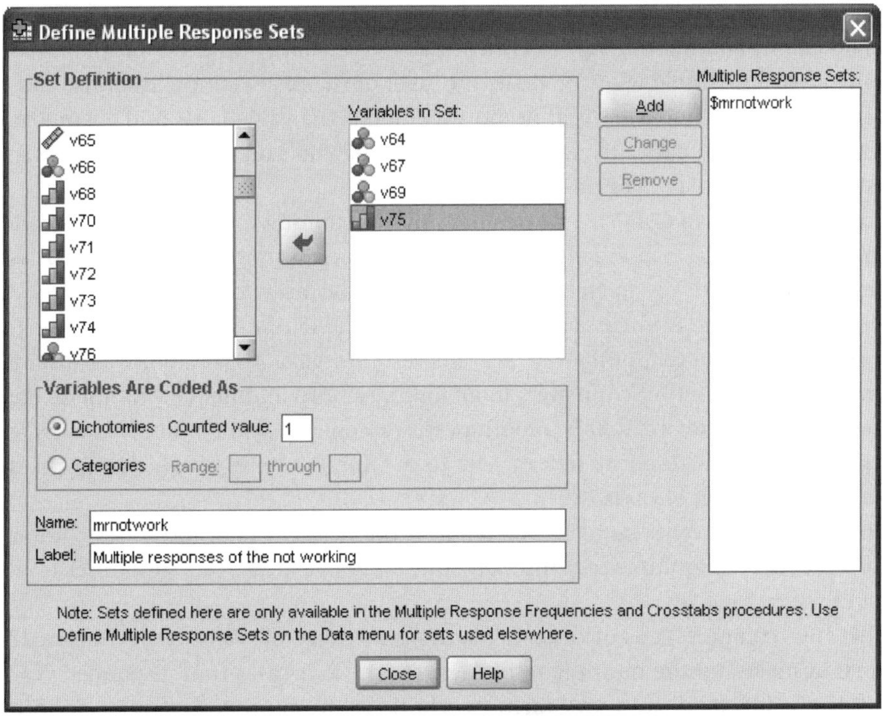

Figure 6.3a *Define Multiple Response Sets window for a group of dichotomous variables*

$mrnotwork Frequencies

		Responses		
		N	Percent	Percent of Cases
$mrnotwork Multiple responses of the not working	v64 Not currently workg: had paid job for 1 year or more	222	35.7%	64.3%
	v67 Not workg:like to have a paid job now or in future	156	25.1%	45.2%
	v69 Not workg: Resp currently looking for a job?	145	23.3%	42.0%
	v76 Not workg: past 12 months traing to improve job skills	98	15.8%	28.4%
	Total	621	100.0%	180.0%

Figure 6.3b *Frequency count for $mrnotwork, a dichotomous response set*

The resulting multiple response set can be seen at the top of Figure 6.3b, the frequency count for **$mrnotwork**. (Instructions on how to generate frequency tabulations and crosstabulations of of multiple response sets are given in the sections below.)

Since the frequency counts of multiple response sets are not based upon a single variable, interpreting them requires some care. In Figure 6.3b, the name of the dichotomous multiple response set is given as **$mrnotwork** with the label 'Multiple responses of the not working'.

For a multiple response set created from a group of dichotomous variables, the 'value labels' come from the variable label and name given to each variable that makes up the multiple response set. For instance, going across the first row of the table, the label of the first multiple response category is 'Not currently working: had paid job for 1 year or more', which is the value label of the variable **v64**. The *N* of 222 is the number of not currently working respondents who said 'Yes' to **v64** (you can check this against the simple frequency tabulation of **v64** in Figure 6.1a).

The count column sums to 621. This figure does not refer to individual cases but instead to the total number of 'Yes' *responses* that respondents gave summed up across the variables **v64**, **v67**, **v69** and **v75**. Some people could have said 'Yes' to all four questions and have been 'counted' four times, others could have said 'Yes' to only one question and only have been 'counted' once, with the rest falling somewhere in between, depending upon the number of 'Yes' answers they gave. In fact, quite a substantial number of respondents have given only 'No' answers to all four questions and hence will not be included at all in the construction of **$mrnotwork**. It is important to remember that the numbers in any tabulation or crosstabulation of a multiple response set can refer to the number of responses that fit the definition of the set *instead of* the number of cases.

The second column, 'Percent', sums to 100.0 and is the percentage of responses coming from each variable that makes up the multiple response set. For example, the 222 'Yes' responses to **v64** make up 35.7 per cent of the 621 responses.

Finally, the third column, 'Percent of cases', is the percentage of 'valid cases' that can be found in each variable that makes up the multiple responses set. The 222 cases that responded 'Yes' to **v64** are 64.3 per cent of the 345 valid cases for **$mrnotwork**. (Here, in multiple response, 'valid cases' means cases where at least one of the four original variables in a case had a 'Yes' answer that multiple response will count.) Since quite a lot of cases had respondents who answered 'Yes' to more than one question, the number of responses is considerably higher than the number of valid cases. This is the reason that the sum of the 'Percent of cases' column adds to 180.0 per cent instead of 100.0 per cent.

Creating a multiple response set from a group of categorical variables where each variable has a unique code

Multiple response sets can also be based upon a group of categorical variables. Figure 6.4a shows how this is done. Here, the six 'job-seeking' variables are used to create a multiple response set called **$job-seek**. The variables **v70** to **v75** are selected from the 'Set definition' column and brought into the centre **Variables in Set** box. The 'Categories' option is ticked and SPSS is told the range of values to include in the multiple response set. (In this example, the range is 1 to 32.) The name of the multiple response set is **$mrjobseek**, which appears in the 'Multiple Response Sets' box once the Add button is clicked.

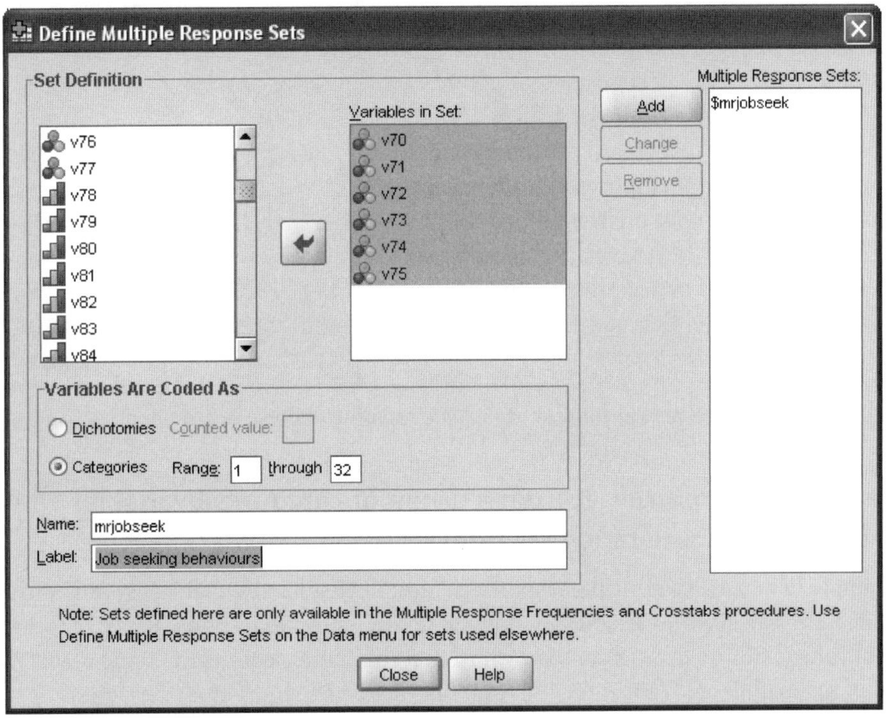

Figure 6.4a   *Define Multiple Response Sets window for a group of categorical variables, each with a unique code*

The resulting multiple response set can be seen in Figure 6.4b, the frequency count for **$jobseek**. What SPSS has done is look across the responses to the variables **v70** to **v75**, including all the values in the range from 1 to 32 that it finds in the six variables and summarizing all the responses it finds in **$mrjobseek**. The frequency count for a multiple response set created from categorical variables more resembles a 'traditional' frequency count since each row in the table is based upon one value in the range of allowed values. In this example, since each variable only has one of the values in the range, an exact correspondence can be seen between the values and counts in the multiple response set and the values and counts of the individual variables that make up the set. For instance, row 1 is the 47 respondents coded as '1 – Registered at a public employment agency' in **v70**, row 2 is the 38 respondents coded as '2 – Registered at a private employment agency' in **v71** and so on. (SPSS takes its 'value labels' for the multiple response variable **$mrjobseek** from the variable labels used in each of the variables that define the multiple response set. Hence, you must take care that the original variables' labels are sensible for explaining the meaning of each code in the multiple response variable (here, they are sensible).)

The 'Percent' and 'Percent of cases' columns have the same meanings as before. In this example, the total number of responses (the total number of job-seeking *behaviours*, not respondents) is 410. Many respondents appear to have tried more than one means of job-seeking; so this 410 is considerably greater than the number of *cases* – respondents who mentioned at least one job-seeking behaviour (193 respondents). Consequently, the 'Percent of cases' column sums to 212.4 per cent.

$mrjobseek Frequencies

		Responses		
		N	Percent	Percent of Cases
$mrjobseek Job seeking behaviours	1 Registered at public employment agency	47	11.5%	24.4%
	2 Registered at private employment agency	38	9.3%	19.7%
	4 Answered job ads	52	12.7%	26.9%
	8 Advertised in newspapers	26	6.3%	13.5%
	16 Applied to employers	111	27.1%	57.5%
	32 Asked relative, friends	136	33.2%	70.5%
	Total	410	100.0%	212.4%

Figure 6.4b   *Frequency counts for $mrjobseek, a multiple response variable based upon discrete codings*

Creating a multiple response set from a group of categorical variables where each variable has the same range of codes

The next example of creating a multiple response set from categorical variables is shown in Figure 6.5a. In this instance, the categorical variables used to create the multiple response set, **v37** to **v40**, have the same range of values, from 1 to 5 (as can be seen in their frequency counts in Figure 6.1c). The multiple response set, **$mrhardjob**, adds together the responses across the individual variables.

The frequency count in Figure 6.5b shows the result. **$mrhardjob** gives the combined distribution of answers that respondents gave when they were asked four questions about how often they experience adverse working conditions. This application of Multiple Response can be particularly useful when the goal is to discover the aggregate pattern of responses across a range of values over a number of variables. For instance, in the example here, we see that only 1 in 10 (10.8 per cent) of responses about adverse conditions at work were where respondents said they 'Never' experienced adverse conditions, with the most common response being adverse conditions being experienced 'Sometimes' (32 per cent) and significant proportions of responses being that adverse conditions held 'Often' or 'Always' (21 per cent and 15.5 per cent, respectively). (Here, 'Percent of cases' is less useful. There are 628 valid respondents (people in work who answered the four questions); for example, there were 802 'Sometimes' responses, which translates to 127.7 per cent of valid cases.)

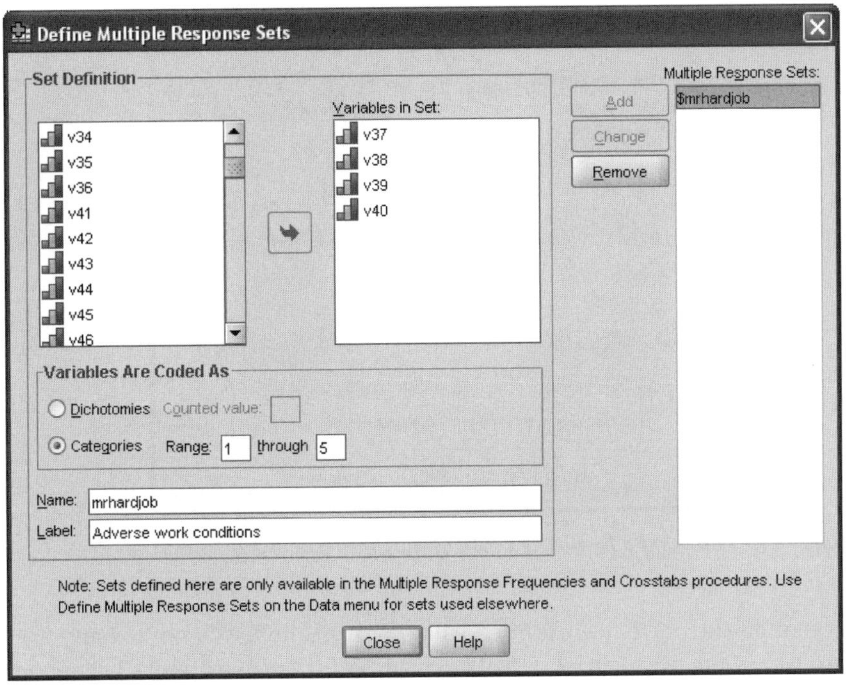

Figure 6.5a   *Define Multiple Response Sets window for a range of category variables, each with the same range of codes*

$mrhardjob Frequencies

		Responses		
		N	Percent	Percent of Cases
$mrhardjob Adverse work conditions	1 Always	388	15.5%	61.8%
	2 Often	527	21.0%	83.9%
	3 Sometimes	802	32.0%	127.7%
	4 Hardly ever	522	20.8%	83.1%
	5 Never	270	10.8%	43.0%
	Total	2509	100.0%	399.5%

Figure 6.5b   *Frequency counts for **mrhardjob**, a multiple response variable based upon common codings*

Tabulating and crosstabulating multiple response sets

Once multiple response sets have been created, they can be viewed through tabulations or crosstabulations.

Tabulations

The window for obtaining frequency counts of multiple response variables is accessed by clicking on **Frequencies...** on the Multiple Response procedure and a window like Figure 6.6 comes up. **Multiple**

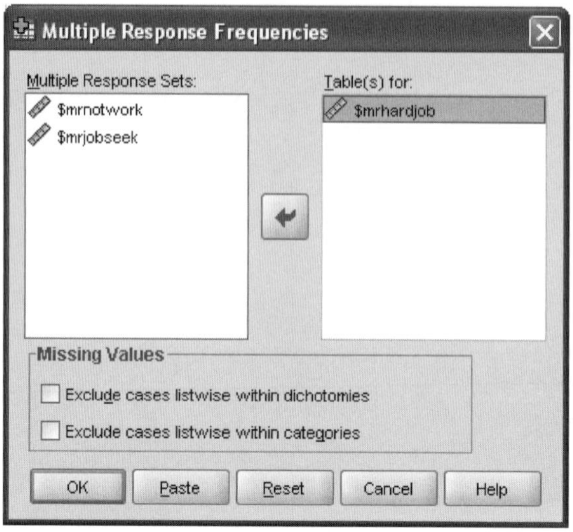

Figure 6.6 *Window for obtaining a frequency count of multiple response variables*

Response Sets that already have been defined will appear in the left-hand box and are brought into the **Table(s) for:** box. (Here, we have requested Frequencies for **$mrhardjob**.) Clicking on **OK** will then produce a frequency count like that in Figure 6.5b. The interpretation of frequency counts has already been discussed at some length above.

Crosstabulations

Multiple response sets also can be viewed in crosstabulations. The Crosstabs window is assessed by clicking on **Crosstabs...** on the Multiple Responses procedure. A main window like that in Figure 6.7a will appear.

The multiple response sets and variables that will be used to make up the tables are defined in the same manner as for a normal Crosstabs table. Multiple response sets or 'normal' variables can be used to define the rows, columns and/or layers of the crosstabulation table. Any combination of multiple response sets and 'normal' variables are allowed (subject to the usual considerations of good table design). In the example here, the rows will be defined by the multiple response set **$mrhardjob**. In order to keep the example simple, no layers will be used and the columns will be defined by a 'normal' variable, **sex**: (1) 'Male' and (2) 'Female'.

The range of values that the 'normal' variable **sex** can take needs to be defined by clicking on the **Define Ranges...** button, bringing up the **Define Variable** sub-window in Figure 6.7b and putting in '1' as the 'Minimum' and '2' as the 'Maximum'.

To choose the kind of percentages we want in the crosstabulation table, we click on the **Options...** button to bring up the sub-window in Figure 6.7c. Here, **Row** and **Column** percentages are chosen and the percentages will be based upon the number of **Responses** to the questions that make up the multiple response variable rather than **Cases**.

To run the procedure, click on **OK**. Figure 6.8 is the result. The table has the same appearance as a 'normal' crosstabulation table, but there is an important difference. Since the crosstabulation is of a multiple response set, the numbers upon which the cell frequencies and percentages are based have only an oblique relation to the number of cases. The total *N* of the table is the number of responses to the four original 'adverse conditions at work' variables, not the number of respondents.

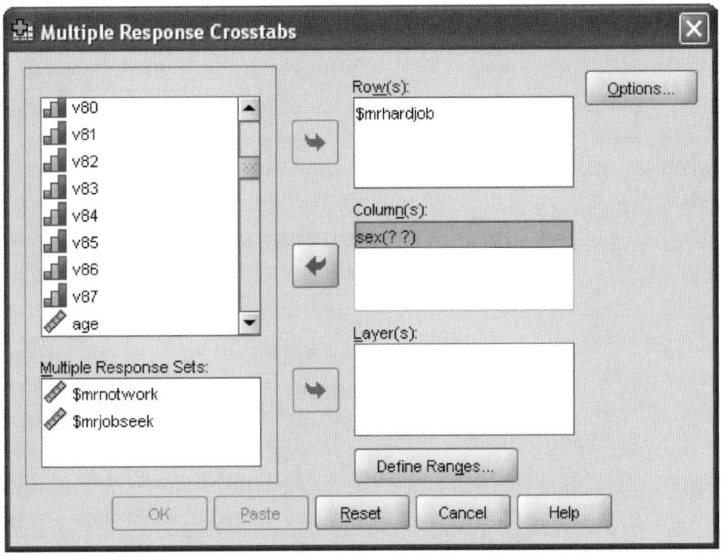

Figure 6.7a   *Multiple Response Crosstabs window*

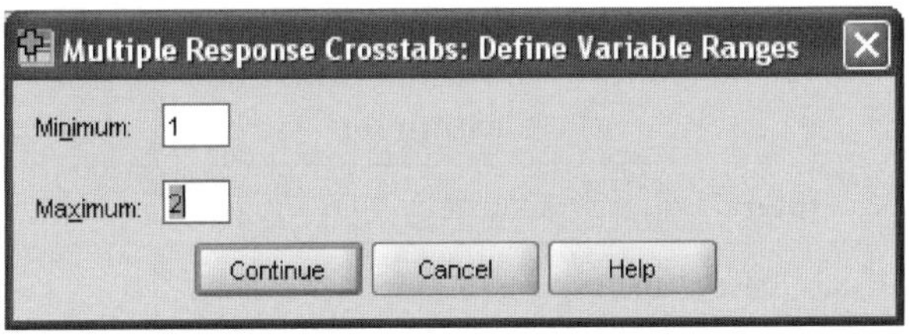

Figure 6.7b   *Multiple Response Crosstabs: Define Variable sub-window*

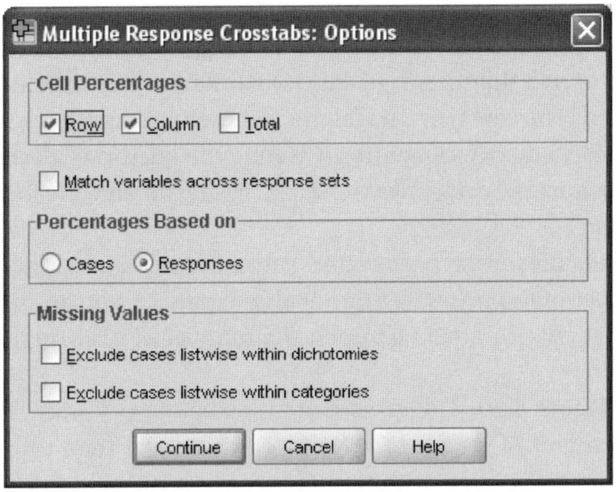

Figure 6.7c   *Multiple Response Crosstabs: Option sub-window with column percentages based upon the number of responses*

$mrhardjob*sex Crosstabulation

			sex R: Gender		
			1 Male	2 Female	Total
$mrhardjob Adverse work conditions	1 Always	Count	295	93	388
		% within $mrhardjob	76.0%	24.0%	
		% within sex	17.8%	11.0%	
	2 Often	Count	390	137	527
		% within $mrhardjob	74.0%	26.0%	
		% within sex	23.5%	16.2%	
	3 Sometimes	Count	557	245	802
		% within $mrhardjob	69.5%	30.5%	
		% within sex	33.5%	28.9%	
	4 Hardly ever	Count	285	237	522
		% within $mrhardjob	54.6%	45.4%	
		% within sex	17.2%	27.9%	
	5 Never	Count	134	136	270
		% within $mrhardjob	49.6%	50.4%	
		% within sex	8.1%	16.0%	
Total		Count	1661	848	2509

Percentages and totals are based on responses.

Figure 6.8 *Crosstabulation of a multiple response set ($mrhardjob) by a categorical variable (sex), with percentages based upon the number of responses*

That said, one can look for patterns in the table. Looking down the columns, we can see that proportionately more men reported that they had adverse working conditions 'Always' or 'Often' with the reverse holding for women. The row percentages are less useful since there are approximately twice as many men as women in work and consequently answering the questions. (But even here the preponderance of women in the 'less adverse' categories shows up, with women contributing over half the 'Never' adverse conditions answers.)

There is scope for altering the format of the table. Percentages can be based upon the number of cases instead of upon the number of responses. Figure 6.9 also requests a **$mrhardjob** by **sex** crosstabulation table, only with percentages which are based upon the number of cases (respondents) rather than the number of responses.

The result appears in Figure 6.10. The same pattern as before is visible, only displayed differently (and, arguably, more strikingly). Since the base *N* of cases is smaller than the number of responses, the row percents in this table are quite large, with several exceeding 100 per cent of the cases. Again, women predominate in the 'Never' and 'Hardly ever' categories and men in the 'Always' and 'Often' categories of adverse working conditions.

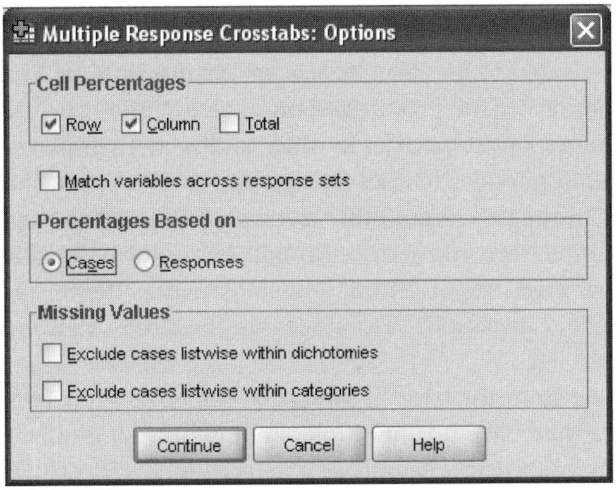

Figure 6.9   *Multiple Response Crosstabs: Option sub-window with percentages based upon the number of cases*

$mrhardjob*sex Crosstabulation

			sex R: Gender		
			1 Male	2 Female	Total
$mrhardjob Adverse work conditions	1 Always	Count	295	93	388
		% within $mrhardjob	76.0%	24.0%	
		% within sex	70.9%	43.9%	
	2 Often	Count	390	137	527
		% within $mrhardjob	74.0%	26.0%	
		% within sex	93.8%	64.6%	
	3 Sometimes	Count	557	245	802
		% within $mrhardjob	69.5%	30.5%	
		% within sex	133.9%	115.6%	
	4 Hardly ever	Count	285	237	522
		% within $mrhardjob	54.6%	45.4%	
		% within sex	68.5%	111.8%	
	5 Never	Count	134	136	270
		% within $mrhardjob	49.6%	50.4%	
		% within sex	32.2%	64.2%	
	Total	Count	416	212	628

Percentages and totals are based on respondents.

Figure 6.10   *Crosstabulation of a multiple response set (**$mrhardjob**) by a categorical variable (**sex**), percentages based on the number of cases*

Summary

Using multiple response sets can be an effective way of seeking patterns in data in situations such as the above in which a series of variables all are responses to essentially a single question and the analyst wishes to combine the responses together in order to display their pattern. The multiple response procedure, however, does not provide facilities for hypothesis-testing based upon probability statistics. For instance, neither the Chi-square test nor other 'goodness of fit' statistics are available with the cross-tabulation facility for multiple response sets, cell residuals cannot be calculated, and the frequencies facility can provide neither measures of central tendency such as the mean or median nor measures of dispersion such as standard deviation. Percentages are the closest that multiple response comes to statistical analysis.

The reasons for this stem from the basic premise that underlies probability-based statistical testing and the nature of the data that make up a multiple response set. All probability statistics are designed to test whether a pattern observed in a sample of data accurately reflects the true pattern that would be observed if the researcher had access to complete information for the whole population. Since the number of responses that each case contributes to the construction of a multiple response set varies unpredictably (from zero responses up to the maximum possible), reliable generalization from a multiple response set to a whole population is not possible. The basic premise of probability-based statistical testing does not hold for multiple response sets; consequently, statistical testing cannot be valid. Hence, the multiple response procedure is basically a useful tool for data exploration.

SPSS EXERCISES FOR MULTIPLE RESPONSE SET

1. Picking another country or countries of your choice, repeat the creation of the multiple response variables generated here and produce frequency counts and crosstabulations for them.

   Do you obtain different patterns of response? What could be the reasons for these differences in comparison to the Philippines?

2. Create a new multiple response variable based upon some completely different 'normal' variables in your dataset. (Unless you create some new variables through recoding, the new multiple response variable will have to be one based upon a group of ordinal variables that have the same code. While there are many variables of that type in the dataset, we are afraid that we have used the only viable instances of variables with binary codes and categorical variables with unique codes. Sorry!)

   Compare the patterns of its frequency count with the frequency counts for the original 'normal' variables that generated it. Note that two different frequency percentages are produced: one based on the percentages of *responses* and one based on the percentage of *cases*.

3. Generate crosstabulation tables using the multiple response variable or variables that you have created. (You can crosstabulate the multiple response variable with a 'normal' categorical or ordinal variable or, if you have created two multiple responses variables, you could try crosstabulating them with each other.

   First, generate the table requesting percentages based upon *cases*.

   Second, generate the same table, only requesting that the percentages be based upon *responses*.

   Note that row percentages in the two tables are not the same, and consider why they differ.

'Geometric' coding

The multiple response procedure can be a valuable tool for exploratory analysis where the researcher wishes to combine together responses across a range of variables, but it does have some weaknesses. First, as noted above, multiple response sets cannot be used in a *confirmatory statistical analysis*. Second, sometimes the main reason a researcher wants to combine the responses across a range of variables together is to see *which* responses group together. Multiple response allows us to discover the gross numbers of responses to each category, but it cannot tell us whether linkages exist between the responses so that certain categories tend to fall together.

'Geometric coding' is a way of coding data that results in a single variable that displays the combinations of categorical responses to a question. This variable is amenable to confirmatory statistical analysis.

An example of geometric coding

The ISSP datasets do not contain any examples of geometric coding, but we have adapted the job-seeking questions to show how the approach works. You may already have noticed that the codings for the six job-seeking variables in Figure 6.1b, **v70** to **v75**, are a bit unusual. If a respondent did not exhibit a type of job-seeking behaviour, they were coded '0' for 'Did not do this activity'. If a respondent did exhibit a type of job-seeking behaviour, they were given the values in rising sequence: 1; 2; 4; 8; 16; 32. This is a 'geometric progression', each value is a doubling of the previous value (so the **v70** job-seeking behaviour ('registered at a public agency') was coded '1', the **v71** job-seeking behaviour was coded '2' ('registered at a private agency'), the **v72** job-seeking behaviour was coded '4' ('answered job advertisements') and so on). But the values of these individual variables is not the geocode. To arrive at the coding of the variable **geojobseek** for a respondent, the coder adds together the values of all the types of job-seeking behaviour the respondent said they did. The *sum of the values* is the code of the variable **geojobseek**. Each combination of job-seeking behaviours will produce a *unique sum* that *cannot* come from any other combination. For example:

- If a respondent who currently is not working has not reported any job-seeking behaviours, their codes for the variables **v70** through **v75** are all zero ('0') and the sum of these variables, the geocode **geojobseek** also will be coded as zero ('0').
- If a respondent has reported only one type of job-seeking behaviour, their geocode will be the value for that variable. For instance, if a respondent's only job-seeking behaviour was 'asking help from a friend or relative', their code for variable **v75** would be '32', their codings for the variables **v70** through **v74** would all be '0' and their coding for **geojobseek** would be '32' (0 + 0 + 0 + 0 + 0 + 32).
- If a respondent has reported two or more job-seeking behaviours, the geocode will be the sum of the value codings for those behaviours (and here's the neat bit) *the value of that sum will be unique in that only that particular combination of behaviours can produce that particular code*. For instance, if a respondent's only job-seeking behaviours have been two: to register with a public employment agency (coded in **v70** as '1') and to register with a private employment agency (coded in **v71** as '2'), the value of **geojobseek** will be '3' (1 + 2 + 0 + 0 + 0 + 0). There is no other combination of responses that can produce the code '3'.
- This will work with any combination of codes. For instance, there is one individual in the Philippines dataset whose code for **geojobseek** is '61'; they have reported a combination of five different types of job-seeking behaviour: 'registering with a public agency' (coded '1'); 'answering job advertisements'

('4'); 'advertising in newspapers' ('8'); 'applying directly to employers' ('16'); 'asking relative or friends' ('32') (1 + 4 + 8 + 16 + 32 = 61).

Figure 6.11, 'Frequency output for a "geometric" variable, **geojobseek**', shows the result when the resulting geometric code for the 564 not currently working respondents who answered all the job-seeking

Geojobseek Geometric code of job seeking behaviour

		Frequency	Percent	Valid Percent	Cumulative Percent
Valid	.00 No job seeking activity	371	30.9	65.8	65.8
	1.00 Registered at public agency	4	.3	.7	66.5
	3.00 = 1 + 2 (registered at public & private agencies)	4	.3	.7	67.2
	4.00 Answered job advertisements	4	.3	.7	67.9
	7.00 = 1 + 2 + 4	1	.1	.2	68.1
	8.00 Advertised in newspapers	1	.1	.2	68.3
	10.00 = 8 + 2	1	.1	.2	68.4
	12.00 = 8 + 4	1	.1	.2	68.6
	15.00 = 8 + 4 + 2 + 1	1	.1	.2	68.8
	16.00 Applied to employers directly	25	2.1	4.4	73.2
	17.00 = 16 + 1	2	.2	.4	73.6
	18.00 = 16 + 2	3	.2	.5	74.1
	19.00 = 16 + 2 + 1	3	.2	.5	74.6
	20.00 = 16 + 4	2	.2	.4	75.0
	22.00 = 16 + 4 + 2	1	.1	.2	75.2
	28.00 = 16 + 8 + 4	3	.2	.5	75.7
	31.00 = 16 + 8 + 4 + 2 + 1	1	.1	.2	75.9
	32.00 Asked relatives, friends	54	4.5	9.6	85.5
	33.00 = 32 + 1	1	.1	.2	85.6
	36.00 = 32 + 4	4	.3	.7	86.3
	37.00 = 32 + 4 + 1	2	.2	.4	86.7
	44.00 = 32 + 8 + 4	2	.2	.4	87.1
	45.00 = 32 + 8 + 4 + 1	1	.1	.2	87.2
	46.00 = 32 + 8 + 4 + 2	1	.1	.2	87.4
	48.00 = 32 + 16	26	2.2	4.6	92.0
	49.00 = 32 + 16 + 1	4	.3	.7	92.7
	50.00 = 32 + 16 + 2	3	.2	.5	93.3
	51.00 = 32 + 16 + 2 + 1	3	.2	.5	93.8
	52.00 = 32 + 16 + 4	6	.5	1.1	94.9
	53.00 = 32 + 16 + 4 + 1	5	.4	.9	95.7

Figure 6.11 *Frequency output for a 'geometric variable', geojobseek*

	54.00 = 32 + 16 + 4 + 2	1	.1	.2	95.9
	55.00 = 32 + 16 + 4 + 2 + 1	9	.8	1.6	97.5
	56.00 = 32 + 16 + 8	4	.3	.7	98.2
	58.00 = 32 + 16 + 8 + 2	1	.1	.2	98.4
	59.00 = 32 + 16 + 8 + 2 + 1	2	.2	.4	98.8
	60.00 = 32 + 16 + 8 + 4	3	.2	.5	99.3
	61.00 = 32 + 16 + 8 + 4 + 1	1	.1	.2	99.5
	63.00 All six types of job seeking behaviours	3	.2	.5	100.0
	Total	564	47.0	100.0	
Missing	-1.00 Currently working	636	53.0		
Total		1200	100.0		

Figure 6.11   *Continued*

questions is tabulated. The combination of values that produced each unique code is given in the table. You may want to examine these.

A code of '0' is given to 371 respondents, 65.8 per cent of the 564 cases; that is, they did not report any job-seeking behaviours. The most common code for those who reported at least one job-seeking behaviour was the 54 respondents who said they had 'asked a relative or friend', but had not done anything else. The most common combination of behaviours was '48': 'asking relative or friends' ('32') and 'applying directly to employers' ('16').

Working with geometric codes

The ability to portray combinations of answers precisely is the great advantage of geometric coding. One should note, however, that the strategy of using geometric coding does have its limitations. Since the number of unique combinations doubles with each additional value, there are limits to the number of categories that can be used (7 values mean as many as 127 unique combinations, 8 values could yield up to to 255 unique combinations, 9 values 511, and so on). Note, however, that all of the combinations that are possible in theory may not actually come up. For instance, the six circumstances in our example did not generate all the theoretically possible combinations.

When coding, it is good practice to give the options that are expected to occur most often the lower values. This should reduce the number of high codes, which are harder to interpret. Also, giving adjacent values to responses that you expect to group together is good practice. In our example, registering with public and private employment agencies were given adjacent values, followed by two advertising-linked options.

When a geometric coding procedure does produce a variable with a large number of codes, it may be possible to simplify the analysis by recoding the rarer codes into groups. For example, most of the codes of **geojobseek** have only a couple of cases. If we are interested in comparing the people who exhibited no job-seeking behaviour with those who used their 'informal' contacts with relatives or friends either singly or in combination with other behaviours and in turn contrasting them with those who relied solely on more 'formal' strategies, this can be clarified by recoding.

Figure 6.12 shows the results of doing this. **geojobseek** has been recoded into three categories: (1) respondents who did not report any job-seeking behaviour; (2) those who only reported some

recjobseek geojobseek recoded * v67 Not workg:like to have a paid job now or in future
Crosstabulation

| | | | v67 Not workg:like to have a paid job now or in future | | |
			1 Yes	2 No	Total
recjobseek geojobseek recoded	1.00 No job seeking behaviours	Count	74	61	135
		% within v67 Not workg: like to have a paid job now or in future	47.4%	92.4%	60.8%
		Adjusted Residual	-6.3	6.3	
	2.00 'Formal' behaviours	Count	29	2	31
		% within v67 Not workg: like to have a paid job now or in future	18.6%	3.0%	14.0%
		Adjusted Residual	3.1	-3.1	
	3.00 Relations & friends in combination with others	Count	53	3	56
		% within v67 Not workg: like to have a paid job now or in future	34.0%	4.5%	25.2%
		Adjusted Residual	4.6	-4.6	
Total		Count	156	66	222
		% within v67 Not workg: like to have a paid job now or in future	100.0%	100.0%	100.0%

Figure 6.12 *Crosstabulation of the recoded job-seeking variable (**recjobseek**) by whether respondent would like to have a paid job in the future (**v67**)*

combination of one or more 'formal' behaviours; (3) those whose job-seeking behaviours included using contacts with relatives or friends either singly or in combination with other behaviours. The association between whether a respondent would like to have a job and the recoded job-seeking variable is highly significant ($p < 0.001$). Not surprisingly, the great majority (92.4 per cent) of those who were not interested in finding a job reported no job-seeking behaviours. Interestingly, while significantly more of those who would like to have a job reported job-seeking behaviours, almost half (47.4 per cent) did not.

CONCLUSION

In situations where a central goal of an analysis will be to identify the combinations of responses to a general question, geometric coding can be a solution. Furthermore, unlike multiple response sets, a variable whose values result from geometric coding can be used in a confirmatory statistical analysis wherever categorical data are appropriate.

SPSS EXERCISE FOR GEOMETRIC CODING

Design some hypothetical 'geometric' coding questions for a draft questionnaire on a topic of your choice. Note that the type of questions that would be appropriate for a geometric code would be ones for which: (1) respondents are likely to choose more than one answer out of a set of options and (2) the focus of the analysis would be more upon the *combinations* of answers people give rather than a simple tabulation of the categories they pick.

7 Analysis of Variance (ANOVA)

INTRODUCTION

ANalysis Of VAriance (ANOVA), or F test, is an extension of the independent groups *t*-test. Analysis of variance is a more general statistical procedure than the groups *t*-test. You will remember, the *t*-test was used when we had two levels of the independent variable (males and females) and we wanted to see how the groups differed on an interval/ratio variable. However, often there are categorical variables which have more than two levels. In the ISSP datasets, for instance, these include marital status (**marital**), education level (**degree**), current employment status (**wrkst**) and religious affiliation (**religgrp**). Analysis of Variance is similar to the independent groups *t*-test but is employed when there are more than two levels of an independent variable.

ANOVA compares whether the average values or levels of one variable (the means of the dependent variable) differ significantly across the categories of another variable or variables (the independent variable). The way in which ANOVA calculates this is to see how the values that go into making up the means in each category are dispersed. If the variance in each category is very high (that is, each category has cases with a good spread of high and low values), the chances of a person with a high or low value being in any one particular category is not large and therefore there probably is not a significant difference between groups. However, if the variance in each category is relatively low, some categories will have almost all of the high values, and other categories will have almost all the low values. That is, whether or not a case has a high value or a low value is likely to be determined by the category and there is probably a significant difference between groups. To put it another way, what an ANOVA does is to compare the variance *between* groups (or categories) with the variance *within* groups (or categories). If there is more difference between groups than there is between individuals within groups, it must be the groups that make the difference and the result is likely to be statistically significant.

What does a significant result with an ANOVA mean? Figure 7.1 is a pictorial example of a *significant* result (on the left) and a *non-significant* result (on the right), where we have 3 groups (A, B, C) and an interval/ratio variable called X. In the diagram in Figure 7.1, the vertical boxplots represent the distributions of scores on variable X. The boxes indicate the middle 50 per cent of values on variable X and the lines above and below the boxes each represent, respectively, the upper and lower 25 per cent of values on variable X. There are three box plots on each side of the diagram to represent the distribution for each of the three groups, A, B and C (see Module 2 for a more detailed discussion of boxplots).

On the left is a diagram of a significant result. Here, as depicted by the relatively 'short fat' boxes and short lines, the range of scores for each of the three groups are closely bunched together. Once we know a person's group (A, B or C), we would be close to knowing their score on variable X. The diagram on the

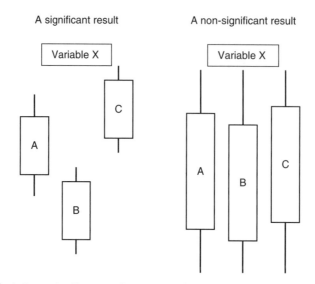

Figure 7.1   *Diagram depicting a significant and a non-significant ANOVA result*

right of the figure is an example of a non-significant result. The range of scores for each of the groups is quite wide, as depicted by the 'long thin' boxes and the relatively long lines. There is a little variance *between* groups, but a lot of variance *within* groups for scores on variable X – therefore even when we know the group, we would not necessarily know what the level of an individual's score on variable X is going to be.

This is precisely what ANOVA does. It compares the variance *between* groups with the variance *within* groups to arrive at a number called the **F-ratio**. The greater the variance *between* groups in comparison to the variance *within* groups, the larger the F-ratio. Hence, we use the F-ratio statistic to see whether the difference between groups is significant.

HOW TO DO A SIMPLE ANOVA USING SPSS

For this module we are going to use the ISSP dataset for South Africa and we will begin with a relatively straightforward example. We want to find out whether there is a significant difference in the length of time employees in the different job sectors spent in education. In other words, the ANOVA used here will examine whether the mean scores on the variable **educyrs** (years of education) are significantly different across five categories of **wrktype** (type of work).

To carry out ANOVA go to the **Analyze** menu, select **Compare Means** and then **One-Way ANOVA**. This will open the One-Way ANOVA dialog box shown in Figure 7.2.

Select the variable you want to calculate the means of (**educyrs** in this example) and click and drag it across to the **Dependent List** box. Then select the variable that contains the categories you want to compare (**wrktype**) and click and drag it across to the **Factor** box.

We could now run the ANOVA at this point. However, there are a number of options we can choose. As the ANOVA compares the mean scores of certain groups, it is a good idea to ask SPSS to produce details of these. Click on **Options** to open the One-Way ANOVA: Options dialog box (shown in Figure 7.3).

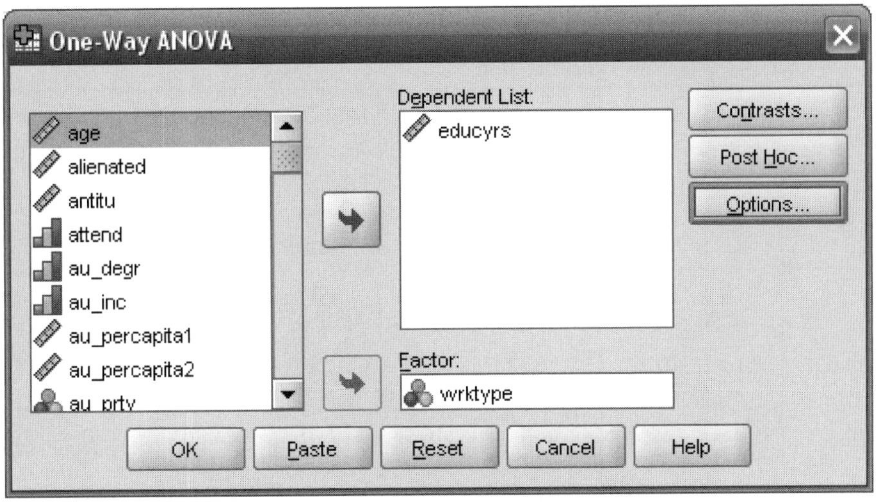

Figure 7.2   *One way ANOVA dialog box*

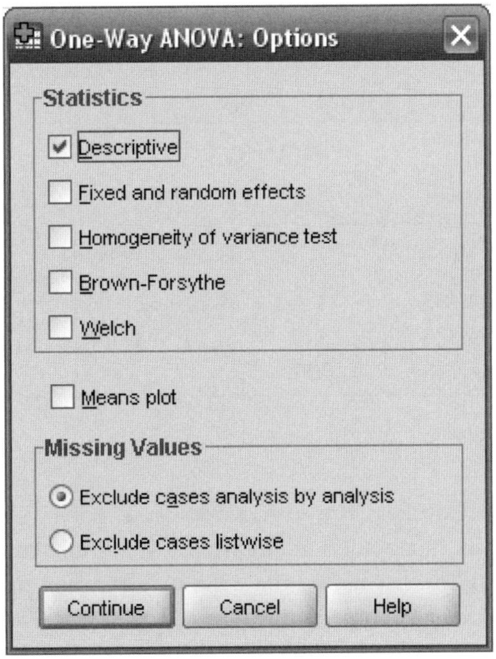

Figure 7.3   *One-Way ANOVA: Options dialog box*

As we want the means for each group, it is necessary to put a tick in the **Descriptive** box. Then click on **Continue** to return to the main ANOVA window. We are now ready to run the ANOVA, so click on **OK**. The results of the ANOVA are shown in Figure 7.4. To interpret these we need to examine the mean scores for **educyrs** across the five categories of **wrktype**.

We can see that there is considerable variation in the average time spent in education ranging from a mean of 9.66 years (standard deviation = 3.4) for employees of private firms to 11.59 (standard

Descriptives

educvrs R: Education I: years of schooling

	N	Mean	Std. Deviation	Std. Error	95% Confidence Interval for Mean		Minimum	Maximum
					Lower Bound	Upper Bound		
1 Work f government	216	11.59	3.219	.219	11.16	12.02	0	23
2 Public owned firm, nat. ind	113	10.85	2.342	.220	10.41	11.29	5	18
3 Private firm, others	1095	9.66	3.404	.103	9.45	9.86	0	21
4 Self employed	141	10.60	3.167	.267	10.07	11.12	0	19
5 ZA Other, BG: Cooperative, GB: Other, charity, voluntarys	336	9.68	3.379	.184	9.32	10.04	0	34
Total	1901	10.02	3.371	.077	9.87	10.17	0	34

ANOVA

educvrs R: Education I: years of schooling

	Sum of Squares	df	Mean Square	F	Siq.
Between Groups	842.483	4	210.621	19.250	.000
Within Groups	20744.675	1896	10.941		
Total	21587.158	1900			

Figure 7.4 *One-Way ANOVA output*

deviation = 3.2) for government workers. However, we do not know if the differences we have observed in the sample are also present in the population as a whole. The results in the ANOVA box immediately below the descriptives table inform us whether the difference between the means is significant. Here F is 19.25 (always report the value of F). The Significance of F is .000 ('.000' means that the result is 'off the scale' and we can read this as less than .0005) and this level of significance means that there is less than a 5 in 10,000 chance that the difference between employment categories came about by chance. Therefore we accept that there genuinely is a significant overall difference between employment sectors in terms of the length of time employees spent in education.

However, at present the findings provide an unclear interpretation of exactly where the differences lie. Looking at the gross differences between the average length of time spent in education we see that a couple of categories are particularly low. For example, those working in 'private firms' (9.66) and 'others' (9.68) appear to have spent considerably less time in education than government employees (11.59). Yet we are really unable to say which of these differences between the groups are the source of the significant F value; that is, are all the differences we note significant, or just some of them?

SPSS gives us facilities for locating the patterns of any significant differences found in an ANOVA. We are able to make contrasts that break down the differences between groups. Within SPSS there are two types of comparisons using ANOVA:

■ **Contrasts** – used when you are making predictions about the relationships between the variable before you perform the ANOVA; and
■ **Post-Hoc comparisons** – used when you have *not* made any predictions about the relationships between the variables before you perform the ANOVA.

(Note, of course, that there is no need to make comparisons when you find no significant overall difference in the ANOVA.)

Let us consider the last example. Here we may have decided that it would be difficult for us to make any strong a-priori statements (i.e. to make predictions before carrying out our analysis) about the relationship between job type and length of time spent in education. Under these circumstances we would use post-hoc comparisons to compare the means. To access the various options we need to go back to One-Way ANOVA (**Analyze** → **Compare Means** → **One-Way ANOVA**). The variables should still be in their boxes, but this time click on **Post Hoc** (see Figure 7.2 again) to open the Post Hoc Multiple Comparisons dialog box (see Figure 7.5). There is a wide range of options to choose from, but we are going to select the **Scheffe test**, a commonly used comparison. Put a tick in the checkbox beside **Scheffe** and click on **Continue**.

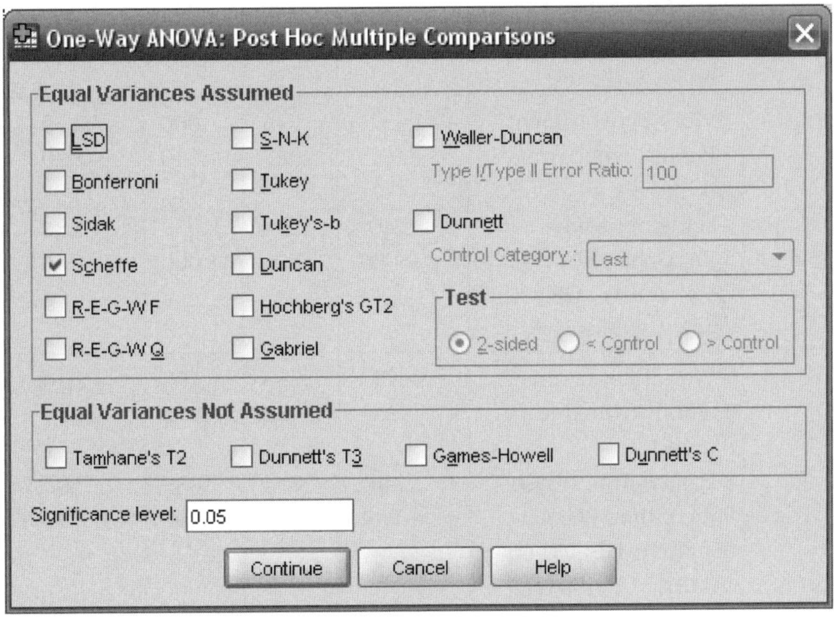

Figure 7.5 *One-Way ANOVA: Post Hoc Multiple Comparisons window*

You will get the same output as before, but you also get some additional information in the **Multiple Comparisons** table (shown in Figure 7.6).

You will notice that the table is divided into five sections, corresponding to the categories of **wrktype**, and each section contains the comparisons for that group's mean with each of the other category means: (1) '**government**', with 'public-owned firm', 'private firm', 'self-employed' and 'other'; (2) '**public-owned firm**' with 'government', 'private firm', 'self-employed' and 'other'; (3) '**private firm**'

Multiple Comparisons

educyrs R: Education I: years of schooling
Scheffe

(1) wrktype R: Workg f priv., pub sector. selfempl.	(J) wrktype R: Workg f priv. pub sector. selfempl.	Mean Difference (I–J)	Std. Error	Sig.	95% Confidence Interval	
					Lower Bound	Upper Bound
1 Work f government	2 Public owned firm, nat. ind	.743	.384	.442	−.44	1.93
	3 Private firm, others	1.937*	.246	.000	1.18	2.70
	4 Self employed	.997	.358	.102	−.11	2.10
	5 ZA: Other, BG: Co-operative, GB: Other, charity, voluntarys	1.911*	.288	.000	1.02	2.80
2 Public owned firm, nat.ind	1 Workf government	−.743	.384	.442	−1.93	.44
	3 Private firm, others	1.194*	.327	.010	.19	2.20
	4 Self employed	.254	.418	.985	−1.03	1.54
	5 ZA: Other, BG: Co-operative, GB: Other, charity, voluntarys	1.168*	.360	.033	.06	2.28
3 Private firm, others	1 Work f government	−1.937*	.246	.000	−2.70	−1.18
	2 Public owned firm, nat. ind	−1.194*	.327	.010	−2.20	−.19
	4 Self employed	−.940*	.296	.039	−1.85	−.03
	5 ZA: Other, BG: Co-operative, GB: Other, charity, voluntarys	−.026	.206	1.000	−.66	.61
4 Self employed	1 Work f government	−.997	.358	.102	−2.10	.11
	2 Public owned firm, nat. ind	−.254	.418	.985	−1.54	1.03
	3 Private firm, others	.940*	.296	.039	.03	1.85
	5 ZA: Other, BG: Co-operative, GB: Other, charity, voluntarys	.914	.332	.108	−.11	1.94
5 ZA Other, BG: Co-operative, GB: Other, charity, voluntarys	1 Work f government	−1.911*	.288	.000	−2.80	−1.02
	2 Public owned firm, nat. ind	−1.168*	.360	.033	−2.28	-.06
	3 Private firm, others	.026	.206	1.000	−.61	.66
	4 Self employed	−.914	.332	.108	−1.94	.11

* The mean difference is significant at the 0.05 level.

Figure 7.6 *Post-Hoc comparison using Scheffe*

with 'government', 'public-owned firm', 'self-employed' and 'other'; (4) **'self-employed'** with 'government', 'public-owned firm', 'private firm' and 'other'; (5) **'other'** with 'government', 'public-owned firm', private firm', and 'self-employed'.

This layout inevitably leads to some replication, but the task of interpreting this table is made easier as any results with a significance value less than .05 are marked with an asterisk. So if we look at the first section of the table in Figure 7.6 we can see that, in terms of the length of time spent in education, there is a significant difference between **government** employees and those who work for a **private firm** (a mean difference of 1.937 years and a significance value of .000). There is also a significant difference between **government** employees and **'other'** workers (a mean difference of 1.911 years and a significance value of .000), but the differences between **government** employees and the other two categories (those who work for **public-owned firms** and the **self-employed**) are *not* significant. The second section of the table examines the differences between those who work for public-owned firms and the other four categories of employees and the only significant results relate to employees of private firms (a mean difference of 1.194 years and a significance value of .01) and other workers (a mean difference of 1.168 years and a significance value of .033). The only other significant difference is between those who work for private firms and the self-employed (a mean difference of .940 years and a significance value of .039) as the other results with an asterisk in table simply replicate those we have already discussed.

SPSS EXERCISE FOR ONE-WAY ANOVA

Now try some ANOVAs by yourself.

- Carry out the ANOVA again (that is, with the same two variables), but this time use an ISSP dataset from a different country and compare your results with the results of the South African data outlined in this module.
- Choose two variables from a dataset of your choice – one categorical (the independent variable) and one interval/ratio (the dependent variable) – and perform an ANOVA. If a significant result is obtained, use post-hoc comparisons to break down the pattern of significant relationships.

TWO-WAY ANALYSIS OF VARIANCE (ANOVA)

We have just dealt with the One-Way ANOVA; however, analysis of variance can also be employed to address more complicated questions. Two-Way ANOVA allows us to deal simultaneously with the effect of two or more independent variables on the dependent variable. We will stick with the South African dataset and in the example outlined below we are going to examine the impact of two independent variables, **degree** (highest education level) and **v27** (respondent currently working for pay), on one dependent variable, **topbot** (respondent's self-placement on a scale of social standing). The aim of the Two-Way ANOVA is to examine the effect of education level (degree) and being in paid employment (**v27**) on **topbot**. With Two-Way ANOVA we can establish the unique effects of each of the independent variables on the dependent variable and (an important addition) also determine whether the effect of one of the independent variables is actually being caused or modified in some way by the other independent variable – whether or not there is an *interaction* between two independent variables.

Knowing what an 'interaction' means will help us interpret the results of Two-Way ANOVAs. Interaction is the expression of the linkage or association between two or more independent variables. This linkage or association is beyond what would be expected by chance. If one does have a statistical interaction, this means that one cannot just add together the effects of each independent variable upon a dependent variable; instead the effect of each independent variable *varies* depending on the other independent variable.

Or to put it more simply, it may be, as for example in the case of the analysis reported here, that unemployed respondents with a degree hold a significantly different view of their social standing than the rest of the sample, with this difference not just being a simple addition of the effect of having a degree and not being in paid employment. (We will discuss interaction further in the coming module on 'Correlation and Regression'.)

A Two-Way ANOVA using SPSS

To carry out a Two-Way ANOVA we need to go to the **Analyze** menu and select **General Linear Model** and then **Univariate**. This will open the Univariate dialog box (Figure 7.7) where you can click and drag the variables to their appropriate locations. As **topbot** is the dependent variable it should be transferred to the **Dependent Variable** box. However, we have two independent variables this time (**degree** and **v27**) and these should be transferred to the **Fixed Factor(s)** box (see Figure 7.7).

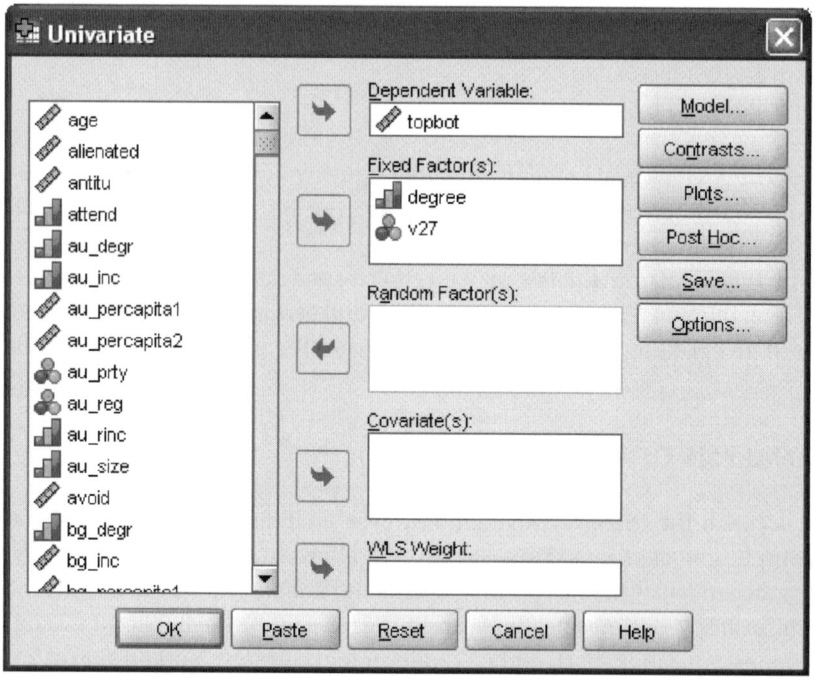

Figure 7.7 *Univariate dialog box*

We again want means and other descriptive statistics and to ensure that these are included in the output, click on the **Options** button. This will open the Univariate: Options dialog box (see Figure 7.8) and you should put a tick beside **Descriptive statistics** in the Display section of the window. Click on **Continue** to return to the main dialog box and then select **OK** to run the procedure.

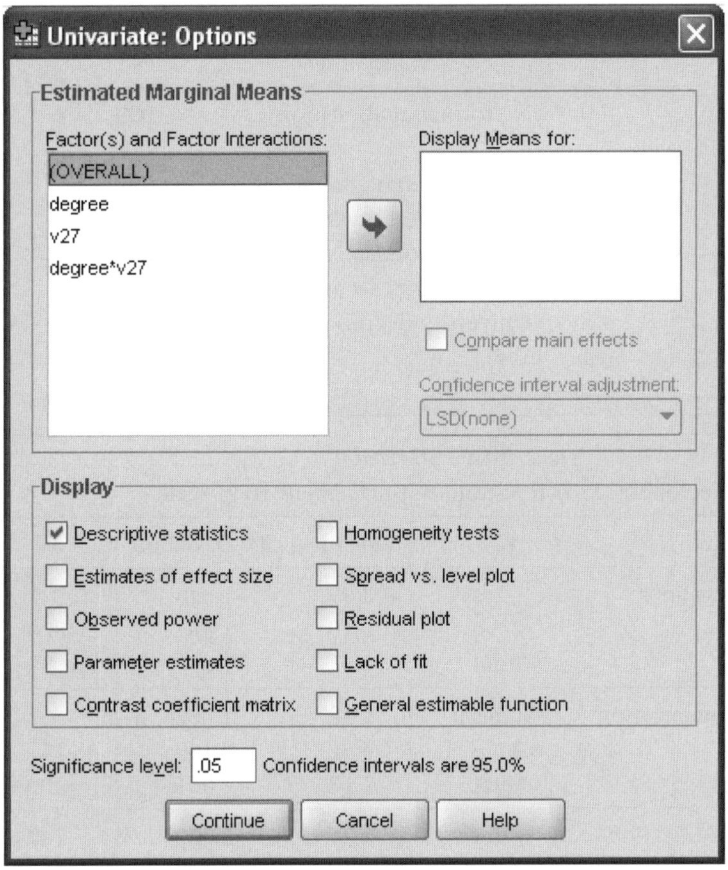

Figure 7.8   *Univariate: Options dialog box*

The results of the Two-Way ANOVA are displayed in Figure 7.9. To begin, the **Between Subject Factors** box gives the counts for each category of the dependent variables. Next, we focus on the 'Descriptive Statistics' section of the output, which provides the means and standard deviations for each group. Here we are able to determine how mean scores on the self-rating scale of social standing vary between the categories of each group *and* between each combination of categories for both groups. For example, the lowest score (3.99) relates to respondents who have no formal qualifications and are currently working for pay. By contrast, the respondents that rate themselves highest (7.07) are those who possess a university degree but are not currently in paid employment.

If we look at the bottom section of the table (the **Tests of Between-Subjects Effects** box) we can see that the F values indicate that the contribution of level of education (**degree**) to the ANOVA is significant (F=87.944, Sig.=.000) and the contribution of whether the respondent is in paid employment (**v27**) to the ANOVA is also significant (F=5.77, Sig=.016).

Looking at the bottom rows of the **Descriptive Statistics** box, we can see that, as we would expect, those currently in work have a higher self-estimation of their standing than those who are not in work (5.31 compared to 4.72), and now we know this difference is significant even when the effect of education is taken into account. There are more than two categories to compare for **degree**, however, so we need to apply a post-hoc test again. To do this, we return to the main **Univariate** window, click on **Post**

Between-Subjects Factors

		Value Label	N
degree R: Education II-highest education level	0	No formal qualification	1099
	1	Lowest formal qualification	209
	2	Above lowest qualification	609
	3	Higher secondary completed	647
	4	Above higher secondary level	125
	5	University degree completed	118
v27 Respondent currently working for pay	1	Yes	866
	2	No	1941

Descriptive Statistics

Dependent Variable: topbot R: Top Bottom self-placement 10 pt scale

degree R: Education II-...	v27...	Mean	Std. Deviation	N
0 No formal qualification	1 Yes	3.99	1.618	275
	2 No	4.10	1.857	824
	Total	4.07	1.800	1099
1 Lowest formal qualification	1 Yes	4.92	1.702	52
	2 No	4.52	2.189	157
	Total	4.62	2.081	209
2 Above lowest qualification	1 Yes	5.25	2.022	142
	2 No	5.10	2.087	467
	Total	5.14	2.071	609
3 Higher secondary completed	1 Yes	6.10	1.823	245
	2 No	5.23	2.026	402
	Total	5.56	1.996	647
4 Above higher secondary level	1 Yes	6.49	1.578	77
	2 No	5.90	2.013	48
	Total	6.26	1.774	125
5 University degree completed	1 Yes	6.73	1.528	75
	2 No	7.07	2.017	43
	Total	6.86	1.721	118
Total	1 Yes	5.31	2.016	866
	2 No	4.72	2.083	1941
	Total	4.90	2.080	2807

Figure 7.9   *Univariate Analysis of Variance results*

Tests of Between-Subjects Effects

Dependent Variable: topbot R: Top Bottom self-placement 10 pt scale

Source	Type III Sum of Squares	df	Mean Square	F	Sig.
Corrected Model	1907.722[a]	11	173.429	47.356	.000
Intercept	36684.372	1	36684.372	10016.939	.000
degree	1610.360	5	322.072	87.944	.000
v27	21.131	1	21.131	5.770	.016
degree * v27	101.497	5	20.299	5.543	.000
Error	10235.944	2795	3.662		
Total	79576.000	2807			
Corrected Total	12143.665	2806			

a. R Squared = .157 (Adjusted R Squared = .154)

Figure 7.9   *Continued*

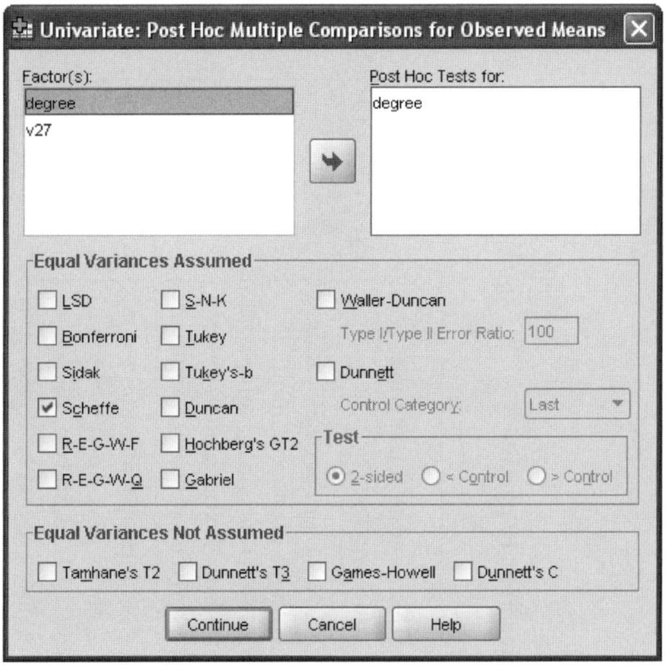

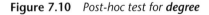

Figure 7.10   *Post-hoc test for **degree***

Hoc... in order to bring up the sub-window in Figure 7.10. Here, we request a 'Post Hoc Test for:' **degree** by moving that variable into the right-hand box and ticking **Sc**heffe.

When we rerun the ANOVA we should obtain the results displayed in Figure 7.11 on the next pages, where we can see that there are significant different between all of the **degree** level categories except for the two highest, 'University degree completed' and 'Above higher secondary level' (n.b. there is not a significant difference between these two categories because the sig. value of .326 is greater than our cut-off point of .05).

Multiple Comparisons

topbot R:Top Bottom self-placement 10 pt scale

Scheffe

(I) R: Education II-highest education level	(J) R: Education II-highest education level	Mean Difference (I-J)	Std. Error	Sig.	95% Confidence Interval	
					Lower Bound	Upper Bound
0 No formal qualification	1 Lowest formal qualification	-.55*	.144	.013	-1.03	-.07
	2 Above lowest qualification	-1.06*	.097	.000	-1.39	-.74
	3 Higher secondary completed	-1.49*	.095	.000	-1.80	-1.17
	4 Above higher secondary level	-2.19*	.181	.000	-2.79	-1.59
	5 University degree completed	-2.78*	.185	.000	-3.40	-2.17
1 Lowest formal qualification	0 No formal qualification	.55*	.144	.013	.07	1.03
	2 Above lowest qualification	-.51*	.153	.047	-1.03	.00
	3 Higher secondary completed	-.94*	.152	.000	-1.44	-.43
	4 Above higher secondary level	-1.64*	.216	.000	-2.36	-.92
	5 University degree completed	-2.23*	.220	.000	-2.97	-1.50
2 Above lowest qualification	0 No formal qualification	1.06*	.097	.000	.74	1.39
	1 Lowest formal qualification	.51*	.153	.047	.00	1.03
	3 Higher secondary completed	-.42*	.108	.010	-.78	-.06
	4 Above higher secondary level	-1.13*	.188	.000	-1.75	-.50
	5 University degree completed	-1.72*	.192	.000	-2.36	-1.08

3 Higher secondary completed	0 No formal qualification	1.49*	.095	.000	1.17	1.80
	1 Lowest formal qualification	.94*	.152	.000	.43	1.44
	2 Above lowest qualification	.42*	.108	.010	.06	.78
	4 Above higher secondary level	−.71*	.187	.014	−1.33	−.08
	5 University degree completed	−1.30*	.192	.000	−1.94	−.66
4 Above higher secondary level	0 No formal qualification	2.19*	.181	.000	1.59	2.79
	1 Lowest formal qualification	1.64*	.216	.000	.92	2.36
	2 Above lowest qualification	1.13*	.188	.000	.50	1.75
	3 Higher secondary completed	.71*	.187	.014	.08	1.33
	5 University degree completed	−.59	.246	(.326)	−1.41	.23
5 University degree completed	0 No formal qualification	2.78*	.185	.000	2.17	3.40
	1 Lowest formal qualification	2.23*	.220	.000	1.50	2.97
	2 Above lowest qualification	1.72*	.192	.000	1.08	2.36
	3 Higher secondary completed	1.30*	.192	.000	.66	1.94
	4 Above higher secondary level	.59	.246	(.326)	−.23	1.41

Based on observed means.
The error term is Mean Square(Error) = 3.662.
* The mean difference is signifcant at the .05 level.

Figure 7.11 *Scheffe test of effects of different education levels (**degree**) upon topbot*

In addition to the main effects of both variables, we can see in Figure 7.9 that there is also a significant interaction between the two independent variable; **degree * v27** is significant (F=5.543, Sig=.000). By going back to the **Descriptive Statistics** box (Figure 7.9) and examining the means carefully we can begin to interpret the source of the significant interaction. As you might expect, in general those in paid employment tend to rate themselves higher than those who are not in work. It is equally predictable that respondents' self-placement rating will increase as their level of education increases (see the *total* scores for **degree** in the Descriptive Statistics section of the table). However, it is respondents who have 'no formal qualifications' but who *are* in paid employment (rather than those who don't have a job) who rate themselves lowest (with a mean of 3.99) and *unemployed* university graduates (rather than employed university graduates) who rate themselves highest (with a mean of 7.07). That is, there is an *interaction* – in addition to the direct effect of the two independent variables, once the effects of level of education and being in paid employment are considered in tandem we can see that there is a variation in their combined effect.

As well as identifying the interaction by carefully inspecting the means for all the combinations of the groups, we can also take advantage of a graphical display provided by SPSS. SPSS can plot the means of the dependent variable for each combination of categories of two independent variables in a graphical representation of an interaction. To do this, run the Two-Way ANOVA again as before, but before clicking **OK**, click on **Plots** in the Univariate dialog box. This will open the Univariate Profile Plots dialog box shown in Figure 7.12.

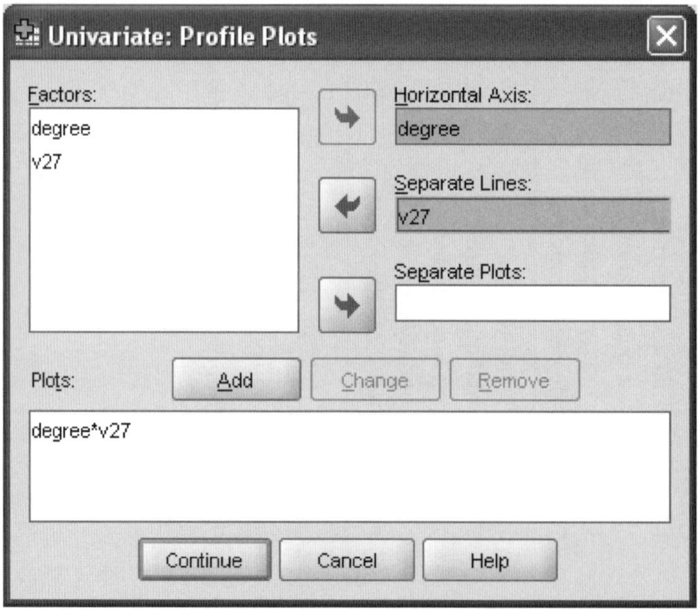

Figure 7.12   *Univariate: Profile Plots*

Transfer **degree** over to the **Horizontal Axis** box, and **v27** to the **Separate Lines** box (if one of the variables has more categories than the other, put the one with the least categories into the Separate Lines box). Then click on the **Add** button (to 'activate' the plot by transferring the variables to the **Plots** box at the bottom of the window) and '**Continue**' to return to the main Univariate window. Finally click on **OK** to rerun the analysis. This time, in addition to the tables we have already discussed, the SPSS output should include the graph shown in Figure 7.13.

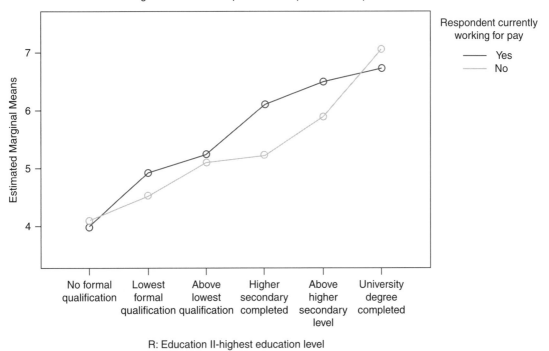

Figure 7.13   *Profile Plot*

In this graph, the employed and unemployed categories are plotted as lines and these should be colour-coded on your computer screen. The vertical Y axis is the mean value of the dependent variable (**topbot**, self-rating scale of social status).

The differences between the groups and the form of the statistical interaction can be seen clearly. The patterns highlighted in the 'total' scores in the table in Figure 7.9 indicated that in general those in work rated themselves higher than those who were unemployed, as did respondents who had a higher level of qualification. In graphical terms this is represented by the two lines sloping upwards from left to right. Note that the two lines broadly run in parallel. However, for the **degree** categories at each end of the scale (university graduates and those with no formal qualifications) the general pattern is reversed and the lines cross each other at the lower left-hand and upper right-hand parts of the chart. So, the graph clearly shows the main sources of the significant statistical interaction: employed people with no formal qualifications have a lower score than we would expect and unemployed graduates have a higher score than we would expect.

So, in our final interpretation of the results, we would note that education level and paid employment, when considered together, are each having an independent significant effect on self-rating of social standing. Furthermore, while educational level and employment each separately reveals differences in self-rating scores, a more complete analysis that takes account of statistical interaction shows that employed rather than unemployed people with no formal qualifications rate themselves lower than all other groups and it is the unemployed graduates rather than the employed graduates who have the highest self-rating score.

CONCLUSION

Analysis of variance is a powerful tool for disentangling the effects of categorical variables upon scalar variables, particularly in the case of Two-Way ANOVA. You should note that 'Two-Way ANOVA' should be more accurately described as '*N-Way* ANOVA'. It is quite feasible to use ANOVA to examine the effects of three, or four or even more independent categorical variables upon a dependent variable at the same time. This can be done by simply adding in more than two independent variables into the **Fixed Factor(s)** box in the main window. In this way it is possible, with care, to begin to produce a multivariate statistical analysis that begins to approach being a genuine model of social reality (in the sense that the model will begin to reflect reality in a simplified manner while highlighting some of its essential characteristics).

SPSS EXERCISES FOR TWO-WAY ANOVA

Now try some Two-Way ANOVAs yourself.

- Carry out the Two-Way ANOVA again (that is, with the same three variables), but this time using an ISSP dataset from a different country of your choice. Compare your results with those for this module.
- Choose two new categorical variables and an interval/ratio variable, and perform a different Two-Way ANOVA. Remember to produce means and try using a plot to help you interpret your findings if there is a significant statistical interaction.
- Repeat the ANOVA, only adding in some additional independent variables in order to produce an N-Way ANOVA (take care that there are a reasonable number of cases in each category of the independent variables).

8   Correlation and Regression

Before considering the correlation and regression statistics, we will look at some of the 'logic' behind what is generally known as 'general linear modelling'. The basic idea behind general linear modelling, which includes both correlation and regression, is that you can depict the relationship between two quantitative variables (whose codes are numbers representing true numeric values: interval or ratio variables) by 'drawing' straight lines. For this module we are going to use the ISSP data for **Russia** and we will begin by looking at scattergrams (or scatterplots) which provide a visual representation of the relationship between two scale variables.

SCATTERGRAMS

Figure 8.1a provides an example of a positive relationship between two variables. Here SPSS has produced a scattergram of the relationship between two variables:

    1. **revision**: how much studying an individual did for an exam (scored from 0 to 30 hours)

by

    2. **score**: exam score, marked out of 30.

When you have a 'positive relationship', the low values on one variable tend to go with low values on the other variable and high values on one variable tend to go with high values on the other. Here we would expect that people doing only a small amount of revising for an exam should tend to score low on the exam, and people doing a lot of studying should achieve higher scores. Therefore a positive relationship on a scattergram will look like that in Figure 8.1a, the plotted points moving from the lower left-hand corner upwards to the upper right-hand corner of the chart.

With a negative relationship you would find the opposite pattern. In Figure 8.1b SPSS has produced a scattergram which displays a negative relationship between two variables:

    1. **out**: how many hours individuals spent socializing the week before the exam (scored from 0 to 30 hours)

by

    2. **score**: exam score, marked out of 30.

When you have a 'negative relationship', the low values on one variable tend to go with high values on the other variable and high values on one variable tend to go with low values on the other. Here,

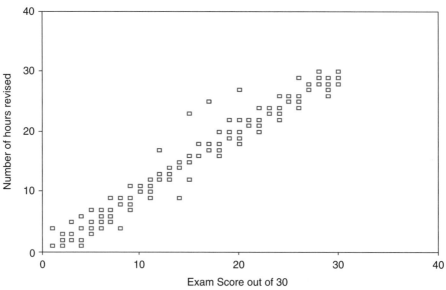

Figure 8.1a *A positive relationship between two variables*

Figure 8.1b *A negative relationship between two variables*

people socializing a lot in the week before an exam should tend to score low on the exam, and people not going out (and presumably doing a lot of revision) before an exam tend to achieve much higher scores. Therefore a negative relationship on a scattergram will look like that in Figure 8.1b, the plotted points moving from the upper left-hand corner downwards to the lower right-hand corner of the chart.

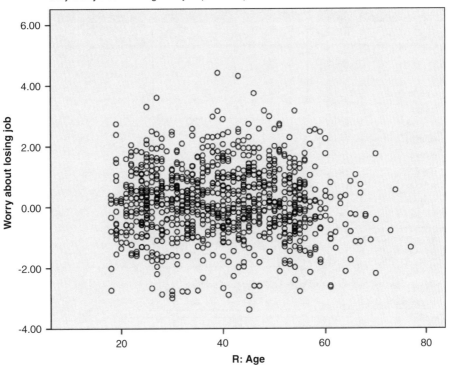

Scattergram plotting scores between respondents age (AGE) and the extent to which they worry about losing their job (WORRY).

Figure 8.1c   *No significant relationship*

However, with most data the relationships aren't this clear, and it is quite possible that two variables will not be strongly related in either a positive or a negative sense. We can see an example of a scattergram of two variables from the ISSP dataset that are not related in Figure 8.1c. Here we have plotted age scores (**age**) against the extent to which a respondent worries about losing their job (**worry**). Note that the scattergram is more or less a random scatter of points with no clear linear pattern.

Producing scattergrams with SPSS

Now, let us produce that last scattergram with SPSS. Respondent's age (**age**) and the degree to which a respondent worries about losing their job (**worry**) are the scale variables that will be used in this example. We will use the Chart Builder in SPSS to produce the scattergram and, although we covered this in Module 2, it will do no harm to recap on the process here.

Click on **Chart Builder** in the **Graphs** menu to open up the Chart Builder dialog box (shown in Figure 8.2). Select the **Scatter/Dot** option from the list of charts and then click and drag the Simple Scatter icon from the gallery (bottom panel) to the canvas (the top panel).

We now need to select our two quantitative variables from the variable list and transfer one to the Y axis and one to the X axis. First click on **age** and drag it to the X axis drop zone and then click on **worry** and drag it to the Y axis drop zone (as shown in Figure 8.2). Run the procedure by clicking on **OK**. A scattergram like the one we have already seen in Figure 8.1c should appear in the Viewer window.

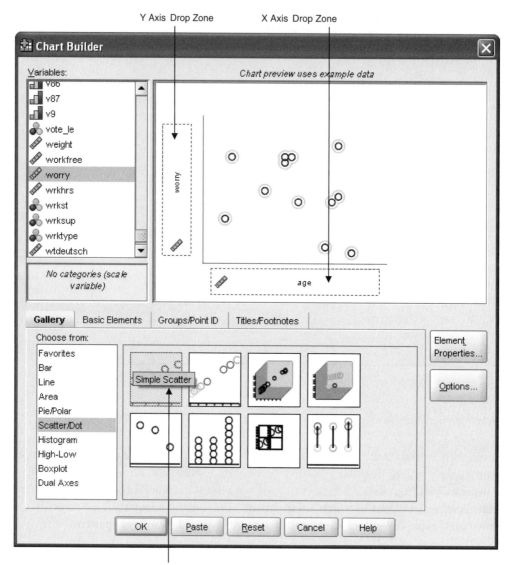

Figure 8.2　*Chart Builder dialog box: Scatterplot*

Points about scattergrams

A scattergram can be thought of as an exploratory data analysis-type technique since it provides a visual depiction of the relationship between two quantitative variables. Note that the scattergram alone is not a confirmatory statistical procedure. The scattergram allows you to check visually the validity of a general linear confirmatory procedure that you are using (such as correlation or regression below). There are instances where a quick inspection of the scattergram can alert you to problems with the data that could invalidate the use of a statistical procedure based upon linear assumptions. Two problems are worth mentioning specifically.

Outliers

Correlation and regression statistics can be inordinately affected by the presence of a few extremely low or high values in the data. That is, the presence of cases with outliers can lead to a misleading or inaccurate result. For example, in our earlier description of a strong positive relationship between time spent revising and exam score, it might be that one individual could have spent hours and hours revising, but may have felt ill on the day and received a very low mark. This score then might be viewed as an outlier. One way of spotting these extreme 'outliers' is to look at a scattergram: one or two points located out on their own some distance from the rest of the data indicate outliers. An analyst may then decide to exclude this small number of outlier cases from the analysis. While outliers may arise as a result of coding errors another common cause is forgetting to declare a missing value. For instance, respondents given a missing value code of '999' for their age would appear as a confusing group of extremely elderly Methuselahs if the analyst forgot to put down '999' as a missing value for age. Inspecting the scattergram can alert the analyst to outliers of these types, which can then be fixed or removed.

Curviliear trends

General linear statistics initially assume that relationships between variables can be depicted by straight lines. It is possible, however, to have a strong linear relationship where the line is not straight. Sometimes these curvilinear relationships become apparent when one inspects the scattergram. Figure 8.3, a graph of 'Age of woman' by 'Likelihood of having a child in the next year', shows an example of a curvilinear relationship – the odds of a young teenage girl having a child are quite low; this rises steeply to a peak for women in their mid/late twenties and then gradually tails off through the thirties into the forties. The value of a simple correlation or regression coefficient for the data depicted in this graph (which assumes a straight-line relationship) would be quite low; hence, underestimating what is in fact a very strong, but curvilinear, relationship.

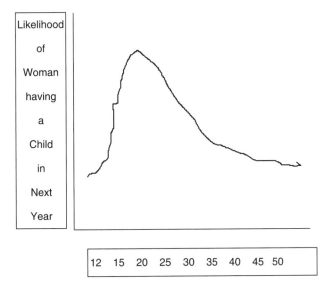

Figure 8.3   *An example of a strong curvilinear relationship*

SPSS EXERCISE FOR SCATTERGRAMS

Select some pairs of variables from one of the ISSP datasets and have SPSS produce scattergrams of the relationships between them. Remember to choose quantitative variables where the codings are genuine numbers in order to produce meaningful scattergrams.

Hints:

- Choose pairs of variables where there is good reason to assume that the relationships will be either strongly positive or strongly negative.
- The scattergrams will look better and be more informative if you select quantitative variables where there are a large number of numeric codes for both variables in a pair rather than just a few codes.

PEARSON'S PRODUCT-MOMENT CORRELATION COEFFICIENT (r)

The usefulness of the scattergram for examining the relationship between two quantitative variables, however, is rather limited. You may have noted when doing your own scattergrams that, while the apparent presence of a pattern in the scattergram plot gave a feeling of the direction of the relationship between the two variables, you are unable to determine whether there actually is a genuine relationship or not.

The aim of the correlation coefficient is to determine:

(1) whether there is a *real relationship* between two interval/ratio variables,
(2) the *direction* of the relationship, and
(3) the *strength* of the relationship.

Pearson's product–moment correlation coefficient is a parametric test. We use hypothesis-testing criteria and confidence levels in order to determine whether a significant correlation occurs between two variables, and the direction of this correlation (positive or negative).

The correlation coefficient can take values ranging from +1.00 through 0.00 to – 1.00.

- A correlation of +1.00 would be a 'perfect' positive relationship.
- A correlation of 0.00 would indicate no relationship (no single straight line can sum up the almost random distribution of points).
- A correlation of –1.00 would be a 'perfect' negative relationship.

Since the correlation coefficient digests all of the information contained in a scatterplot into a single number, it is a statistic that is very efficient at describing the data. (Statistics that are 'efficient' in this manner are sometimes called *powerful* statistics.)

Assumptions of the correlation coefficient

The data used in correlations (and regressions and *all* versions of the General Linear Model) must meet some assumptions:

- the data should be interval/ratio data. (However correlation is *robust*, which means that the assumption does not have to be strictly met for the statistic still to perform reasonably well. So this condition can be 'bent' to some degree; for example, by correlating ordinal variables);
- *homoscedasticity.* That is, if the intersection points between variables are plotted around the correlation 'line', they will be 'normally' distributed around the line – some will be above the line, some will be below it and more points will be close to the 'line' than far away;
- the relationship between the variables in question can be adequately portrayed by straight lines.

Correlating with SPSS

Although a bivariate correlation by definition focuses on the relationship between only two variables, SPSS can produce a correlation matrix which allows you to carry out a number of bivariate correlations simultaneously. This is what we are going to do in the current example, using four scale variables from the ISSP dataset:

age– respondent's age

educyrs – years of schooling

isea – International Socio-economic Index

siops – Standard Occupational Prestige Scale

To open up the Bivariate Correlations dialog box (Figure 8.4) go to the **Analyze** menu and click on **Correlate** and then **Bivariate**. Click and drag each of the variables (**age, educyrs, isea** and **siops**) into the target variable list as shown in Figure 8.4. *Don't* press OK yet. You need to adapt the correlation window to suit your needs. Tick the box next to the type of correlation coefficient you want to obtain. Here click on the **Pearson** box.

You also need to decide here whether to carry out a 'two-tailed' or 'one-tailed' test of significance. There are two types of 'tailed' tests (the rather peculiar use of the word 'tailed' refers to either one or both ends, or 'tails', of a normal distribution of possible correlations):

- with a two-tailed test, SPSS assumes that you do not have any idea before you begin whether the correlation will be positive or negative (two possibilities, hence 'two-tailed');
- with a one-tailed test, SPSS assumes that you anticipate beforehand whether the correlation is going to be positive or negative. What you are testing, then, is not whether the correlation will be positive or negative, but whether the correlation will be statistically significant or not (only one possible 'direction' to the correlation, hence 'one-tailed). Because you 'have gone further out on a limb' (when you predicted beforehand the direction of the correlation), the size of the correlation coefficient needed to reach statistical significance for a one-tailed test is not as large (or, to put it another way, the criteria for a one-tailed test to be significant is more lenient).

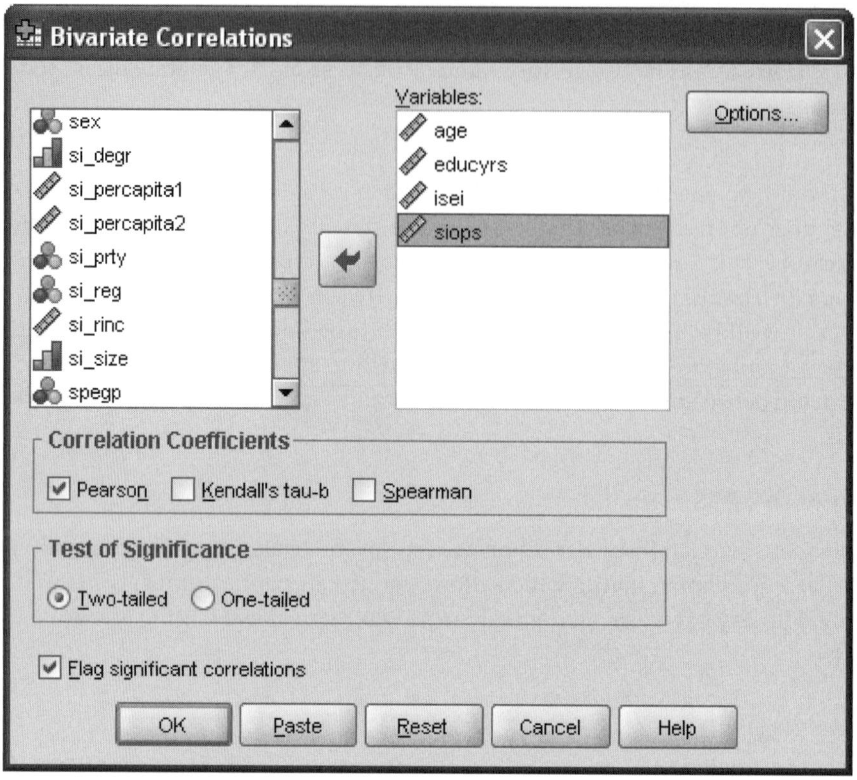

Figure 8.4 *Bivariate Correlations dialog box*

To select a one- or a two-tailed test of significance, specify in the **Test of Significance** box at the bottom of the Bivariate Correlations window whether you want a One-tailed or Two-tailed test of significance. This time we will use a two-tailed test; that is, we are not making any predictions in advance about whether the relationship will be positive or negative.

You can also manipulate the **Variables** box in other ways. For instance, by pasting more than two variable names into the Variables box, as in this example, SPSS will correlate each variable with *every other* variable in the Variables box to produce what is called a *correlation matrix*.

Run the correlation by clicking on **OK**. You will obtain an Output which looks like Figure 8.5.

Each 'box' contains:

The correlation coefficient: Pearson correlation

The statistical significance, Sig (2 tailed) = .xxx

The number of cases: N

(Note: ' . ' is printed if a coefficient cannot be computed)

Interpretation of the correlation coefficient (r)

At first sight the table in Figure 8.5 looks very complicated, but if we focus on each of the individual cells it becomes much more manageable. Although there are 16 cells in this table a lot of this information is redundant. For a start, the four boxes on the diagonal running from the top left to the bottom

Correlations

		age R: Age	educyrs R: Education I: years of schooling	isei Internatl socio-economic index	siops Standard Occ Prestige Scale
age R: Age	Pearson Correlation	1.000	−.322**	−.075**	−.049
	Sig. (2-tailed)		.000	.005	.068
	N	1605	1421	1379	1379
educyrs R: Education I: years of schooling	Pearson Correlation	−.322**	1.000	.510**	.489**
	Sig. (2-tailed)	.000		.000	.000
	N	1421	1421	1285	1285
isei Internatl socio-economic index	Pearson Correlation	−.075**	.510**	1.000	.906**
	Sig. (2-tailed)	.005	.000		.000
	N	1379	1285	1379	1379
siops Standard Occ Prestige Scale	Pearson Correlation	−.049	.489**	.906**	1.000
	Sig. (2-tailed)	.068	.000	.000	
	N	1379	1285	1379	1379

**. Correlation is significant at the 0.01 level (2-tailed).

Figure 8.5 *Pearson product–moment correlation coefficient between respondents' Age, Years of schooling, International Socio-economic Index and Standard Occupational Prestige Scale*

right are only reporting the relationship between each variable and itself (so the correlation in all of those boxes is 1.000 and N is the number of valid cases for the variable). Moreover, as the boxes on either side of this diagonal mirror each other (i.e. those in the lower left-hand side of the table replicate those in the upper right-hand side), we are only really interested in six cells in total. It is also important to remember that this is a correlation matrix and, as such, represents a series of individual bivariate correlations. In other words, we only need to focus on one cell at a time and identify the information relating to three things: (1) the direction of the relationship; (2) whether the relationship is significant; and (3) the strength of the relationship.

Interpreting the results

1. The first cell we are interested in is the correlation between **age** and **educyrs**. The Pearson correlation (r) is −.322, the Sig (2 tailed) is .000, and $N = 1421$. This minus sign tells us that there is a negative (or inverse) relationship between age and years of schooling. In other words older people tend to have fewer years of schooling than younger people. This may appear counter-intuitive but if you think about it, those from an older generation are likely to have left school at an earlier age than young people today. A significance level of .000 indicates that the probability of the correlation not being statistically significant is very low. However, the Pearson's r value (−.322) suggests that this is a weak to moderate relationship.

2. The next cell on the top row provides information on the relationship between age and the respondent's ranking on the International Socio-economic Index. The Pearson's r result (−.075) represents

another negative relationship, but this time it is extremely weak (i.e. less than .1). This indicates that as respondent's age increases their ranking on the International Socio-economic Index decreases and the result is significant at the .01 level ($p=.005$).

3. The final cell in the top row of the table relates to the correlation between age and occupational prestige. However there is not a significant relationship between these two variables as the two-tailed significance level is *greater than* .05 (i.e. $p=.068$).

4. The next cell we are interested in is the third cell on the second row. This provides information on the relationship between years of schooling and the respondents' ranking on the International Socio-economic Index. We can see from Figure 8.5 that there is a significant relationship between these two variables ($p<.001$) and that the correlation is positive and relatively strong (i.e. Pearson's $r = .510$). This indicates that the longer the respondent has spent in school the higher their score on the International Socio-economic Index.

5. The final cell on the second row of the table also shows a significant result ($p<.001$). The Pearson's r value of .489 is similar to the previous result, indicating a relatively strong positive correlation between years of schooling and occupational prestige. This suggests that those who have spent longer in school are employed in more prestigious occupations.

6. The final bivariate correlation can be found in the last cell in the third row of the table and concerns the relationship between the International Socio-economic Index and the Standard Occupational Prestige Scale. This Pearson's r value of .906 represents an extremely strong positive correlation between these two variables and this result is highly significant ($p<.001$). In other words, those respondents who are in occupations that are ranked towards the bottom of the International Socio-economic Index also score poorly on the Standard Occupational Prestige Scale, and those respondents that have high scores on the International Socio-economic Index also rank highly on the Standard Occupational Prestige Scale.

As the preceding discussion demonstrates, it is necessary to take account of the strength of relationships, not just the direction and their statistical significance. Remember correlations can range from highly negative (–1.00) to highly positive (+1.00). Within this range, we use the actual value of r to determine the strength of relationship. Therefore a correlation of 0.50 (regardless of whether it is either positive or negative) is stronger than one of only 0.10. Note here that some of the results in the correlation matrix were very high (e.g. $r = .906$ is very close to a perfect positive correlation of 1.00) while some others, even though *statistically* significant, were very low (e.g. –.075 is relatively close to zero).

While the conventions for deciding when a result is statistically significant are clear, with $p<0.05$, $p<0.01$ and $p<0.001$ being the commonly accepted 'cut off' points, there are no such agreed conventions for statistically significant weak relationships. Deciding when a statistically significant correlation is so weak that it should be considered to have little substantive importance is a matter of judgement. One helpful indicator may be that the square of the correlation coefficient (r^2) provides an indication of the amount of variance in one variable that may be considered to be linked to the values of the other variable in a correlation pair. So, with our results above, the correlation of .510 means that over one-quarter (26 per cent) of the variance in the International Socio-economic Index can be linked to the number of years the respondent spent in school. While, in contrast, the weak correlation of **age** with **isei** ($r = -.075$) implies that only half of one per cent of the variance in the International Socio-economic Index can be linked to the respondent's age. So although this correlation is statistically significant it is of doubtful substantive importance. It might help to note that a correlation must be above .30 in order to account for at least ten per cent of variance.

SPSS EXERCISES IN PRODUCING CORRELATIONS

▪ Select a pair of quantitative variables from an ISSP dataset of your choice and correlate them using SPSS.
▪ Then, choose a list of variables and produce a correlation matrix.
▪ Try doing the correlation matrix with a one-tailed test and then a two-tailed test and note how the levels of significance change.

Hint:
Use the same variables that you used for the scattergrams and you will be able to compare the correlation coefficients with the plots of the variables that produced the coefficients.

A final point on correlation coefficient

With Pearson's product–moment correlation, you have examined the *association* between variables. However, it is important to remember that you have not shown that one *causes* another. For example, the correlation matrix we have just looked at suggested a significant relationship between years of schooling and occupational prestige. It does not follow from the significant correlation results, however, that you can assert that one causes the other. We may have sound theoretical reasons for hypothesizing such a causal link and if we want to pursue this further we could use regression statistics.

REGRESSION

The assumptions for regression are the same as for correlation:

1. interval/ratio data (but, like correlation, regression is *robust* and can tolerate violations of its assumptions with ordinal variables);
2. homoscedasticity; and
3. the relationships between variables are linear; that is, they can be portrayed by straight lines.

What makes regression different from correlation is that regression assumes that the *independent* (x) variable is, at least in part, a *cause* or a *predictor* of the *dependent* (y) variable. For instance, we could have a hypothesis that more years of education will *cause* people to be in a higher-ranked occupation. So, years of education will be the independent/causal x variable and occupational rank will be the dependent/caused y variable.

Hence, regression is a version of the General Linear Model that allows us to test hypotheses in which *causality* is asserted. Regression assumes that an *independent* (x) variable is, at least in part, a cause of a *dependent* (y) variable.

Using SPSS to carry out a simple regression

For this example we will stick to one of the variables used in the correlation example (**siops**, the Standard International Occupational Prestige Scale). Here, the argument is that the amount of years of education a person has (**educyrs**) affects their ranking on the **siops**. So, **siops** is the dependent variable and **educyrs** is the independent variable.

Pull down the **Analyze** menu and select **Regression** and then **Linear....** A Linear Regression window like that in Figure 8.6 will come up.

Here, in order to have SPSS carry out a simple regression of the effect of years of education upon the ranking of the respondent's occupation, the variable **siops** has been placed in the **Dependent** box and the variable **educyrs** into the **Independent[s]:** box. When you click on **OK**, SPSS will carry out the regression and produce the output in Figure 8.7.

When reporting the regression it is good practice that you note and write the following statistics in any report. Though some may not seem relevant now it is common practice to provide information on all the following:

1. Look in the **Model Summary** box. R (*r*) (Pearson product–moment correlation) is .489;
2. R square (*r*²), the percentage variance that the two variables share (out of possible maximum of 100 per cent if the same variable in effect was correlated with itself), is calculated by squaring the *r* figure. In this example, this figure is .239, representing per cent of shared variance. Just under a quarter (23.9 per cent) of the variance in occupational prestige can be explained by years of education;

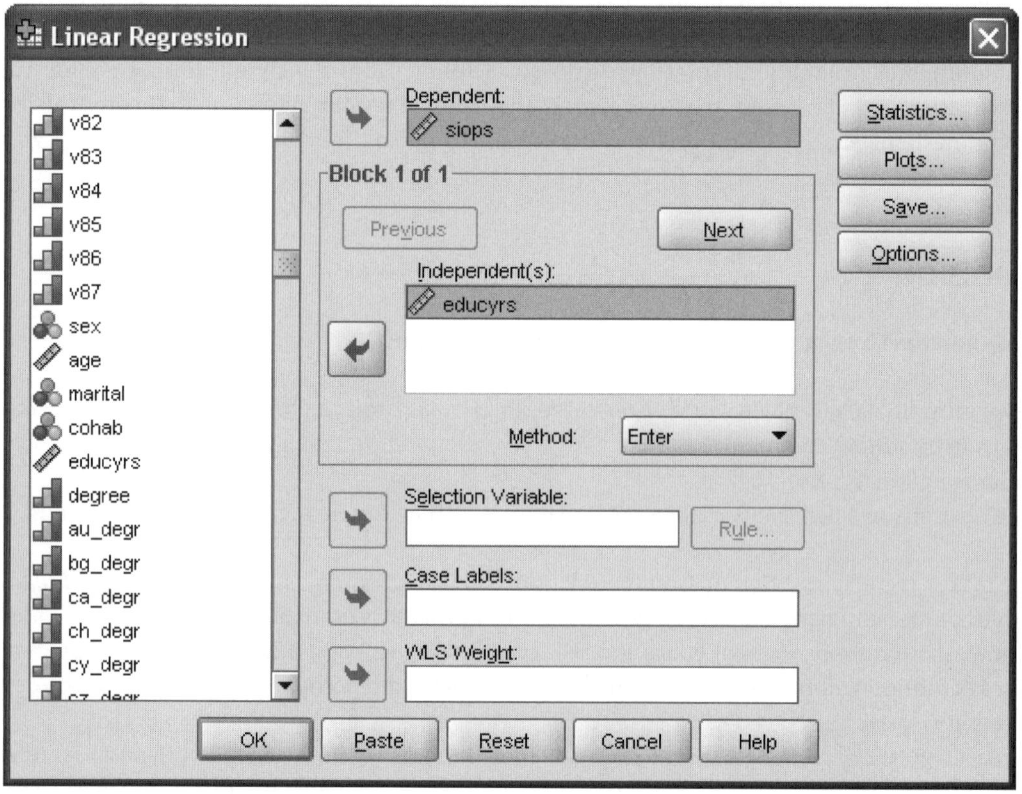

Figure 8.6 *Linear regression* window

Regression

Variables Entered/Removed[b]

Model	Variables Entered	Variables Removed	Method
1	**educyrs** R: Education I: years of schooling[a]	.	Enter

a. All requested variables entered.
b. Dependent Variable: **siops** Standard Occ Prestige Scale

Model Summary

Model	R	R Square	Adjusted R Square	Std. Error of the Estimate
1	.489[a]	.239	.238	12.70376

a. Predictors: (Constant), **educyrs** R: Education I: years of schooling

ANOVA[b]

Model		Sum of Squares	df	Mean Square	F	Sig.
1	Regression	64993.544	1	64993.544	402.722	.000[a]
	Residual	207057.620	1283	161.386		
	Total	272051.164	1284			

a. Predictors: (Constant), **educyrs** R: Education I: years of schooling
b. Dependent Variable: **siops** Standard Occ Prestige Scale

Coefficients[a]

Model		Unstandardized Coefficients		Standardized Coefficients	t	Sig.
		B	Std. Error	Beta		
1	(Constant)	14.100	1.362		10.352	.000
	educyrs R: Education I: years of schooling	2.260	.113	.489	20.068	.000

a. Dependent Variable: **siops** Standard Occ Prestige Scale

Figure 8.7   *Regression results*

3. adjusted R square. The r^2 figure may not always be reliable, and instead the adjusted r^2 figure is used. Here, at .238 it is very close to the unadjusted r^2 in the model summary box;
4. look in the **ANOVA^b** box. ANOVA is used to establish whether our findings might have arisen from a sampling error. Here we establish whether our regression line is different from zero. If it is, then we can claim that our findings have not arisen simply from a sampling error. In the present table (ANOVA) we look at the F and Sig columns. Here the F value is 402.722 and the confidence value $=.000$ (very significant, $p<0.005$). The result is not due to sampling error;
5. look in the **Coefficients** box. B is the slope of the regression line. For the present example on the **educyrs** row it is 2.260;
6. also in the coefficients box is a t value (20.068) and its confidence value (Sig.<0.0005). This shows you the statistical significance of the predictor value (in this case, it is highly significant).

The standard regression formula is: $y = a + bx$

This can be translated into English as: 'The value of the dependent variable (y) is predicted to be a constant (a) plus a coefficient (b) times the independent variable (x)'.

We can take the values from the table in Figure 8.7 and insert their values in the standard regression formula to produce: $y = 14.1 + 2.26x$

In terms of interpreting the results, we first note the statistic found for the slope, B $= +2.26$. This means that every rise of one unit for the independent variable **yrseduc** predicts a rise on the dependent variable **siops** of 2.26 units (that is, more education predicts a higher job ranking). The constant of 14.1 is the hypothetical predicted score of **siops** (occupational prestige units) if a respondent had no education at all (if **yrseduc** = 0). The Analysis of Variance shows that the regression result is significantly different from zero (F $= 402.7$, $p < 0.0005$). Hence, our result did not occur by chance and, consistent with our research hypothesis, the amount of years of education significantly raises the ranking of the respondent's occupation.

Multiple regression

Regression is a *multivariate* statistical technique. The regression equation can be extended to take in more than one independent causal x variable. We can depict this by extending the regression formula: $y = a + b_1x_1 + b_2x_2 + b_3x_3 + ... + b_nx_n$. Each independent variable x will explain some of the variance in the dependent variable y. To put it another way, multiple regression is testing the extent to which each independent x variable will play a part in predicting what the most likely value of the dependent variable y will be.

This is a great advantage because true models of social relationships can be tested by quantitative statistical estimation. However, there are two cautions.

1. The result produced by a multivariate computer program, such as a multiple regression result, will be *reliable* (since SPSS goes through a set mathematical routine in order to produce its results).
2. *But* it may not necessarily be *valid*. A change in the mathematical procedure *or* the independent, causal variables in the model could produce a different, equally reliable result. And, more significantly, like any statistical calculation program, SPSS cannot provide any information on the conceptual validity of the variables being included in a model. A poorly specified or just stupidly conceived model may produce a mathematically elegant solution.

Figure 8.8 attempts to depict visually the amount of variance in a single dependent variable y that three independent x variables could explain. Each circle in Figure 8.8 is intended to show a unique part

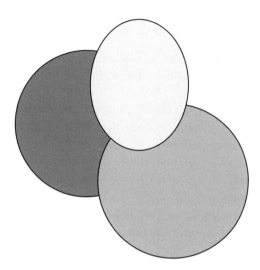

Figure 8.8   *How variables may overlap*

of the variance in y that is explained by each of three x variables (the part of each circle that does not overlap with the other two circles is meant to be the variance unique to each x variable). The problem, however, is that, as indicated by the overlap of the circles, some of the explained variance in y can be attributed to a combination of two or even all three of the x variables.

SPSS will apportion this shared variance between the three independent x variables; *but* the proportion of the variance that it 'gives' to each is no more than an 'educated guess' of how it should be divided up. If a large amount of the total variance is shared between the variables, a slight change in the mathematical (iterative) routine that apportions the shared variance can result in a radically different result. This problem, called multicollinearity, can be serious if two or more independent variables are too highly correlated with each other. If a large number of independent variables are being entered into a multivariate analysis, there is a good chance that some of them will be correlated.

An SPSS example of multiple regression

These ideas can be applied to our example of the effect of respondents' education (**educyrs**) on the standing of their job (**siops**). So far we have speculated that years of education influences occupational standing. However, obviously there may be variables other than education that also influence occupational standing. For example, age may be a causal factor. Older respondents have been in the labour market longer and have had longer in their careers to move up job ladders (alternatively, given the immense changes in Russia over the last decades, it may be that younger people may have job advantages due to entering directly into a post-socialist market economy). Similarly, people whose jobs earn high incomes can be expected to have jobs that consequently have a higher social status; those whose working conditions are unpleasant could be expected to be in jobs with low status (and the reverse, those whose working conditions are pleasant could be expected to be in jobs with higher status; and so on).

A multiple regression allows you work through these speculations by establishing which of a number of potential causal variables are most important by ascertaining which of the variables explain a significant amount of variance in the dependent variable that is unique (that is, variance that is not shared with one of the other independent variables). In summary, by using multiple regression, we can establish which of the independent factors (education, age, amount of income, pleasant or hard working conditions, etc.) might be important independent influences upon the respondents' occupational standing.

Producing a multiple regression with SPSS is basically the same as producing a simple regression. Pull down the <u>A</u>nalyze menu and select **Regression** and then **Linear....** A Linear Regression window like that in Figure 8.9 will come up.

As before, the variable **siops** is the dependent y variable. Here, however, instead of testing to establish the effect of a single independent variable, a number of other independent variables in addition to **educyrs** have been included in the regression:

- **age**: respondent's age in years;
- **ru_rinc**: respondent's earnings;
- **jobhard**: an index score of how unpleasant the respondent reports their working conditions to be;
- **jobgood**: an index score of how pleasant the respondent reports their working conditions to be;
- **hompop**: the number of persons living in the respondent's household.

To carry out this multiple regression, you put all six of the variables into the **Independent(s):** box. Click on **OK** and SPSS will carry out the multiple regression. The results can be seen in Figure 8.10.

All the columns of statistics are the same as with the simple linear regression, only now we will see the results for a number of independent variables combined.

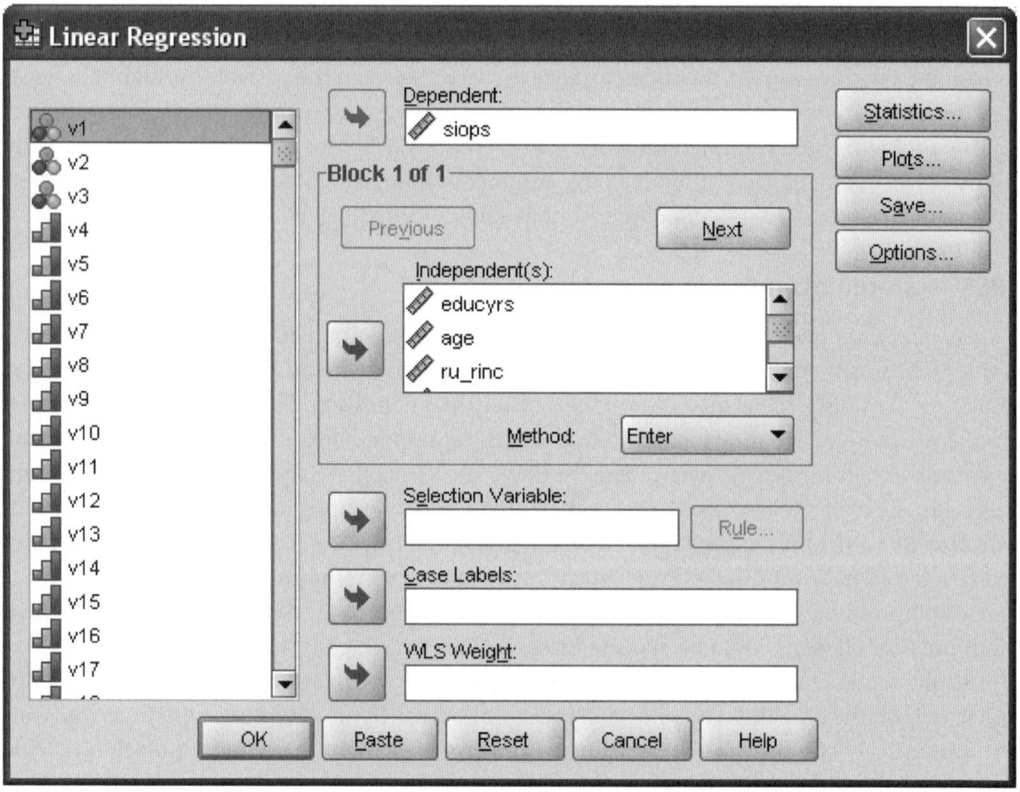

Figure 8.9 *Multivariate linear regression window*

Regression

Variables Entered/Removed[b]

Model	Variables Entered	Variables Removed	Method
1	**hompop** How many persons in household, **educyrs** R: Education I: years of schooling, **jobgood** Job has rewarding conditions, **jobhard** Job conditions hard, **age** R: Age, **ru_rinc** Respondent's Earnings: Russia[a]	.	Enter

a. All requested variables entered.
b. Dependent Variable: siops Standard Occ Prestige Scale

Model Summary

Model	R	R Square	Adjusted R Square	Std. Error of the Estimate
1	.556[a]	.310	.303	12.20652

a. Predictors: (Constant), hompop How many persons in household, educyrs R: Education I: years of schooling, jobgood Job has rewarding conditions, jobhard Job conditions hard, age R: Age, ru_rinc Respondent's Earnings: Russia

ANOVA[b]

Model		Sum of Squares	df	Mean Square	F	Sig.
1	Regression	43508.052	6	7251.342	48.667	.000[a]
	Residual	96998.410	651	148.999		
	Total	140506.462	657			

a. Predictors: (Constant), hompop How many persons in household, educyrs R: Education I: years of schooling, jobgood Job has rewarding conditions, jobhard Job conditions hard, age R: Age, ru_rinc Respondent's Earnings: Russia

Figure 8.10 *Multivariate regression results*

Coefficients[a]

Model	Unstandardized Coefficients		Standardized Coefficients		
	B	Std. Error	Beta	t	Sig.
1 (Constant)	12.676	3.182		3.983	.000
educyrs R: Education I: years of schooling	2.426	.185	.450	13.111	.000
age R: Age	.010	.040	.008	.250	.803
ru_rinc Respondent's Earnings: Russia	.000	.000	.074	2.083	.038
jobhard Job conditions hard	−1.985	.361	−.188	−5.498	.000
jobgood Job has rewarding conditions	.624	.353	.062	1.767	.078
hompop How many persons in household	−.943	.387	−.080	−2.436	.015

a. Dependent Variable: **siops** Standard Occ Prestige Scale

Figure 8.10 *Continued*

1. Look in the **Model Summary** box. Note that with additional predictive independent variables coming into the regression, the amount of explained variance (r^2) in the dependent variable (**siops**) has gone up; the 'Adjusted R Square' has risen from 23.8 per cent to 30.3 per cent (when there is more than one independent variable in a regression, 'adjusted r^2' gives a more accurate indication of the amount of explained variance).
2. Look in the **ANOVA**[b] box. As in the univariate regression the value of F shows us that the regression statistic was significantly different from zero (F = 48.667, $p<0.0005$). We can be confident that our results did not occur by chance.
3. Look in the **Coefficients** box. Here, we now are able to determine the *relative importance* (by using the statistics in the Sig. column) of each of the independent variables in accounting for variance in the respondents' occupational standings (**siops**). We discover the following things regarding our independent variables.
4. Consistent with our earlier finding, we find that the respondents' education (**educyrs**) continues to explain a significant amount of variance in their occupational standing (Sig. = .000, $p<0.0005$). The direction of the effect is as before, more education predicts the respondents will have a higher occupational ranking.
5. In addition, we also discover that some of the other independent variables also have significant effects upon occupational standing:

- **jobhard** is the next most important (Sig. = .000, $p < 0.0005$). For each increase of one unit on the **jobhard** index, the equation predicts that occupational standing will *drop* by almost two units (−1.985);
- **hompop** has a significant effect, though the level of significance is lower (Sig.=.015, $p < 0.015$). For each extra person in the respondent's household, the equation predicts that, on average, the respondent's occupational ranking index will drop by almost one unit (−.943);

- finally, **ru_rinc**, the respondent's income also has a significant effect, though the level of significance just makes it below the 0.05 cut-off (Sig. = .038). Higher earnings is linked to higher occupational ranking. (You might be puzzled by the value of the Unstandardized Coefficient, B, for **ru_rinc** being '.000'. Remember, however, that the literal meaning of 'B' is 'the amount of change in the dependent variable y caused by an increase of one unit in the independent variable x'. Here, **ru_rinc** is expressed in roubles. While increased income does have the effect of raising occupational standing, *one* rouble is a minuscule amount, so the effect of 1 rouble on the dependent variable, **siops**, will be tiny.)

7. Continue to look in the **Coefficients** box. Note that, *once the effects of the other independent variables have been taken into account*, two of the independent variables do *not* exert significant effects upon the dependent variable.

- **jobgood**, the index of whether the respondent's job has rewarding working conditions, is just over the 0.05 cut-off (Sig. = .078);
- **age** with Sig. = .803 (that is, an over 80 per cent chance that any effect is spurious) is completely eliminated.

Therefore, in summary, a number of independent variables – **educyrs**, **jobhard**, **hompop** and **ru_rinc** – account for unique variance in the dependent variable **siops**, but also two of the independent variables – **jobgood** and **age** – have no statistically significant effect.

To return to the general format for the multiple regression formula, $y = a + b_1x_1 + b_2x_2 + b_3x_3 + ... + b_nx_n$. we can put the individual significant variables into the equation and depict the result like this: **siops** = 12.676 + 2.426**educyrs** –1.985**jobhard** – 0.943**hompop** + 0.000**ru_rinc**. For instance, if a person had 10 years of education, a score of +2 on the **jobhard** index, lived with 3 other people in their household and had an income of 6500 roubles, the equation's prediction for **siops**, the ranking of their occupation, would be **18.404** (= 24.26 + (2.426*10) –3.97 (–1.985*2) –1,886 (–0.943*4) + 0 (+0.000*6500).

In effect, what we have done with the multiple regression is to test six hypotheses: whether, once the effect of the other independent variables are taken into account, each independent variable has a significant effect upon the dependent variable. The results were the following.

- Education in years has an independent effect, raising the amount of occupational standing of the respondent (CONFIRMED, highly significant).
- Hard working conditions has an independent effect, lowering the amount of occupational standing of the respondent (CONFIRMED, highly significant).
- Number of people in the household has an independent effect, lowering the amount of occupational standing of the respondent (CONFIRMED, significant).
- Amount of the respondent's earnings has an independent effect, raising the amount of occupational standing of the respondent (CONFIRMED, but barely significant).
- Does rewarding job conditions have an independent effect, raising the amount of occupational standing of the respondent? (REJECTED, not quite significant).
- Does age have an independent effect on the amount of occupational standing of the respondent? (REJECTED, not significant at all).

Further considerations

Standardized coefficients

In multiple regression, the 'Standardized Coefficients (Beta)' column in the output becomes important. Remember that the literal interpretation of 'B', the unstandardized coefficient, is 'the amount of change in y caused by a change of one unit in x'. If an x variable has values that are much higher or lower than the dependent y variable or the other independent x variables, the values taken by B for different independent variables in a multiple regression solution can be wildly different. This can make direct comparison between different independent variables quite difficult. (Our above example illustrates this very clearly, where **ru_rinc** (respondent's income in roubles) is significant but B paradoxically apparently is zero (.000). Even though **ru_rinc** is significant, it is in effect impossible to compare its B coefficient directly with the other variables because its values are so different.) Regression coefficients for the independent variables in a regression equation can be standardized so that each independent variable has a mean of zero and a standard deviation of one. The effect of this is to place the 'betas' for different variables onto basically the same scale and make comparison between the 'betas' for different variables much more direct and easier. 'Standardized' regression coefficients (normally) will range between +1.00 and –1.00 like correlation coefficients.

Note how the standardized 'betas' in our example above are much more directly comparable than their unstandardized counterparts. The largest standardized 'beta' is .450 for **educyrs**, the most statistically significant independent variable. This is followed by **jobhard** at –.188, which is still highly statistically significant (although the effect upon the dependent variable is less strong). This is followed by **hompop** at –.080 and finally by **ru_rinc**, the smallest significant coefficient with a beta of .074. Note how we now can compare the standardized **ru_rinc** coefficient directly with the other variables. The two non-significant variables, **jobgood** and **age**, then follow with smaller standardized betas of .062 and .008, respectively.

'Listwise' vs. 'Pairwise' deletion of missing cases

In simple regression, if either variable has a missing value, the case in question is excluded from the analysis. The default for multiple regression, however, is 'listwise' deletion of cases: if *any* of the variables used in the multiple regression has a missing value, the case is deleted. Problems can arise if different variables all have only a small proportion of missing values *but* each case has its values being missing on *different* variables.

For example, let us say you have six variables in your multiple regression and each of these six variables has 10 per cent missing values. If it is the same 10 per cent of cases that have the 10 per cent missing values for all six variables, you lose only about 10 per cent of the cases from the analysis – no big problem. *But*, if *different* cases have missing values on *different* variables, you could find SPSS deleting up to <u>60 per cent</u> of the cases from the analysis:

10% + 10% + 10% + 10% + 10% + 10% = 60% – a big problem!

One way around this is to use 'pairwise' deletion of cases: basically, SPSS computes a correlation matrix on its way to producing a multiple regression result. With 'pairwise' deletion, SPSS is told to use the correlations in the matrix with only those cases being excluded from calculating the correlations when one or the other variable in each individual correlation is missing. So, with 10 per cent missing values in each of six variables, the maximum loss of cases from any single correlation would be 20 per cent (10 per cent + 10 per cent).

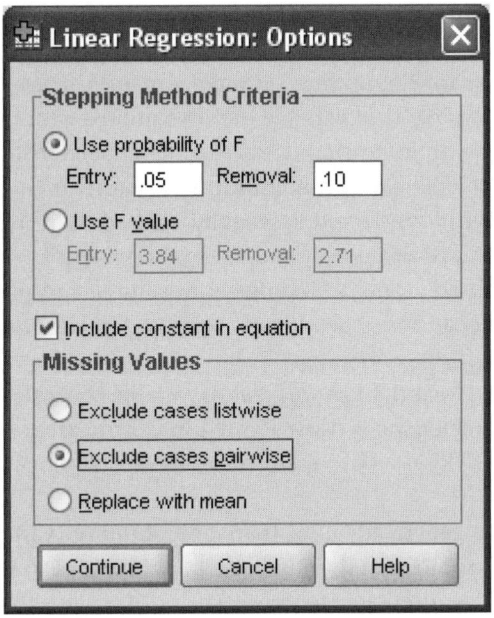

Figure 8.11 *Linear regression: Options sub-window with 'Exclude cases pairwise'*

You can obtain 'pairwise' deletion by clicking on the **Options...** button in the Linear Regression window. A Linear Regression: Options window like that in Figure 8.11 will come up. As has been done here, click the **Exclude cases pairwise** button in the **Missing Values** box, then on the **Continue** button to get back to the Linear Regression window.

We have introduced 'Pairwise' vs. 'Listwise' deletion of cases here with the multiple regression procedure, but note that the problem of losing a large proportion of cases applies to *any* multivariate procedure. Version 17 of SPSS is introducing a new way of dealing with the problem of multiple missing cases by providing what amounts to allowing SPSS Statistics to use regression-like prediction in order to make an 'educated guess' as to what the missing values of a variable might be.

'Dummy' variables

By now you see how regression is a powerful means of carrying out a causal analysis. As you may note from the introduction to this module on correlation, there is, however, a significant limitation: linear regression assumes scalar (normally, interval or ratio) variables in which the values are numeric in character. The statistic is *robust* (that is, it can tolerate some violation of its assumptions) so that, thanks to the Central Limit Theorum, if we have a reasonably large sample size (100 cases or more) it is possible to introduce ordinal variables into regression, particularly as independent variables. However, this cannot extend to nominal/categorical variables in which the codings have no implicit numerical sense.

For instance, there is a categorical variable in the Russian dataset, **ru_reg**, that breaks the country down into seven geographic regions. These are coded 1 to 7 but obviously these number codes have no numerical meaning. At the same time, due to differences in wealth, economic structure, etc., we might expect that people living in some regions would tend to have jobs of a higher or lower occupational ranking than people in other regions and that this 'region effect' could be separate from the effects of the other independent variables in our example above. Just inserting the **ru_reg** variable as it stands into the regression as an independent variable would be an absolute nonsense. What is required is a way of legitimately bringing categorical variables into regression analyses.

Thankfully, there is a means for doing this: 'dummy' variables. These rather curiously named variables are created by recoding a categorical variable into two groups with the code '1' indicating *presence* of a characteristic and the code '0' indicating *absence* of the characteristic. For instance, gender could be recoded into a 'dummy' variable called **maledummy** in which men are coded '1' and women are coded '0'. The resulting variable is considered to be quasi-numerical in that people coded '1' absolutely possess the characteristic 'manness' and people coded '0' (also known as women) absolutely do not possess the characteristic. (We ask the reader to indulge our example and please overlook the last quarter century's theorization of gender and transgender and hark back to a simpler time when men were men and women were women.)

In the example in Figures 8.12a and 8.12b we create a variable **centraldummy** from the original variable **ru_reg**, in which the characteristic is those located in central areas contrasted with the rest. Note how we can use the statement, 'Else = 0' to easily generate the 'absence' category. Figure 8.12c shows the before and after results.

Notice that we could have generated more than one 'dummy' variable based upon the Russian regions. For instance, a 'Far East/Siberian dummy' also could have been constructed in contrast to the rest of the country. It is perfectly acceptable to do so. The only proviso that needs to be kept in mind is that there always must be one group of substantial size that is never made into a 'dummy' variable. If all the categories of the original variable are made into separate 'dummies', a causal analysis that tries to include them all will crash.

In addition, to make it easier to discuss results (and to think about them) it is good practice to make the unused 'comparator' category a group that is logically sensible against which to contrast all the

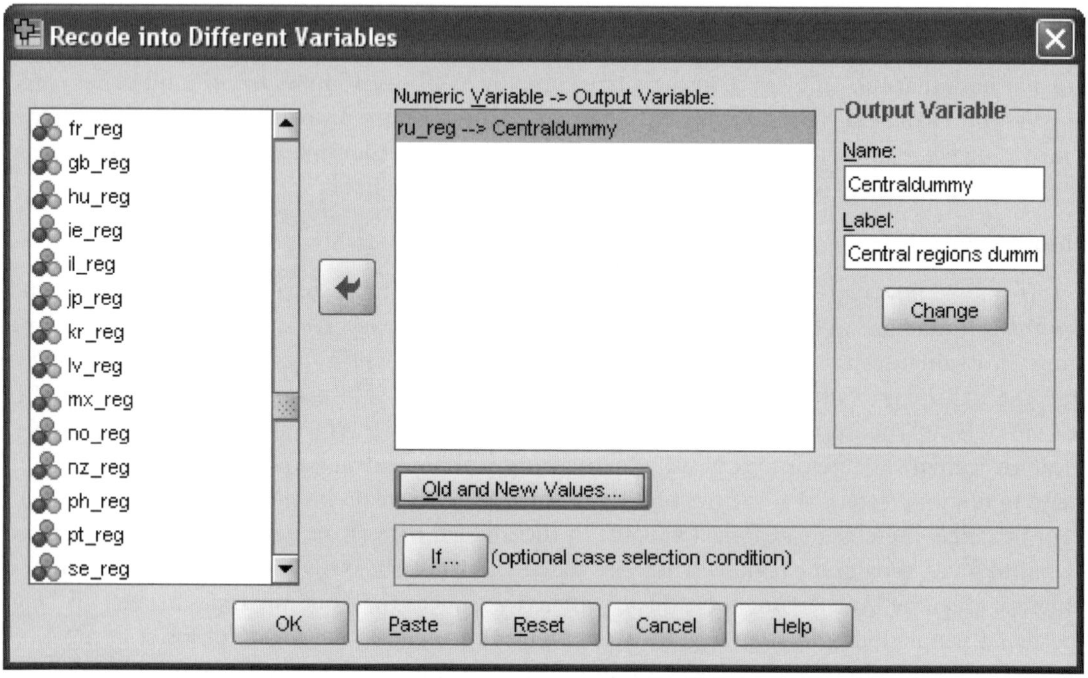

Figure 8.12a *Creating a dummy variable, **Centraldummy**, through Recode*

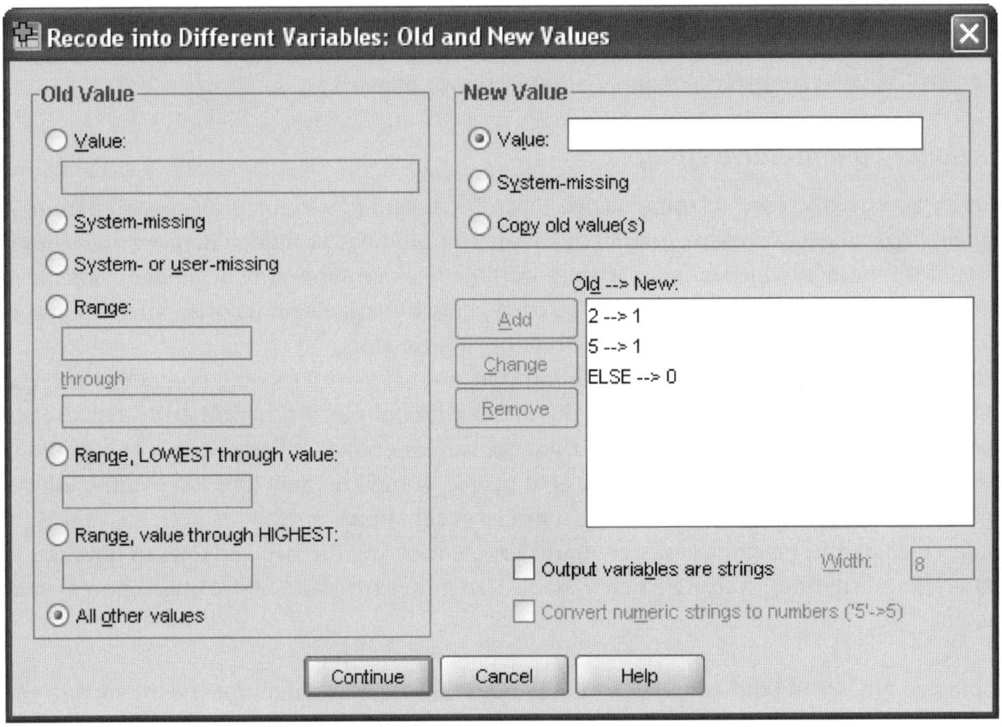

Figure 8.12b   *Recoding **ru_reg** values in dummy values*

'Before' ru_reg Region: Russia

		Frequency	Percent	Valid Percent	Cumulative Percent
Valid	1 North-West (Severo-Zapadnyi)	158	9.8	9.8	9.8
	2 Central	446	27.8	27.8	37.6
	3 Southern	205	12.8	12.8	50.4
	4 Povolzhskiy	354	22.1	22.1	72.5
	5 Ural	143	8.9	8.9	81.4
	6 Siberian	224	14.0	14.0	95.3
	7 Far East	75	4.7	4.7	100.0
	Total	1605	100.0	100.0	

'After' Centraldummy Central regions dummy

		Frequency	Percent	Valid Percent	Cumulative Percent
Valid	.00 Other regions	1016	63.3	63.3	63.3
	1.00 Central or Ural	589	36.7	36.7	100.0
	Total	1605	100.0	100.0	

Figure 8.12c   *Before and after variables, original and 'dummy'*

dummy variables. For instance, if you were creating a series of 'dummy' variables based on marital status, the 'dummies' might be: (1) 'Married or living together as a couple'; (2) 'Separated or divorced'; (3) 'Widowed'. A good comparator would be 'Single, never married'.

Interactions of quantitative variables

As we have already discussed to some degree towards the end of Module 5, 'Crosstabulation' and in 'Interaction effects' under 'Two-way Analysis of Variance in Module 7, causal variables can *interact* so that the effect of two or more independent variables working *in concert* upon the dependent variable may be different from the simple additive effect of each independent variable on its own. Interactions between two quantitative variables are of particular relevance to regression.

For instance, in our above example, we found that education and income both affect occupational ranking with both raising the predicted rank. One additionally could hypothesize that the effect of these two variables together might be more than the sum of each effect singly; that is, it could be that the effect on the job rankings of highly educated people in high income jobs is a *multiple* effect rather than a simple addition so that they make up a special occupational elite.

This interaction effect is quite easily computed by multiplying the two variables in question (in this case, **educyrs** and **ru_rinc**) to create a new variable that is an expression of the interaction of education and income.

- People that are low in both education and income will have low values for the interaction variable.
- People that are in the middle range for both variables will have middle range values for the interaction variable.
- People who are high on one variable and low on the other *also* will have middle range values for the interaction variable.
- People who are high on both variables will have extremely higher values on the interaction value since their value for the interaction will be the multiplicative product of two large numbers.

'Dummy' variables also can be used in the creation of quantitative interaction variables, but the generation and interpretation of the resulting variable takes some care. For instance, we can produce an interaction of being male and having a high income by multiplying **ru_inc** by **maledummy**. The resulting interaction variable will be coded 'zero' for all women but will have the values for personal income for all men. If it then appears to have a significant effect as an independent variable in a regression, the interpretation would be that there is some 'extra' effect of higher income for men that does not apply for women.

Finally, two 'dummy' variables may be multiplied together to generate a variable that represents their interaction. In this case, the caution about taking care in the generation and interpretation of the resulting interaction still applies, only doubly so. This is illustrated in Figure 8.13 using our two existing 'dummies':

	Maledummy	
Centraldummy	Male (= 1)	Female (= 0)
Central (= 1)	1	0
All other regions (= 0)	0	0

Figure 8.13 *Generating an interaction variable from two 'dummy' variables*

Here, the interaction variable can only take the value '1' for men located in the central regions. All others, men in other regions and all women, have a value of '0'. If this variable then appears to have a significant effect as an independent variable in a regression, the interpretation would be that there is some 'extra' effect of being a man located in the Central regions that does not apply to men in other regions or to women no matter where they are located. (Note how the value that is coded as '1' (presence of the characteristics) is dependent upon which category of each generating 'dummy' variable is coded as '1'. If you were interested in a different combination, you would have to use generating dummy variables with different codes for '1'.)

Method

The default method of carrying out a regression is to have SPSS enter all of the variables into the regression equation simultaneously. This default is called 'Enter' and is the one we have used above.

There are other ways of introducing independent x variables into a regression equation. The one you might want to consider is called 'Stepwise', where the x variables that have a significant effect upon the dependent y variable are put in one at a time (that is, 'step by step'), starting with the most significant, until none are left. A fairly lengthy printout results where you can see the effect that each variable has upon the overall result as it is added in. The final solution of the 'stepwise' procedure will be the inclusion of all independent variables in the regression equation that SPSS finds to have a statistically significant effect upon the dependent variable.

'Stepwise' is handy if there are a lot of independent variables since those variables that are initially most significant will get 'first shot' at explaining the variance in the dependent variable. The net result tends to be a somewhat more parsimonious solution than that produced by the 'Enter' method with a smaller number of variables each explaining proportionately more variance.

'Stepwise' is also useful if you suspect there may be multicollinearity with a lot of variance being shared between the independent x variables. By looking at how the coefficients change as each new variable is added in turn and observing how the relative strengths of the effects of the remaining independent x variables change, it is possible to spot variables that are correlated – if the addition of a new variable generates some drastic shifts in the coefficients of other variables, they probably are linked in some way.

An SPSS example of stepwise multiple regression with diagnostics

Figure 8.14a shows the top Linear Regression window, only this time we are requesting the 'Stepwise' Method of entry for independent variables. Also, this example now includes the new 'dummy' and 'interaction' variables that were introduced in the previous section.

Figure 8.14b shows the 'Results of a stepwise multiple regression with dummy and interaction variables'. Note that in the **Variables Entered/Removed** box we now have six models instead of just one. The stepwise procedure goes through six steps, adding a new variable each time and hence produces six models. (In our example, the stepwise procedure has only added variables and has not dropped any variables. This is not unusual. Variables are only dropped if their coefficient becomes non-significant due to the effects of other, additional, independent variables that are added in during later steps. This is a fairly rare occurrence.)

The **Model Summary** box shows how the general 'fit' of the regression improves with each step from Model 1 to Model 6. Note how the 'Adjusted R Square' gradually rises from 26.0 per cent to 32.4 per cent of explained variance in the dependent variable, **siops**. The Durbin–Watson statistic that appears at the

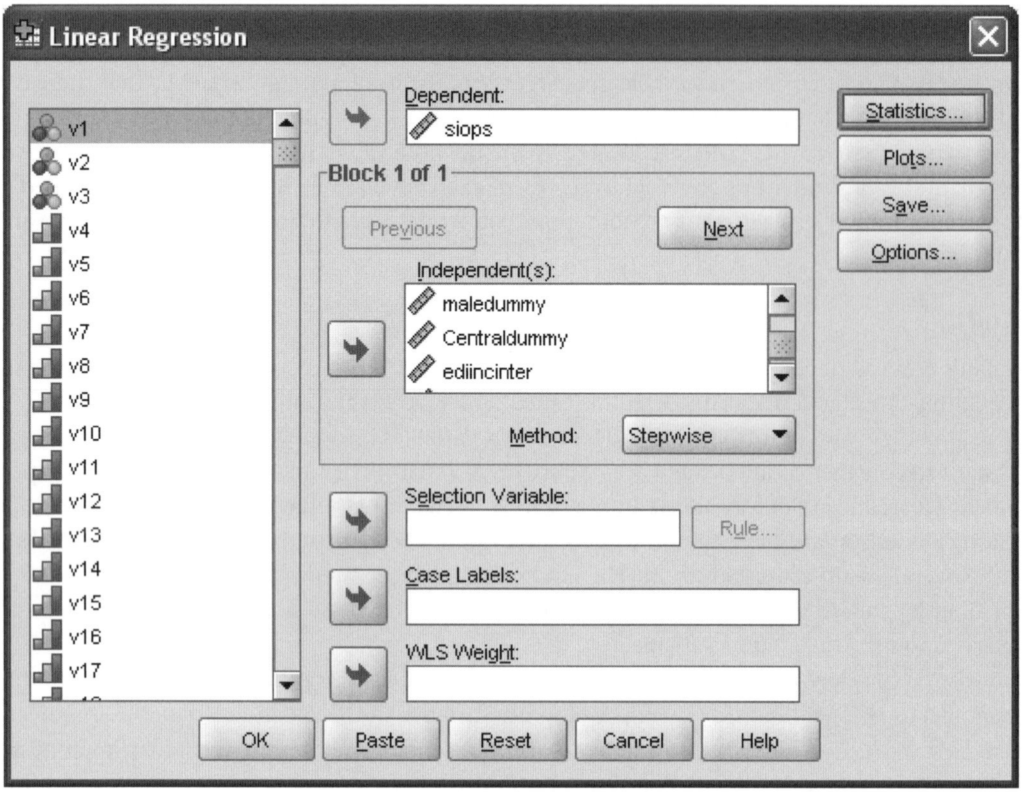

Figure 8.14a *Stepwise multiple regression with interaction variables and residual analysis*

final stage is an indicator of the overall extent of multicollinearity between the variables. If it is less than 1.0, there may be problems. Here it is well above that at 1.905, so we are on safe grounds.

The **ANOVA** box is as before, only with the six models shown now. The fit remains acceptable throughout. The **Coefficients** box is the real core of the results. If you look down the models, you can see the order that SPSS chose independent variables for inclusion and how the inclusion of each new variable slightly alters the coefficients of the variables that are already in.

The final solution in the **Coefficients** box is Model 6, on page 229. The basic pattern in Model 6 is not radically different from the solution we had with the 'Enter' method in the previous example. While the coefficients differ slightly, all of the variables from the 'Enter' reappear, and **jobgood**, which was just excluded last time, manages to squeak in at $p < 0.03$. Of all the new 'dummy' and 'interaction' variables, only **maledummy** is significant. Interestingly, being a man implies a quite substantial *drop* in likely standing of one's occupation.

In a similar way to following the inclusion of variables in the **Coefficients** box, you can also trace the variables that are left out of models in the **Excluded Variables** box. Again, the final sub-box for Model 6, on page 231 is the most informative. None of the excluded variables at the stage of the final solution are anywhere near statistical significance.

Regression

Variables Entered/Removed[a]

Model	Variables Entered	Variables Removed	Method
1	**educyrs** R: Education I: years of schooling		Stepwise (Criteria: Probability-of-F-to-enter <= .050, Probability-of-F-to-remove >= .100).
2	**jobhard** Job conditions hard		Stepwise (Criteria: Probability-of-F-to-enter <= .050, Probability-of-F-to-remove >= .100).
3	**maledummy** Dummy variable for males		Stepwise (Criteria: Probability-of-F-to-enter <= .050, Probability-of-F-to-remove >= .100).
4	**ru_rinc** Respondent's Earnings: Russia		Stepwise (Criteria: Probability-of-F-to-enter <= .050, Probability-of-F-to-remove >= .100).
5	**hompop** How many persons in household		Stepwise (Criteria: Probability-of-F-to-enter <= .050, Probability-of-F-to-remove >= .100).
6	**jobgood** Job has rewarding conditions		Stepwise (Criteria: Probability-of-F-to-enter <= .050, Probability-of-F-to-remove >= .100).

a. Dependent Variable: **siops** Standard Occ Prestige Scale

Model Summary[g]

Model	R	R Square	Adjusted R Square	Std. Error of the Estimate	R Square Change	F Change	df1	df2	Sig. F Change	Durbin-Watson
						Change Statistics				
1	.511[a]	.261	.260	12.58186	.261	231.578	1	656	.000	
2	.541[b]	.293	.291	12.31680	.032	29.538	1	655	.000	
3	.550[c]	.303	.300	12.23684	.010	9.588	1	654	.002	
4	.563[d]	.317	.313	12.12007	.014	13.662	1	653	.000	

Figure 8.14b *Results of stepwise multiple regression with interaction variables and residual analysis*

Model Summary^g *(Continue)*

Model	R	R Square	Adjusted R Square	Std. Error of the Estimate	Change Statistics					Durbin-Watson
					R Square Change	F Change	df1	df2	Sig. F Change	
5	.570[e]	.325	.320	12.06120	.008	7.390	1	652	.007	
6	.574[f]	.330	.324	12.02689	.005	4.726	1	651	.030	1.905

a. Predictors: (Constant), educyrs R: Education I: years of schooling
b. Predictors: (Constant), educyrs R: Education I: years of schooling, jobhard Job conditions hard
c. Predictors: (Constant), educyrs R: Education I: years of schooling, jobhard Job conditions hard, maledummy Dummy variable for males
d. Predictors: (Constant), educyrs R: Education I: years of schooling, jobhard Job conditions hard, maledummy Dummy variable for males, ru_rinc Respondent's Earnings: Russia
e. Predictors: (Constant), educyrs R: Education I: years of schooling, jobhard Job conditions hard, maledummy Dummy variable for males, ru_rinc Respondent's Earnings: Russia, hompop How many persons in household
f. Predictors: (Constant), **educyrs** R: Education I: years of schooling, **jobhard** Job conditions hard, **maledummy** Dummy variable for males, **ru_rinc** Respondent's Earnings: Russia, **hompop** How many persons in household, **jobgood** Job has rewarding conditions
g. Dependent Variable: **siops** Standard Occ Prestige Scale

ANOVA^g

Model		Sum of Squares	df	Mean Square	F	Sig.
1	Regression	36659.593	1	36659.593	231.578	.000[a]
	Residual	103846.869	656	158.303		
	Total	140506.462	657			
2	Regression	41140.580	2	20570.290	135.595	.000[b]
	Residual	99365.882	655	151.704		
	Total	140506.462	657			
3	Regression	42576.348	3	14192.116	94.778	.000[c]
	Residual	97930.114	654	149.740		
	Total	140506.462	657			

		Sum of Squares	df	Mean Square	F	Sig.
4	Regression	44583.310	4	11145.828	75.876	.000[d]
	Residual	95923.152	653	146.896		
	Total	140506.462	657			
5	Regression	45658.292	5	9131.658	62.772	.000[e]
	Residual	94848.170	652	145.473		
	Total	140506.462	657			
6	Regression	46341.939	6	7723.657	53.397	.000[f]
	Residual	94164.523	651	144.646		
	Total	140506.462	657			

a. Predictors: (Constant), educyrs R: Education I: years of schooling

b. Predictors: (Constant), educyrs R: Education I: years of schooling, jobhard Job conditions hard

c. Predictors: (Constant), educyrs R: Education I: years of schooling, jobhard Job conditions hard, maledummy Dummy variable for males

d. Predictors: (Constant), educyrs R: Education I: years of schooling, jobhard Job conditions hard, maledummy Dummy variable for males, ru_rinc Respondent's Earnings: Russia

e. Predictors: (Constant), educyrs R: Education I: years of schooling, jobhard Job conditions hard, maledummy Dummy variable for males, ru_rinc Respondent's Earnings: Russia, hompop How many persons in household

f. Predictors: (Constant), educyrs R: Education I: years of schooling, jobhard Job conditions hard, maledummy Dummy variable for males, ru_rinc Respondent's Earnings: Russia, hompop How many persons in household, jobgood Job has rewarding conditions

g. Dependent Variable: siops Standard Occ Prestige Scale

Figure 8.14b   *Continued*

Coefficients[a]

Model		Unstandardized Coefficients		Standardized Coefficients	t	Sig.	Collinearity Statistics	
		B	Std. Error	Beta			Tolerance	VIF
1	(Constant)	7.173	2.317		3.096	.002		
	educyrs R: Education I: years of schooling	2.754	.181	.511	15.218	.000	1.000	1.000
2	(Constant)	10.202	2.336		4.368	.000		
	educyrs R: Education I: years of schooling	2.522	.182	.468	13.841	.000	.945	1.058
	jobhard Job conditions hard	-1.937	.356	-.184	-5.435	.000	.945	1.058
3	(Constant)	11.816	2.378		4.968	.000		
	educyrs R: Education I: years of schooling	2.513	.181	.466	13.878	.000	.945	1.058
	jobhard Job conditions hard	-1.572	.373	-.149	-4.214	.000	.851	1.175
	maledummy Dummy variable for males	-3.128	1.010	-.107	-3.097	.002	.893	1.120
4	(Constant)	11.982	2.356		5.085	.000		
	educyrs R: Education I: years of schooling	2.360	.184	.438	12.822	.000	.897	1.115
	jobhard Job conditions hard	-1.658	.370	-.157	-4.477	.000	.848	1.180
	maledummy Dummy variable for males	-4.236	1.044	-.145	-4.056	.000	.819	1.221
	ru_rinc Respondent's Earnings: Russia	.000	.000	.128	3.696	.000	.866	1.154

Model								
5	(Constant)	15.298	2.643		5.788	.000		
	educyrs R: Education I: years of schooling	2.347	.183	.435	12.810	.000	.897	1.115
	jobhard Job conditions hard	-1.575	.370	-.149	-4.259	.000	.842	1.188
	maledummy Dummy variable for males	-4.417	1.042	-.151	-4.241	.000	.816	1.226
	ru_rinc Respondent's Earnings: Russia	.000	.000	.137	3.957	.000	.858	1.165
	hompop How many persons in household	-1.034	.381	-.088	-2.718	.007	.983	1.018
6	(Constant)	15.781	2.645		5.967	.000		
	educyrs R: Education I: years of schooling	**2.362**	.183	.438	12.919	.000	.895	1.117
	jobhard Job conditions hard	**-1.517**	.370	-.144	-4.104	.000	.838	1.194
	maledummy Dummy variable for males	**-4.624**	1.043	-.158	-4.434	.000	.809	1.236
	ru_rinc Respondent's Earnings: Russia	**.000**	.000	.114	3.148	.002	.783	1.277
	hompop How many persons in household	**-1.068**	.380	-.091	-2.812	.005	.981	1.019
	jobgood Job has rewarding conditions	**.746**	.343	.074	2.174	.030	.880	1.137

a. Dependent Variable: siops Standard Occ Prestige Scale

Figure 8.14b   *Continued*

Excluded Variables[d]

Model		Beta In	t	Sig.	Partial Correlation	Collinearity Statistics		
						Tolerance	VIF	Minimum Tolerance
1	age R: Age	.020[a]	.603	.547	.024	1.000	1.000	1.000
	ru_rinc Respondent's Earnings: Russia	.057[a]	1.683	.093	.066	.968	1.033	.968
	jobhard Job conditions hard	-.184[a]	-5.435	.000	-.208	.945	1.058	.945
	jobgood Job has rewarding conditions	.078[a]	2.328	.020	.091	.999	1.001	.999
	hompop How many persons in household	-.086[a]	-2.571	.010	-.100	.999	1.001	.999
	maledummy Dummy variable for males	-.153[a]	-4.606	.000	-.177	.992	1.009	.992
	Centraldummy Central regions dummy	.015[a]	.447	.655	.017	.999	1.001	.999
	ediincinter Interaction of Education & Income	.062[a]	1.717	.087	.067	.861	1.162	.861
	maleincinter Male & Income interaction	-.052[a]	-1.548	.122	-.060	.999	1.001	.999
	centmaleinter Central male interaction	-.062[a]	-1.835	.067	-.072	.996	1.004	.996

For reasons of space, Models 2–4 have been removed from the Excluded Variables table.

Model	Predictor	B	t	Sig.	Beta	Tolerance	VIF	
5	age R: Age	-.006[b]	-.192	.848	-.008	.954	1.048	.815
	jobgood Job has rewarding conditions	.074[b]	2.174	.030	.085	.880	1.137	.783
	Centraldummy Central regions dummy	.002[b]	.067	.946	.003	.994	1.006	.815
	ediincinter Interaction of Education & Income	-.175[b]	-.994	.320	-.039	.033	29.954	.033
	maleincinter Male & Income interaction	-.044[b]	-.559	.576	-.022	.166	6.023	.166
	centmaleinter Central male interaction	.007[b]	.198	.843	.008	.779	1.284	.681
6	age R: Age	.007[c]	.211	.833	.008	.922	1.085	.782
	Centraldummy Central regions dummy	-.001[c]	-.031	.975	-.001	.992	1.008	.781
	edincinter Interaction of Education & Income	-.122[c]	-.685	.493	-.027	**.033**	**30.613**	.033
	maleincinter Male & Income interaction	-.034[c]	-.427	.669	-.017	.165	6.046	.165
	centmaleinter Central male interaction	.005[c]	.136	.892	.005	.778	1.285	.678

a. Predictors in the Model: (Constant), educyrs R: Education I: years of schooling

b. Predictors in the Model: (Constant), educyrs R: Education I: years of schooling, jobhard Job conditions hard, maledummy Dummy variable for males, ru_rinc Respondent's Earnings: Russia, hompop How many persons in household

c. Predictors in the Model: (Constant), educyrs R: Education I: years of schooling, jobhard Job conditions hard, maledummy Dummy variable for males, ru_rinc Respondent's Earnings: Russia, hompop How many persons in household, jobgood Job has rewarding conditions

d. Dependent Variable: siops Standard Occ Prestige Scale

Figure 8.14b *Continued*

Testing for multicollinearity

In addition to the Durbin–Watson statistic, it is also possible to ascertain whether there are multicollinearity problems between individual variables. We do this by bringing up the Linear Regression: Statistics … sub-window and ticking the **Durbin–Watson** and **Collinearity diagnostics** boxes. This brings up the two 'Collinearity Statistics' columns, 'Tolerance' and 'VIF', that appear on the right-hand side in the **Coefficients** and **Excluded Variables** boxes in the output. As a rule of thumb, if 'Tolerance' is greater than .4 and 'VIF' is less than 10, we are on safe grounds. Looking at Model 6 in the **Coefficients** box, we can see that there is no cause for alarm. Interestingly, if we look at the **Variables Excluded** for Model 6, you will note that **ediincinter**, the interaction of education and income, does appear potentially very problematic with a Tolerance of .033 and a VIF of 30.613, both vastly beyond the acceptable margins. Given that this variable is made up of a composite of two other variables that do appear in the solution, it is not surprising that it is correlated with them. Fortunately, it does not come anywhere close to being included in the regression solution.

Residual analysis

There is one final topic we need to consider before closing this module. As we now know, the final regression solution is an equation that predicts the likely value of the dependent variable for any given combination of values on the independent variables. It can be considered to be a (very) 'educated guess' that has been arrived at through careful statistical analysis of patterns in the data. However, the predicted values of the dependent variable are estimates of the most likely average figure – the actual cases in the data will not all correspond exactly to what the equation predicts. The predicted values are the 'fit' to the data that the regression has produced. The difference between the values of the dependent variable that are predicted by that 'fit' and the actual observed values are the 'residual', that which is not 'fit'. In a good 'fit' to the data, the residual differences between the actual, observed values and the predicted values will be homoscedastic, normally distributed above and below the predicted value with most differences being fairly small and only a few, if any, being 'outliers' that are far from their predicted values.

As you would expect, SPSS has procedures that allow us to analyse the residuals. 'Casewise diagnostics', locating any individual cases that diverge widely from their predicted value, are procured by ticking the appropriate box in the Linear Regression: Statistics sub-window in Figure 8.14c. Visual plots of residuals are produced by bringing up the Linear Regression: Plots sub-window shown in Figure 8.14d by ticking the **Plots** … button on the main Linear Regression window. Here, we ask for a **Histogram** of residuals and a **Normal probability plot**.

The **Casewise Diagnostics** box in Figure 8.14e shows us that there is one person, Case Number 14770, whose actual value for the dependent variable **siops** (a '20') varies widely from the value that the equation predicts (a '65'). We could remove this 'outlier' case and recompute the analysis. However, one case out of over 600 is not a disaster and, since the person probably is a legitimate case (most likely someone with a large amount years of education who is in a low status job), we decided to leave it in.

The visual plots of residuals appear in Figures 8.14f and 8.14g. Residuals should be normally distributed around a central point of zero. The histogram in Figure 8.11f reflects this ideal pattern quite well.

The scatterplot of standardized residuals against standardized predicted values should take the form of a straight line running at a 45 degree angle from (0,0) on the lower left to (1.0,1.0) on the upper right. As we can observe in Figure 8.14g, the actual plot conforms very closely to this.

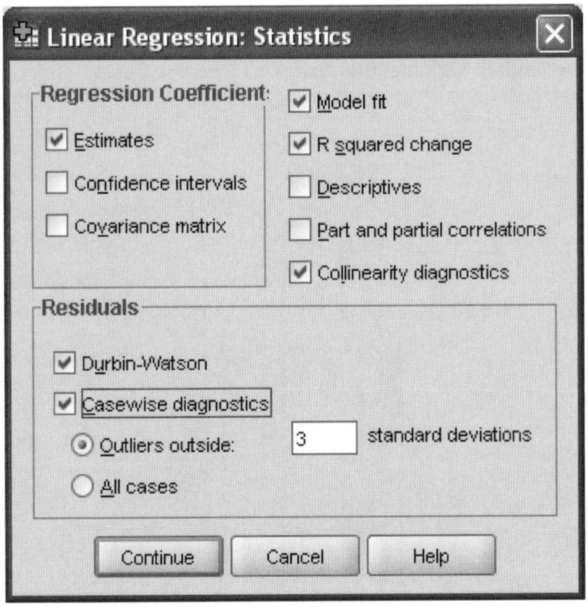

Figure 8.14c   *Linear regression statistics*

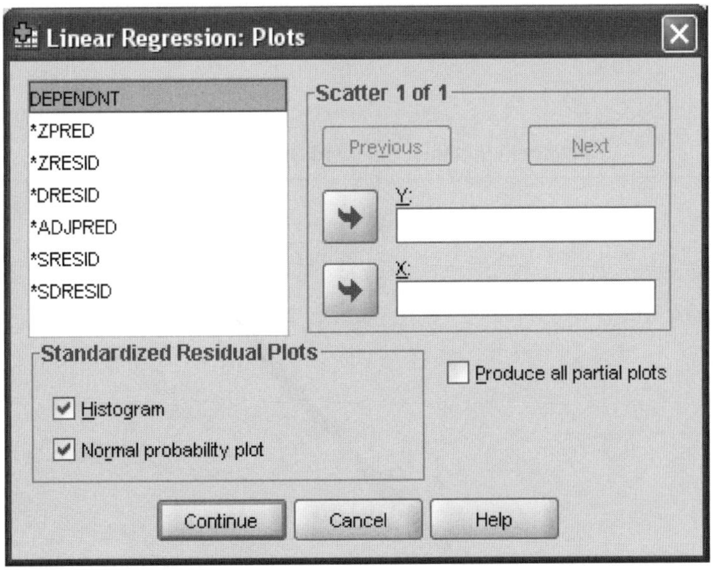

Figure 8.14d   *Linear regression residuals plots*

Casewise Diagnostics[a]

Case Number	Std. Residual	siops Standard Occ Prestige Scale	Predicted Value	Residual
14770	–3.744	20.00	65.0274	–45.02745

a. Dependent Variable: siops Standard Occ Prestige Scale

Figure 8.14e   *Regression residual output*

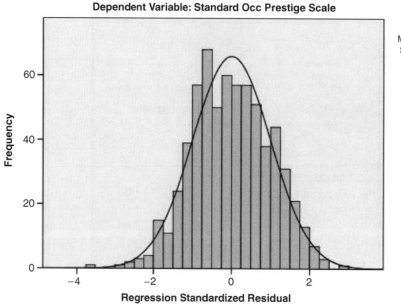

Figure 8.14f *Histogram of residuals*

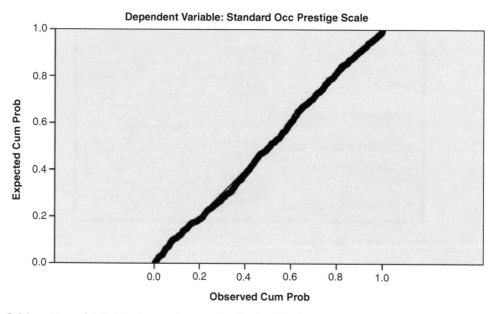

Figure 8.14g *Normal P-P plot of regression standardized residual*

A deliberately problematic regression

So far, we have presented an example of a multivariate regression that has worked quite well. However, we are aware that when you try your own regression analyses, you might not be so lucky. To show you what to look out for, we will conclude the module by showing output from a multivariate regression analysis that has some problems.

We will continue to use some of the same variables. In this example, however, the dependent variable will be **ru_rinc**, the respondent's income in roubles. The independent variables will be: **siops**, the measure of occupational ranking that we have been using as a dependent variable; **isei**, another ranking of occupational standing; **educyrs**; plus two additional measures of the respondent's educational attainment, **degree**, a general ranking of educational qualification and **ru_degr**, a coding of level of educational qualification that is specific to Russia; **urbrural**, a rating by the respondent of their community on a continuum from urban to rural; **ru_size**, a specific coding for Russia of the size of communities. The 'Enter' method has been used and multicollinearity and residual analyses are requested as before. Figure 8.15 shows the relevant output.

In the 'Model Summary' we note that the adjusted r^2 is rather low, 11.0 per cent of variance in the dependent variable, **ru_rinc**, is explained by the regression. The Durbin–Watson statistic is lower than our previous example, at 1.642, but this is still above 1.000. The ANOVA shows that the regression equation gives a fit to the data that is significantly better than by chance. It is when we examine the **Coefficients** box that we come across some cause for unease. Only two of the independent variables,

Model Summary[b]

Model	R	R Square	Adjusted R Square	Std. Error of the Estimate	Durbin-Watson
1	.346[a]	.119	.110	5017.701	1.642

a. Predictors: (Constant), **urbrural** Type of comm.: R.s self-asses., **isei** Internatl socio-economic index, **degree** R: Education II-highest education level, **ru_degr** Country specific education: Russia, **educyrs** R: Education I: years of schooling, **siops** Standard Occ Prestige Scale, **ru_size** Size of community: Russia
b. Dependent Variable: **ru_rinc** Respondent's Earnings: Russia

ANOVA[b]

Model		Sum of Squares	df	Mean Square	F	Sig.
1	Regression	2.305E9	7	3.293E8	13.080	.000[a]
	Residual	1.699E10	675	2.518E7		
	Total	1.930E10	682			

a. Predictors: (Constant), **urbrural** Type of comm.: R.s self-asses., **isei** Internatl socio-economic index, **degree** R: Education II-highest education level, **ru_degr** Country specific education: Russia, **educyrs** R: Education I: years of schooling, **siops** Standard Occ Prestige Scale, **ru_size** Size of community: Russia
b. Dependent Variable: **ru_rinc** Respondent's Earnings: Russia

Figure 8.15 *Deliberately problematic multivariate regression result*

Coefficients[a]

Model		Unstandardized Coefficients		Standardized Coefficients			Collinearity Statistics	
		B	Std. Error	Beta	t	Sig.	Tolerance	VIF
1	(Constant)	5723.037	1085.051		5.274	.000		
	isei Internatl socio-economic index	−40.917	26.947	−.133	−1.518	.129	.169	5.906
	siops Standard Occ Prestige Scale	57.626	31.858	.158	1.809	.071	.170	5.868
	educyrs R: Education I: years of schooling	96.835	169.302	.049	.572	.568	.178	5.620
	degree R: Education II-highest education level	112.782	416.109	.019	.271	.786	.253	3.950
	ru_degr Country specific education: Russia	220.219	289.007	.056	.762	.446	.237	4.211
	ru_size Size of community: Russia	−1149.173	222.650	−.553	−5.161	.000	.114	8.795
	urbrural Type of comm.: R.s self-asses.	1249.475	443.323	.301	2.818	.005	.115	8.719

a. Dependent Variable: ru_rinc Respondent's Earnings: Russia

Figure 8.15 *Continued*

Casewise Diagnostics[a]

Case Number	Std. Residual	ru_rinc Respondent´s Earnings: Russia	Predicted Value	Residual
14205	3.381	25000	8032.74	16967.260
14354	7.472	48010	10518.14	37491.855
14683	9.856	60000	10547.48	49452.522
14789	3.263	25000	8629.66	16370.341
14841	6.276	40000	8506.83	31493.168
14845	3.400	25000	7941.90	17058.103
14846	4.388	30000	7980.29	22019.706
14856	4.539	30000	7225.03	22774.971
15098	3.293	23000	6477.22	16522.777
15326	3.804	25000	5913.43	19086.567

a. Dependent Variable: **ru_rinc** Respondent´s Earnings: Russia

Histogram

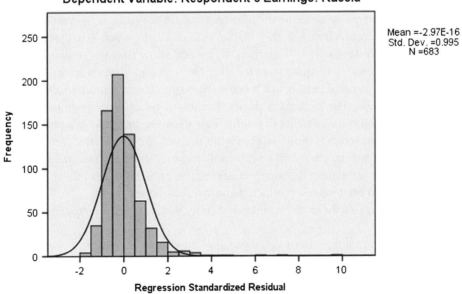

Dependent Variable: Respondent´s Earnings: Russia

Mean =-2.97E-16
Std. Dev. =0.995
N =683

Figure 8.15 *Continued*

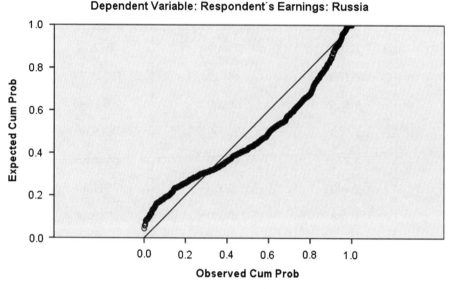

Figure 8.15 *Continued*

ru_size and **urbrural**, have significant effects on the dependent variable. That in itself would be accept-able but, at .114 and .115, respectively, the 'Tolerance' statistics for both of these are well below the .200 cut-off and while 'VIF' for each is below 10, at 8.795 and 8.719, they are not that much below 10. There appears to be a multicollinearity problem here. In addition, there are clear signs of multicollinearity among the other independent variables, with 'Tolerance' values hovering at (and mainly below) .200.

There also seem to be problems with the residual differences between actual observed values for **ru_rinc** and the predicted values. The 'Casewise Diagnostics' show that ten respondents are outliers. The residual difference appear to be quite large for all these cases and, more worryingly, in *all* ten cases the regression has underestimated their actual income. These problems with the residuals are confirmed when we inspect the charts. The histogram shows that the distribution of residual values is neither Normal nor centred around zero. The bulk of residuals are negative, but there is a pronounced positive upwardly skewed 'tail' (our ten rich outliers). Finally, in marked contrast to the previous example, the plot of expected versus observed cumulative probabilities clearly diverges from the straight 45 degree line. The equation is over-estimating the lower values; but this quickly turns into the equation under-estimating the middle and high values, producing an inverse S-shaped curve.

Confronted with results like these, the wise analyst (if they didn't give up altogether) might:

- try to discover some variables other than those associated with community size/'urbrurality' that would help predict **ru_rinc**;
- consider removing the correlated variables from the equation so they settle on only one measure of education, one measure of 'urbrurality', and one measure of occupational ranking;
- produce histograms of all the variables to see if any of them are skewed and, if they are, try using mathematical transformations to make them more symmetric;
- consider excluding the ten 'outlier' cases from the analysis.

CONCLUSION

When it works well, a good solution to a multivariate regression approaches being a true model in that it very powerfully concentrates facets of the data and reveals their interrelationships in a dynamic manner. It moves towards genuine prediction that can be extrapolated into the real world. Through the construction of dummy variables and interactions, the technique allows great flexibility in its analysis. One feature linear regression cannot easily cope with is situations where the dependent variable is categorical, but logistic regression, covered in Module 10, provides this vital extension.

SPSS EXERCISES FOR REGRESSION

1. Working your way from the more basic to the final example, repeat the analyses carried out in this module, only using data from the country of your choice. How do your results differ from those for Russia? Can you think of explanations why this is the case?

2. Take your analyses further by dropping the variables that were not close to significance in your final solution to (1) and add in some additional variables of your own choosing, either by selecting some from those already available in the dataset and/or by constructing some new 'dummy' or 'interaction' variables. Carry out a stepwise regression, paying close attention to potential problems of multicollinearity and how the coefficients alter as SPSS inserts new variables into the regression.

3. Think of a causal hypothesis that can be tested using some of the quantitative variables in the dataset you have chosen. You need a dependent (y) variable and at least three independent (x) variables that could conceivably be a 'cause of' or have an effect upon the y variable:

   a. do simple regressions of each independent x variable in turn upon the dependent y variable. Note whether or not each independent variable has a significant effect (the significance level) and the extent of the effect (the regression coefficient (b) and the 'constant' (a));

   b. then run a multiple regression upon the dependent variable of all the independent variables at the same time. Note the overall significance of this multiple regression and how the extent of the effect of each independent variable changes when it must 'compete' with other independent variables in a multiple regression. Since all the independent variables are 'competing' with each other in the multiple regression, what probably will happen is that each independent x variable in the multiple regression will show a smaller effect on the dependent y variable than it did on its own in a simple regression. It is quite possible that some independent variables that were shown as having significant effects upon the dependent variable in the simple regressions may lose out to other independent variables in the multiple regression to the extent that they are no longer significant. If this happens, their previous significant effect can be considered to have been spurious.

9 Factor Analysis

INTRODUCTION

Factor analysis is a statistical technique that allows us to simplify the correlational relationships between a number of continuous variables. As demonstrated in Module 8, the correlation procedure can be used to generate a correlation matrix – the correlations of a large number of variables, each with all the others. Once a correlation matrix is produced, however, it can be difficult to systematically identify reliable patterns of correlation between the variables. Factor analytic techniques are a solution to this type of problem, allowing us to look at the patterns that underlie the correlations between a number of variables. In that sense, factor analysis is a *data reduction* technique. Its logic is that the variation observed in a variety of individual variables reflects the patterns of a smaller number of some deeper, more fundamental, features, the 'factors'.

Why would you wish to look for these unobserved underlying factors? Imagine if you wanted to look at all of the patterns of association, or correlation, between ten quantitative variables (Variables 1 to 10). This would imply having to interpret 52 relationships between variables. (For example, Variable 1 can be correlated with Variables 2 to 10. And, Variable 2 can be separately associated with Variables 3 to 10, Variable 3 with Variables 4 to 10 and so on.) Identifying real patterns is complicated further because the relationship between, for example, Variables 1 and 2 may be affected by the separate relationships each of these variables have with Variable 3, with Variable 4, and so on. This leads to a complicated explanation of 52 relationships, similar to the shared variance problem discussed in previous modules. The analyst will find it difficult to explain which variable is actually related to what other variables, as she or he may be uncertain whether the apparent relationship between two variables is genuine, or simply a facet of both variables' relationships with another, third, variable.

Indeed, even writing an explanation of multiple correlations is difficult. What factor analysis does is provide reliable means of simplifying the relationships and identifying within them what *factors*, or common components of association between groups of variables, underlie the relationships.

A simple way of explaining the process of factor analysis is depicted in Figure 9.1.

We use the main principle of factor analysis all the time. Imagine that the top line of Figure 9.1 represents all the musicians and music groups in the world. What we do is group certain types of music into categories. So, Beethoven, Mozart and others fall under a category of Classical Music; Miles Davis, Charlie Parker and others fall into a Jazz category; and so on. In the same way that themes such as Classical Music, Jazz, Pop, HipHop, Dance, Indie and so on can be used to identify underlying groupings that categorize musicians and music groups, factor analysis will work to establish common features underlying the relationships between the variables in a dataset.

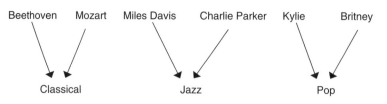

Figure 9.1 *Simple example of what factor analysis does*

USING FACTOR ANALYSIS IN SPSS

The main aim of this chapter is to present the main two features of factor analytic techniques:

1. **Extraction** – The process by which we determine the factors underlying a collection of variables;
2. **Rotation** – A second step, used in order to simplify structure when the extraction techniques have identified more than one factor underlying the relationships between a number of variables.

Extraction

Extraction techniques allow you to determine the factors underlying the relationship between a number of variables. There are many extraction procedures, but the most common one is called 'Principal Component Analysis'.

Let us use an example from the **South Korean** dataset. There are eight questions in which respondents are asked to state what is personally important to them about a job.

1. **v11**, Job security is personally important.
2. **v12**, High income is personally important.
3. **v13**, Opportunity for advancement is personally important.
4. **v14**, Having an interesting job is personally important.
5. **v15**, Being able to work independently is personally important.
6. **v16**, Having the opportunity to help other people is personally important.
7. **v17**, Having a job that is useful to society is personally important.
8. **v18**, Being able to decide the time of day when one works is personally important.

Figure 9.2 shows the Pearson product–moment correlation matrix statistics for correlations between all eight variables.

You will notice that all the correlations are statistically significant but the correlations between some pairs of variables are higher than those between other pairs. High correlations between a number of variables suggest that they may reflect a single underlying factor. Therefore, to test for this, we will perform a factor analysis on these variables.

Pull down the **Analyze** menu and then click on **Dimension Reduction** (or **Data Reduction** in versions of SPSS prior to 17.0) and then **Factor** .... You should obtain a screen that looks like Figure 9.3. Factor analysis is found under the general heading termed Dimension or Data Reduction because, by condensing the information in a large number of variables into a smaller number of factors, it can be considered to be *reducing* the complexity of the raw data. Transfer the variables **v11** to **v18** into the **Variables** box.

Correlations

		v11 Personally important: job security	v12 Personally important: high income	v13 Personally important: opport f advancement	v14 Personally important: an interesting job	v15 Personally important: work independently	v16 Personally important: help other people	v17 Personally important: a job useful to society	v18 Personally important: decide time of work
v11 Personally important: job security	Pearson Correlation	1.000	.250**	.337**	.289**	.239**	.250**	.241**	.187**
	Sig. (2-tailed)		.000	.000	.000	.000	.000	.000	.000
	N	1559	1553	1543	1551	1533	1553	1546	1542
v12 Personally important: high income	Pearson Correlation	.250**	1.000	.291**	.184**	.158**	.110**	.117**	.175**
	Sig. (2-tailed)	.000		.000	.000	.000	.000	.000	.000
	N	1553	1574	1548	1563	1543	1563	1560	1553
v13 Personally important: opport f advancement	Pearson Correlation	.337**	.291**	1.000	.505**	.352**	.346**	.312**	.221**
	Sig. (2-tailed)	.000	.000		.000	.000	.000	.000	.000
	N	1543	1548	1554	1550	1535	1548	1543	1542
v14 Personally important: an interesting job	Pearson Correlation	.289**	.184**	.505**	1.000	.372**	.319**	.312**	.258**
	Sig. (2-tailed)	.000	.000	.000		.000	.000	.000	.000
	N	1551	1563	1550	1568	1542	1561	1556	1553
v15 Personally important: work independently	Pearson Correlation	.239**	.158**	.352**	.372**	1.000	.417**	.344**	.462**
	Sig. (2-tailed)	.000	.000	.000	.000		.000	.000	.000
	N	1533	1543	1535	1542	1546	1542	1536	1536
v16 Personally important: help other people	Pearson Correlation	.250**	.110**	.346**	.319**	.417**	1.000	.737**	.353**
	Sig. (2-tailed)	.000	.000	.000	.000	.000		.000	.000
	N	1553	1563	1548	1561	1542	1569	1560	1553
v17 Personally important: a job useful to society	Pearson Correlation	.241**	.117**	.312**	.312**	.344**	.737**	1.000	.338**
	Sig. (2-tailed)	.000	.000	.000	.000	.000	.000		.000
	N	1546	1560	1543	1556	1536	1560	1565	1549
v18 Personally important: decide time of work	Pearson Correlation	.187**	.175**	.221**	.258**	.462**	.353**	.338**	1.000
	Sig. (2-tailed)	.000	.000	.000	.000	.000	.000	.000	
	N	1542	1553	1542	1553	1536	1553	1549	1558

**. Correlation is significant at the 0.01 level (2-tailed).

Figure 9.2 *Correlation matrix between all variables used in the factor analysis*

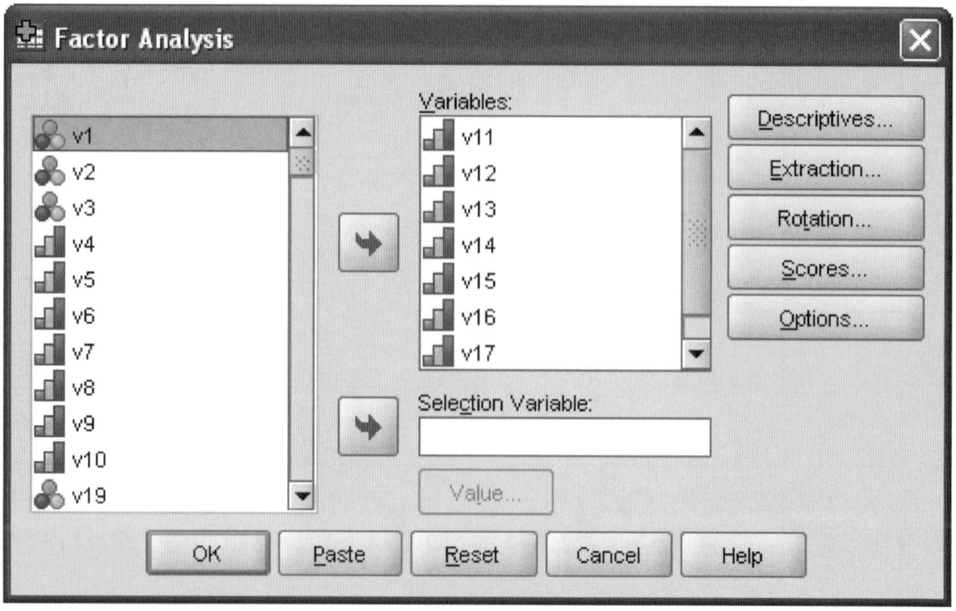

Figure 9.3 *Factor Analysis main window*

There are two types of criteria that are most commonly used to determine the number of factors to extract. The first is *Eigenvalues*, a measure of the amount of variability in the data explained by a given factor. SPSS calculates the potential factors, and assigns each, in descending order, an 'Eigenvalue'. Factors with Eigenvalues above 1 explain more variation in the data than an individual variable and traditionally are seen as significant factors. SPSS will extract that number of factors. However, some statisticians prefer to use the Scree Test. What the Scree Test does is plot the Eigenvalues by size in order to provide a visual assessment that allows the analyst to see which factors should be accepted. We will use both in this example.

Click on **Extraction** in the main Factor Analysis window and you should obtain Figure 9.4.

Note that the default setting on SPSS is to extract all factors with Eigenvalues over 1. However, we also want to plot a Scree plot so tick the **Scree plot** box. Click on **Continue** in order to go back to the main window.

We need to ascertain that the data's characteristics are appropriate for a factor analysis. Click on **Descriptives** to bring up the sub-window in Figure 9.5 and under **Statistics** tick **Initial solution** and under **Correlation matrix** tick **KMO and Bartlett's test of sphericity**.

Rotation

Before moving on to run the procedure, we need to consider one additional feature of factor analysis: rotation. 'Rotation' is necessary when extraction techniques suggest there are two or more factors. The rotation of factors is designed to give us an idea of how the factors we initially extracted differ from each other and to provide a clearer picture of which items are associated with each factor. Basically, the axes of two factors are 'spun', or rotated, around their centre point so that each variable becomes more clearly associated with one factor and not the other.

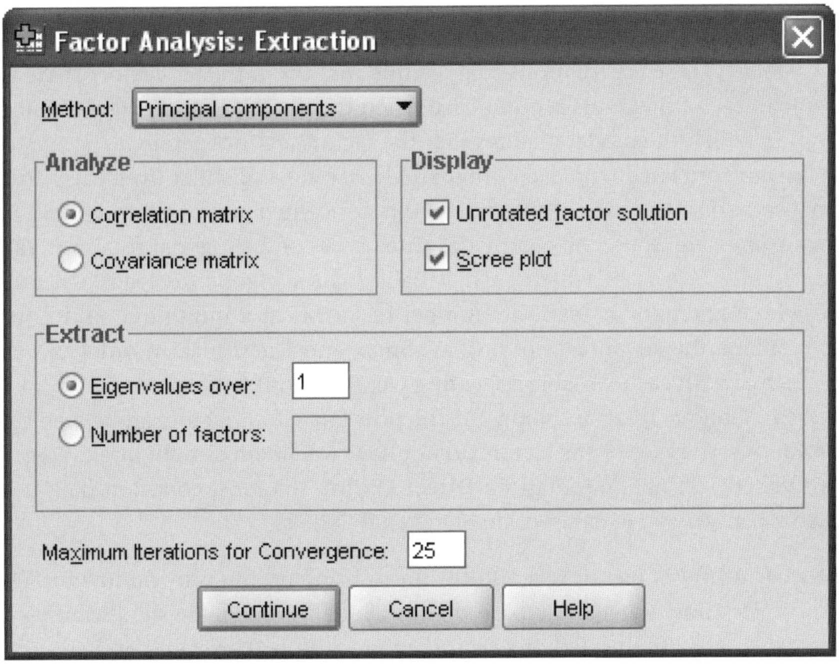

Figure 9.4 *Factor Analysis: Extraction sub-window*

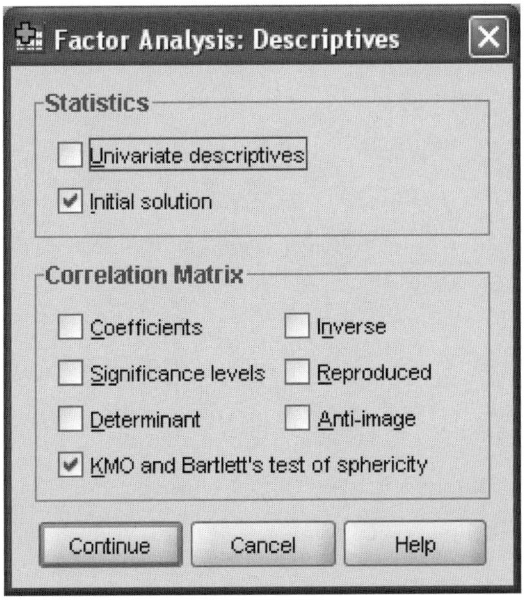

Figure 9.5 *Factor Analysis: Descriptives sub-window*

There are two basic types of rotation techniques.

1. *Orthogonal Rotations.* These are rotations that assume that the extracted factors share no association and are unique to each other. This is often used when the analyst is applying a theoretical model to factor analysis in which the model predicts that the factors are independent. The goal is to produce factors that are not correlated with each other and hence are as distinct from each other as possible. In orthogonal rotations, the axes of the two factors concerned are forced to remain at right angles to each other as they are 'spun'. SPSS provides three types of orthogonal rotation: **Varimax**, which attempts to produce factors in which each variable scores highly, or 'loads' on only one factor; **Quartimax**, which attempts to keep the number of factors at a minimum; and **Equamax**, which attempts to combine the advantages of both Varimax and Quartimax in order to produce a result that has few factors with each variable appearing clearly on only one factor.
2. *Oblique Rotations.* Oblique rotations allow for the possibility that factors are related one to another. In oblique rotations, the axes of the factors do not have to remain at right angles to each other. SPSS provides two varieties of oblique rotation: **Direct Oblim**, the most common oblique method, and **Promax**, used when very large datasets are being analysed.

From the top **Factor Analysis** menu, select **Rotation** to bring up the sub-window in Figure 9.6. Since we note from the correlation matrix that all of the individual variables are significantly correlated with each other, we suspect that the underlying factors might also be correlated and so decide to use the **Direct Oblimin** rotation.

Now we are ready to do the factor analysis. Go back to the main menu and press **OK** to run the procedure. You should then get an output like that shown in Figure 9.7a.

The first thing we see on the output is a box with the Kaiser–Meyer–Olkin (KMO) measure of sampling adequacy and Bartlett's Test of Sphericity. The KMO index tells you how effectively the variables can be grouped into a smaller number of underlying factors. KMO has a maximum of 1.0 and the larger

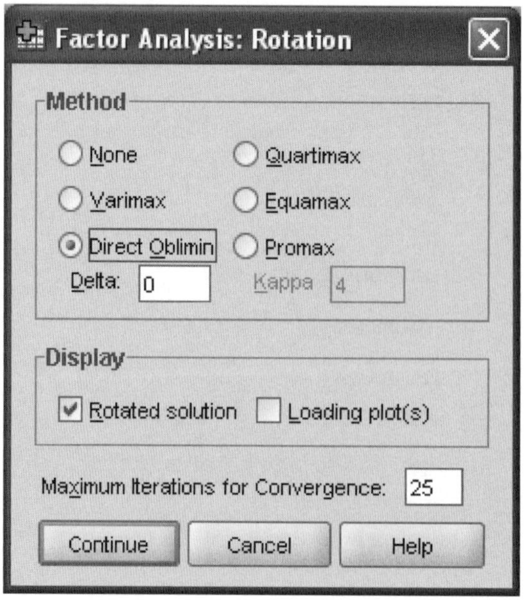

Figure 9.6 *Factor Analysis: Rotation sub-window*

KMO and Bartlett's Test

Kaiser-Meyer-Olkin Measure of Sampling Adequacy.		.768
Bartlett's Test of Sphericity	Approx. Chi-Square	3182.597
	df	28
	Sig.	.000

Communalities

	Initial	Extraction
v11 Personally important: job security	1.000	.457
v12 Personally important: high income	1.000	.488
v13 Personally important: opport f advancement	1.000	.575
v14 Personally important: an interesting job	1.000	.480
v15 Personally important: work independently	1.000	.485
v16 Personally important: help other people	1.000	.743
v17 Personally important: a job useful to society	1.000	.694
v18 Personally important: decide time of work	1.000	.412

Extraction Method: Principal Component Analysis.

Figure 9.7a   *Factor Analysis output, initial sections*

it is the better the prospects are for a successful factor analysis. Sources vary about how large KMO needs to be but, as a general rule of thumb, we suggest a value of at least 0.60. In our example, KMO is large enough, 0.768.

Bartlett's Test of Sphericity tests whether the correlation matrix of the variables going into the factor analysis are significantly different from an *identity matrix* (a correlation matrix in which the correlation between variables other than themselves is close to zero). If none of the variables in the attempted factor analysis are correlated there are no underlying common factors and factor analysis won't work. A small significance level indicates that the matrix shows correlations between variables. Here, the significance level is .000, indicating that the odds are very high that the matrix is not an identity matrix of close to zero correlations. Taken together, these results indicate that it is reasonable to proceed with a factor analysis.

Look in the **Total Variance Explained** box in Figure 9.7b. This is where you obtain information on the number of factors to extract. Here, you will notice two sets of three columns ('Total', 'per cent of variance' and 'Cumulative per cent') under 'Initial Eigenvalues' and under 'Extraction sums of squared loading'. Those columns under 'Initial Eigenvalues' show all values of Eigen and those under 'Extraction

Total Variance Explained

Component	Initial Eigenvalues			Extraction Sums of Squared Loadings			Rotation Sums of Squared Loadings[a]
	Total	% of Variance	Cumulative %	Total	% of Variance	Cumulative %	Total
1	3.162	39.528	39.528	3.162	39.528	39.528	2.795
2	1.171	14.642	54.170	1.171	14.642	54.170	2.217
3	.869	10.861	65.031				
4	.840	10.500	75.531				
5	.703	8.785	84.316				
6	.520	6.496	90.812				
7	.480	5.997	96.809				
8	.255	3.191	100.000				

Extraction Method: Principal Component Analysis.

a. When components are correlated, sums of squared loadings cannot be added to obtain a total variance.

Figure 9.7b *Factor Analysis output, variance explained*

sums of squared loading' show what SPSS has selected. In each case, the column 'Total' is the Eiganvalue, the ' per cent of Variance' is the amount of variance (up to a maximum of 100 per cent explanation of the relationship between the variables) each factor takes up, and 'Cumulative per cent' is the amount of variance for each factor added together in ascending order. Here, we can see that only the first two factors have Eigenvalues over 1. Therefore SPSS is suggesting we extract two factors that account for 54.170 per cent of the variance of the relationship between variables.

The number of factors the method of using Eigenvalues chooses can be slightly inaccurate – sometimes selecting too many factors when the number of variables used is below 20. Therefore another way of determining factor is through the use of the **Scree Plot**. What the Scree Plot does is plot the Eigenvalues in order to provide visual criteria which we use to determine the number of factors. The Scree Plot takes its name after the debris, or scree, that collects at the bottom of a rocky slope on a mountain. As we can see in Figure 9.7c, the Scree Plot does resemble the side of a mountain. We determine the number of factors to retain by selecting those whose Eigenvalues occur before the plot straightens outs (or roughly straightens out). Here we choose only the first two factors, as the plot starts to straighten out after point 2 on the axis. Another way is to imagine the plot as an arm with a bend at the elbow. You would select all points from above the elbow bend.

As we must acknowledge from the above, using Scree Plots to choose the best number of factors is hardly an exact science; however, many believe the Scree Test is a more reliable way of determining factors. We suggest that you use both Eigenvalues and the Scree Plot to come to a decision about the number of factors to retain.

Finally, look at the figures contained in the three matrices in Figure 9.7d. These tables contain three versions of the 'Factor Loadings' of each of the variables on the two factors. Loadings are the strength of each variable in defining the factor. The reason we used the word 'defining' is that factor analysis does not tell you the conceptual meaning of the factor; you must decide that for yourself. That is, you look at what variables 'load' on a factor. Hopefully, these variables have some meanings or features in common which you can use as clues to the common conceptual feature of the factor. Based upon your assessment

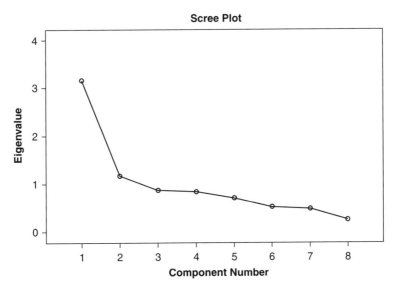

Figure 9.7c   *Factor Analysis output, Scree Plot*

Component Matrix[a]

	Component	
	1	2
v11 Personally important: job security	.527	.422
v12 Personally important: high income	.357	.600
v13 Personally important: opport f advancement	.659	.374
v14 Personally important: an interesting job	.640	.265
v15 Personally important: work independently	.681	−.142
v16 Personally important: help other people	.758	−.410
v17 Personally important: a job useful to society	.720	−.420
v18 Personally important: decide time of work	.595	−.242

Extraction Method: Principal Component Analysis.
a. 2 components extracted.

Figure 9.7d   *Factor Analysis output, component matrices*

Pattern Matrix[a]

	Component	
	1	2
v11 Personally important: job security	.061	.651
v12 Personally important: high income	−.202	.745
v13 Personally important: opport f advancement	.197	.665
v14 Personally important: an interesting job	.267	.551
v15 Personally important: work independently	.613	.176
v16 Personally important: help other people	.878	−.048
v17 Personally important: a job useful to society	.857	−.075
v18 Personally important: decide time of work	.627	.040

Extraction Method: Principal Component Analysis.
Rotation Method: Oblimin with Kaiser Normalization.
a. Rotation converged in 5 iterations.

Structure Matrix

	Component	
	1	2
v11 Personally important: job security	.295	.673
v12 Personally important: high income	.065	.672
v13 Personally important: opport f advancement	.435	.735
v14 Personally important: an interesting job	.465	.647
v15 Personally important: work independently	.676	.396
v16 Personally important: help other people	.861	.267
v17 Personally important: a job useful to society	.830	.233
v18 Personally important: decide time of work	.641	.265

Extraction Method: Principal Component Analysis.
Rotation Method: Oblimin with Kaiser Normalization.

Figure 9.7d *Continued*

Component Correlation Matrix

Component	1	2
1	1.000	.358
2	.358	1.000

Extraction Method: Principal Component Analysis.
Rotation Method: Oblimin with Kaiser Normalization.

Figure 9.7d *Continued*

of what this common conceptual feature may be, the practice is for the analyst to give that factor a name. What you call the factor is up to you, it is usually a general term representing the factor.

CAUTION: Note that all SPSS has done is identify which variables have codings that appear to 'hang together' in a *numerical* sense. It is the judgement of the human analyst that decides upon what the *meaning* of the factor may be. Since a characteristic of humans is to see patterns where there may be none, or just to make a mistake, you must be cautious when attributing meaning to a factor. Once a factor is given a name, that name may begin to take on a spurious reality.

Loadings on factors can be positive or negative, ranging from zero to a maximum absolute value of one (±1.0). The larger the absolute value, the stronger the link between that variable and the factor. A negative loading indicates that the variable has an inverse relationship with the factor. Opinions are fairly arbitrary about at which point loadings become important to a factor. However, Comrey (1973: 1346) suggests that anything above 0.44 can be considered salient, with increased loadings becoming more vital in determining the factor.

The boxes in Figure 9.7d (Component, Pattern and Structure Matrix) all relate to the rotation. For interpretation, we concentrate upon the **Pattern Matrix**, which yields the most distinct factors.

To define each factor, we will decide to include those variables with salient loading on the factors (above .44). On Factor 1, the variables: **v16**, 'Personally important: Help other people' (.878); **v17**, 'Personally important: A job useful to society' (.857); **v18**, 'Personally important: Decide time of work' (.627); **v15**, 'Personally important: Work independently' (.613) load above .44. On Factor 2: **v12**, 'Personally important: High income' (.745); **v13**, 'Personally important: Opportunity for advancement' (.665); **v11**, 'Personally important: Job security' (.651); **v14**, 'Personally important: An interesting job' (.551) load above .44. We could argue that each factor represents conceptually distinct features of jobs.

Now we must name each factor. Looking at the items, those variables loading on Factor 1 all represent features of jobs to do with making a contribution to society or personal control and hence could be labelled '*Self-actualization*'. Factor 2 contains variables that in the main seem to have something to do with the concrete benefits of jobs and hence could be labelled '*Instrumental*'. (The variable **v14** does not quite fit this attribution, but one could argue that it is instrumental to want to have a job that is interesting rather than boring. Note also that **v14** is the variable that 'loads' least on Factor 2 and has the largest value of the variables that do not 'load' on Factor 1. This is what is sometimes referred to a crossloading (where variables are pulled onto two factors).)

Our interpretation of the results of this factor analysis would be that among the general population in South Korea, two main types of features are important for how people personally evaluate jobs: first, the extent to which a job gives them opportunities for self-actualization, in terms of making a contribution to society and having personal control of their work timing and tasks; second, instrumental features of jobs in terms of income, chances for advancement and job security are also important for South Koreans. Interestingly, South Koreans also appear to see having an interesting job as a practical instrumental benefit rather than as an idealistic benefit.

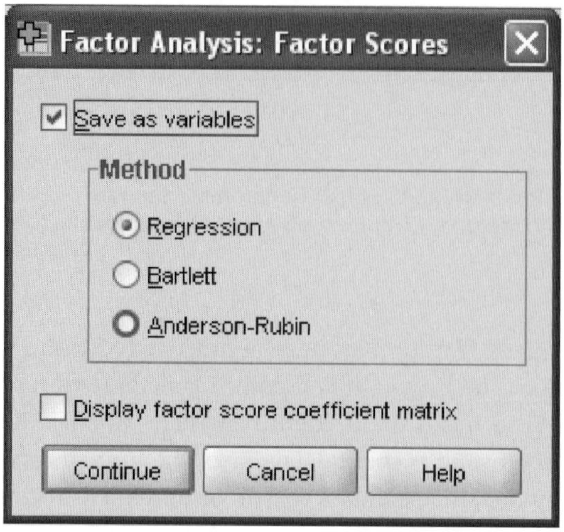

Figure 9.8 *Saving factor analysis scores*

Moving on – using factor scores in other analyses

SPSS gives the analyst the option of saving the factor scores as variables in their own right. This is effected by going to **Scores...** to bring up the **Factor Analysis: Factor Scores** sub-window as shown in Figure 9.8 and checking the **Save as** variables box. When the factor analysis is run, two new variables, **FAC1_1** and **FAC1_2** that are variables representing Factor 1 ('Self-actualization') and Factor 2 ('Instrumentality') will appear in the Data Grid. These variables will have been computed by multiplying each variable, **v11** to **v18**, by its factor score and adding together the result. Because factor scores themselves are standardized, each factor variable will have a mean of zero and a standard deviation of one (although their distributions can be skewed and may not conform precisely to a Normal distribution).

Factor score variables can be quite useful as they are, in effect, scales of the variables that make them up and can be used in subsequent analyses as they can be presumed to be more reliable than one of the individual variables. For instance, one could carry out analyses in which **FAC1_1** and **FAC1_2** are dependent variables in order to see what are the characteristics of respondents that cause them to view 'Self-actualization' or 'Instrumentality' as personally important for the jobs they seek.

While it is beyond the scope of this book, when you begin to use factor scores in this manner as variables in their own right, you are moving into the realm of 'latent variable analysis', a whole suite of complex techniques where factor analytic techniques are used to generate composite 'unobserved' variables that are presumed to more accurate reflections of conceptual ideas since they are more free of the measurement error associated with any single 'observed' variable. Analyses of relationships among these latent unobserved variables are argued to be 'purer' representations of reality and structure.

More about rotation

Now that we have presented the results of a factor analysis, let us return to the idea of 'rotation'. The process of rotation can be best explained by diagrams. Figure 9.9 attempts to depict unrotated and rotated factors. The first diagram, 'Unrotated (Principal component matrix)' shows the factors prior to

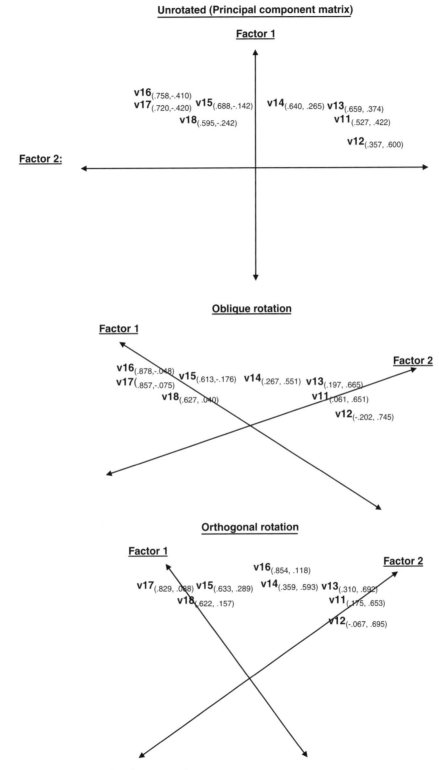

Figure 9.9 *Diagrams representing factor rotation*

rotation, with the factors orthogonal (or uncorrelated, at right angles to each other). (The terms 'component' and 'factor' can be considered equivalent. Some writers tend to use 'component' to refer to unrotated factors and 'factor' to refer to components after they are rotated.) Note how, while we can see that the eight variables in the factor analysis appear to fall into the two factors of the solution we have been discussing, their values, as reference points on the grid determined by these two unrotated factors, overlap considerably. Identifying which variables go to make up each factor is not easy at this point.

See what happens when we 'rotate' the axes of the two factors obliquely (in effect, spinning the axes of two factors around their centre point and no longer requiring them to be at right angles to each other). The lines of the rotated factors now go through the two sets of points and the grid reference points are such that variables that have a high value on one factor have a low value on the other factor. It is much easier to identify which variables go with which factor.

Finally, let's look at an orthogonal rotation. Here, the axes again have been 'spun' around their centre point, but they are constrained to remain at right angles to each other. The orthogonally rotated axes fit the data considerably better than the unrotated axes but not quite as well as the oblique rotation.

Here, the oblique rotation worked better because the variables are correlated with each other. ('Better' being defined as yielding factors that more easily allowed a clear interpretation of which variables belong with which factor.) This just happened to be a feature of the batch of data we have used in this example. With other data, it is possible that one of the orthogonal rotation techniques will produce a 'better' (that is, an easier to interpret) result.

In fact, it has been our experience over the years that, in the main, either oblique or orthogonal rotation usually works about as well with most batches of data in the sense that both will produce

Rotated Component Matrix[a]

	Component	
	1	2
v11 Personally important: job security	.175	.653
v12 Personally important: high income	–.067	.695
v13 Personally important: opport f advancement	.310	.692
v14 Personally important: an interesting job	.359	.593
v15 Personally important: work independently	.633	.289
v16 Personally important: help other people	.854	.118
v17 Personally important: a job useful to society	.829	.088
v18 Personally important: decide time of work	.622	.157

Extraction Method: Principal Component Analysis.
Rotation Method: Varimax with Kaiser Normalization.
a. Rotation converged in 3 iterations.

Figure 9.10 *An orthogonal (Varimax) rotated matrix*

similar factors that lead to the same substantive interpretation of the data. For instance, in Figure 9.10, a **Varimax** orthogonal rotation of these eight variables, you will note that, while the two resulting factors are not quite as 'pure' as those that came from the oblique rotation, the same four-variable by four-variable split results. If we had carried out the orthogonal **Varimax** rotation, we still would have reached the same substantive conclusion that there are two distinct factors called 'Self-actualization' and 'Instrumentality' that are the main features that are personally important when South Koreans think about jobs.

Other considerations

Remember that factor analysis is a very descriptive procedure. It requires us to describe things and to attach conceptual ideas to its statistical results; this is not always an exact science.

Your goal with factor analysis is a clear interpretation. As we said above, what is meant by a 'clear interpretation' is that the variables that make up each factor ideally: (a) should load highly on one factor, and low on all other factors and (b) the variables that go to make up each factor should form a group that goes together conceptually as well as statistically.

If you have a number of variables which load on several factors, or variables that load on none of the factors, then there is something wrong with your extraction techniques. The loading of a number of variables across different factors suggests you have not extracted enough factors, while if a number of variables do not load on any factor then you have extracted too many. However, don't concern yourself overly if you have a result like the one above where only a single variable tends to load on two factors. The crossloading of a single variable may be due to that variable being ambiguous, or genuinely applicable to both factors.

This type of factor analysis is an *exploratory* technique and hence it is quite all right if you wish to perform a number of extractions and different rotation techniques during the same analysis. Therefore revisiting extraction techniques and extracting more or fewer factors in order to see whether this has a substantial effect on the final results is perfectly acceptable and useful.

So, how then do you know you have made a good analysis? There are some generally accepted criteria. The first was mentioned immediately above – all variables loading on only one factor and low on all other factors. Other criteria are less certain: if you have an interpretation that is consistent with theory, or just makes common sense, then it is useful. Factor analysis is as much an art form as it is a science!

SPSS EXERCISES FOR FACTOR ANALYSIS

1. Continuing on with the example in this module, try a factor analysis using the same variables, **v11** to **v18**, only on one or more different countries. Do you get the same two factors? If different factors result, what could this indicate to you about the attitudes of people in different societies towards work?
2. Using a different selection of variables taken from the dataset of your choice, carry out a completely new factor analysis of your own. (Remember to select variables that are scalar (interval/ratio) preferably, but are at least clearly ordinal.)
   - How many factors now emerge from the analysis?
   - What names can you give to the rotated factors?

10   Logistic Regression

Logistic regression can be considered an extension of normal least squares regression to situations where the dependent variable is a nominal variable of two or more categories. In ordinary linear regression, the dependent variable ideally should be interval or ratio in which its values represent genuine numerical quantities. While normal regression is known to be robust and can often tolerate the violation of this requirement, continuing to yield reliable results when the dependent variable is ordinal (particularly if the ordinal values are many and tend to cluster around a centre point in a 'normal' way), this toleration cannot extend to unordered, categorical variables. The assumption of homoscedasticity, that most of the true observed values of the dependent variable will fall close to those predicted by the linear regression equation and cluster around the predicted line in an approximation to a normal distribution, becomes nonsensical with a categorical variable. With a categorical dependent variable, predictions will be either 100 per cent correct (the category of the dependent variable is what is predicted) or 100 per cent wrong (the category of the variable is some other category than what is predicted) – there can be no 'near' or 'far' from the observed.

Logistic regression gets around this problem by expressing its solution in terms of the odds or probability that a case with a given set of characteristics will fall into the category of interest. These odds are the summed product of the effects of a number of independent variables. So that the solution will appear as a set of distinct, additive coefficients, these effects are expressed as logs.

Having the regression coefficients appear as logs is a decidedly mixed blessing. While each coefficient appears separately, can be identified as statistically significant or not, and the direction of the effect, positive or negative, is known from its sign, having the coefficients appear as a log does make their concrete interpretation more difficult than with linear regression. As we will see from the worked examples, however, while logistic regression is less intuitive than normal regression, it is possible to arrive at an interpretation of the magnitude of a coefficient as well as its direction and statistical significance.

While the algorithms that drive the computation of the coefficients are different and the coefficients appear as logs, the application of the procedure is remarkably similar to that we already have introduced for linear regression in Module 8, 'Correlation and Regression'. As with linear regression, the independent variables still need to be either quantitative interval/ratio variables (or ordinal variables if we are willing to accept a violation of assumptions) or 'dummy' presence/absence variables based upon recoding categories. 'Interaction' independent variables, including ones based partly or wholly upon 'dummy' variables, can be introduced. The goal of an analysis can be either to discover which of a list of independent variables continues to exert a significant causal effect upon the dependent variable once all the potential candidate variables are included in the same multivariate model and/or to establish a predictive equation that will allow us to make an 'educated guess' about the likely value of the dependent variable for a new case that is based upon the values of that case's independent variables. Tests of significance for each individual variable and measures of the overall 'fit' of the regression result are given. All the independent variables can either be entered simultaneously or SPSS allows both 'forward' and 'backward' elimination of variables either individually or in groups.

SPSS provides two types of logisitic regression procedures:

- Binary (or binomial) logistic regression in which the dependent variable is binary – the presence or absence of some category or characteristic and
- Multinomial Logistic regression in which the dependent variable is categorical with more than two categories.

Perhaps the best way to explain logistic regression is by specific examples. Here, we will use data from the **USA** dataset. Americans were asked to state their political party affiliation, which produced the variable **us_prty**, coded into seven categories: (1) 'strong Democrat'; (2) 'not very strong Democrat'; (3) Independent, close to Democrat'; (4) 'Independent'; (5) 'Independent, close to Republican'; (6) 'not very strong Republican'; (7) 'strong Republican'. For this example, we have used recode to create a binary dependent variable, **Republican**, in which the categories 'not very strong Republican' and 'strong Republican' are combined into a single group, 'Republican', which will be contrasted with all others in the USA dataset. A binary logistic regression will be carried out to establish which of a variety of characteristics predispose a person to be a supporter of the Republican Party.

BINARY LOGISTIC REGRESSION – WORKED EXAMPLE

Run the binary logistic regression procedure as shown in Figure 10.1, go to **Analyze**, select **Regression** and then choose **Binary Logistic...** The Logistic Regression window in Figure 10.2a will come up. We select the new binary variable **Republican** from the variable list and move it into the **Dependent:** box. A number of independent variables are entered into the **Covariates:** box:

- two new variables created by Recode from the variable **ethnic: (1) African**, whether or not the respondent considers themself or their family to be of African origin or to have an African-American ethnic identity; **(2) Latino**, whether or not the respondent considers themselves to be of Latin American origin or ethnic identity. African-Americans have tended to vote Democrat and so may be hypothesized not to have a Republican Party affiliation. The situation for Hispanics is more complex, with their traditionally more conservative values pointing towards Republican support, but this being offset by their lower socioeconomic profile that could be linked to Democrat support;
- higher social status can be hypothesized to cause more conservative attitudes and Republican Party support. To that effect two variables of respondent's social standing are entered: **isei**, an externally assigned International Socio-economic Index score based upon occupation and **topbot**, the respondent's self-placement on a ten-level scale of social standing. Two other variables that could be considered oblique measures of social standing, **v27**, whether or not the respondent currently is in paid work and **us_degr**, an ordinal variable of educational attainment, are also entered;
- **vote_le**, was entered on the grounds that those who voted in the last election would be more likely to be affiliated to a political party;
- **age** was entered on the hypothesis that older respondents could tend to be more conservative and Republican supporters. Similarly, **attend**, the frequency of attendance at religious services and **prounion**, a scale of the extent of anti-labour union attitudes were entered;

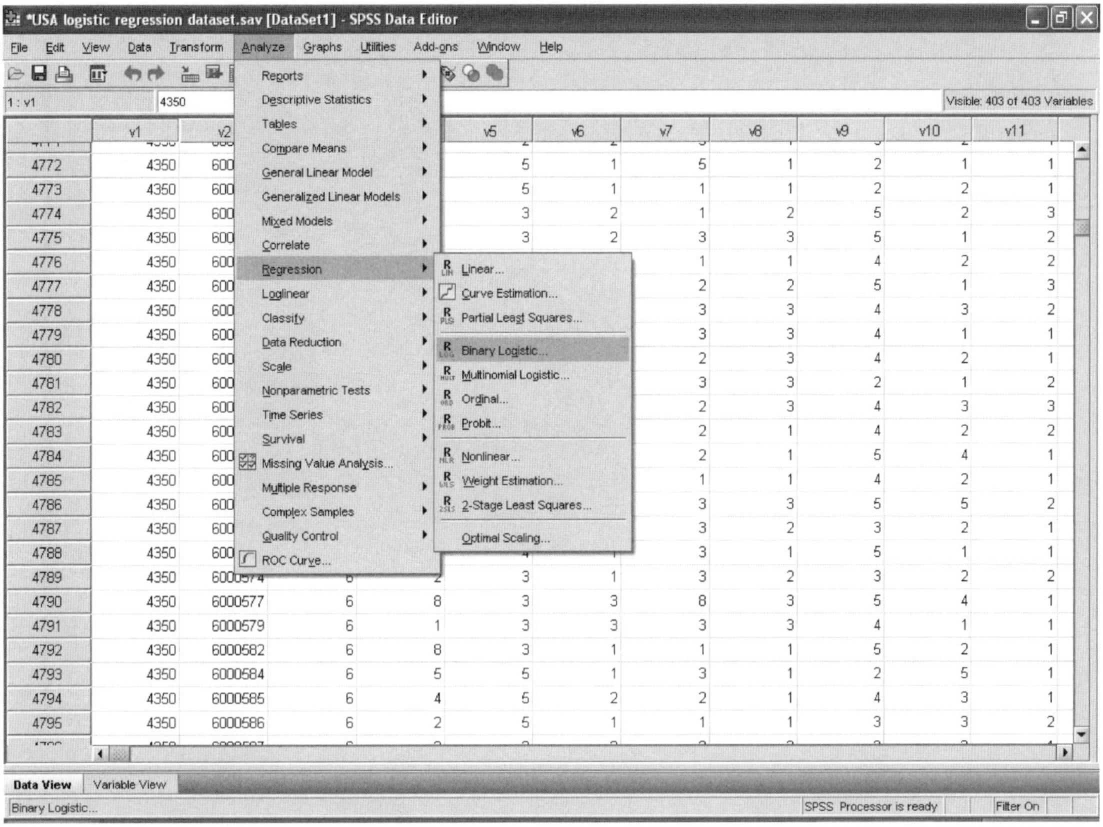

Figure 10.1 *Accessing logistic regression*

■ other variables entered are: **sex**, respondent's gender; **us_size**, an ordinal variable of the size of the respondent's community; **positive**, a scale of respondent's own opinion about whether they have a generally positive outlook on life; and **relaxed**, a scale of the respondent's self-assessment about whether they have a relaxed view of life.

Taken as a group, these variables can be considered a set of hypotheses of the characteristics that might cause a person to see themselves as affiliated to the Republican Party.

By default, SPSS considers the independent 'Covariate' variables to be scalar. Some, however, are ordinal and a number are unambiguously categorical and need to be so designated. To do this, click on the **Categorical...** button to bring up the 'Logistic Regression: Define Categorical Variables' sub-window, Figure 10.2b. We designate the variables **Latino**, **African**, **v27**, **sex** and **vote_le** as categorical by moving them into the **Categorical Covariates:** box. The ordinal variables can be left as scalar Covariates (if we are willing to tolerate bending the rules a bit) or designated as categorical. Here, for purposes of demonstration, we have left the ordinal **topbot** scale and **attend** as 'scalar' and designated **us_size** and **us_degr** as categorical.

Some optional output will help us interpret the results. Go to the Options sub-window in Figure 10.2c by clicking on the **Options...** button and then ticking **Classification plots** and **Hosmer–Lemeshow goodness-of-fit**. To run the procedure, we click on **Continue** to return to the main window. Sticking

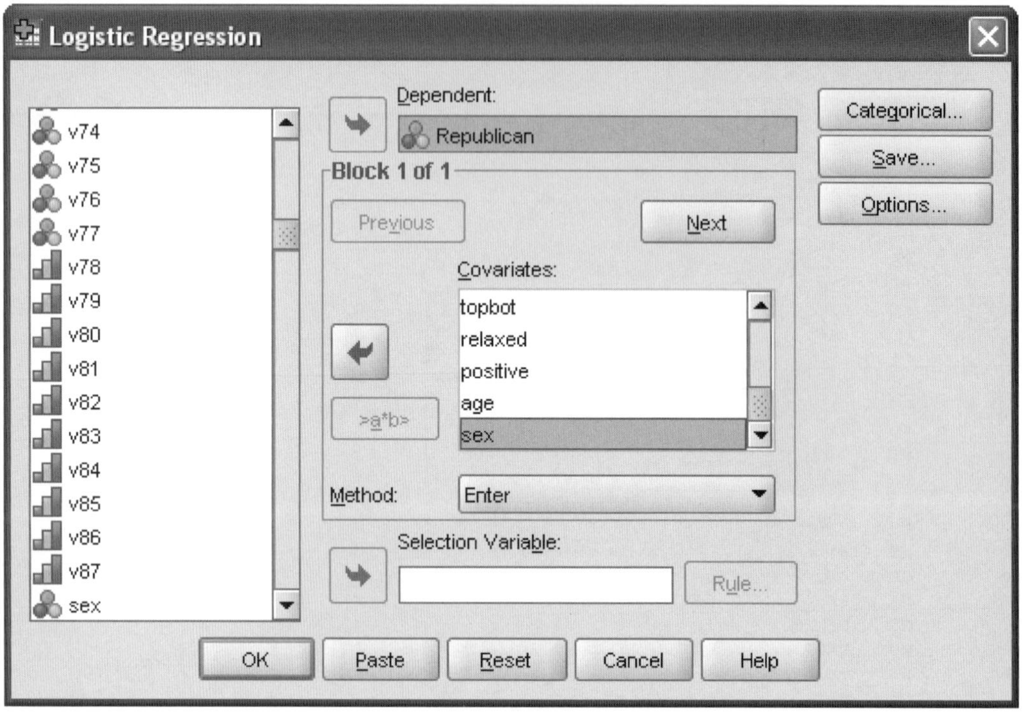

Figure 10.2a *Logistic regression window*

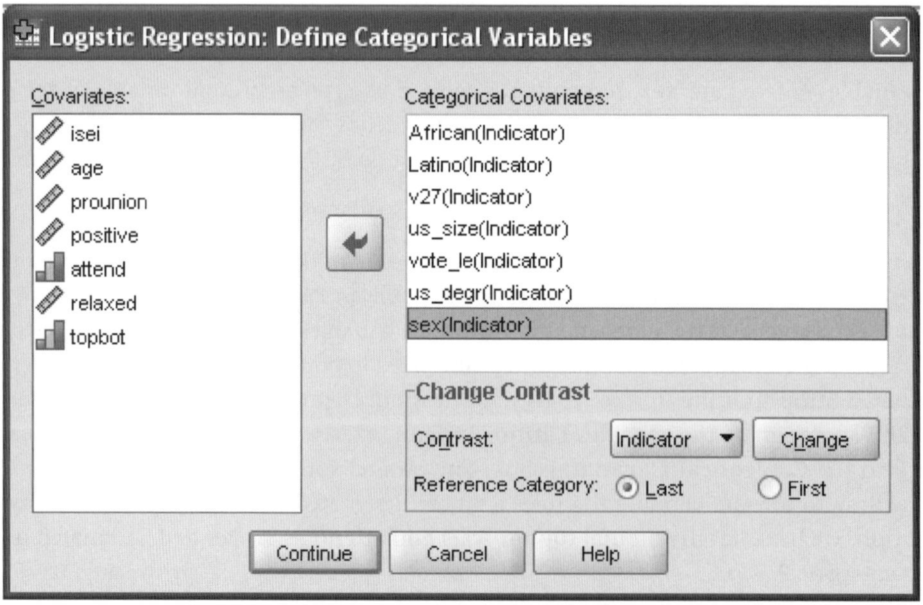

Figure 10.2b *Logistic regression sub-window: defining variables as categorical*

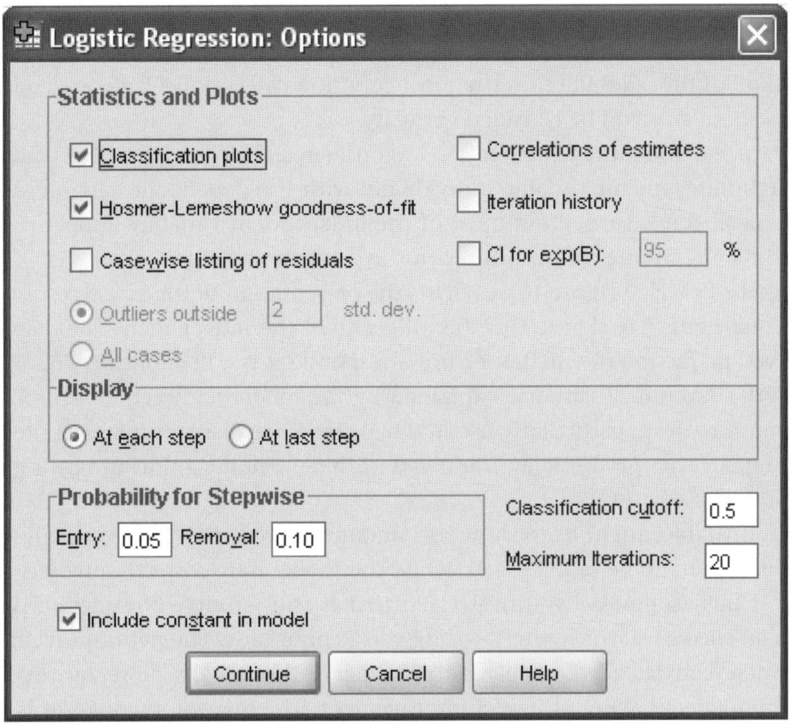

Figure 10.2c   *Logistic regression sub-window: optional output*

with the SPSS default **Method** of **Enter**ing all independent variables at once instead of opting for entering variables in steps, we click on **OK** to run the procedure.

Interpretation of results

The first bit of output is the Case Processing Summary in Figure 10.3a, which shows that even though a large number of variables are being included in this analysis, the 'listwise' loss of cases due to missing values is fairly small, with 87.7 per cent of cases remaining in the analysis. This is followed by a table of the Categorical Variables' Codings. As well as listing the number that falls into each category (thereby providing a check whether any categories are prohibitively small for an analysis), note that the table indicates which category of each variable is the reference category against which any effects will be contrasted. The reference categories for each variable were left as the last category, SPSS's default.

One idiosyncrasy of SPSS's binary regression procedure is that it automatically recodes the two values of the dependent variable to 0 and 1, arbitrarily setting the lowest value 0 and the highest to 1. This means that the category of interest *must* be given the higher coding to avoid SPSS inadvertently conducting an analysis that focuses on the 'absence' category rather than the category of interest. In order to avoid any confusion, the safest procedure is to code the two categories of the dependent variable into 0 and 1 yourself, with the category of interest being coded '1'. This is what we have done here, with 'Republican' being coded '1' and 'All others' being coded '0'. The box with the 'Dependent Variable Encoding' shows this.

'Block O: Beginning Block' in Figure 10.3b shows the state of play prior to the analysis proper and is mainly useful as a baseline against which to compare results. The 'Classification Table' shows that if we assume that all of the cases fall into the most common category (in this case code '2.00 Others'), 77.2 per cent of respondents will be classified correctly.

The table of 'Variables not in the Equation' can be considered analogous to a table of simple correlation coefficients of each independent variable individually with the dependent variable. Note that before the multivariate regression is carried out most of the independent variables appear to be significantly associated when in a one-to-one relationship with the dependent variable.

'Block 1: Method = Enter' in Figure 10.3c begins the presentation of the actual results. The 'Omnibus Tests of Model Coefficients' are significant; the influence of the independent variables produces a significantly improved prediction of whether or not a respondent is a Republican. The 'R squares' are an attempt to show the amount of variance explained by the model (between 21 and 32 per cent). The 'Hosmer and Lemeshow Test', particularly useful when there are a large number of predictor variables, also indicates the model has produced an improved fit (here, a non-significant result greater than 0.05 indicates an improved prediction).

The 'Classification Table' attempts to show the amount of predictive improvement from the model. The improvement appears to be rather small; while the model now correctly predicts that 106 people are Republicans, it misses almost two-thirds (198) that it still wrongly considers to be 'Others' and, furthermore, has labelled 61 of the 'Others' wrongly as Republicans. The net improvement is marginal, 80.6 per cent now correctly labelled compared to 77.2 per cent originally. Note, however, that this table can give only an imperfect picture of model improvement. The regression equation is giving the odds of whether each person is a Republican or not. However, the table arbitrarily applies a .5 cut-off so that all those with odds even slightly above .50 being attributed as Republican and all those with odds even slightly below .50 being attributed as 'Others'. There is no way of knowing from the table whether large proportions of respondents are close to the cut-off point.

Logistic Regression

Case Processing Summary

Unweighted Cases[a]		N	Percent
Selected Cases	Included in Analysis	1332	87.7
	Missing Cases	186	12.3
	Total	1518	100.0
	Unselected Cases	0	.0
	Total	1518	100.0

a. If weight is in effect, see classification table for the total number of cases.

Dependent Variable Encoding

Original Value	Internal Value
0	0
1.00 Republican	1

Figure 10.3a *Binary logistic regression: initial output*

Categorical Variables Codings

		Frequency	Parameter coding					
			(1)	(2)	(3)	(4)	(5)	(6)
us_size Size of community: USA	1 1-9 millions	77	1.000	.000	.000	.000	.000	.000
	2 500 000-999 999	75	.000	1.000	.000	.000	.000	.000
	3 100 000-499 999	155	.000	.000	1.000	.000	.000	.000
	4 50 000- 99 999	178	.000	.000	.000	1.000	.000	.000
	5 10 000- 49 999	443	.000	.000	.000	.000	1.000	.000
	6 1 000- 9 999	383	.000	.000	.000	.000	.000	1.000
	7 Less than 1 000	21	.000	.000	.000	.000	.000	.000
us_degr Country specific education: USA	1 Less th High school	193	1.000	.000	.000	.000		
	2 High school	698	.000	1.000	.000	.000		
	3 Junior college	101	.000	.000	1.000	.000		
	4 Bachelor	218	.000	.000	.000	1.000		
	5 Graduate	122	.000	.000	.000	.000		
sex R: Gender	1 Male	632	1.000					
	2 Female	700	.000					
Latino Latin ethnic identity	1.00 Latin	120	1.000					
	2.00 All others	1212	.000					
v27 Respondent currently working for pay	1 Yes	937	1.000					
	2 No	395	.000					
vote_le R: Vote last election: yes, no	1 Yes	936	1.000					
	2 No	396	.000					
African African ethnic identity	1.00 African	186	1.000					
	2.00 All other	1146	.000					

Figure 10.3a *Continued*

Block 0: Beginning Block

Classification Table[a,b]

Observed			Predicted		
			Republican		
			0	1.00 Republican	Percentage Correct
Step 0	Republican	0	1028	0	100.0
		1.00 Republican	304	0	.0
		Overall Percentage			77.2

a. Constant is included in the model.
b. The cut value is .500

Variables in the Equation

		B	S.E.	Wald	df	Sig.	Exp(B)
Step 0	Constant	−1.218	.065	348.258	1	.000	.296

Variables not in the equation

			Score	df	Sig.
Step 0	Variables	African(1)	52.451	1	.000
		Latino(1)	7.979	1	.005
		isei	21.593	1	.000
		v27(1)	1.357	1	.244
		vote_le(1)	47.750	1	.000
		Us_size	12.492	6	.052
		us_size(1)	1.637	1	.201
		us_size(2)	2.100	1	.147
		Us_size(3)	4.462	1	.035
		us_size(4)	.014	1	.905
		Us_size(5)	5.481	1	.019
		us_size(6)	.053	1	.819
		Us_degr	32.190	4	.000
		Us_degr(1)	15.240	1	.000
		Us_degr(2)	1.479	1	.224
		Us_degr(3)	.055	1	.815
		Us_degr(4)	21.451	1	.000

Figure 10.3b *Beginning block of binary logistic regression output*

Variables not in the equation *(Continued)*

	Score	df	Sig.
prounion	163.770	1	.000
attend	30.313	1	.000
topbot	5.931	1	.015
relaxed	6.402	1	.011
positive	2.095	1	.148
age	4.778	1	.029
sex(1)	2.783	1	.095
Overall Statistics	278.507	22	.000

Figure 10.3b *Continued*

Block 1: Method = Enter

Omnibus Tests of Model Coefficients

		Chi-square	df	Sig.
Step 1	Step	314.883	22	.000
	Block	314.883	22	.000
	Model	314.883	22	.000

Model Summary

Step	−2 Log likelihood	Cox & Snell R Square	Nagelkerke R Square
1	1116.022[a]	.211	.320

a. Estimation terminated at iteration number 7 because parameter estimates changed by less than .001.

Hosmer and Lemeshow Test

Step	Chi-square	df	Sig.
1	7.308	8	.504

Figure 10.3c *Binary logistic regression solution*

Contingency Table for Hosmer and Lemeshow Test

		Republican = .00		Republican = 1.00 Republican		Total
		Observed	Expected	Observed	Expected	
Step 1	1	130	131.572	3	1.428	133
	2	128	128.321	5	4.679	133
	3	126	124.152	7	8.848	133
	4	119	119.954	14	13.046	133
	5	118	114.594	15	18.406	133
	6	108	106.752	25	26.248	133
	7	101	98.390	32	34.610	133
	8	79	87.317	54	45.683	133
	9	78	71.909	55	61.091	133
	10	41	45.038	94	89.962	135

Classification Table[a]

				Predicted		
				Republican		
Observed				0	1.00 Republican	Percentage Correct
Step 1	Republican	0		967	61	94.1
		1.00 Republican		198	106	34.9
		Overall Percentage				80.6

a. The cut value is .500.

Figure 10.3c *Continued*

Variables in the Equation

		B	S.E.	Wald	df	Sig.	Exp(B)
Step 1	African(1)	−2.785	.528	27.809	1	.000	.062
	Latino(1)	−.563	.336	2.815	1	.093	.569
	isei	−.003	.005	.419	1	.518	.997
	v27(1)	.055	.193	.082	1	.775	1.057
	vote_le(1)	.982	.211	21.728	1	.000	2.670
	us_size			5.905	6	.434	
	us_size(1)	−.435	.699	.388	1	.534	.647
	us_size(2)	−.742	.695	1.141	1	.285	.476
	us_size(3)	−.923	.646	2.042	1	.153	.397
	us_size(4)	−.492	.629	.610	1	.435	.612

Figure 10.3d *Binary logistic regression solution, Variables in the equation*

Variables in the Equation   (*Continued*)

	B	S.E.	Wald	df	Sig.	Exp(B)
us_size(5)	−.416	.607	.471	1	.493	.660
us_size(6)	−.701	.607	1.336	1	.248	.496
us_degr			2.461	4	.652	
us_degr(1)	−.209	.392	.284	1	.594	.812
us_degr(2)	.106	.284	.139	1	.709	1.112
us_degr(3)	.250	.365	.469	1	.493	1.284
us_degr(4)	.243	.293	.690	1	.406	1.276
prounion	−.780	.079	97.750	1	.000	.458
attend	−.172	.033	27.335	1	.000	.842
topbot	−.037	.046	.646	1	.422	.964
relaxed	−.172	.067	6.521	1	.011	.842
positive	.094	.069	1.839	1	.175	1.099
age	−.002	.006	.103	1	.748	.998
sex(1)	.212	.155	1.880	1	.170	1.237
Constant	−.480	.870	.304	1	.581	.619

Figure 10.3d   *Continued*

The real meat of the results is in the 'Variables in the Equation' table in Figure 10.3d. Since we used the 'Enter' method, all variables are included. In this table of multivariate results, the number of variables that show statistical significance has halved from ten to five. Most notably, the three indicators of social status – objective and subjective rankings of status and educational attainment, **isei**, **topbot** and **us_degr**, respectively – are no longer significant. Of the remainder, four – **prounion**, **African**, **attend** and **vote_le** – are significant at $p<0.0005$. Here we can use the Wald coefficients to rank these in order of importance; the larger the Wald value, the more significant the variable. Hence, the largest single determinant of being a Republican is **prounion**. The beta (B) coefficients in the left-hand column are the logged odds of being in the category of interest (in this example, being a Republican). The sign of the beta (B) coefficient indicates whether the effect of an independent variable is positive, raising the odds of being in the category of interest, or negative, lowering the odds of being in the category of interest. The beta coefficient for **prounion** is negative, so possessing pro-labour union opinions makes a respondent less likely to be attributed Republican. The other three variables with a 'Sig.' of '.000' all have Wald coefficients in close proximity, each just above 27. The beta for **African** is negative, indicating that respondents with an African identity are less likely to be Republicans. The beta for **vote_le** is positive, which indicates that those who voted in the last election are more likely to have a Republican Party affiliation. The 'B' for **attend** is also negative, but because the variable has been coded so that higher values signify less attendance, this indicates that the odds are that those who attend religious services more often are more likely to be Republican. In addition, those with a self-attributed 'relaxed' view of life appear to have a lower probability of being Republican.

The 'Exp(B)' column on the right-hand side is another way of looking at the same results, only allowing a somewhat more direct interpretation. Exp(B) can be interpreted as the predicted change in odds when there is an increase of one unit in the independent variable. An Exp(B) less than one means that the odds of

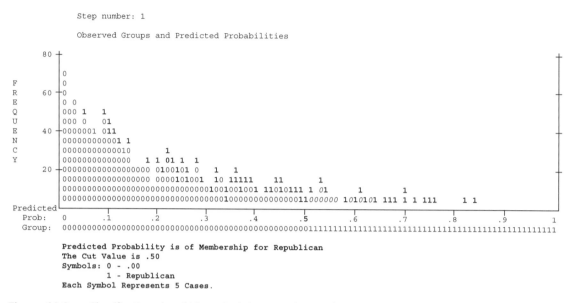

Figure 10.3e *Classification plot of binary logistic regression result*

being in the category of interest decrease and an Exp(B) greater than one means that the odds increase. So, looking at these results, the Exp(B) column is predicting that: an increase of one unit on the **prounion** scale will cut the odds of the respondent being a Republican by a bit more than half (.458); having an **African** ethnic identity will lower the odds of being a Republican considerably to less than a tenth in comparison to others (.062); having voted in the last election will raise the odds of being a Republican more than two and a half times (2.670) and so forth. To sum up, the findings of this binary logistic regression analysis are that being anti-union, having voted in the last election and being a regular attender at religious service will raise the odds of a respondent being affiliated to the Republican Party, while having an African ethnic identity or assessing oneself as being a relaxed person will lower the odds of being a Republican.

Finally it is worth remembering that the variables that have been eliminated in the multivariate analysis in effect represent hypotheses that have been disproven. Remarkably, there is no indication that higher social status links to being a Republican. In addition to the three variables that stand directly or obliquely for social status being eliminated, having a Hispanic identity (**Latin**), **age**, **sex**, community size (**us_size**) and having a **positive** attitude to life all fall out as determinants of Republican identification.

The 'classification plot' in Figure 10.3e gives a visual representation of the correspondence between observed and predicted values for the dependent variable that is an improvement over the 'Classification Table' in Figure 10.3c. The '1's in the plot represent the actual observed category of interest, 'Republicans' and the '0's represent 'All others'. The horizontal 'x' axis is a scale of probability of being in the category of interest (Republicans) and ranges between 0.0 (no chance of being a Republican) and 1.0 (100 per cent chance of being a Republican). The vertical 'y' axis is the frequency of cases. An ideal solution would be a 'U'-shaped distribution with all the '0's clustering on the left and all the '1's clustering on the right. A terrible solution would be a Normal-shaped distribution that peaked in the centre around 0.5 on the scale with the '0's and '1's all mixed up. The actual distribution that is displayed in the plot depicts the middling quality of the result of the analysis. The plot is far from a perfect result. There is a considerable portion of the '1's (that is, actual Republicans) whose predicted value falls below 0.5 and hence are predicted to be in the 'All others' category and also some '0's whose predicted values are above 0.5 and hence are wrongly predicted to be Republicans. Nevertheless, the distribution definitely is not peaked in the middle, shows at least half the 'U' shape on the left and the zeros tend to cluster towards the left and ones towards the right of the scale. Not a perfect solution, but perhaps a reasonable one.

MULTINOMIAL LOGISTIC REGRESSION – WORKED EXAMPLE

In order to provide an example of multinomial logistic regression in which the dependent variable is nominal but with more than two categories, we will return to our original United States political party affiliation variable, **us_prty**, and use Recode to create a new variable, **Parties**, with three categories: Republicans; Independents; and Democrats. We will use this new variable as the dependent variable in a multinomial logistic regression that essentially will repeat the analysis we have just carried out on the Republicans.

As before, we go to the **Analyze** menu, select **Regression**, and then select **Multinomial Logistic…** This brings up the Multinomial Logistic Regression main window in Figure 10.4a.

Multinomial logistic regression seems to have been designed by SPSS a bit later as the interface is somewhat more 'user-friendly' than that for binary logistic regression. Move the variable **Parties** into the **Dependent** box, move the same categorical variables that we used in the previous example into the **Factor(s):** box and the scalar variables into the **Covariate(s):** box.

We need to specify the model that we desire. Click on the **Model…** button to bring up the Model sub-window (Figure 10.4b).

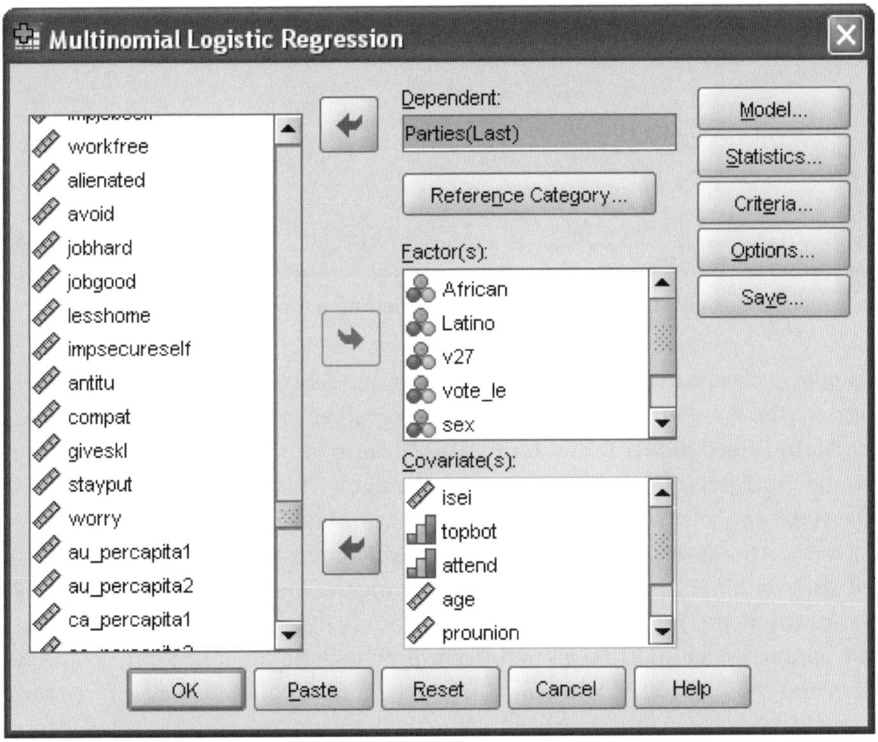

Figure 10.4a *Multinomial logistic regression*

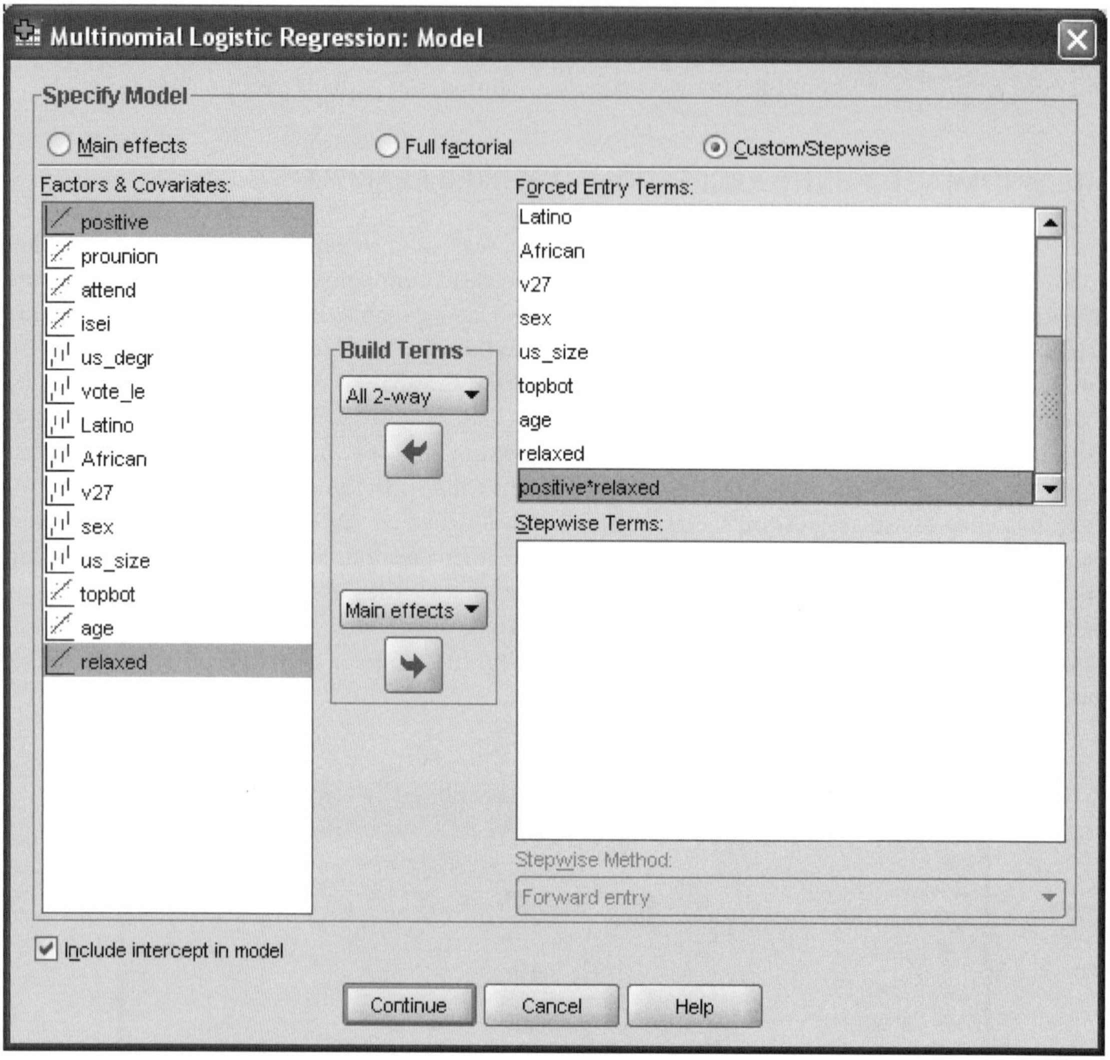

Figure 10.4b *Multinomial logistic regression sub-window: setting a model*

In this example, we want to continue with an 'Enter' model in which all independent variables are put in simultaneously. We do this by selecting all the variables in the left-hand **Factors & Covariates:** box, selecting **Main Effects** under **Build Terms** and clicking on the right-hand arrow to move all the variables into the top **Forced Entry Terms:** box on the right. This will generate a multinomial logistic regression that is the equivalent of our previous example for binary logistic regression.

The format of the Multinomial Logistic Regression: Model sub-window allows for interaction variables to be specified easily within the procedure rather than having to generate them beforehand using Compute under the **Transform** menu. For example, to create a two-way interaction variable, select **All 2-way** from the drop-down options under **Build Terms** in the centre, choose the variables for the two-way interactions that are desired and then click the right-hand arrow; the interaction variables will appear in the right-hand list of terms. We have done this to produce one 2-way interaction variable, **relaxed*positive**, which can be seen on the bottom of the independent variables listed in the **Forced Entry Terms:** box.

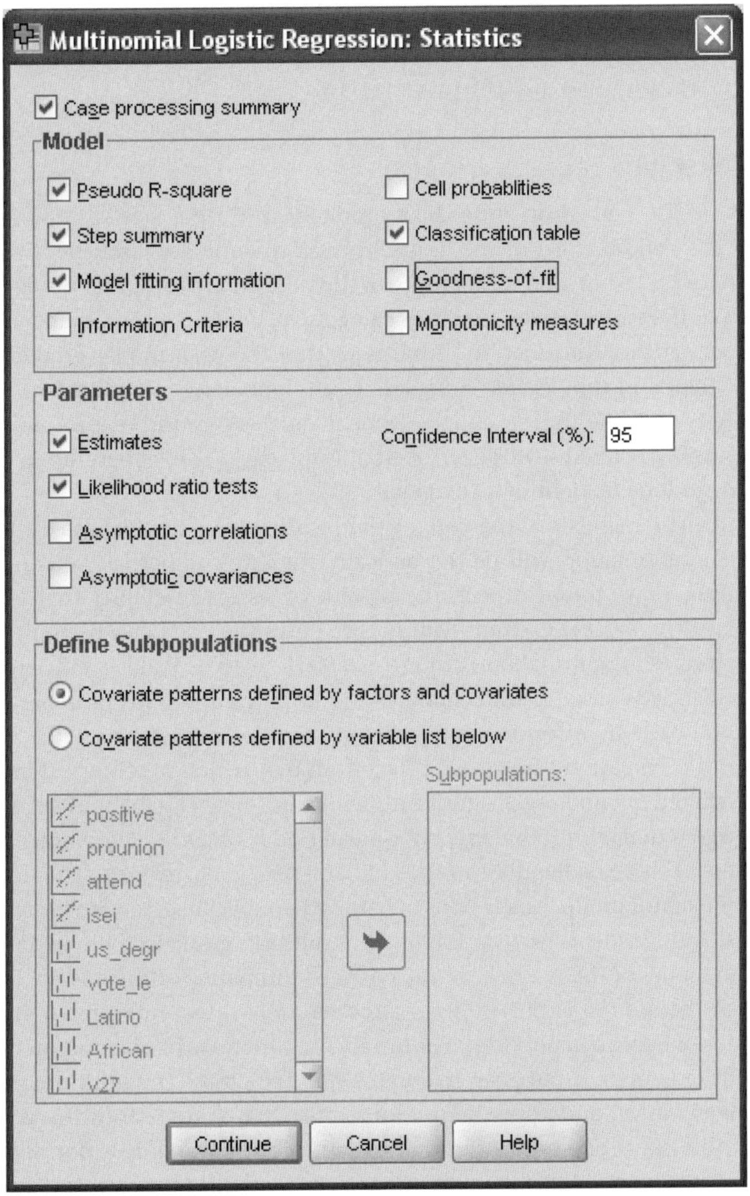

Figure 10.4c *Multinomial logistic regression sub-window: selecting statistics*

If we wanted to carry out a stepwise logistic regression, this would be done by entering the desired independent variables into the lower box on the right side, **Stepwise Terms:**. The **Stepwise Method:** menu at the bottom right would then 'light up' and the desired stepwise method could be specified. (An example of stepwise regression is given with linear regression in Module 8. The discussion in that module of the 'logic' behind using a stepwise approach and when it could be useful would apply equally well to this module. Here, to keep from further complicating what is a difficult module, we have restricted ourselves to only using the 'Enter' method.)

Returning to the main window, we click on the **Statistics...** button to bring up the Statistics sub-window in Figure 10.4c. We keep the defaults and also tick the **Classification table** button. We then return to the main window and, as usual, run the procedure by clicking **OK**.

Interpretation of results

The multinomial logistic regression procedure produces a 'Case Processing Summary' (shown in Figure 10.5a) that is a combination of the 'Case Procession Summary' and the 'Categorical Variables Codings' in the binary procedure and rather more to the point than both. The number and percentages in each category of all the variables designated as categorical, including the dependent variable **Parties**, is shown. The 'Model Fitting Information' informs us that the final model produces a significant fit to the data (Sig. = .000) and the 'Pseudo R-Square' equivalents range from 19.5 to 38.5 per cent. The 'Likelihood Ratio Tests' indicate that seven independent variables – **positive**, **prounion**, **attend**, **vote_le**, **African**, **age** and possibly **relaxed** – will exert a significant effect somewhere upon the odds of being either a Republican, an independent or a Democrat.

As with binary logistic regression, the core of the results are in the 'Parameter Estimates' table in Figure 10.5b. Their interpretation will be the basically the same as before. Looking first at the odds of being a Republican, as we might expect, the pattern of results resembles that which we found in the binary regression. The most important feature that raises the odds of a person being a Republican as before is **prounion**, being anti-labour union ($p<0.0005$, with a Wald coefficient of 145). Having an **African** ethnic identity comes second, significantly lowering the odds of being a supporter of the Republican Party, followed by **attend**ance at religious services, which raises the chance of being a Republican. The rest of the pattern, however, differs from that which we observed in the Binary regression. **vote_le** and **relaxed** are no longer significant, while four new variables (albeit at levels more than $p<0.0005$) appear: **age** (younger respondents have greater odds of being Republicans, $p<0.01$), **positive** ($p<0.05$), **Latino**, less likely to be Republican ($p<0.05$) and **sex** (male, $p<0.05$). The reason for the differences is that the comparator group for the odds of being a Republican is now no longer 'All others' but is instead 'Democrats'. Independents now appear in the results as a group in their own right, and when we examine their results some of the reasons for the changed estimates for the odds of being a Republican become apparent. As before the Exp(B) column allows a more direct interpretation of each variable's effects upon the odds of being a Republican. For instance, an increase of one unit on the **prounion** scale will reduce the odds of being a Republican to about a quarter (.288). The multinominal logistic regression output also gives a lower and upper bound for Exp(B). If 1.0 falls within the range of these upper and lower bounds, this is a strong indication that the effect of the variable is not significant.

Looking at the results for the Independents, as with the Republicans **prounion** appears as the single most important independent variable (Wald = 63, $p<0.0005$). **African** again comes second and in this case as with the Republican results, having an African ethnic identity makes one less likely to be an Independent. This is followed closely by **vote_le** but here *not* having voted in the last election raises the odds of now being an Independent. **age** is also significant ($p<0.0005$) with less affiliated younger respondents having greater odds of being Independents. Finally, having a **positive** opinion of oneself appears to raise the chances of being an Independent ($p<0.05$).

Finally, you should note that Democrats by virtue of being coded the highest (3) are the 'reference category' against which the Republicans and Independents have been compared. While there are no results directly available for the Democratic Party supporters, the factors that define them can be inferred in contrast to the Republicans and Independents. Hence, respondents who have pro-labour

Nominal Regression

Case Processing Summary		N	Marginal Percentage
Parties Main split of parties	1.00 Republicans	304	22.8%
	2.00 Independents	604	45.3%
	3.00 Democrats	424	31.8%
African African ethnic identity	1.00 African	186	14.0%
	2.00 All other	1146	86.0%
Latino Latin ethnic identity	1.00 Latin	120	9.0%
	2.00 All others	1212	91.0%
v27 Respondent currently working for pay	1 Yes	937	70.3%
	2 No	395	29.7%
vote_le R: Vote last election: yes, no	1 Yes	936	70.3%
	2 No	396	29.7%
sex R: Gender	1 Male	632	47.4%
	2 Female	700	52.6%
us_degr Country specific education: USA	1 Less th High school	193	14.5%
	2 High school	698	52.4%
	3 Junior college	101	7.6%
	4 Bachelor	218	16.4%
	5 Graduate	122	9.2%
us_size Size of community: USA	1 1-9 millions	77	5.8%
	2 500 000-999 999	75	5.6%
	3 100 000-499 999	155	11.6%
	4 50 000- 99 999	178	13.4%
	5 10 000- 49 999	443	33.3%
	6 1 000- 9 999	383	28.8%
	7 Less than 1 000	21	1.6%
Valid		1332	100.0%
Missing		186	
Total		1518	
Subpopulation		1332[a]	

a. The dependent variable has only one value observed in 1332 (100.0%) subpopulations.

Figure 10.5a *Multinomial logistic regression preliminary output*

Model Fitting Information

Model	Model Fitting Criteria	Likelihood Ratio Tests		
	−2 Log Likelihood	Chi-Square	df	Sig.
Intercept Only	2.824E3			
Final	2.272E3	551.853	46	.000

Pseudo R-Square

Cox and Snell	.339
Nagelkerke	.385
McFadden	.195

Likelihood Ratio Tests

Effect	Model Fitting Criteria	Likelihood Ratio Tests		
	−2 Log Likelihood of Reduced Model	Chi-Square	df	Sig.
Intercept	2.272E3	.000	0	.
positive	2.278E3	5.995	2	.050
prounion	2.452E3	179.416	2	.000
attend	2.301E3	28.465	2	.000
isei	2.274E3	1.495	2	.473
us_degr	2.279E3	6.244	8	.620
vote_le	2.336E3	63.430	2	.000
Latino	2.277E3	4.331	2	.115
African	2.381E3	108.294	2	.000
v27	2.274E3	1.295	2	.523
sex	2.277E3	4.123	2	.127
us_size	2.281E3	8.960	12	.706
topbot	2.273E3	.708	2	.702
age	2.293E3	20.610	2	.000
relaxed	2.278E3	5.902	2	.052
relaxed * positive	2.273E3	.286	2	.867

The chi-square statistic is the difference in -2 log-likelihoods between the final model and a reduced model. The reduced model is formed by omitting an effect from the final model. The null hypothesis is that a ll parameters of that effect are 0.

a. This reduced model is equivalent to the final model because omitting the effect does not increase the degrees of freedom.

Figure 10.5a *Continued*

Parameter Estimates

Parties Main split of parties[a]	B	Std. Error	Wald	df	Sig.	Exp(B)	95% Confidence Interval for Exp(B)	
							Lower Bound	Upper Bound
1.00 Republicans								
Intercept	2.289	1.074	4.539	1	.033			
positive	.180	.081	4.936	1	.026	1.197	1.021	1.403
prounion	-1.243	.103	144.718	1	.000	.288	.236	.353
attend	-.172	.039	19.390	1	.000	.842	.780	.909
isei	-.007	.006	1.152	1	.283	.993	.981	1.006
[us_degr=1]	-.064	.454	.020	1	.887	.938	.385	2.282
[us_degr=2]	.009	.337	.001	1	.980	1.009	.521	1.951
[us_degr=3]	.385	.437	.778	1	.378	1.470	.625	3.458
[us_degr=4]	.134	.351	.145	1	.703	1.143	.574	2.275
[us_degr=5]	0[b]	.	.	0	.	.	.	.
[vote_le=1]	.157	.249	.397	1	.529	1.170	.718	1.908
[vote_le=2]	0[b]	.	.	0	.	.	.	.
[Latino=1.00]	-.795	.389	4.170	1	.041	.452	.211	.969
[Latino=2.00]	0[b]	.	.	0	.	.	.	.
[African=1.00]	-3.573	.544	43.135	1	.000	.028	.010	.082
[African=2.00]	0[b]	.	.	0	.	.	.	.
[v27=1]	-.085	.227	.141	1	.707	.918	.588	1.433
[v27=2]	0[b]	.	.	0	.	.	.	.
[sex=1]	.365	.184	3.947	1	.047	1.440	1.005	2.063
[sex=2]	0[b]	.	.	0	.	.	.	.
[us_size=1]	-.254	.865	.086	1	.769	.776	.142	4.232
[us_size=2]	-.841	.853	.971	1	.324	.431	.081	2.297
[us_size=3]	-1.079	.806	1.793	1	.181	.340	.070	1.650
[us_size=4]	-.699	.790	.783	1	.376	.497	.106	2.337
[us_size=5]	-.515	.767	.449	1	.503	.598	.133	2.690
[us_size=6]	-.808	.768	1.106	1	.293	.446	.099	2.009
[us_size=7]	0[b]	.	.	0	.	.	.	.
topbot	-.025	.053	.215	1	.643	.976	.879	1.083
age	-.017	.007	6.586	1	.010	.983	.970	.996
relaxed	-.154	.081	3.648	1	.056	.857	.732	1.004
relaxed * positive	-.021	.067	.101	1	.750	.979	.859	1.116

Figure 10.5b *Multinomial logistic regression parameter estimates*

Parties Main split of parties[a]		B	Std. Error	Wald	df	Sig.	Exp(B)	95% Confidence Interval for Exp(B)	
								Lower Bound	Upper Bound
2.00 Independents	Intercept	3.010	.877	11.775	1	.001			
	positive	.125	.062	4.040	1	.044	1.133	1.003	1.281
	proumion	-.686	.086	63.337	1	.000	.504	.425	.596
	attend	.001	.031	.002	1	.963	1.001	.942	1.064
	isei	-.005	.005	1.146	1	.284	.995	.985	1.005
	[us_degr=1]	.196	.348	.317	1	.574	1.216	.615	2.405
	[us_degr=2]	-.145	.279	.269	1	.604	.865	.501	1.495
	[us_degr=3]	.208	.360	.334	1	.563	1.232	.608	2.496
	[us_degr=4]	-.159	.300	.282	1	.596	.853	.474	1.535
	[us_degr=5]	0[b]	.	.	0	.	.	.	.
	[vote_le=1]	-1.083	.175	38.069	1	.000	.339	.240	.478
	[vote_le=2]	0[b]	.	.	0	.	.	.	.
	[Latino=1.00]	-.352	.280	1.579	1	.209	.703	.406	1.218
	[Latino=2.00]	0[b]	.	.	0	.	.	.	.
	[African=1.00]	-1.465	.212	47.784	1	.000	.231	.152	.350
	[African=2.00]	0[b]	.	.	0	.	.	.	.
	[v27=1]	-.197	.177	1.234	1	.267	.821	.580	1.163
	[v27=2]	0[b]	.	.	0	.	.	.	.
	[sex=1]	.206	.147	1.955	1	.162	1.229	.921	1.640
	[sex=2]	0[b]	.	.	0	.	.	.	.
	[us_size=1]	.287	.699	.168	1	.682	1.332	.338	5.246
	[us_size=2]	-.152	.689	.049	1	.825	.859	.222	3.315
	[us_size=3]	-.215	.664	.105	1	.746	.807	.220	2.962
	[us_size=4]	-.304	.658	.213	1	.644	.738	.203	2.680
	[us_size=5]	-.141	.643	.048	1	.827	.869	.246	3.063
	[us_size=6]	-.156	.644	.059	1	.808	.855	.242	3.023
	[us_size=7]	0[b]	.	.	0	.	.	.	.
	topbot	.015	.040	.130	1	.718	1.015	.938	1.098
	age	-.024	.005	20.006	1	.000	.976	.966	.987
	relaxed	.018	.063	.082	1	.774	1.018	.899	1.153
	relaxed * positive	-.027	.051	.282	1	.595	.973	.881	1.075

a. The reference category is: 3.00 Democrats.
b. This parameter is set to zero because it is redundant.

Figure 10.5b   Continued

Classification

Observed	Predicted			
	1.00 Republicans	2.00 Independents	3.00 Democrats	Percent Correct
1.00 Republicans	148	113	43	48.7%
2.00 Independents	79	405	120	67.1%
3.00 Democrats	35	143	246	58.0%
Overall Percentage	19.7%	49.6%	30.7%	60.0%

Figure 10.5b   *Continued*

union views, or have an African ethnic identity or who are older rather than younger are more likely to be Democrats. Looking at the results as a whole, it is also apparent why the variable **vote_le**, that helped define Republicans in the binary regression is no longer significant for Republicans in this multinomial analysis. Supporters of either political party, Republican or Democrat, are more likely to have voted in the last election than the more apathetic Independents.

The multinomial logistic regression output concludes with the requested classification table. The diagonal running from the upper left to the bottom right shows the numbers correctly predicted to be in the same party category as their actual affiliations. While only 60 per cent have been classified correctly, this is better than the potential benchmarks of a random attribution (which would generate one-third correct classifications) or attributing all respondents to the most common category, the 50 per cent who are Independents.

SPSS EXERCISES FOR LOGISTIC REGRESSION

1. Using the dataset for the country of your choice, try to recreate approximations of the 'political party affiliation' analyses that have been presented in this module.

   (a) For the binary logistic regression, recode your country's political party affiliation variable so that one of the larger parties, preferably the largest conservative party on 'the right' is contrasted with all others, including those who support no political party. Then recreate the binary logistic regression with this new dichotomous variable as the dependent variable using the same independent variables as those in this module.

   Three issues may arise when recreating the analyses in this module.

   ■ It is possible that some of the categories in the ordinal independent variables in your country may have very small numbers. If this is the case and you are using the variable as a categorical variable in the logistic regression, consider collapsing categories together.

   ■ Not all countries have the scalar variables for respondent's self-assessment about how **positive** and **relaxed** they were. These came from a section of the interview schedule that was optional for nations. If you are using a dataset that does not have them, simply omit them from the analysis.

- There may not be groups that can be given ethnic identity codes like the two in the analyses in this module. If this is not possible, you will have to omit that part of the analysis.
- Compare your results with those for the United States, noting the similarities and any differences. What could be possible explanations for the differences between the two nations?

(b) For the multinomial logistic regression, Recode the political party affiliation variable and create three or more categories based upon the larger political parties or political groupings. (You may have an unaffiliated neutral or middle group like the Independent category for the USA.) Try to do the recode so that the highest code goes to a party or political grouping on 'the left'. It is important that there is a reasonable proportion of cases in the highest code (say, a minimum of 5 per cent) since this will be the 'reference group' against which all other categories of the dependent variable are contrasted. (Depending upon which country's dataset you are using, there may be smaller parties or groupings that do not fit validity into any larger categorization. If so, you may need to make them 'missing values' and exclude them from the analysis altogether.)

Again, compare your results with those for the United States, noting the similarities and any differences. What could be possible explanations for the differences between the two nations?

2. Using the country and categorical dependent variables of your own choosing, carry out binary and multinomial logistic regressions to answer a research question of your own.

Loglinear Analysis

INTRODUCTION

Loglinear analysis is a prime example of necessity being the mother of invention. By the early 1970s, the development of multivariate techniques for the analysis of quantitative or interval/ratio data in the social sciences was well in hand. Analysis of variance, multiple regression and factor analysis, all techniques covered in earlier modules in this text, were firmly established and made up part of the battery of statistical techniques available in SPSS at that time. Most of the variables available in a typical set of social science data, however, are categorical or ordinal variables with a limited number of distinct levels and hence are not suitable for parametric techniques. Social scientists had learned to think about data analysis in terms of multivariate problems but often were frustrated from carrying out multivariate analyses due to the lack of a technique suitable for nominal or ordinal data. Loglinear analysis was created expressly to fill this gap.

We will present the loglinear analysis technique in the following manner. First, the types of problem that loglinear analysis can answer will be discussed in a general manner. Second, the 'logic' underlying the loglinear analysis procedure will be presented in non-statistical terms. Third, to illustrate the general discussions, specific examples will be given of loglinear analyses carried out on the **all nations** ISSP dataset.

Problems that loglinear analysis can answer

The loglinear analysis technique makes possible the multivariate analysis of data in which all the variables in the analysis are made up of categories; either nominal data in which the categories do not fall into any particular order or ordinal data in which they do. The technique can address two basic types of issues.

On the one hand, loglinear analysis can be thought of as an extension of contingency table or crosstabulation analysis in which there are several control variables. Let us take a very basic and general example in order to illustrate this first type of problem. Assume that we have four categorical or ordinal variables, which we call: A; B; C; and D. Each of these four variables can take three distinct values or levels: 1; 2; or 3. We can indicate a variable and level by a subscript. For instance, the three values that variable A can take would be indicated by: A_1, A_2, and A_3; and the three values that variable B can take would be: B_1, B_2 and B_3 and so on. If we think there may be an association between variables A and B, we could put them into a crosstabulation table of A by B and test for an association using the techniques presented in the crosstabulation analysis module – applying a statistical test of association like Chi-square and, if a significant association is found, working out which cells in the table cause the association by using adjusted residuals. If we think the form of the association between A and B might be different depending upon the level of variable C, we could produce three crosstabulation tables of A by B, one for each level of variable C (that is, variable C would be a control variable). Each table could be checked in turn for whether it had a significant association and what the pattern of association in the table's cells might be.

So far so good. However, problems begin to arise if we also suspect that the pattern of associations we find in the A by B tables with C as a control *also* might vary depending upon the value that D takes. If we use both C and D as control variables, we will end up with *nine* separate A by B tables, one for each of the combinations of the variables C and D. Each table could have a different pattern of association, with some of these tables having statistically significant associations while others do not. Also, there may be no real reason why we should not present the data in the form of *C by D* tables with A and B as control variables (or A by C tables with B and D as controls, or B by D tables with A and C as control variables, and so on). This is a multivariate problem – we require a means of deciding which of the many possible associations between these four categorical variables are important so we can concentrate on them and ignore the many other insignificant associations. Loglinear analysis can provide an answer to this problem.

A second version of loglinear analysis can be thought of as a categorical parallel to multiple regression analysis. Staying with our 'A to D variables' format, let us say that variable A can be considered possibly affected or caused by variables B to D. For example, A could be whether a person had decided to take early retirement. B could be a person's sex, C whether the person's health had been good, average or poor, and D whether the person had a pension plan or not. B, C and D could be thought of as existing prior to the decision about early retirement and possibly to have affected the decision. We could produce individual crosstabulation tables of A by B, A by C, and A by D with the association in each table *considered on its own* apparently statistically significant. But if we also suspect or know that B, C and D are strongly associated with each other, the apparent significant links of one or more of these variables with A could in fact be illusory. Again, this is a multivariate problem – we require a means of deciding which of the three associations are important and which are statistical artefacts. A special case of loglinear analysis called logit analysis can provide an answer to this problem.

The 'logic' of loglinear analysis

Continuing with the format that has been followed in the previous modules, now we will give a non-statistical presentation of the 'logic' that underlies loglinear analysis. The basic idea of loglinear analysis is in fact a simple extension of the reasoning behind Chi-square. Let us take another example using four variables – A, B, C and D – only simplify the example even further and have only two levels for each of the four variables so that, for instance, variable A will have two values: A_1 and A_2. So, taking all four of the variables together, there will be 16 possible combinations (or possible cells) of the variables ($2 \times 2 \times 2 \times 2 = 16$). Also, let us say we have a small dataset with 144 people.

Loglinear analysis builds up a model based upon the effects of distribution. These effects can be broken down in the following manner.

1. *Cell frequency/gross effect.*
   First, we would expect to find on average 9 people in each of the sixteen cells ($144/16 = 9$). That is, holding everything else equal, if the 144 people are scattered completely at random across the 16 cells, by chance each cell should have 9 people in it.

2. *Marginal effects.*

    For the sake of argument, let us assume that, for each of our variables A, B, C and D, level 2 has twice as many people as level 1. So, for example, level A_1 will have 48 people and level A_2 will have 96 people (a 1 : 2 ratio), variable B will be the same (B_1 = 48 people and B_2 = 96 people) as will C_1 and C_2 and D_1 and D_2. Holding everything else equal, that means that you would expect to find that any cell associated with level A_2 should have twice as many cases as any equivalent cell associated with level A_1. The same should hold for B_1 cells contrasted with B_2 cells, C_1 cells contrasted with C_2 cells and D_1 contrasted with D_2 cells. These are called *marginal effects*.

3. *Two-way interactions.*

    If any two variables are crosstabulated together, say A by B, the actual, observed distribution of cases in the cells of the crosstabulation may differ significantly from that which would be expected by chance. If this is the case, we have a *two-way interaction* between the two variables. For example, see Figure 11.1.

Expected ratio of cases if A & B are not associated			A hypothetical ratio of cases If A & B are associated		
	B_1	B_2		B_1	B_2
A_1	1	2	A_1	3	1
A_2	2	4	A_2	2	2

Figure 11.1 *A by B, 'chance' and 'actual' distributions*

On the left-hand side, you can see the ratio of how the cases would be distributed by chance in the table, A by B, if there was no association between the two variables. If there is an association, the actual distribution would differ significantly from that expected by chance, yielding a different distribution across the cells of the crosstabulation table. The right-hand table illustrates one such possible different form that this distribution could take.

You will note that the logic of loglinear modelling parallels that which underlies Chi-square; the actual distribution of cases in cells is contrasted with that which you would expect to find by chance.

4. *Three-way interactions.*

    It is also possible that the distribution of cases in the A by B crosstabulation can be different depending upon the level taken by a third variable. If this is the case, that the A by B association varies for different values of a third variable, C, we have a *three-way interaction*. Figures 11.2a and 11.2b illustrate the possible appearance that the absence and presence of a three-way interaction could have.

    Note that the ratio of cell numbers in Figure 11.2a are exactly the same regardless of which value is taken by the third variable, C. In contrast, note that the ratio of cell numbers in Figure 11.2b differ

C_1			C_2		
	B_1	B_2		B_1	B_2
A_1	3	1	A_1	3	1
A_2	2	2	A_2	2	2

Figure 11.2a *A by B for two levels of C, 'three-way' interaction absent*

	C_1					C_2	
	B_1	B_2				B_1	B_2
A_1	2	3			A_1	3	1
A_2	2	7			A_2	2	2

Figure 11.2b *A by B for two levels of C, 'three-way' interaction present*

depending upon the value taken by the third variable, C. That is, when the pattern of association between A and B varies depending upon the value taken by C; there is a three-way interaction between A, B and C.

5. *Four- or N-way interactions.*

The distribution of cases in the A by B crosstabulation tables that are different for each value of C could also vary for each value of a fourth variable, D, yielding *four-way interactions*. This pattern of increasingly complex interactions can be extended for an additional number of *N* extra variables. All this ends up in a linear equation that can be expressed like this:

Any cell's frequency = Gross effect × Marginal effects × Interaction effects

To make the computation easier, the effects are put into terms of logs so they can be added rather than multiplied; hence, the name of the procedure: *Loglinear analysis*.

The goal of a loglinear analysis usually is *parsimony* – to establish the simplest possible loglinear equation that manages to produce predicted frequencies for each cell that do not vary significantly from the actual cell frequencies. This is accomplished by eliminating the most complex interactions in turn. If the cell frequencies predicted after the most complex interaction is removed do not diverge significantly from the actual cell frequencies, the next most complex interaction term is removed and again the predicted frequencies are compared with those that actually occur. This process is repeated until eventually no more interaction terms can be removed without producing a model whose predicted values do not 'fit' the actual cell frequencies well. For instance, taking our A × B × C × D example, it may be possible to remove the most complex four-way interaction term (A × B × C × D) and all of the three-way interactions before arriving at the simplest model that still gives a good 'fit' – a model that includes only two-way interactions. If such a result can be obtained, the interpretation of associations is comparatively easy. You would know that you need not worry about complex tables with one or more control variables and instead would only need to describe what is going on in a series of two-way, relatively simple crosstabulation tables.

We will now demonstrate this procedure through the use of specific examples drawn from the **all nations** ISSP dataset.

LOGLINEAR ANALYSIS – SPECIFIC EXAMPLES WITH SPSS

Three examples of loglinear analysis will be given to illustrate the procedure.

1. First, **Model Selection** will be used to show the steps involved in gradually eliminating more complex interactions from a model until the simplest possible model is found that still gives predictions of the expected frequencies in the individual cells that do not diverge significantly from the actual observed cell frequencies.

2. Second, a **General** loglinear analysis will be used to show how a too-simple set of interactions produces a model whose predicted cell frequencies match the actual frequencies poorly.
3. Third, a **Logit** model will be given in order to illustrate a 'regression-style' predictive analysis in which one variable can be considered dependent upon several other variables.

The same set of variables will be used in all three analyses:

- **sex.** The gender variable in the ISSP dataset where code '1' is 'Male' and '2' is 'Female';
- **nation.** A collapsing together of the national datasets that make up the all nations ISSP dataset into four categories where code '1' is 'Western developed nations' (e.g. the United States, Finland, Australia, etc.), '2' is 'Eastern developed nations' (South Korea, Japan and Taiwan), '3' is 'Post-socialist countries' (e.g. former East Germany, Hungary, Slovenia, etc.) and '4' is 'Developing nations' (e.g. South Africa, Dominican Republic, etc.);
- **strata.** A collapsing together of the ten EGP class categories into three groupings where code '1' is 'Upper middle class', '2' is 'Intermediates' and '3' is 'Menials';
- **agecats.** A collapsing together of age into three categories – '1' '30 or younger', '2' 'Aged 31 to 50' and '3' 'Aged 51 or older';
- **security**. A variable based upon **v11**, a respondent's statement of how important job security is to them personally in which **v11** is collapsed into three categories – '1' 'Very important', '2' 'Important' and '3' 'Indifferent or not very important'.

This recoding of the original variables in the **all nations** ISSP dataset in order to produce fewer, larger categories is advisable due to the multiplication of cells in a multivariate crosstabulation. For instance, the number of categories in these five recoded variables in combination implies 216 cells ($216 = 2 \times 4 \times 3 \times 3 \times 3$). If the original variables had been used, even if we had restricted age to only its three categories 9150 cells would have been implied ($2 \times 31 \times 10 \times 3 \times 5 = 9150$). If the 43,440 respondents in the very large **all nations** dataset were scattered equally across all categories, just under 5 people on average would be found in each cell. (And, since people will be clustered rather than scattered at random across the cells, many cells would have no one at all.) In a multivariate loglinear analysis which involves a number of variables with a large number of categories, it is quite easy to generate more potential cells than there are cases – even for datasets such as the ISSP **all nations** sample with a very large number of cases. In general, if the number of categories of variables can be collapsed without losing much information, it is advisable to do so.

Deciding how much, and where, to combine categories without losing information is, however, more of an art than a science; that is, a matter of judgement and familiarity with the data. Generally, the analyst wishes to keep the number of empty cells or cells with almost no cases to a minimum, but this must be balanced against the need to retain the substantive discrimination between categories.

'Model selection'

In the first example, 'Model Selection' will be used to show the steps involved in gradually eliminating more complex interactions from a model. Here the goal is *parsimony* – to find the simplest possible model that still gives predictions of the expected frequencies in the individual cells that do not diverge significantly from the cell frequencies actually observed. Before beginning, we can anticipate that the five variables – **sex**, **nation**, **strata**, **agecats** and **security** – will be associated with each other and, furthermore, that the patterns of association could be quite complex. For instance, **nation** and **strata** are almost surely associated so that people in the higher class stratum are more likely to be found in the developed nations categories and it is quite possible that the exact form or strength of this link between class and nation could vary depending, for example, upon gender. By starting with a set of complex patterns of associations (here, all four-way interactions between the five variables) and gradually simplifying the model by removing the most complex associations in turn, a solution will be reached – the model that posits the smallest number of least complex associations (interactions) between the five variables.

As shown in Figure 11.3, begin by opening the **Analyze** menu, clicking on **Loglinear** and selecting the **Model Selection** window.

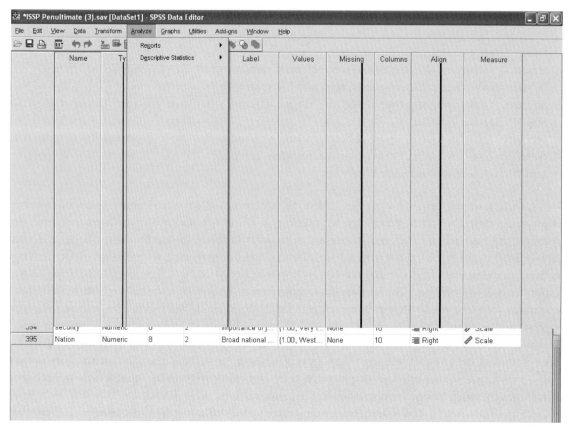

Figure 11.3 *Selecting loglinear*

Your first step with the Model Selection window (Figure 11.4a) is to choose the variables for the analysis from the list on the left-hand side and use the arrow to insert them into the list of 'Factor[s]' in the middle of the window. Here, **Nation, security, strata, agecats** and **sex** have all been inserted.

Next, you need to define the range of values for each variable that will be used in the analysis. The range of values for **security** (1 3), **strata** (1 3), **agecats** (1 3) and **sex** (1 2) have been set and **Nation** (? ?) shows this range needs to be defined. To do that, click on the **Define Range** button to bring up the sub-window shown in Figure 11.4b.

Type in 1 and 4 as the Minimum and Maximum values for the variable **Nation** and then click on the **Continue** button to return to the main window.

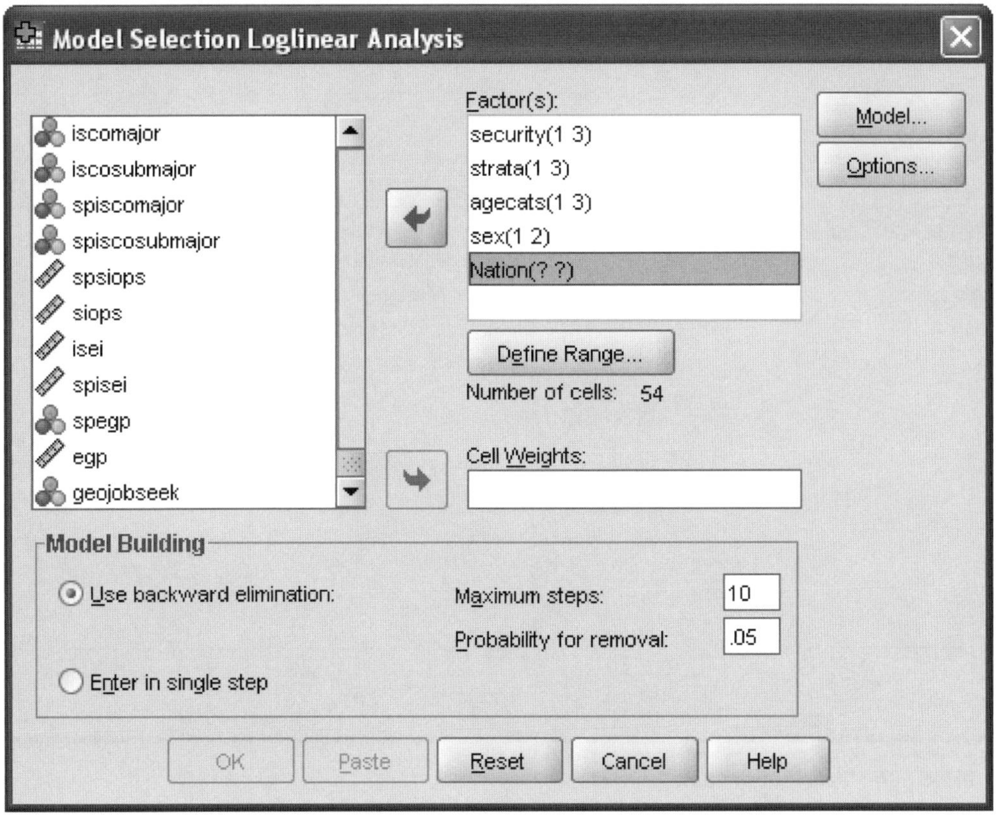

Figure 11.4a   *The Model Selection window*

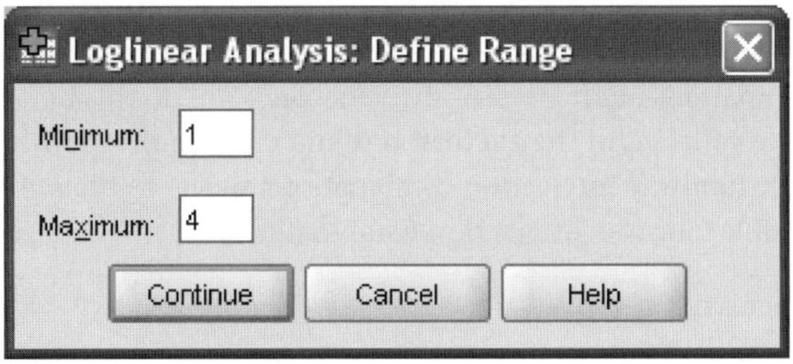

Figure 11.4b   *The Define Range sub-window*

Note that the range of values should not have any gaps. For instance, a variable with three codes, 1, 3 and 5 would pose problems. The range would be 1 to 5 and SPSS would assume that the variable had *five* levels, 1, *2*, 3, *4* and 5 and would seek cell combinations for the non-existent levels 2 and 4 (and consequently would find many empty cells). All of the codes implied by a range must have genuine values. (The gaps could be rectified by recoding the codes 1, 3, and 5 into three consecutive numbers.)

Next, you have to specify a loglinear model. Click on the **Model** button in the Model Selection window (Figure 11.4a) to bring up the sub-window in Figure 11.4c. The default is the 'Saturated' model – all

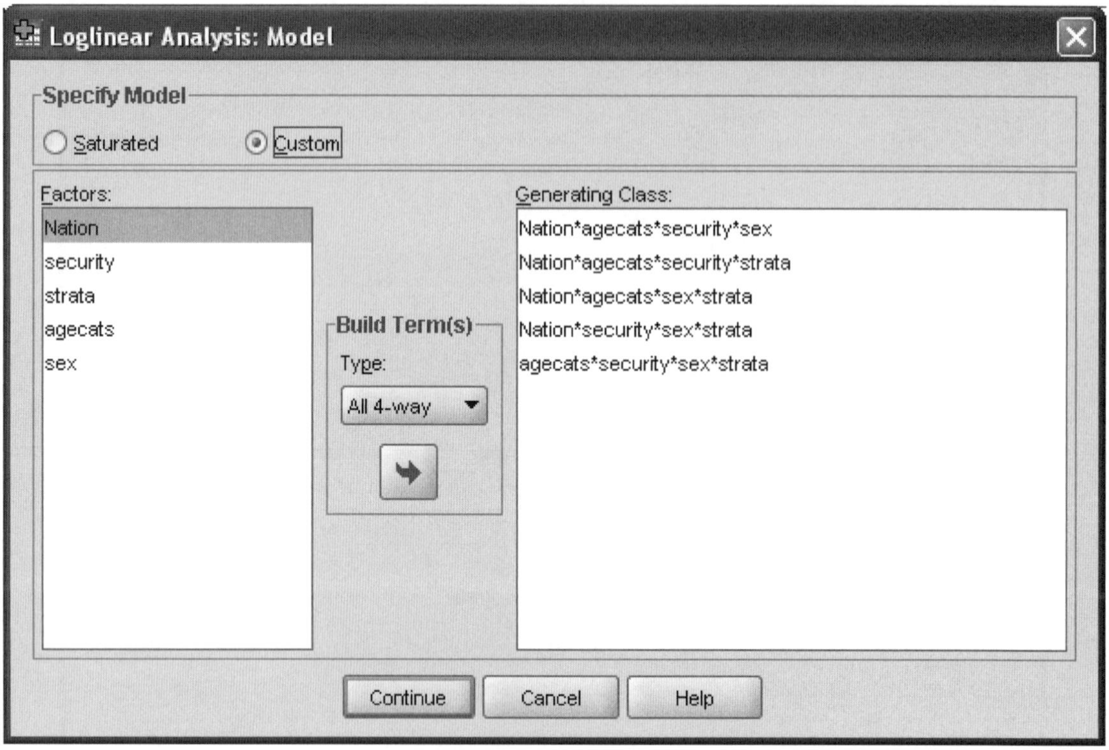

Figure 11.4c *The Model sub-window*

possible associations between all variables. You do not want this, but rather the simplest possible model. Click on the **Custom** button. Next, you need to give SPSS a starting point from which to work backwards to reach the simplest possible model. You do this by bringing down the small sub-menu in the middle of the window that is initially set on 'Interaction '. Here, we decide to begin with 'All 4-way' interactions (that is, all possible combinations of any four of the variables). You do this by selecting 'All 4-way', then highlighting all five of the variables in the **Factors:** box and clicking the right-hand arrow button under **Build term[s]**. All possible four-way interaction combinations appear in the right-hand box, **Generating Class**. There are five possible four-way interaction combinations:

■ **Nation * agecats * security * sex**
■ **Nation * agecats * security * strata**
■ **Nation * agecats * sex * strata**
■ **Nation * security * sex * strata**
■ **agecats * security * sex * strata**

Now, click on **Continue** to go back to the main window.

Sometimes you may want to change the default settings. To do this, click on the **Options** button to bring up the sub-window in Figure 11.4d. Here, the default is to include cell frequencies and residuals in the output. This has the potential for producing a massive amount of output, so we want to simplify the output for this illustration by removing these. This is accomplished by removing the ticks in the **Frequencies** and **Residuals** boxes under Display. Click on **Continue** to return to the main window.

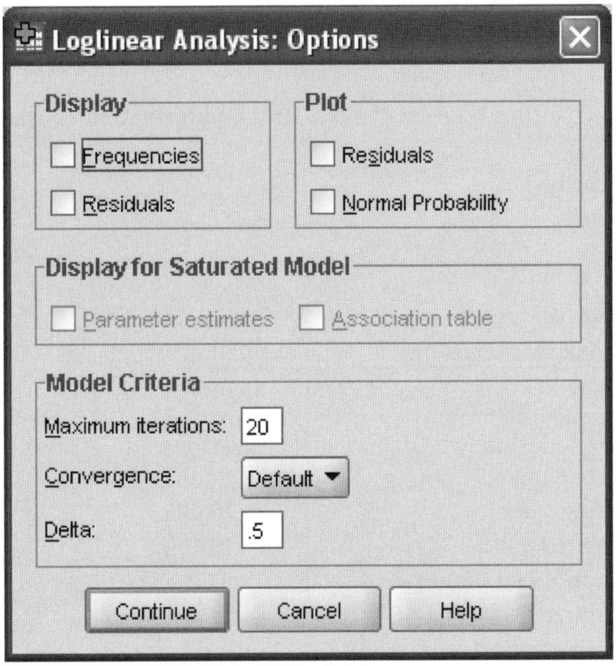

Figure 11.4d   *The Options sub-window*

You are now prepared to run the loglinear model selection. Note that the **Model Building** button for 'Use backward selection' is switched on. As usual, run the procedure by clicking **OK**.

The output begins with 'Data Information', reporting that 33,877 cases were valid and 9563 cases were rejected (due to the values for one or more of the variables in a case falling outside the ranges we stated – in this example these 'out of range' cases are in fact missing values, mainly those who could not be assigned a **strata** category due to not currently working). The variables in the analysis and the number of levels in each variable's range is given.

SPSS then moves to 'Backward elimination' and begins to check whether there are any interactions that can be taken out. The analysis begins at Step 0 with the most complex model that we specified, all four-way interactions of the variables. The clearest candidate for an interaction that can be removed is the fifth one, **agecats * security * sex * strata**. The removal of this interaction will produce a loss in 'fit' that is very far from significant (.957). The program then moves through seven stages of removing interactions, each time eliminating the interaction whose removal will have the least significant effect upon the 'fit' to the data. For instance, in the next step, the interaction whose removal will have the least effect is **Nation * agecats * security * sex** with a significant effect of its removal of .126; again, far from significant. The final stage is reached at Step 6/7 when there are no more interactions whose removal would not have a significant effect on the 'fit' to the data. This is the Final Model, and appears towards the end of Figure 11.5. Since there are no other interaction terms that can be removed without producing a significant loss in 'fit', this model becomes the 'best' model and the final solution to the loglinear analysis.

The final model is the simplest set of interactions that can accurately depict the pattern of associations (the cell frequencies) between the five variables in the analysis. Unfortunately for the goal of parsimony (a simple set of interactions), the final solution, shown in the **Convergence Information** box at the bottom of Figure 11.5, is rather complex:

- a four-way interaction: **Nation * agecats * sex * strata**, plus three three-way interactions:
- security * sex * strata;
- Nation * agecats * security;
- agecats * security * strata.

Hierarchical Loglinear Analysis

Data Information

		N
Cases	Valid	33877
	Out of Range[a]	0
	Missing	9563
	Weighted Valid	33877
Categories	**Nation** Broad national groupings	4
	security Importance of job security	3
	strata Crude class groupings	3
	agecats Age categores	3
	sex R: Gender	2

a. Cases rejected because of out of range factor values.

Design 1
Backward Elimination Statistics

Step Summary

Step[a]			Effects	Chi-Square[c]	df	Sig.	Number of Iterations
0	Generating Class[b]		Nation*agecats*security*sex, Nation*agecats*security*strata, Nation*agecats*sex*strata, Nation*security* sex*strata, agecats*security* sex*strata	26.944	24	.307	
	Deleted Effect	1	Nation*agecats*security*sex	16.654	12	.163	3
		2	Nation*agecats*security* strata	35.489	24	.061	3
		3	Nation*agecats*sex*strata	43.510	12	.000	4
		4	Nation*security*sex*strata	18.761	12	.094	3
		5	agecats*security*sex*strata	2.606	8	.957	3

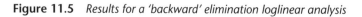

Figure 11.5 *Results for a 'backward' elimination loglinear analysis*

1	Generating Class[b]		Nation*agecats*security*sex, Nation*agecats*security*strata, Nation*agecats*sex*strata, Nation*security*sex*strata	29.550	32	.591	
	Deleted Effect	1	**Nation*agecats*security*sex**	17.672	12	.126	3
		2	Nation*agecats*security*strata	35.935	24	.056	4
		3	Nation*agecats*sex*strata	43.843	12	.000	4
		4	Nation*security*sex*strata	18.678	12	.097	4
2	Generating Class[b]		Nation*agecats*security*strata, Nation*agecats*sex*strata, Nation*security*sex*strata, agecats*security*sex	47.222	44	.342	
	Deleted Effect	1	Nation*agecats*security*strata	35.806	24	.057	4
		2	Nation*agecats*sex*strata	42.970	12	.000	4
		3	Nation*security*sex*strata	18.595	12	.099	4
		4	**agecats*security*sex**	1.737	4	.784	4
			—Several more steps of deletions until, at Step 6, there are no more suitable interactions for removal—				
6	Generating Class[b]		Nation*agecats*sex*strata, security*sex*strata, Nation*agecats*security, Nation*security*strata, agecats*security*strata	112.950	90	.051	
	Deleted Effect	1	Nation*agecats*sex*strata	43.033	12	.000	4
		2	security*sex*strata	22.247	4	.000	4
		3	Nation*agecats*security	77.922	12	.000	4
		4	Nation*security*strata	134.252	12	.000	3
		5	agecats*security*strata	52.220	8	.000	4
7	Generating Class[b] THE FINAL MODEL		**Nation*agecats*sex*strata, security*sex*strata, Nation*agecats*security, Nation*security*strata, agecats*security*strata**	112.950	90	.051	

a. At each step, the effect with the largest significance level for the Likelihood Ratio Change is deleted, provided the significance level is larger than .050.

b. Statistics are displayed for the best model at each step after step 0.

c. For 'Deleted Effect', this is the change in the Chi-Square after the effect is deleted from the model.

Figure 11.5   *(Continued)*

Convergence Information[a]

Generating Class	Nation*agecats*sex*strata, security*sex*strata, Nation*agecats*security, Nation*security*strata, agecats*security*strata
Number of Iterations	0
Max. Difference between Observed and Fitted Marginals	.135
Convergence Criterion	1.007

[a.] Statistics for the final model after Backward Elimination.

Goodness-of-Fit Tests			
	Chi-Square	df	Sig.
Likelihood Ratio	112.950	90	.051
Pearson	112.252	90	.056

Figure 11.5 (*Continued*)

The procedure concludes with two versions of 'Goodness-of-fit test statistics'. The gist of each is the same: the final model is the simplest possible set of associations that will yield predicted cell frequencies that are not significantly different from those actually observed (Sig. = .051 and Sig. = .056).

The above output demonstrates the usual procedure that you would follow in a loglinear analysis, using the changes in the significance of 'fit' to indicate the goodness of fit of successively simpler models.

There are instances, however, where you may wish to try out a specific loglinear model; for example, instead of seeking the simplest model, you may want to compare the 'fit' of two contrasting model specifications. In these instances, you would conduct a general loglinear analysis.

General loglinear analysis

In the next example, we will carry out a general loglinear analysis using the same five variables – **Nation**, **security**, **strata**, **agecats** and **sex**. We will produce a loglinear analysis restricted only to two-way interactions in order to see how much worse the fit is than the previous 'final/best' solution we found above.

For a general loglinear analysis, you select **General** from the types of loglinear analysis shown in Figure 11.3. The window shown in Figure 11.6a will appear.

The general loglinear analysis procedure allows us to construct more complex models than those possible with a hierarchical loglinear analysis. One feature available in the inclusion of the effects of one or more quantitative variables into a loglinear model as covariates.

In an extension to the above example, we will replace **agecats** by bringing across an interval/ratio variable, **age** (respondent's age), as a **Cell Covariate**. Covariates are quantitative variables that are likely to affect the distribution of cases across the cells defined by the categorical variables in a loglinear model. Covariates must be interval/ratio variables. Here, by including **age** as a covariate, we are anticipating that the respondent's age may be affecting the associations between the other variables. For instance, for the variable **security**, it may be that older respondents are more likely to worry about losing their job and not finding another one. Including an appropriate quantitative covariate into a loglinear model can help improve its 'fit'.

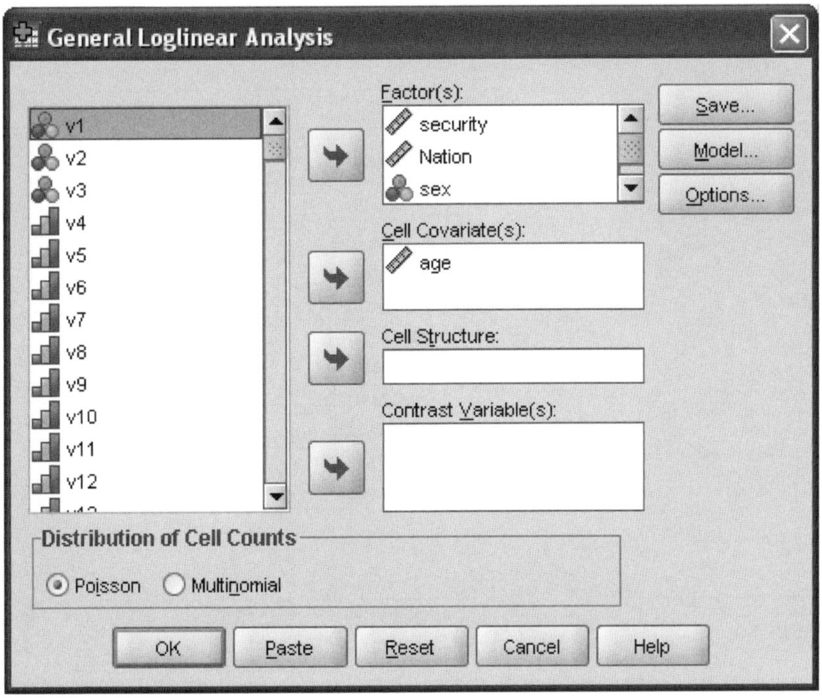

Figure 11.6a *General loglinear analysis*

Aside from that, as in our previous example, the four variables **security**, **Nation**, **sex** and **strata** have been brought as 'Factor[s]' into the model by selecting them from the list of variables in the left-hand column and clicking on the right-pointing arrow.

We want to produce a general loglinear model of all two-way interactions. To do so, click on the **Model** button to bring up the window in Figure 11.6b. Click the **Custom** button.

To produce the model of all two-way interactions, select 'All 2-way' from the drop-down menu under 'Build Term[s]', then highlight all the variables in the 'Factors and Covariates' list on the left and click on the right-hand **Build Term[s]** button. All of the two-way interactions will appear on the right-hand 'Terms in Model' list. Then click the **Continue** button in order to return to the main window.

If you wish, the options can be changed from their default values. For instance, here we decide not to have plots printed in the output. To do this, go to the Option sub-window by clicking on the **Options** button to bring up the sub-window in Figure 11.6c. Deselect the plots by switching off the ticks for the plots of 'Adjusted residuals' and 'Normal probability for adjusted'. Note that unlike the previous example, we have left the ticks for the Display of **Frequencies** and **Residuals**, so we will obtain these in the output this time.

Click **Continue** to return to the main window and run the model by clicking **OK**.

The output for a general loglinear analysis shown in Figure 11.7 provides a bit more information than that for a 'backward elimination' analysis. As before, the number of cases, valid and missing, and the labels for each of the variables in the analysis are given.

The output provides the goodness-of-fit statistics. This model of two-way interactions fits the data very poorly. (The 'Sig.' of 0.000/0.000 means that the probability is virtually nil that the differences between the actual cell frequencies and the frequencies predicted by the model could be only due to

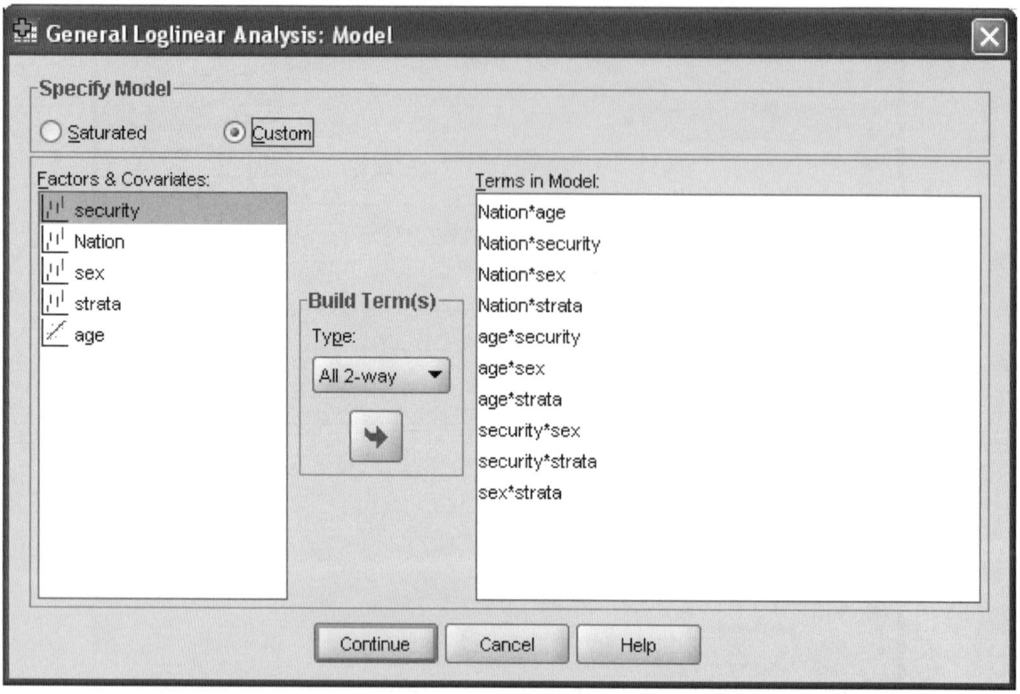

Figure 11.6b *General loglinear analysis model of two-way interactions*

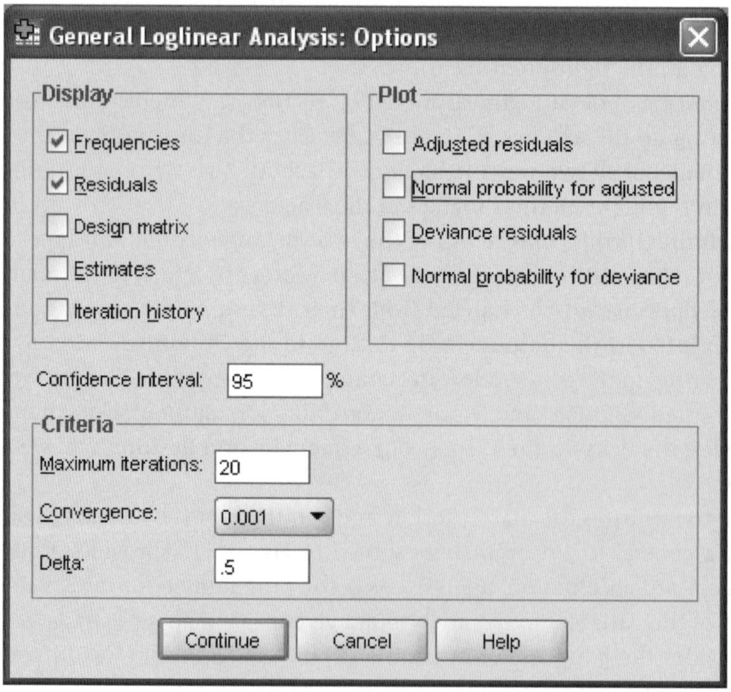

Figure 11.6c *The Options sub-window*

Data Information

		N
Cases	Valid	33757
	Missing	9683
	Weighted Valid	33757
Cells	Defined Cells	72
	Structural Zeros	0
	Sampling Zeros	0
Categories	**security** Importance of job security	3
	Nation Broad national groupings	4
	sex R: Gender	2
	strata Crude class groupings	3

Convergence Information[b,c]

Maximum Number of Iterations	20
Converge Tolerance	.00100
Final Maximum Absolute Difference	.00049[a]
Final Maximum Relative Difference	.17242
Number of Iterations	7

a. The iteration converged because the maximum absolute changes of parameter estimates is less than the specified convergence criterion.

b. Model: Poisson

c. **Design:** Constant + **Nation * age** + **security * Nation** + **Nation * sex** + **Nation * strata** + **security * age** + **sex * age** + **strata * age** + **security * sex** + **security * strata** + **sex * strata**

Goodness-of-Fit Tests[a,b]

	Value	df	Sig.
Likelihood Ratio	197.863	31	**.000**
Pearson Chi-Square	199.311	31	**.000**

a. Model: Poisson

b. **Design:** Constant + **Nation * age** + **security * Nation** + **Nation * sex** + **Nation * strata** + **security * age** + **sex * age** + **strata * age** + **security * sex** + **security * strata** + **sex * strata**

Figure 11.7 *Results for a general loglinear analysis*

Cell Counts and Residuals

security Importance of job security	Nation Broad national groupings	sex R: Gender	strata Crude class groupings	Observed Count	Observed %	Expected Count	Expected %	Residual	Standardized Residual	Adjusted Residual	Deviance
1.00 Very important	1.00 Western developed	1 Male	1.00 UMC	1787	5.3%	1863.744	5.5%	-76.744	-1.778	-4.386	-1.790
			2.00 Middle groupings	1871	5.5%	1825.654	5.4%	45.346	1.061	1.960	1.057
			3.00 Menials	922	2.7%	870.598	2.6%	51.402	1.742	3.289	1.725
		2 Female	1.00 UMC	1820	5.4%	1902.342	5.6%	-82.342	-1.888	-4.336	-1.902
			2.00 Middle groupings	2385	7.1%	2339.293	6.9%	45.707	.945	1.870	.942
			3.00 Menials	1010	3.0%	993.369	2.9%	16.631	.528	1.021	.526
	2.00 Eastern developed	1 Male	1.00 UMC	411	1.2%	371.339	1.1%	39.661	2.058	3.456	2.023
			2.00 Middle groupings	447	1.3%	452.709	1.3%	-5.709	-.268	-.435	-.269
			3.00 Menials	181	.5%	174.978	.5%	6.022	.455	.642	.453
		2 Female	1.00 UMC	265	.8%	279.020	.8%	-14.020	-.839	-1.374	-.846
			2.00 Middle groupings	454	1.3%	463.438	1.4%	-9.438	-.438	-1.003	-.440
			3.00 Menials	128	.4%	144.515	.4%	-16.515	-1.374	-2.270	-1.401
	3.00 Post−socialist	1 Male	1.00 UMC	485	1.4%	537.200	1.6%	-52.200	-2.252	-4.378	-2.290
			2.00 Middle groupings	730	2.2%	704.333	2.1%	25.667	.967	1.540	.961
			3.00 Menials	510	1.5%	567.956	1.7%	-57.956	-2.432	-5.520	-2.475
		2 Female	1.00 UMC	781	2.3%	667.061	2.0%	113.939	4.412	7.174	4.294
			2.00 Middle groupings	1037	3.1%	1107.622	3.3%	-70.622	-2.122	-4.079	-2.145
			3.00 Menials	633	1.9%	591.829	1.8%	41.171	1.692	4.119	1.673

			Count	%		%				
4.00 Developing	1 Male	1.00 UMC	561	1.7%	539.377	1.6%	21.623	.931	1.561	.925
		2.00 Middle groupings	1045	3.1%	1019.198	3.0%	25.802	.808	1.402	.805
		3.00 Menials	402	1.2%	424.913	1.3%	-22.913	-1.112	-2.756	-1.122
	2 Female	1.00 UMC	478	1.4%	427.918	1.3%	50.082	2.421	3.656	2.376
		2.00 Middle groupings	1021	3.0%	1077.753	3.2%	-56.753	-1.729	-3.214	-1.744
		3.00 Menials	348	1.0%	365.841	1.1%	-17.841	-.933	-1.868	-.941
2.00 Important 1.00 Western developed	1 Male	1.00 UMC	1624	4.8%	1464.316	4.3%	159.684	4.173	8.559	4.100
		2.00 Middle groupings	1001	3.0%	1128.027	3.3%	-127.027	-3.782	-5.984	-3.857
		3.00 Menials	464	1.4%	504.710	1.5%	-40.710	-1.812	-2.984	-1.837
	2 Female	1.00 UMC	1332	3.9%	1376.702	4.1%	-44.702	-1.205	-3.014	-1.211
		2.00 Middle groupings	1432	4.2%	1362.225	4.0%	69.775	1.891	3.276	1.875
		3.00 Menials	529	1.6%	546.021	1.6%	-17.021	-.728	-1.219	-.732
2.00 Eastern developed	1 Male	1.00 UMC	304	.9%	311.234	.9%	-7.234	-.410	-.612	-.412
		2.00 Middle groupings	343	1.0%	371.064	1.1%	-28.064	-1.457	-2.455	-1.476
		3.00 Menials	122	.4%	123.393	.4%	-1.393	-.125	-.168	-.126
	2 Female	1.00 UMC	196	.6%	213.017	.6%	-17.017	-1.166	-1.627	-1.182
		2.00 Middle groupings	350	1.0%	311.009	.9%	38.991	2.211	3.176	2.167
		3.00 Menials	122	.4%	107.282	.3%	14.718	1.421	1.871	1.390
3.00 Post–socialist	1 Male	1.00 UMC	242	.7%	274.285	.8%	-32.285	-1.949	-3.742	-1.990
		2.00 Middle groupings	368	1.1%	314.215	.9%	53.785	3.034	4.205	2.953
		3.00 Menials	273	.8%	229.584	.7%	43.416	2.865	4.067	2.781

Figure 11.7 (Continued)

Cell Counts and Residuals

security Importance of job security	Nation Broad national groupings	sex R: Gender	strata Crude class groupings	Observed Count	Observed %	Expected Count	Expected %	Residual	Standardized Residual	Adjusted Residual	Deviance
4.00	Developing	2 Female	1.00 UMC	343	1.0%	350.201	1.0%	-7.201	-.385	-.568	-.386
			2.00 Middle groupings	476	1.4%	496.281	1.5%	-20.281	-.910	-1.391	-.917
			3.00 Menials	268	.8%	305.433	.9%	-37.433	-2.142	-4.093	-2.188
		1 Male	1.00 UMC	319	.9%	371.074	1.1%	-52.074	-2.703	-3.866	-2.771
			2.00 Middle groupings	602	1.8%	590.839	1.8%	11.161	.459	.723	.458
			3.00 Menials	270	.8%	249.260	.7%	20.740	1.314	2.109	1.296
		2 Female	1.00 UMC	257	.8%	256.172	.8%	.828	.052	.070	.052
			2.00 Middle groupings	556	1.6%	554.339	1.6%	1.661	.071	.113	.070
			3.00 Menials	239	.7%	221.317	.7%	17.683	1.189	1.642	1.173
3.00 Indifferent or not important	1.00 Western developed	1 Male	1.00 UMC	397	1.2%	372.240	1.1%	24.760	1.283	2.540	1.269
			2.00 Middle groupings	184	.5%	205.277	.6%	-21.277	-1.485	-2.591	-1.512
			3.00 Menials	70	.2%	85.433	.3%	-15.433	-1.670	-2.458	-1.724
		2 Female	1.00 UMC	260	.8%	240.656	.7%	19.344	1.247	1.934	1.231
			2.00 Middle groupings	180	.5%	192.524	.6%	-12.524	-.903	-1.402	-.913
			3.00 Menials	82	.2%	76.869	.2%	5.131	.585	.736	.579
	2.00 Eastern developed	1 Male	1.00 UMC	60	.2%	56.561	.2%	3.439	.457	.617	.453
			2.00 Middle groupings	54	.2%	55.591	.2%	-1.591	-.213	-.284	-.214
			3.00 Menials	14	.0%	19.130	.1%	-5.130	-1.173	-1.399	-1.232

2 Female	1.00 UMC	26	.1%	30.829	.1%	-4.829	-.870	-1.085	-.894
	2.00 Middle groupings	40	.1%	34.188	.1%	5.812	.994	1.250	.968
	3.00 Menials	14	.0%	11.701	.0%	2.299	.672	.764	.652
3.00 Post–socialist	1 Male 1.00 UMC	48	.1%	58.057	.2%	-10.057	-1.320	-1.611	-1.361
	2.00 Middle groupings	71	.2%	54.455	.2%	16.545	2.242	2.852	2.141
	3.00 Menials	42	.1%	28.915	.1%	13.085	2.433	3.056	2.278
2 Female	1.00 UMC	44	.1%	56.197	.2%	-12.197	-1.627	-2.002	-1.692
	2.00 Middle groupings	53	.2%	58.094	.2%	-5.094	-.668	-.822	-.678
	3.00 Menials	36	.1%	38.282	.1%	-2.282	-.369	-.450	-.373
4.00 Developing	1 Male 1.00 UMC	50	.1%	68.574	.2%	-18.574	-2.243	-2.793	-2.358
	2.00 Middle groupings	102	.3%	96.637	.3%	5.363	.546	.718	.541
	3.00 Menials	51	.2%	42.128	.1%	8.872	1.367	1.669	1.323
2 Female	1.00 UMC	29	.1%	30.885	.1%	-1.885	-.339	-.415	-.343
	2.00 Middle groupings	77	.2%	64.234	.2%	12.766	1.593	1.982	1.544
	3.00 Menials	29	.1%	35.541	.1%	-6.541	-1.097	-1.710	-1.134

a. Model: Poisson

Figure 11.7 (*Continued*)

chance.) We must conclude that the original result found by the 'backward elimination' procedure which included a four-way interaction and three three-way interactions is in fact the 'best' solution that is capable of explaining the patterns of association between the variables.

Since we ticked **Frequencies** and **Residual** in the Options sub-window, a table of Cell Counts and Residuals is given. Since the model does not fit the data well the numbers of residuals (the differences between the Observed counts in each cell and the Expected counts) are high in many cells.

'Logit' analysis

In our third example, we demonstrate a **logit** analysis to carry out a regression-style causal analysis. To do this we will treat **security**, the extent to which respondents are worried about losing their job, as the dependent variable since it may be considered logically to follow (or to be affected by) people's **sex**, their social class/**strata**, their **age cat**egory and/or the **Nation** in which they are located.

Pull down the **A**nalyze menu, select **Loglinear** and this time choose **Logit**. The main window will come up as shown in Figure 11.8a. Here, we select **security** from the list of variables on the left-hand side and use the arrow button to insert it in the **Dependent** box. **Nation**, **strata**, **agecats** and **sex** are inserted in the **F**actor[s] box.

Then, you click on the **Model** button to set up the logit model. When the sub-window in Figure 11.8b comes up, click the **Custom** button. Then, select 'All 2-way' in the small pull-down list under Build Term(s), highlight all four of the variables (**Nation**, **strata**, **agecats** and **sex**) in the **F**actors & **Covariates** box on the left and click the right-hand **Build Terms(s)** button to generate a model of all two-way interactions of the 'causal' variables. Then, click **Continue**.

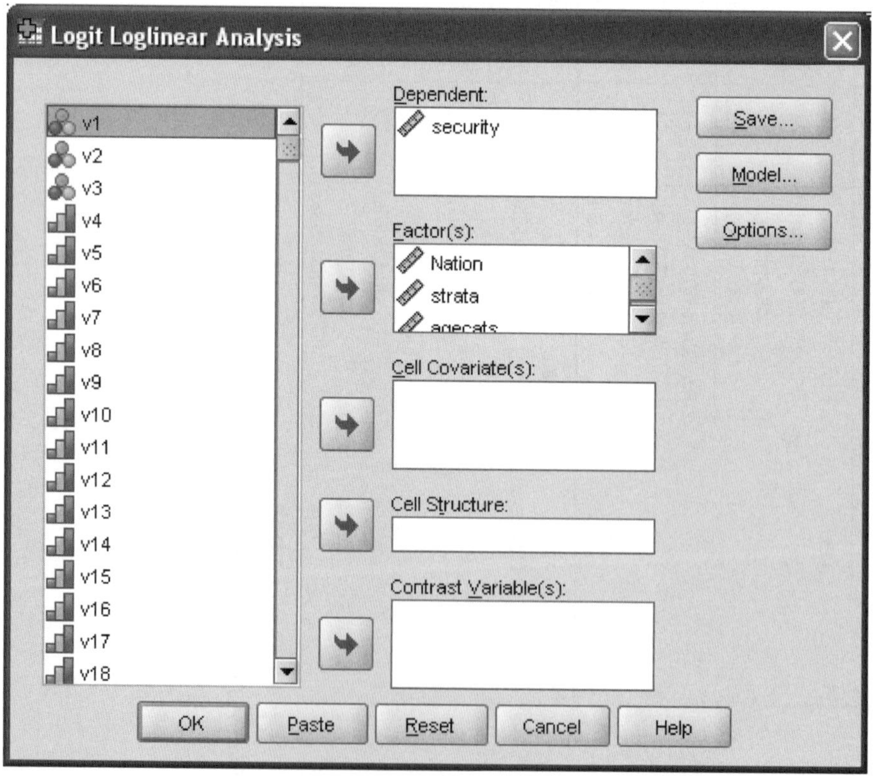

Figure 11.8a *Logit main window*

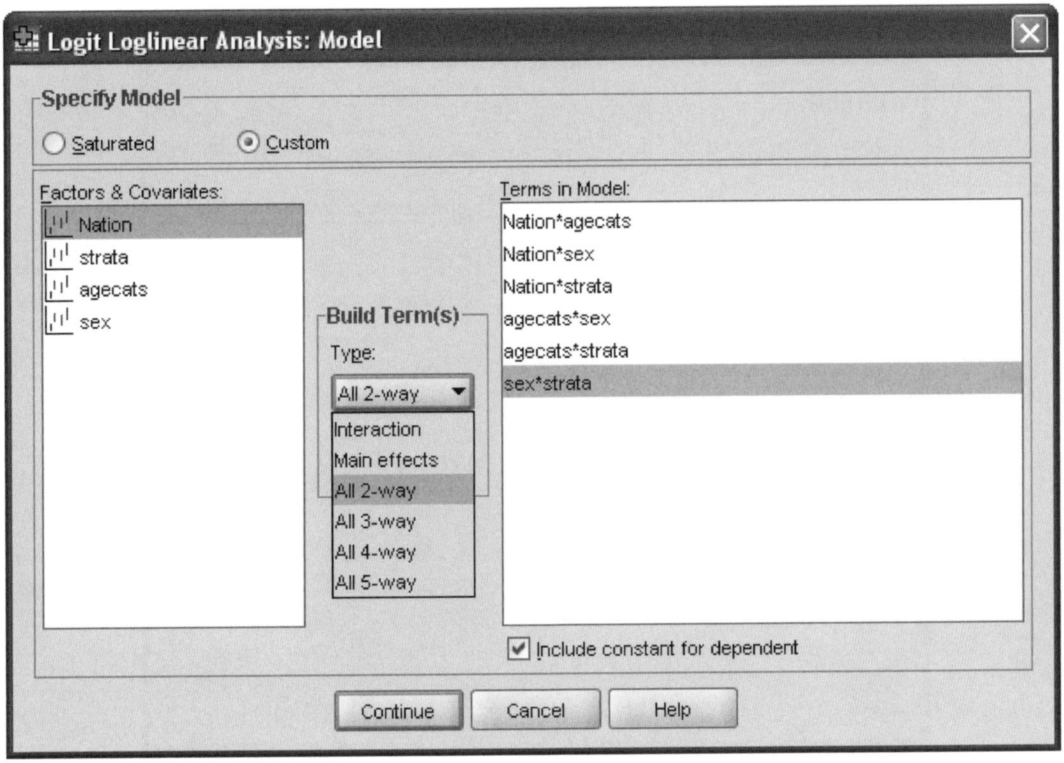

Figure 11.8b   *Logit model*

We decide to keep the output to a minimum since the purpose of this analysis is to assess the 'fit' of the model. To do this, you click on the **Options** button to bring up the Options sub-window (Figure 11.8c) and switch off the Display and Plot ticks. Press the **Continue** button in order to return to the main Logit window.

Once you return to the main window, click **OK** to run the first model. Its results appear below.

You will now be familiar with the beginning of the output, which shows the numbers of cases in the analysis and the labelling of the variables included in the analysis.

The form of the model design is different. What a logit analysis does is model the interactions between the 'dependent' variable (here, **security**) and the 'independent' variables (here, **Nation**, **strata**, **agecats** and **sex**). Since this logit model is a 'causal' model of the effect of the four independent variables upon the dependent variable **security**, the only terms of interest are interactions between **security** and the independent variables. All other interactions (which are those solely between the independent variables) are of no interest and, in effect, are allowed to take place without any limitations. So, since we have four independent variables, any logit analyses we do will have (unseen) modellings of four-way interactions between the four independent variables – even if the interactions between the independent and the dependent variable are kept quite tightly restricted. You can see this in the Design in Figure 11.9, where all of the interactions shown include **security**.

This model with its set of interactions between **security** and the complete set of two-way interactions with the four independent variables provides a reasonably good 'fit' to the distribution of responses to the question about the personal importance of job security that are given across the range of countries in the ISSP 'all nations' dataset. The significance of the Chi-squares are .059 and .062, respectively.

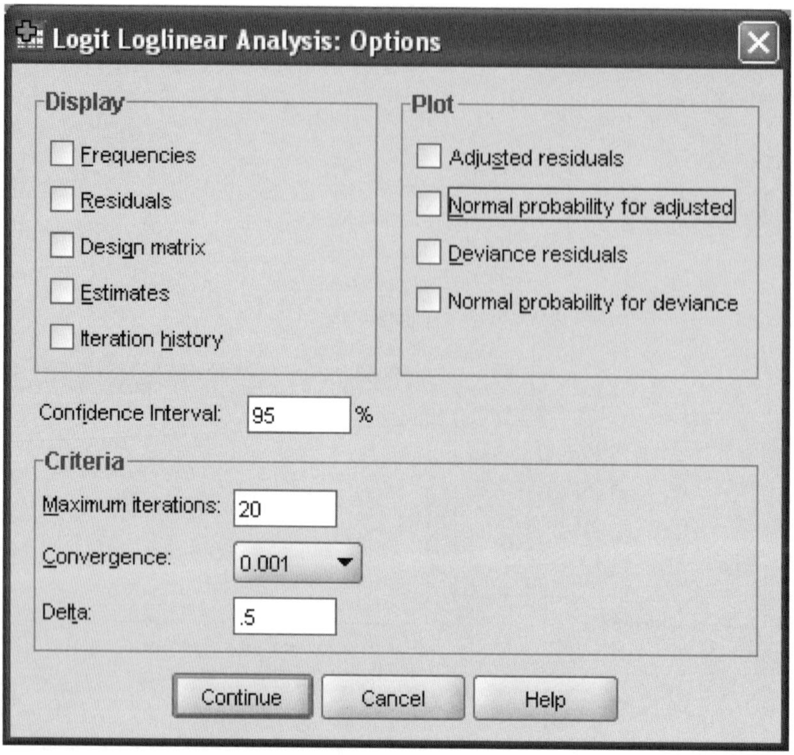

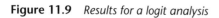

Figure 11.8c *Logit Options sub-window*

Data Information

		N
Cases	Valid	33877
	Missing	9563
	Weighted Valid	33877
Cells	Defined Cells	216
	Structural Zeros	0
	Sampling Zeros	0
Categories	**security** Importance of job security	3
	Nation Broad national groupings	4
	strata Crude class groupings	3
	agecats Age categories	3
	sex R: Gender	2

Figure 11.9 *Results for a logit analysis*

Convergence Information[b,c]

Maximum Number of Iterations	20
Converge Tolerance	.00100
Final Maximum Absolute Difference	2.50230E-6
Final Maximum Relative Difference	8.67643E-5
Number of Iterations	6

a. The iteration converged because the maximum absolute changes of parameter estimates is less than the specified convergence criterion

b. Model: Multinomial Logit

c. **Design**: Constant + **security**
+ **security * Nation*agecats**
+ **security * Nation*sex**
+ **security * Nation*strata**
+ **security * agecats*sex**
+ **security * strata*agecats**
+ **security * strata*sex**

Goodness-of-Fit Tests[a,b]			
	Value	df	Sig.
Likelihood Ratio	100.723	80	0.59
Pearson Chi-Square	100.296	80	0.62

a. Model: Multinomial Logit

b. **Design**: Constant + **security** + **security * Nation * agecats** + **security * Nation * sex** + **security * Nation * strata** + **security * agecats * sex** + **security * strata * agecats** + **security * strata * sex**

Figure 11.9 (*Continued*)

Analysis of Dispersion[a,b]

	Entropy	Concentration	df
Model	348.244	225.097	62
Residual	28449.372	17676.022	67690
Total	28797.616	17901.118	67752

a. Model: Multinomial Logit
b. Design: Constant + security + security * Nation * agecats + security * Nation * sex + security * Nation * strata + security * agecats * sex + security * strata * agecats + security * strata * sex

Measure of Association[a,b]

Entropy	.012
Concentration	.013

a. Model: Multinomial Logit
b Design: Constant + security + security * Nation * agecats + security * Nation * sex + security * Nation * strata + security * agecats * sex + security * strata * agecats + security * strata * sex

Figure 11.9 (*Continued*)

CONCLUSION

As with most of the statistical procedures available in SPSS, more complex loglinear analyses are possible. For instance, it is possible to construct loglinear models in which the interactions in some cells are more likely than in other cells or to exclude cells from the analysis in which it is unlikely or impossible that anyone will be found, however, these procedures are beyond the scope of this general textbook. What this module has done is give you an introduction to loglinear analysis with SPSS. Following its instructions, you should be able to carry out some basic multivariate analyses with categorical data, either:

 'disentangling' the complex interplay of associations between a collection of categorical variables, or

■ carrying out a simple causal analysis in which one categorical variable is seen as being potentially caused by some combination of a number of independent categorical variables.

SPSS EXERCISES FOR *LOGLINEAR ANALYSIS*

1. Try repeating a simplified version of our analyses here, only without Nation and using the dataset from the country of your choice. Do you obtain patterns of results that differ from those observed here?

2. Using either the country dataset of your choice or the **all nations** dataset, try out some loglinear analyses for yourself.

   a. *Model selection.* Choose three or more categorical or ordinal variables that are made up of a small number of categories that you believe are related, one with the other (you may need to use Recode carefully to reduce the number of categories in a variable). Carry out a 'model selection' loglinear analysis in order to establish the simplest set of associations between the variables that still gives close estimations of the true observed frequencies in each cell ('a good fit to the data').

   b. *General.* Choose three or more categorical or ordinal variables that are made up of a small number of categories that you believe are related, one with the other. Carry out two or more general loglinear analyses of these variables in which you set up at least two different models or descriptions of patterns of inter-relationships that you believe could produce good descriptions of the data. Compare the results of the analyses to establish: (i) which of the models you have proposed produce good 'fits' to the data (none, some, or all of the models you test may fit the data well); (ii) compare the results from each model to see which model (if any!) produced the best 'fit' to the data. (You compare the models by seeing which model generates the greater *p* value that indicates the best fit. If two models fit the data equally well, pick the one that has the simpler set of relationships.)

   c. *Logit.* Select one categorical or ordinal variable that you believe may be affected (or 'caused') by two or more other categorical or ordinal variables and carry out two or more logit analyses to see which is the simplest combination of 'causal' variables that can model or explain adequately the distribution in the 'dependent' variable.

Hints:

- It is best to begin your experimentation with loglinear analysis by investigating simple or obvious relationships between a small number of variables. Try more complex models later on when you have become more familiar with the technique.

- Do not expect the loglinear analysis technique to work miracles. A model with too many variables and/or too many empty cells will fail. Remember that the number of cells rises exponentially with each extra variable you add to a model. Similarly, a variable with a large number of categories greatly increases the complexity of model estimation. Keep the number of variables to a minimum and use Recode to combine categories in order to keep the number of categories in the variables you include in your models at the minimum possible without losing significant information.

Conclusion

You have now worked your way systematically through an introduction to the main procedures available within SPSS and have had practical experience of carrying out various types of analyses. This final section collates the material that has been presented so that you will be ready to carry out a complete analysis from start to finish.

A central feature of this workbook has been its reliance upon the analysis of datasets drawn from the International Social Survey Program (ISSP). The suggested exercises at the end of each module have dealt with the procedures covered in that section of the workbook. While this means that you have had experience of the genuine sorts of problems and issues that would confront a 'real' researcher, in one crucial respect all that you have done so far has been artificial. Each module has covered the conditions under which it would be appropriate to use its statistical procedure, both in terms of the problem that the statistics are designed to answer and the levels of measurement that the procedures require. While you have had to develop ideas for analyses and then choose appropriate variables from the datasets in order to test those ideas, the type of problem and *which* statistical tests to use have never been at issue in each module's exercises.

A 'real' researcher, however, would not have these advantages. In 'real-world' research, quantitative analysts will have an idea or research problem which leads them to develop anticipated empirical findings – hypotheses. Before any statistical analysis can even be contemplated, the analyst has to locate quantitative information that will shed light on their research problem. This may mean generating completely new quantitative material through a sample survey or some other means of generating primary data or, if they are lucky, locating an existing quantitative dataset that already contains the information they need. The creation of a completely new dataset or the selection of an existing source of data for a secondary analysis involves the careful *operationalization* of theoretical concepts – establishing variables in the dataset that validly represent the conceptual ideas which one wishes to test. Only when the information has been generated or located will the researcher have a dataset that contains quantitative material which can be analysed to establish whether hypothetically predicted findings actually are confirmed in a variable analysis. You have not had to face these problems here since the ISSP datasets have been provided 'ready-made'.

CHOOSING THE CORRECT STATISTICAL TEST

Once a research problem has been identified, hypotheses have been derived, and a dataset that contains information which will allow the statistical testing of these hypotheses has been obtained, the researcher confronts a different kind of dilemma – which statistical tests from the extensive battery of those available should be used? It is not uncommon for a student to complete one or more statistics courses quite successfully, only to encounter an unexpected 'block' the first time they attempt to carry out an independent analysis as part of a dissertation project or thesis. The source of the problem is quite simple – during their statistics training, they would have been given advice on which statistical procedure to use in any given exercise. In a real analysis, however, there is no one there to tell the researcher which procedures to apply – they have to work this out for themselves. If students have never been faced with this problem before it can be a daunting task!

The process that one goes through in order to decide upon the correct statistical procedure for an analysis can be thought of as a triangular relationship. The researcher will have a 'research problem' – the question or hypothesis which they wish to resolve through their analysis. The information they use to resolve this research problem hopefully will be contained in the data that are available for their analysis. If the data cannot provide variables for analysis that are conceptually valid operationalizations of the ideas in the research problem, attempting an analysis is pointless. If the data are suitable, their characteristics (for instance, the level of measurement of each variable in the analysis) and the exact nature of the research question will determine which statistical test or tests that are chosen as being most appropriate (see Figure C.1).

The characteristics of the variables that will be used in an analysis and the exact nature of the statistical question that the analysis seeks to answer, taken together, determine the possible statistical procedures which are appropriate. Figure C.2 collates the requirements of each procedure together into a single table in order to make the task of selecting the appropriate statistic easier.

In order to use the table systematically to select an appropriate statistic, go through the following steps.

1. *Establish whether the 'analysis problem' involves looking at one variable at a time, or at a connection between two or more variables.*

   If the 'problem' involves only one variable, the appropriate statistic or procedures should be found in the **Only one variable** column. If the 'problem' involves two or more variables simultaneously, the appropriate statistic should be located in one of the cells that are a combination of a '*1st or Dependent variable*' and '*2nd or Independent variables*'.

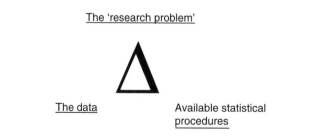

The 'research problem'

The data   Available statistical procedures

Figure C.1 *The triangular relationship between research problem, data and statistical procedures*

2nd or Independent Variables are:

1st or _Dependent Variable:_	Only one variable	Nominal/Categorical	Ordinal	Interval/Ratio
Nominal/Categorical	Frequency count Bar chart, Pie chart Mode	Crosstabs Chi-square (χ^2), Phi (ϕ), Cramer's V, Contingency coefficient, Lambda, McNemar's test, Uncertainty coefficient Loglinear analysis	Crosstabs Chi-square (χ^2), Phi (ϕ), Cramer's V, Contingency coefficient, Lambda, McNemar's test, Uncertainty coefficient, Loglinear analysis	Logistic regression
Ordinal	Median (Md) Quartiles, Deciles, Interquartile deviation (dq) Box 'n' dot plot	Crosstabs Eta Loglinear analysis	Crosstabs Kendall's Tau (T), Gamma, Somer's d, Kappa, Spearman's correlation coefficient (Rho) Loglinear analysis	Scattergram plot Correlation coefficients Regression
Interval/Ratio	Histogram Mean Standard deviation (sd), Variance Skewness, Kurtosis Stem 'n' leaf diagram Box 'n' dot plot	_t_-test Analysis of Variance (ANOVA) Box 'n' dot plot for two or more groups	_t_-test Analysis of Variance (ANOVA)	Scattergram plot Pearson's correlation coefficient (r) Regression

Figure C.2 _Choosing the correct statistical procedure_

2. *Use the level of measurement of the variable or variables to select the appropriate cell of statistical procedures.*

   If the 'problem' involves only one variable, this is relatively simple. You go down the **Only one variable** column to the appropriate row. For instance, if the variable of interest is **age**, it is an interval/ratio variable, and the appropriate statistic will be one or more of those in the bottom row: histogram; mean; standard deviation; variance; skewness, kurtosis; stem 'n' leaf diagram or box 'n' dot plot.

   If the 'problem' involves two or more variables, you have to decide whether one of the variables can be considered the 'first' or 'dependent' (caused) variable, while the other variable(s) can be considered the 'second' or 'independent' (causal) variable(s). You then establish the level of measurement of each variable and locate the appropriate cell in the table. For instance, if both the 'first' and the 'second' variable are interval/ratio, you will be led to the statistics listed in the bottom right-hand cell: scattergram plot; Pearson's correlation coefficient (*r*); regression.

3. *Depending upon the nature of the 'analysis problem', select an appropriate procedure or statistic.*

   Continuing with the above 'one variable' example, if the 'problem' was to indicate the average or central point of the distribution of respondents' ages, you would select the mean. If the problem was to examine the distribution of ages around the central point, you could choose the standard deviation or the variance. If you wished to produce a visual depiction of the age distribution, a histogram, a stem 'n' leaf diagram or a box 'n' dot plot could be in order.

In the case of the 'two variable' example above, if you believed that the second variable could be an independent cause of the first, dependent, variable, regression could be used to test this.

(Figure C.2 only shows the statistical and graphing procedures that are available in SPSS and covered in this book. You will have noted that there are other statistical procedures in SPSS that this workbook does not discuss. There are also of course many additional statistical procedures which SPSS does not cater for. Both of these groups of additional procedures can be considered comparatively exotic or specialized relative to those that we have covered.)

A NOTE OF CAUTION

Finally, we would like to end with a note of caution. The process of becoming proficient in SPSS can be described as 'having a steep learning curve'. That is, at the beginning, the novice can feel overwhelmed by the amount of detail that must be absorbed in order to get SPSS to work and by the necessity of understanding all facets of carrying out even a simple statistical procedure before they can begin to gain an overall understanding of how to use the package. Very quickly, however, the basics of running an SPSS analysis begin to make sense and a feeling of mastery can follow quickly. This feeling of mastery, however, can be illusory. SPSS is the type of computer package that can be called a TOM (Totally Obedient Moron). It will carry out a completely nonsensical analysis in a very efficient and completely reliable manner. As long as the numerical characteristics of the variables specified in an analysis allow it, SPSS usually will produce the statistics that have been requested, even if the rationale underlying the analysis is completely illogical. It is rare that SPSS will give a warning equivalent to asking the researcher '*Are you really sure this is what you want to do?!*'

This is partially due to SPSS being designed to cater to a very broad constituency of users who will be working with many radically different types of data across a wide variety of disciplines, from the social sciences through marketing and commercial applications to the biological sciences. A manifestation of this is the tendency (which you may have noticed) of SPSS to provide more, rather than less, information in its output than most users will need. That, and the scientific appearance of an impressively designed bit of output, can impart a (perhaps false) sense of proficiency to the novice user. For example, if you asked SPSS to correlate the variables **relig** (religious denomination) and **ethnic** (ethnic group), both of which are multiple-category variables in which the codes in no way fall into an interval or ratio or even an ordinal scale, SPSS would gladly oblige, reporting a correlation coefficient with its associated level of significance without any warning or indication that this was a completely invalid procedure to have carried out. SPSS leaves it up to the researcher to understand the characteristics of the variables in their data and to know enough about the statistical procedures they are requesting to realize when a procedure is utterly incorrect. While it is rewarding to carry out an SPSS analysis that 'works', in the sense of producing output without error messages, you must remember that it is up to you to request sensible tasks and to interpret the resulting output properly. In this respect, the flexibility and ease of use of SPSS can be a mixed blessing.

That said, SPSS is first and foremost a very powerful and flexible tool for the analysis of social data. By the time you have completed the modules in this workbook and carried out analysis exercises using the practice datasets, you will have developed an important skill. The ability to analyse data using SPSS can provide an immediate 'payback' on the other courses that you will be taking as part of your degree – particularly if any of these require the analysis of quantitative data. Possessing knowledge of SPSS can also be vital for the successful completion of a postgraduate degree. An even more significant area is that of employment. The SPSS package is, without doubt, *the* package for social science data analysis and is recognized as such throughout the world in academia, the public services and in private enterprise. In practical terms, being able genuinely to claim and demonstrate a proficient understanding of SPSS can be the decisive factor in a job interview. But more than that, however you decide to employ your newly acquired skills, the ability to analyse statistical data opens up a whole new world of research possibilities.

APPENDIX 1
The Data Set Variables:
A Quick Guide

The 'Quick Guide' below provides summary information on the variables included in the ISSP dataset that we have selected for inclusion in the teaching datasets. The first five columns summarize information contained within the SPSS 'Variable grid': Variable name; Variable label; Value labels (if they are used); Missing values; Level of measurement. The next column 'Location in questionnaire' gives the question and page number of the original question wordings used in the ISSP Work Orientation module. This questionnaire can be accessed as a *.pdf file located at: http://www.za.uni-koeln.de/data/en/issp/codebooks/ZA4350_bq.pdf. The questionnaire can be viewed directly but we recommend that you download and print it for future reference. Note that, since each national survey used its own methodology to ask the additional 'background' on items such as age, gender, educational level etc., only the work orientation questions are in the central questionnaire. To link to the GESIS website where an extensive collection of additional information about the 2005 Work Orientation survey and about the ISSP generally can be found, go to: http://www.gesis.org/en/data_service/issp/data/2005_Work_Orientations_III.htm.

The final 'Comments' column gives additional information that we felt was necessary to help you understand the variables in the datasets. We have used this column to point out the existence of some variables that are particular only to the separate national datasets. Also, in order to widen the scope of potential analyses that you can carry out, we generated a significant number of attitude scales and indices of social standing that are not in the original ISSP dataset. Information about the meanings of these additional variables and how to interpret them can be found in the 'Comments' column.

Finally, we must point out that the datasets we provide are *teaching* datasets derived from the original ISSP data. We have modified them for teaching purposes by creating additional variables and in some cases simplifying the original data. As part of this simplification, the teaching datasets do not contain all of the variables in the original ISSP dataset. If you desire to carry out analyses of these data for research purposes, we *strongly* advise you to apply to and download the original data from the ISSP website where it is freely available.

Variable name*	Variable label	Value labels	Missing values	Level of measurement	Location in questionnaire	Comments
v2*	Respondent ID number	None	None	Nominal		
v3	Country		None	Nominal		Only appears in the dataset for all 32 countries
v10	Enjoy a paid job even if I did not need money	1 Strongly agree 2 Agree 3 Neither agree nor disagree 4 Disagree 5 Strongly disagree	8, 9	Ordinal	2 (Q2), page 1	
v11	Personally important: job security	1 Very important 2 Important 3 Neither important nor unimportant 4 Unimportant 5 Very unimportant	8, 9	Ordinal	3 (Q4), page 2	
v12	Personally important: high income	1 Very important 2 Important 3 Neither important nor unimportant 4 Unimportant 5 Very unimportant	8, 9	Ordinal	3 (Q4), page 2	
v13	Personally important: opportunity for advancement	1 Very important 2 Important 3 Neither important nor unimportant 4 Unimportant 5 Very unimportant	8, 9	Ordinal	3 (Q4), page 2	

v14	Personally important: an interesting job	1 Very important 2 Important 3 Neither important nor unimportant 4 Unimportant 5 Very unimportant	8, 9	Ordinal	3 (Q4), page 2
v15	Personally important: work independently	1 Very important 2 Important 3 Neither important nor unimportant 4 Unimportant 5 Very unimportant	8, 9	Ordinal	3 (Q4) , page 2
v16	Personally important: help other people	1 Very important 2 Important 3 Neither important nor unimportant 4 Unimportant 5 Very unimportant	8, 9	Ordinal	2 (Q4), page 2
v17	Personally important: a job useful to society	1 Very important 2 Important 3 Neither important nor unimportant 4 Unimportant 5 Very unimportant	8, 9	Ordinal	3 (Q4), page 2
v18	Personally important: decide time of work	1 Very important 2 Important 3 Neither important nor unimportant 4 Unimportant 5 Very unimportant	8, 9	Ordinal	3 (Q4), page 2

(Continued)

Variable name	Variable label	Value labels	Missing values	Level of measurement	Location in questionnaire	Comments
v19	Personal choice between different kinds of jobs	1 Being an employee 2 Being self-employed	8, 9	Nominal	4 (Q8), page 3	
v20	Personal choice between kinds of firms	1 Working in a small firm 2 Working in a large firm	8, 9	Nominal	4 (Q8), page 3	
v21	Personal choice between different work types	1 Working in private business 2 Working for government or civil service	8, 9	Nominal	4 (Q8), page 3	
v22	Employees have more job security than self-employed	1 Strongly agree 2 Agree 3 Neither agree nor disagree 4 Disagree 5 Strongly disagree	8, 9	Ordinal	5 (N), page 3	
v23	Being employee interferes more with family life	1 Strongly agree 2 Agree 3 Neither agree nor disagree 4 Disagree 5 Strongly disagree	0, 8, 9	Ordinal	5 (N), page 3	
v24	Trade unions are important for job security	1 Strongly agree 2 Agree 3 Neither agree nor disagree 4 Disagree 5 Strongly disagree	8, 9	Ordinal	6 (N), page 4	

v25	Work conditions much worse without trade unions	1 Strongly agree 2 Agree 3 Neither agree nor disagree 4 Disagree 5 Strongly disagree	8, 9	Ordinal	6 (N), page 4
v26	Preference of personal work situation at present	1 A fulltime job, 30 hours or more 2 A part-time job, 10–29 hours 3 Less than 10 hours job 4 No paid job at all	8, 9	Ordinal	7 (Q9), page 4
v27*	Respondent currently working for pay	1 Yes 2 Not	9	Nominal	8 (Q11), page 4
v28	Preference: number of hours working-earning money	1 Work longer, earn more money 2 Same number of hours for same money 3 Work less, earn less	0, 8, 9	Ordinal	9 (Q13), page 5
v29	Apply to Rs job: my job is secure	1 Strongly agree 2 Agree 3 Neither agree nor disagree 4 Disagree 5 Strongly disagree	0, 8, 9	Ordinal	10 (Q14), page 5
v31*	Rs job: opportunities for advancement are high	1 Strongly agree 2 Agree 3 Neither agree nor disagree 4 Disagree 5 Strongly disagree	0, 8, 9	Ordinal	10 (Q14), page 5

(Continued)

Variable name	Variable label	Value labels	Missing values	Level of measurement	Location in questionnaire	Comments
v32*	Apply to Rs job: my job is interesting	1 Strongly agree 2 Agree 3 Neither agree nor disagree 4 Disagree 5 Strongly disagree	0, 8, 9	Ordinal	10 (Q14), page 5	
v34	Apply to Rs job: can help other people	1 Strongly agree 2 Agree 3 Neither agree nor disagree 4 Disagree 5 Strongly disagree	0, 8, 9	Ordinal	10 (Q14), page 5	
v37*	How often: come home from work exhausted	1 Always 2 Often 3 Sometimes 4 Hardly ever 5 Never	0, 8, 9	Ordinal	11 (Q15), page 6	
v38*	How often applies: do hard physical work	1 Always 2 Often 3 Sometimes 4 Hardly ever 5 Never	0, 8, 9	Ordinal	11 (Q15), page 6	
v39*	How often applies: find work stressful	1 Always 2 Often 3 Sometimes 4 Hardly ever 5 Never	0, 8, 9	Ordinal	11 (Q15), page 6	

v40*	How often: work in dangerous conditions	1 Always 2 Often 3 Sometimes 4 Hardly ever 5 Never	0, 8, 9	Ordinal	11 (Q15), page 6
v41	How working hours are decided	1 Employer decides, I can't change 2 I decide within limits 3 Entirely free to decide	0, 8, 9	Ordinal	12 (Q16), page 6
v42	Best describes the organization of daily work	1 Free to decide 2 Can decide within limits 3 Not free to decide	0, 8, 9	Ordinal	13 (N), page 6
v43	How difficult: to take time off during working hours	1 Not difficult at all 2 Not too difficult 3 Somewhat difficult 4 Very difficult	0, 8, 9	Ordinal	14 (N), page 7
v44	How often: demands of job interfere with family life	1 Always 2 Often 3 Sometimes 4 Hardly ever 5 Never	0, 8, 9	Ordinal	15 (N), page 7
v45	How often: family life interferes with job	1 Always 2 Often 3 Sometimes 4 Hardly ever 5 Never	0, 8, 9	Ordinal	15 (N), page 7

(Continued)

Variable name	Variable label	Value labels	Missing values	Level of measurement	Location in questionnaire	Comments
v46	How much use of past work experience and skills	1 Almost none 2 A little 3 A lot 4 Almost all	5–9, 0	Ordinal	16 (Q19), page 7	
v47	How helpful is present work experience for new job	1 Very helpful 2 Helpful 3 Not so helpful 4 Not helpful at all	0, 8, 9	Ordinal	17 (N), page 8	
v48	Training to improve job skills over past 12 months	1 Yes 2 No	0, 8, 9	Nominal	18 (N), page 8	
v49	Relations between management and employees	1 Very good 2 Quite good 3 Neither good nor bad 4 Quite bad 5 Very bad	0, 8, 9	Ordinal	19 (Q21), page 8	
v50	Relations between workmates/colleagues	1 Very good 2 Quite good 3 Neither good nor bad 4 Quite bad 5 Very bad	0, 8, 9	Ordinal	19 (Q21), page 8	
v51	How satisfied are you in your (main) job	1 Completely satisfied 2 Very satisfied 3 Fairly satisfied 4 Neither satisfied nor dissatisfied 5 Fairly dissatisfied 6 Very dissatisfied 7 Completely dissatisfied	0, 8, 9	Ordinal	20 (Q22), page 9	

v52	Willing to work harder to help firm succeed	1 Strongly agree 2 Agree 3 Neither agree nor disagree 4 Disagree 5 Strongly disagree	0, 8, 9	Ordinal	21 (Q23), page 9
v53	Proud to be working for my firm	1 Strongly agree 2 Agree 3 Neither agree nor disagree 4 Disagree 5 Strongly disagree	0, 8, 9	Ordinal	21 (Q23), page 9
v54	I would turn down another job to stay	1 Strongly agree 2 Agree 3 Neither agree nor disagree 4 Disagree 5 Strongly disagree	0, 8, 9	Ordinal	21 (Q23), page 9
v57	How likely you will try to find a job in next 12 months	1 Very likely 2 Likely 3 Unlikely 4 Very unlikely	0, 8, 9	Ordinal	24 (Q25), page 10
v58	Extent of worry about the possibility of losing job	1 Worry a great deal 2 Worry to some extent 3 I worry a little 4 Don't worry at all	0, 8, 9	Ordinal	25 (Q26), page 11
v59	Avoid unemployment: would accept a job that requires new skills	1 Strongly agree 2 Agree 3 Neither agree nor disagree 4 Disagree 5 Strongly disagree	0, 8, 9	Ordinal	26 (N), page 11

(Continued)

Variable name	Variable label	Value labels	Missing values	Level of measurement	Location in questionnaire	Comments
v60	Avoid unemployment: would accept lower position, lower pay	1 Strongly agree 2 Agree 3 Neither agree nor disagree 4 Disagree 5 Strongly disagree	0, 8, 9	Ordinal	26 (N), page 11	
v61	Avoid unemployment: would accept temporary employment	1 Strongly agree 2 Agree 3 Neither agree nor disagree 4 Disagree 5 Strongly disagree	0, 8, 9	Ordinal	26 (N), page 11	
v62	Avoid unemployment: would travel longer to get to work	1 Strongly agree 2 Agree 3 Neither agree nor disagree 4 Disagree 5 Strongly disagree	0, 8, 9	Ordinal	26 (N), page 11	
v63	Do you do any other work for additional income	1 No 2 Yes, mostly as an employee 3 Yes, mostly self-employed 4 Yes, other	0, 8, 9	Nominal	27 (N), page 11	
v64	Not currently working: had paid job for 1 year or more	1 Yes 2 No	0, 8, 9	Nominal	28, page 12	
v65	Not currently working: end (year) of last paid job		0, 9998, 9999	Scale	29, page 12	

v66	Not currently working: main reason for job ending	1 Retired due to age 2 Retired by choice 3 Retired not by choice 4 Became disabled 5 Workplace shut down 6 Dismissed 7 Contract ended 8 Family responsibilities 9 Got married 10 Other reasons	0, 98, 99	Nominal	30, page 12	
v67	Not working; would like to have a paid job now or in future	1 Yes 2 No	0, 8, 9	Nominal	31, page 13	
v68	Not working; how likely to find a job	1 Very likely 2 Likely 3 Unlikely 4 Very unlikely	0, 8, 9	Ordinal	32, page 13	
v69	Not working; Resp currently looking for a job?	1 Yes 2 No	0, 8, 9	Nominal	33, page 13	
v70	Not working; registered at a public agency	0 No 1 Yes	−1, −2, −3	Nominal	34, page 14	Basis for a geocode
v71	Not working; registered at a private agency	0 No 2 Yes	−1, −2, −3	Nominal	34, page 14	Basis for a geocode
v72	Not working; answered advertisements	0 No 4 Yes	−1, −2, −3	Nominal	34, page 14	Basis for a geocode
v73	Not working; advertised in newspapers	0 No 8 Yes	−1, −2, −3	Nominal	34, page 14	Basis for a geocode

(Continued)

Variable name	Variable label	Value labels	Missing values	Level of measurement	Location in questionnaire	Comments
v74	Not working: applied directly to employers	0 No 16 Yes	−1, −2, −3	Nominal	34, page 14	Basis for a geocode
v75	Not working: asked relatives, friends	0 No 32 Yes	−1, −2, −3	Nominal	34, page 14	Basis for a geocode
v76	Not working: training in past 12 months to improve job skills	1 Yes 2 No	0, 8, 9	Nominal	35 (N) page 14	
v77	Not working: Main source of economic support of Resp	1 Pension, private or state 2 Unemployment benefits 3 Spouse/Partner 4 Other family members 5 Social assistance/welfare 6 Occasional work 7 Other	0, 8, 9	Nominal	36, page 15	
v78	Self-assessment: R is reserved	1 Strongly agree 2 Agree 3 Neither agree nor disagree 4 Disagree 5 Strongly disagree	0, 8, 9	Ordinal	page 16	Optional question, not asked in all countries
v79	Self-assessment: R is generally trusting	1 Strongly agree 2 Agree 3 Neither agree nor disagree 4 Disagree 5 Strongly disagree	0, 8, 9	Ordinal	page 16	Optional question, not asked in all countries

v80	Self-assessment: R does a thorough job	1 Strongly agree 2 Agree 3 Neither agree nor disagree 4 Disagree 5 Strongly disagree	0, 8, 9	Ordinal	page 16	Optional question, not asked in all countries
v81	Self-assessment: R is relaxed	1 Strongly agree 2 Agree 3 Neither agree nor disagree 4 Disagree 5 Strongly disagree	0, 8, 9	Ordinal	page 16	Optional question, not asked in all countries
v82	Self-assessment: R has an active imagination	1 Strongly agree 2 Agree 3 Neither agree nor disagree 4 Disagree 5 Strongly disagree	0, 8, 9	Ordinal	page 16	Optional question, not asked in all countries
v83	Self-assessment: R is outgoing, sociable	1 Strongly agree 2 Agree 3 Neither agree nor disagree 4 Disagree 5 Strongly disagree	0, 8, 9	Ordinal	page 16	Optional question, not asked in all countries
v84	Self-assessment: tends to find fault w others	1 Strongly agree 2 Agree 3 Neither agree nor disagree 4 Disagree 5 Strongly disagree	0, 8, 9	Ordinal	page 16	Optional question, not asked in all countries
v85	Self-assessment: R tends to be lazy	1 Strongly agree 2 Agree 3 Neither agree nor disagree 4 Disagree 5 Strongly disagree	0, 8, 9	Ordinal	page 16	Optional question, not asked in all countries

(Continued)

Variable name	Variable label	Value labels	Missing values	Level of measurement	Location in questionnaire	Comments
v86	Self-assessment: R gets nervous easily	1 Strongly agree 2 Agree 3 Neither agree nor disagree 4 Disagree 5 Strongly disagree	0, 8, 9	Ordinal	page 16	Optional question, not asked in all countries
v87	Self-assessment: R has artistic interests	1 Strongly agree 2 Agree 3 Neither agree nor disagree 4 Disagree 5 Strongly disagree	0, 8, 9	Ordinal	page 16	Optional question, not asked in all countries
sex*	R: Gender	1 Male 2 Female	9	Nominal		
age*	R: Age		99	Scale		
marital*	R: Marital status	1 Married or living as married 2 Widowed 3 Divorced 4 Separated, but married 5 Single, never married	9	Nominal		
cohab	R: Steady life-partner	1 Yes 2 No	0, 9	Nominal		
educyrs*	R: Education I: years of schooling		95–99	Scale		

degree*	R: Education II-highest education level	0 No formal qualification 1 Lowest formal qualification 2 Above lowest qualification 3 Higher secondary completed 4 Above higher secondary level 5 University degree completed	7, 9	Ordinal	General coding of educational qualifications that applies across all countries
xx_degr	Country-specific education		0, 9	Ordinal	Each country has a variable, 'xx_degr', that is a unique coding of its own educational qualifications.
wrkst*	R: Current employment status	1 Employed full-time 2 Employed part-time 3 Employed less than part-time 4 Helping family member 5 Unemployed 6 Student in school or vocational training 7 Retired 8 Housewife/Househusband, home duties 9 Permanently disabled 10 Other, not in labour force	97–99	Nominal	
wrkhrs*	R: Hours worked weekly		97–99, 0	Scale	

(*Continued*)

Variable name	Variable label	Value labels	Missing values	Level of measurement	Location in questionnaire	Comments
isco88	R: Occupation International Standard Classification of Occupation (ISCO)1988 4-digit code		9996–9999, 0	Nominal		A complete listing of the ISCO codings and information about its use and construction can be found in English, Spanish and French at: http://www.ilo.org/public/english/bureau/stat/isco88/major.htm
wrktype*	R: Working for private/ public sector or self-employed	1 Work for government 2 Publicly owned firm or nationalized industry 3 Private firm or others 4 Self-employed 5 Other	0, 8, 9	Nominal		
nemploy	R: Self-employed – number of employees		9995–9999, –1	Scale		
wrksup	R: Supervises others at work	1 Yes, supervises 2 No, does not supervise	7–9, 0	Nominal		
union	R: Trade union membership	1 Currently member 2 Once member, not now 3 Never a member	0, 8, 9	Nominal		
spwrkst*	Spouse: Current employment status	1 Employed full-time 2 Employed part-time 3 Employed less than part-time 4 Helping family member 5 Unemployed 6 Student in school or vocational training	97–99, 0	Nominal		

	7 Retired 8 Housewife/Househusband, home duties 9 Permanently disabled 10 Other, not in labour force			
spisco88	Spouse: Occupation ISCO 1988 4-digit code	9996–9999, 0	Nominal	A complete listing of the ISCO codings and information about its use and construction can be found in English, Spanish and French at: http://www.ilo.org/public/english/bureau/stat/isco88/major.htm
spwrktyp	Spouse: Working for private/public sector, self-employed	0, 8, 9	Nominal	
	1 Work for government 2 Publicly owned firm or nationalised industry 3 Private firm or others 4 Self-employed 5 Other			
xx_rinc*	Respondent's earnings	999990 to highest value, 0	Ordinal or Scale	Each country has a variable, 'xx_rinc', that is a unique coding in the local currency of the Respondent's earnings.
xx_inc	Family income	999990 to highest value, 0	Ordinal or Scale	Each country has a variable, 'xx_inc', that is a unique coding in the local currency of the household's income.
hompop*	How many persons in household	0, 96, 99	Scale	

(Continued)

Variable name	Variable label	Value labels	Missing values	Level of measurement	Location in questionnaire	Comments
hhcycle	Household composition: children+adults		0, 95, 99	Nominal		
party_lr	Respondent's party affiliation: left-right (derived)	1 Far left, etc. 2 Left, centre-left 3 Centre, liberal 4 Right, conservative 5 Far right, etc. 6 Other, not specific 7 No party, No preference	6–9, 0	Ordinal	A common political affiliation code applied across all countries	
xx_prty[*]	Respondent's party affiliation, local code		97–99, 0	Nominal	Each country has a variable, 'xx_prty', that is a unique coding of the local political parties.	
vote_le[*]	R: Vote in last election	1 Yes 2 No	7–9, 0	Nominal		
relig[*]	R: Religious denomination		998, 999	Nominal		
religgrp	R: Religious main groups (derived)	1 No religion 2 Roman Catholic 3 Protestant 4 Christian Orthodox 5 Jewish 6 Islam 7 Buddhism 8 Hinduism 9 Other Christian religions 10 Other Eastern religions 11 Other religions	99, 98	Nominal		

attend*	R: Attendance of religious services	1 Several times a week 2 Once a week 3 Two or 3 times a month 4 Once a month 5 Several times a year 6 Once a year 7 Less frequently 8 Never	97–99, 0	Ordinal	
topbot*	Respondent's placement of self on a 10-point scale of social standing	1 'lowest' to 10 'highest'	97–99, 0	Ordinal	
xx_reg*	Region of country		0, 99	Nominal	Each country has a variable, 'xx_reg', that is a unique coding of geographical regions within that country.
xx_size	Size of community		0, 99	Ordinal	Each country has a variable, 'xx_size', that is a unique coding for that country of the size of the community in which R lives.
urbrural*	Type of community: R's self-assessment	1 Urban, a big city 2 Suburb, outskirts of a big city 3 Town or small city 4 Country village 5 Farm or home located in the country	0, 9	Ordinal	

(Continued)

Variable name	Variable label	Value labels	Missing values	Level of measurement	Location in questionnaire	Comments
ethnic*	Family origin, ethnic group, identity		0, 99	Nominal		
mode	Method of data collection	10 Pencil & paper, no visuals 11 Pencil & paper, visuals 12 Pencil & paper, R reads questionnaire 13 Pencil & paper, Interpreter, no visuals 14 Pencil & paper, Interpreter, visuals 20 Computer-assisted, no visuals 21 Computer-assisted, visuals 30 Self completed by pencil & paper, Interviewer attending 31 Self-completed by pencil & paper, Dropped off & picked up later 32 Self-completed, Dropped off & mailed back by R 34 Self-completed, Mailed back by R 40 Telephone interview	99	Nominal		
weight	Weighting factor		None	Scale		

hhadults	Number of adults in household	None	
jobselfact*	Job is self-actualizing	99.00	Scale	An attitude scale of how 'self-actualizing' R finds their work. High values indicate high 'self-actualization'.
impjobself*	Personally important that job self-actualizes	99.00	Scale	An attitude scale of how important it is to the respondent that their job is 'self-actualizing'. High values indicate high importance.
workfree*	Control and freedom at work	99.00	Scale	An attitude scale of the extent of personal control R feels they have of their working environment. High values indicate feelings of high control.
alienated*	Alienation from job	99.00	Scale	A scale of alienation of R from their job. High values indicate high alienation.
avoid*	Will make sacrifice to avoid unemployment	99.00	Scale	A scale of the extent R would make sacrifices to avoid becoming unemployed. High values indicate willingness to make sacrifices.
jobhard*	Job conditions hard	99.00	Scale	A scale of the extent that R reports unpleasant/difficult working conditions. High values indicate adverse conditions reported.

(Continued)

Variable name	Variable label	Value labels	Missing values	Level of measurement	Location in questionnaire	Comments
jobgood*	Job has rewarding conditions		99.00	Scale	A scale of the extent that R reports positive working conditions.	
lesshome*	Less time spent on home and leisure due to job		99.00	Scale	A scale of the extent that R spends less time on personal activities due to work demands. High values indicate job interferes with personal life.	
relaxed*	Self-assessed as relaxed		99.00	Scale	R's personal assessment of whether they are relaxed. Only available if a country asked these optional questions.	
impsecureself	Secure well-paid job is important		99.00	Scale	High values indicate security is more important in a job than risk.	
prounion	Pro labour unions scale		99.00	Scale	Higher values indicate pro-trade union opinions.	
compat*	Job and family compatible		99.00	Scale	A scale of compatibility between work and home life. High values indicate high compatibility.	
giveskl*	Job gives employment skills		99.00	Scale	A scale of the extent R feels that their job gives them skills that would help them find employment	
stayput*	Will stay in present job		99.00	Scale	A scale of R's assessment of the likelihood they will remain in their present job. High values indicate little likelihood of moving on.	

worry*	Worry about losing job	99.00	Scale	A scale of the extent that R is worried about losing their job. High values indicate worry.
positive*	Positive self-assessment	99.00	Scale	A scale of the extent that R assesses themselves as an effective person. High values indicate a positive assessment. Only available if a country asked these optional questions.
xx_percapita1*	Income per person in household	None	Scale	Each country has a variable, 'xx_percapita1', that is a unique coding in the local currency of the income per *person* in the household.
xx_percapita2	Income per adult in household	None	Scale	Each country has a variable, 'xx_percapita2', that is a unique coding in the local currency of the income per *adult* in the household.
jobseek	Amount of job-seeking activities	−1.00	Scale	Number of job-seeking activities.
iscomajor	Respondent: International Standard Classification of Occupations (ISCO), *Major Groups*	None	Nominal	0 Armed forces 1 Legislators, senior officials & managers 2 Professionals 3 Technicians & associated professionals 4 Clerks 5 Service shop & market sales workers

(Continued)

Variable name	Variable label	Value labels	Missing values	Level of measurement	Location in questionnaire	Comments
		6 Skilled agricultural & fishery workers 7 Craft & related trade workers 8 Plant & machine operators, Assemblers 9 Elementary occupations				
iscosubmajor	Respondent: ISCO *sub-Major* Groups	1 Legislators & senior officials 2 Corporate managers 3 General managers 4 Physical, mathematical & engineering science professionals 5 Life science & Health professionals 6 Teaching professionals 7 Other professionals 9 Physical & engineering science Associate professionals 10 Teaching Associate professionals 11 Other Associate professionals 12 Office clerks 13 Customer service clerks 14 Personal & protective service workers	None	Nominal		

15 Salespersons, models & demonstrators
16 Market-oriented skilled agricultural & fishery workers
17 Subsistence agricultural & fishery workers
18 Workers in extraction & building trade
19 Workers in metal, machinery & related trades
20 Workers in precision handicrafts, printing & related trades
21 Workers in other crafts & related trades
22 Stationary plant & related Operators
23 Machine operators & assemblers
24 Drivers & Mobile plant operators
25 Sales & Services elementary occupations
26 Labourers in agriculture & fishing
27 Labourers in mining, construction, manufacturing & transport
28 Armed forces

(Continued)

Variable name	Variable label	Value labels	Missing values	Level of measurement	Location in questionnaire	Comments
spiscomajor	Spouse: ISCO *Major* Groups	0 Armed forces 1 Legislators, senior officials & managers 2 Professionals 3 Technicians & associated professionals 4 Clerks 5 Service shop & market sales workers 6 Skilled agricultural & fishery workers 7 Craft & related trade workers 8 Plant & machine operators, Assemblers 9 Elementary occupations	None	Nominal		
spiscosubmajor	Spouse: ISCO *sub-Major* Groups	1 Legislators & senior officials 2 Corporate managers 3 General managers 4 Physical, mathematical & engineering science professionals 5 Life science & Health professionals 6 Teaching professionals 7 Other professionals 9 Physical & engineering science Associate professionals	None	Nominal		

10 Teaching Associate professionals

11 Other Associate professionals

12 Office clerks

13 Customer service clerks

14 Personal & protective service workers

15 Salespersons, models & demonstrators

16 Market-oriented skilled agricultural & fishery workers

17 Subsistence agricultural & fishery workers

18 Workers in extraction & building trade

19 Workers in metal, machinery & related trades

20 Workers in precision handicrafts, printing & related trades

21 Workers in other crafts & related trades

22 Stationary plant & related Operators

23 Machine operators & assemblers

24 Drivers & Mobile plant operators

(Continued)

Variable name	Variable label	Value labels	Missing values	Level of measurement	Location in questionnaire	Comments
		25 Sales & Services elementary occupations 26 Labourers in agriculture & fishing 27 Labourers in mining, construction, manufacturing & transport 28 Armed forces				
spsiops*	Spouse: Standard Occupational Prestige Scale			Scale	A social standing rating of occupations. Higher values indicate more 'prestige' associated with the occupation.	
siops*	Respondent: Standard Occupational Prestige Scale			Scale	A social standing rating of occupations. Higher values indicate more 'prestige'.	
isei	Respondent: International socio-economic index			Scale	An index of occupational standing based upon the average education and income of a job.	
spisei	Spouse: International socio-economic index			Scale	An index of occupational standing based upon the average education and income of a job.	
spegp*	Spouse: EGP Class categories	1 I Higher 'service' 2 II Lower 'service' 3 III Routine clerical & sales 5 IVa & IVb Self-employed 6 IVc Farmers & Farm Managers	None	Nominal	A set of 'marxian Weberian' social class categories originally developed at Nuffield College, Oxford for England & Wales and subsequently extended by the CASMIN study for international comparison.	

Variable	Label	Values	Missing	Measure	Description
		7 V Manual supervisors 8 VI Skilled manual 9 VIIa Semi & Unskilled manual 10 VIIb Agricultural workers			
egp[*]	Respondent: EGP Class categories	1 I Higher 'service' 2 II Lower 'service' 3 III Routine clerical & sales 4 IVa Small employers 5 IVb Own account self-employed 6 IVc Farmers & Farm Managers 7 V Manual supervisors 8 VI Skilled manual 9 VIIa Semi & Unskilled manual 10 VIIb Agricultural workers	None	Nominal	A set of 'marxian Weberian' social class categories originally developed at Nuffield College, Oxford for England & Wales and subsequently extended by the CASMIN study for international comparison.
geojobseek[*]	Geometric code of job-seeking behaviour	0 No job-seeking activity 1 Registered at public employment agency 2 Registered at private employment agency 3 = 1 + 2 4 Answered job advertisements 8 Advertised in newspapers 16 Applied directly to employers 32 Asked relatives or friend for help	–1.00	Nominal	A 'geometric' coding of job-seeking behaviours in which each code indicates a *unique combination* of behaviours.

[*] Starred variables are those included in the SPSS Student Version datasets.

APPENDIX 2
SPSS Syntax

As this book is aimed primarily at the novice user, the various data analysis and modification procedures that we have covered have been demonstrated using the SPSS menu system. However, it is important to point out that all of these tasks (and many additional procedures) can also be carried out using the program's command syntax and this is generally the preferred method for more experienced users. Although initially less user-friendly than the menu system, the command syntax ultimately provides a quicker and more efficient means of carrying out statistical analysis in SPSS, and it is particularly useful if you want to perform specific procedures repeatedly. Version 17 contains an enhanced syntax editor which includes various features designed to minimise errors and speed up the process of analysis further. While it is only possible to provide a very brief introduction to command syntax here, more detailed information is available through the Help menu in SPSS and context-sensitive help for commands currently in the syntax window can be can be obtained using the F1 key.

DISPLAYING SYNTAX IN THE OUTPUT WINDOW

One way to become more familiar with the command language in SPSS is to ensure that a log of the corresponding syntax always precedes any output in the Viewer Window. If this log doesn't appear in the Viewer Window along with your output you will need to change the settings in SPSS as outlined below.

Select **Options** from the **Edit** drop-down menu and then click on the **Viewer** tab in the Options Dialog box (Figure A2.1). Make sure that the '**Display commands in log**' checkbox is selected, and click OK. From now on the syntax commands relating to any procedures you carry out will appear just before the output in the Viewer Window. You will gradually become more familiar with this command language and you can copy and paste these into the syntax window (see example below).

Example 1

To illustrate this we will reproduce an example from Module 2 (*Listing and Exploring Data*), but this time with the 'Display commands in log' option selected (follow the steps outlined above, if you haven't already done so).

Click **here** to select Viewer tab

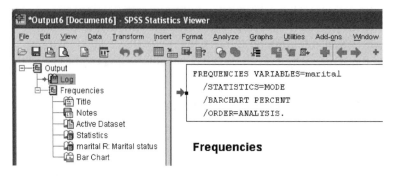

Click **here** to display syntax in output log

Figure A2.1 *Options: Viewer dialog box*

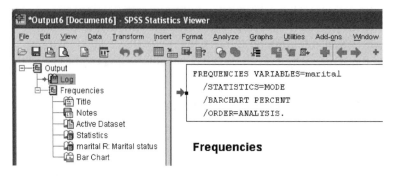

Figure A2.2 *Output log in Viewer Window*

Open up the ISSP dataset for Great Britain and then follow the steps for Example 1 on pp.60–61 to produce a frequency table, mode and bar chart for the marital status variable (**Marital**). As can be seen from Figure A2.2, the output log (containing the syntax commands for the procedures you carried out) appears just before the output in the Viewer Window.

We can save these commands as a syntax file and run them at a later date without having to go through the menu system and dialog boxes. To do this, select the syntax by clicking on **Log** in the Outline Pane (see Figure A2.2) and then copy it to the clipboard in the usual way (i.e. Edit → Copy). To create a new syntax file select **File**, **New** and **Syntax** (Figure A2.3) and then paste the syntax from the clipboard into the Syntax Editor (Figure A2.4) using Edit and Paste.

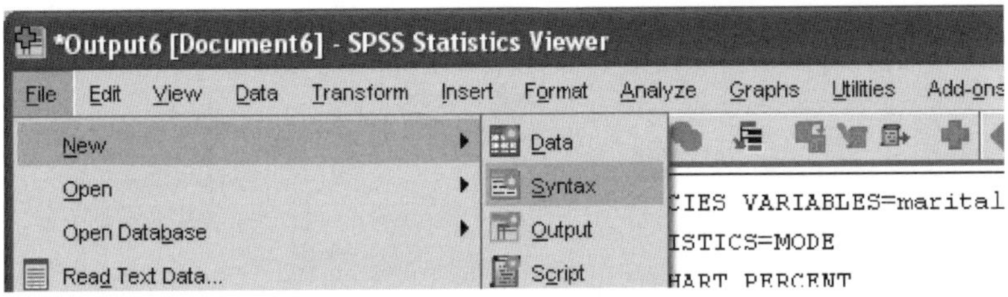

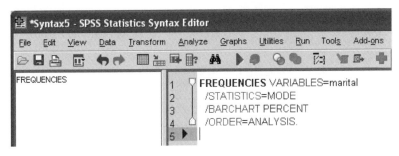

Figure A2.3   *Creating a new syntax file*

Figure A2.4   *Syntax Editor*

The Syntax Editor is examined in more detail below but for the moment we can save this file to run at a later date. Click on **File**, and then **Save As**, before giving the file a name and location. Note that syntax files have the suffix **.sps** to distinguish them from data files (**.sav**) and output files (**.spv**).

PASTING SYNTAX FROM A DIALOG BOX

An alternative way of creating a syntax file is to paste the commands directly into the Syntax Editor from a dialog box. To do this, simply click on the Paste button, rather than the OK button, when ready to run the procedure. We will use the Explore procedure that we carried out in Module 2 (pp.66–68) to illustrate this.

Example 2

Using the ISSP dataset for Great Britain, follow the steps for the Explore procedure as outlined on pp. 66–68 but remember to click on **Paste** (see Figure A2.5), instead of OK, to complete the process. If a syntax file is already open, the commands for the stem and leaf displays and boxplots will be pasted into the Syntax Editor, otherwise a new file will be created automatically.

In Figure A2.6 the commands relating to the Explore procedure have been added to the syntax file that we created in Example 1. You can run this file, edit it or save it to process at a later date.

Once you have created a syntax file you can modify the commands as you see fit. Additional commands can be added, either by copying commands from the output log or pasting them from the dialog boxes, allowing you to build up a very detailed syntax file. The ability to run this file at a later date can save a lot of time and trouble, and speed up the overall process of data analysis. Moreover, as you become more familiar with the language you will be able to type commands directly into the Syntax Editor and create your own files from scratch.

Click **here** to paste the commands into a syntax window.

Figure A2.5 *Explore Dialog box*

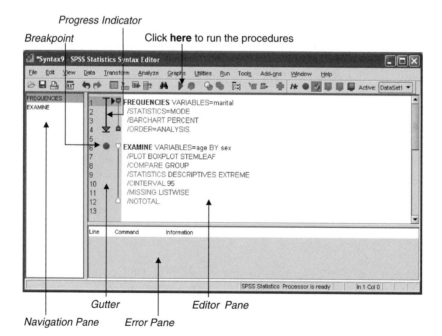

Figure A2.6 *Syntax Editor*

THE SYNTAX EDITOR

The Syntax Editor is used to create new commands, as well as to edit and run existing ones. While a working knowledge of the SPSS syntax rules is necessary for anyone intending to generate their own commands from scratch, the enhanced Syntax Editor in SPSS Statistics 17 makes this task a little easier.

The key features of the Syntax Editor are identified in Figure A2.6. The main area of the window, where syntax is entered and edited, is known as the **Editor Pane**. This has a colour-coding facility which recognises the SPSS command syntax, making it easier to identify errors. SPSS Statistics 17 also has an **Auto-Completion** function which operates in a similar way to predictive text and allows the user to select recognised terms from a context-sensitive list. This helps to speed up the overall process and reduces the possibility of runtime errors.

The **Error Pane** is directly below the Editor Pane and provides information on any errors that occurred in the previous run. Clicking on an error message moves the cursor to the specific line of syntax that caused the problem. (Note: There are no errors in the current example in Figure A2.6).

The **Navigation Pane** performs a similar function to the Outline Pane in the Viewer Window and provides a list of all the commands in the Syntax Editor. In the example in Figure A2.6 the *Frequencies* and *Examine* commands that were created earlier are shown.

Finally, the **Gutter** is the section of the Editor Window located between the Navigation Pane and the Editor Pane. The Gutter in Figure A2.6 shows line numbers along the left-hand side and also includes a **Progress Indicator** and a **Breakpoint**. The progress indicator provides information on how much of a syntax file has been completed. In Figure A2.6 we can see that only the first command (Frequencies) has been carried out, as the progress indicator arrow stops before the Examine command. Breakpoints allow the user to stop the execution of the subsequent command and continue when ready. They can be inserted at any point in a syntax file and are represented by a red circle in the Gutter. The Breakpoint in Figure A2.6 will stop the execution of the syntax run immediately after the Frequencies command has been completed.

Running a command

To run a command in the Syntax Editor, highlight the command you want to run (or place the cursor somewhere within it) and click the **Run Button** on the Toolbar (shown in Figure A2.6). Alternatively, you can use the Run menu, which offers a greater range of alternative options. The output will be displayed in the Viewer Window, just as it would if you had carried out the procedures using the Menu system.

For further information on command syntax you should consult the Help menu in SPSS.

The advantages of SPSS syntax

Now that you have had this brief introduction to SPSS syntax, we will close by systematically listing the advantages that the use of syntax can provide:

1. *Carrying out repeated procedures.* Frequently it can be the case that you want to do the same operation a number of times. In the Windows version of SPSS, this often requires opening a window and going through the same steps over and over again. For instance, suppose you are creating a new dataset based upon a survey of social attitudes that contains 50 Likert-type questions for which the response options are the same: *(1) Strongly agree; (2) Agree; (3) Don't know; (4) Disagree; (5) Strongly disagree.* Attaching Value labels to the 50 variables in 'Variable view' on the data grid would be quite a tedious operation, going to each variable and typing in the same five labels over and over. The following syntax command would have the same result:

```
VALUE LABELS v1 to v50 (1) Strongly agree (2) Agree (3) Don't know (4) Disagree
(5) Strongly disagree.
```

2. *Carrying out procedures that would be difficult or not possible in the windows version.* While they are more complex than the windows versions, syntax commands are also more precise and flexible. This can give you the capacity to carry out a procedure that would not be possible with the windows version of SPSS.

For instance, you may remember from Module 3 that COUNT gives you the ability to count the total number of times a code or range of codes occurs across some variables. However, the windows version of COUNT does not have the capacity to count the total number of times *different* codes appear across different variables. For instance, suppose you would like to create a new variable called **elite** that is the count of the number of 'high status' codes people have across a number of variables, but where the 'high status' code is *different* for each variable. This could not be done in a single windows COUNT statement, but it can be done in SPSS syntax.

Here, we have an example where the variable **elite** will have 1 added to it if **degree** is coded '5 (university degree or higher); **edyrs** (education in years) is 17 years or more; the **egp** coding of social class is '1 or 2 (upper or lower service)'; the **isei** and **siops** rankings of job standing are 75 points or higher; **gbpercapti1**, the household per capita income is £50,000 or more; and **gb_rinc**, the respondent's personal income is £40,000 or more.

```
COUNT elite = degree (5) edyrs (17 thru highest) egp (lowest thru 2) isei
siops (75 thru highest) gbpercapti1 (50000 thru highest) gb_rinc (40000 thru
highest).
```

A person for whom all of these statements for the eight variables concerned are true will have a counted value for **elite** of 8. A person for whom none of these are true will have a score of zero for **elite**. Everyone else will rank somewhere in between.

3. *Keeping an exact record of what you have done.* When you save the syntax commands from a procedure that has been carried out, you have a precise record of exactly what was done. This can be very useful.

It may be that you will want to reproduce the same analysis sometime in the future, perhaps years later. For instance, new, more up-to-date data may be collected and you will want to replicate an analysis that was carried out on a previous dataset. It could be very hard to reproduce the precise format of the windows that you used for the original analysis. However, if the variable names are the same, all you need to do is call up the syntax file and run it on the new data.

4. *Repeating an analysis in a modified form.* A similar problem can arise if you need to repeat an analysis that you carried out before, only with some modifications. For instance, your instructor or a supervisor may have spotted an error and want you to make a slight change to an assignment you have submitted. It can be very hard to reproduce precisely the windows you used the first time. Again, you can call up the syntax file, make the change and rerun the analysis quickly and easily. The capacity to be able to recall the details of an analysis exactly can become crucial in cases where an examiner or the reviewer of an article that has been submitted to a journal demand changes before you receive a pass mark or have the article accepted for publication.

5. *Passing the details of an analysis to someone else.* Similarly, you may want to send the exact details of an analysis to someone else so they can repeat it. For instance, you could carry out an analysis on a dataset from one country in the ISSP datasets, save the syntax record of the analysis, and then send it to a friend in another country so they could reproduce the analysis with the data for their country. Having the syntax file means that the exact details of an analysis can be communicated to another person without any ambiguity. This can be extremely important when people located in places far apart are working together on a joint comparative project.

Glossary

This glossary gives explanations of terms, statistical concepts and features of SPSS that are prominent in this textbook. In order to help you make links between items, we have included suggestions for cross-referencing from one term to another.

Analysis of Variance (ANOVA): A statistical test that determines whether the levels of one variable (the means of a dependent variable) differ significantly across the categories of another (independent) variable or variables. It does so by comparing the variance *between* the different categories of the independent variable(s) with the variance within each of these categories. (See *F-ratio*)

Bar charts: Visual representations of data in which the proportionate frequency of categories is depicted by the length of the bars.

Bartlett's test of sphericity: A test of whether a correlation matrix of variables is significantly different from an identity matrix (a correlation matrix in which the correlations between variables other than themselves is close to zero). The smaller the significance value of the test, the less likely the correlation matrix is an identity matrix. (See *Factor analysis*)

Bimodal: A distribution of scalar values with two distinct modes or 'humps'. (See *Mode* and *Multimodal*)

Binary variable: A categorical/nominal variable in which there are only two categories where one category implies the opposite or absence of the other; e.g., Male/Female or Yes/No. (See *Levels of measurement*)

Bivariate: (See *Multivariate*)

Boolean logic: Logical statements used in SPSS *IF* data modifications and selections in which the parts of the statement are linked by whether any (OR) or all (AND) parts of the statement are true. (See *IF* and *Logical operators*)

Box plot: A depiction of (usually ordinal) data in which the central 50% is indicated by a box and the lower 25% (the lower quartile) and the upper 25% (the upper quartile) are indicated by lines. (See *Exploratory data analysis* and *Outliers*)

Case: A complete individual record or unit of analysis; the rows on an SPSS *Data grid*. (See *Variable*)

Categorical data or variable: (See *Levels of measurement*)

Cell: The intersection between a category of one variable and a category of another variable in a crosstabulation or contingency table. (See *Crosstabulation*)

Central Limit Theorum: *If repeated random samples of size N are drawn from any population, with mean (a certain value) µ and standard deviation σ, then, as N becomes large, the sampling distribution of sampling means will approach normality(take the form of a Normal distribution), with mean µ and standard deviation of σ / √N.'* The Central Limit Theorem is the principle that is the foundation underlying all confirmatory statistical testing and the expression of statistical results in terms of 'p', the *probability* that the result does not mirror the true population difference or relationship.

Central tendency: The middle of a batch of data. 'Middleness' can be conceived of in a variety of ways. (See *Mean, Median* and *Mode*)

Chi-square (X²): A statistical test of association between two variables in which the *expected* values are compared with the *observed* values.

Coding: The process of converting data into a form amenable to computer analysis, usually by assigning numerical values, or codes.

Component matrix: The matrix of components, or factors, in a factor analysis prior to rotation. (See *Factor analysis*)

Compute: The numerical data transformation procedure in SPSS in which arithmetical operations are carried out on variables in order to modify them and/or create new variables. (See *Data transformation, IF* and *Recode*)

Computer packages: Collections of computer algorithms or discrete computer programs that are brought together into a single compatible set. SPSS is a computer package.

Confidence interval: The range within which a true value of a statistical analysis is expected to lie. Normally expressed at a level of probability; e.g., *'We can be 95% sure that the true mean will fall between 4.5 and 8.8.'*

Contingency table: (See *Crosstabulation*)

Control variable: A third variable, the values of which may affect the relationship between two other variables.

Curvilinear relationship: A link between two variables in which the relationship can be depicted as a line, but a *curved* line rather than a straight line.

Correlation coefficient, Pearson's product-moment: A measure of association between two interval/ratio variables, ranging between –1.00 (strong negative association), 0.00 (no association) and +1.00 (strong positive association). (See *Spearman's Rho*)

Correlation matrix: A square grid depicting the correlation coefficients of a group of variables in which each variable is correlated with all other variables.

Count: (a) The number of cases in a cell; (b) A data transformation procedure in SPSS in which all occurrences of a value or group of values across a range of variables is added up.

Cramér's V: An appropriate measure of association when the variables in a crosstabulation table are categorical and either the number of rows or columns exceeds 2. Closely related to chi-square. Values are bounded between 0 and 1, with 0 representing no association and 1 signifying a perfect association. (See *Chi-square* and *Phi*)

Critical value: The lowest value of a statistical test at which we will accept a result as being statistically significant. (See *Statistical significance*)

Crosstabulation: A table depicting the frequencies for each combination of the values of two variables. (For crosstabulation table statistics, see *Chi-square, Cramer's V, Gamma, Goodman and Kruskal's tau, Kendall's tau-b, Lambda, Phi* and *Somer's D*)

Data view: The data spreadsheet in SPSS that shows either the codings or the value labels in an SPSS dataset for each case by each variable. (See *Variable view*)

Data reduction: Applying a statistical technique that is designed to identify underlying features of a batch of data. (See *Factor analysis*)

Data selection: Data manipulation techniques designed to choose a subset of cases.

Data transformation: Data manipulation techniques designed to modify or combine variables in ways that make them more amenable for an analysis. The main data transformation techniques in SPSS are RECODE; COMPUTE; IF; and COUNT. (See *Compute, Count, IF* and *Recode*)

Deduction: Developing (*deducing*) conceptual abstractions or theories from observed data or the results of an analysis. (See *Durkheim, Empiricism, Induction, Operationalization* and *Positivism*)

Degrees of freedom (df): The amount of sources of variation in a batch of data. In general, the greater the degrees of freedom, the more likely that a given value of a statistical test will be significant.

Dependent variable: A variable whose values are hypothesised to be affected by (i.e., *depend upon*) the values of one or more other, 'independent', variables. (See *Independent variable*)

Descriptive statistics: Statistics which solely describe the characteristics of data but do not hypothesize relationships or differences between variables. (See *Inferential statistics*)

Dispersion, measures of: Indicators of the amount of spread around the central point of a batch of data. (See *Interquartile deviation, Range* and *Standard deviation*)

Dummy variables: Variables indicating the presence or absence of a characteristic in which 'presence' is indicated by 1 and 'absence' by 0; e.g., MALEDUMMY where 'Male' = 1 and 'Female = 0. Useful in parametric statistics where the dummy variable may be considered to satisfy the requirement that all variables be 'scalar' or interval/ratio and where the 'presence/absence' is considered to be a quantity.

Durbin-Watson statistic: An indicator of the overall extent of multicollinearity in a multiple regression. (See *Multicollinearity* and *Regression*)

Durkheim, Emile: A 'founding father' of the social sciences who laid fundamental conceptual and empirical groundwork for the Positivistic approach to data analysis. His concept of 'social facts' forms part of the logical basis for statistical analysis. (See *Social fact*)

Eigenvalue: The amount of variance accounted for by a factor. Eigenvalues of more than 1.0 account for more variance than a single variable. (See *Factor analysis)*

Empiricism: Analysis of quantitative data without a conceptual agenda in which the goal is to display significant features of the data. (See *Positivism*)

Extraction: Identifying the underlying factors/components in a factor analysis. (See *Factor analysis*)

Exploratory Data Analysis (EDA): A body of data manipulation techniques that emphasise ease of calculation and visual display that were popularised by John Tukey. They do not have a grounding in statistical theory and instead have the common goal of revealing interesting patterns in batches of data. (See *Box plot* and *Stem and leaf diagram*)

Factor analysis: A statistical technique that allows the simplification of correlational relationships between a number of variables by 'extracting' assumed components, or factors, that underlie the correlations between the individual variables (See *Bartlett's test of sphericity, Component matrix, Data reduction, Eigen value, Extraction, Kaiser-Meyer-Olkin (KMO) sampling adequacy measure* and *Rotation*)

Frequency table: A table showing the frequencies of a variable, the count of the numbers in each category of the variable.

F-ratio: In Analysis of Variance, the ratio of *between* variance to *within* variance. (See *Analysis of Variance*)

Gamma (y): A popular measure of association in crosstabulation tables when both variables are ordinal. A PRE (proportional reduction in error) measure, Gamma takes advantage of the fact that ordinal data can be ranked. The calculation of Gamma is based upon the difference between the number of concordant pairs (two cases that are ranked the same on both variables) and the number of discordant pairs (two cases that are ranked differently on both variables). A negative Gamma score indicates that there are more discordant than concordant pairs, whereas a greater proportion of concordant pairs will produce a positive result (−1 represents a perfect negative association, whereas +1 indicates a perfect positive association). Gamma is a symmetric measure of association; so the result will be the same regardless of which variable is deemed to be dependent/independent. A problem with Gamma is that it ignores all pairs that are tied and so it may overestimate the strength of an association if there is a high percentage of tied cases. (See *Crosstabulation and Proportional reduction in error*)

Geometric codes: A coding system designed to capture all possible combinations of a number of categories. Each initial code in a sequence of categories is the doubling of the previous code; e.g., 1, 2, 4, 8, 16. The 'geometric code' is the sum of all category codes that apply. Every combination of categories will produce a unique value for the geometric code of a case.

General linear model: A collection of parametric statistical procedures with the common perspective that relationships between two or more variables can be depicted by (usually straight) lines.

Goodman and Kruskal's *tau* (T): A proportional reduction in error (PRE) statistic for nominal variables. (See *Gamma, Lambda, Proportional reduction in error* and *Somer's D*)

Goodness of fit: The extent to which a statistical result depicts the actual features of a batch of data. (See *Residual*)

Gross effect: The overall effect of the average number of cases expected across all cells in a loglinear analysis. (See *Loglinear analysis*)

Histogram: A bar chart for interval/ratio data which has many values. Each bar represents the proportionate frequency count for a set range of values.

Homoscedasticity: The extent to which the data in a linear regression cluster around the regression line. The clustering should approximate a Normal distribution, with most values close to the line. (See *Regression*)

Hypothesis: A predictive statement of a relationship between population parameters or variables. The statement typically takes the form of predicting *differences* between groups or *relationships* between variables. The accuracy of the statement is evaluated by statistical analysis. (See *Inferential statistics, Null hypothesis, One-tailed test* and *Two-tailed test*)

Identity matrix: A correlation matrix in which the correlations between variables other than themselves is close to zero. (See *Bartlett's test of sphericity*)

IF: Data transformations or data selections in which a statement is deemed to hold true 'IF' the logical conditions of the statement are met. IF statements are often used to create new variables for analysis that are the logical combinations of two or more existing variables. (See *Boolean logic* and *Logical operators*)

Independent variable: A variable that is hypothesized or predicted to affect or cause another variable, the 'dependent' variable. (See *Dependent variable*)

Induction: Evaluating conceptual abstractions or theories from observed data or the results of an analysis. (See *Deduction, Durkheim, Empiricism, Operationalization* and *Positivism*)

Inferential statistics: Statistics that hypothesise a relationship or difference between variables in a population. (See *Descriptive statistics* and *Hypothesis*)

Interaction: When the effect of two or more independent variables acting together is different than the simple effect of adding each independent effect together. Interactions can take the form of (a) two variables together having more (or *less*) impact than the effect of simply adding their effects together (e.g., a drug interaction where the effect of two innocuous drugs taken together can be lethal) or (b) a particular combination of categories having more (or *less*) effect than the simple additive effect of the categories together (e.g., white Anglo-Saxon Protestants being more likely to be admitted to elite universities than the advantages that would be expected simply by adding together the higher rates of admission for Whites, Anglo-Saxons and Protestants (i.e., the 'WASP effect').

International Social Survey Programme (ISSP): An international collaboration between survey organisations in which the group annually devises a module questionnaire on a different topic. Each nation carries out an independent survey using the module and the responses are collated together into a combined dataset.

Interquartile deviation: The difference between the upper and lower quartiles; i.e., the middle 50% of a distribution. Particularly appropriate for ordinal (ranked) data, the interquartile deviation is less affected by extreme values (outliers) than its interval/ratio equivalent, the standard deviation. (See *Dispersion* and *Standard deviation*)

Interval data or variable: (See *Levels of measurement*)

Kaiser-Meyer-Olkin (KMO) sampling adequacy measure: An index in a factor analysis of how effectively the variables in the correlation matrix can be grouped into a smaller number of factors. The KMO has a maximum value of 1.0 and the larger the value, the better are the prospects for a successful factor analysis. As a general rule of thumb, the KMO should be larger than 0.60. (See *Factor analysis*)

Kendal's tau-b (τ^b): This statistic takes account of tied pairs on both variables (separately) and is therefore a good alternative to Gamma when there is a high proportion of tied ranks. One limitation of Kendall's tau-b is that it can only obtain the values of +1 or –1 if a crosstabulation table has the same number of rows and columns. Kendall's tau-b is also a symmetric measure of association and so can be used when it is not clear which variable is dependent and which variable is independent.

Kuhn, Thomas: A philosopher of science who asserted that scientific progress is not the orderly progression of existing theories being supplanted or modified by empirical testing and evidence. But instead is an essentially political process where outmoded paradigms are replaced when their proponents die out or are removed by a new generation of scientists.

Kurtosis: A measure of the extent to which the data values are clustered around a central point. Normal distributions have a kurtosis value of zero but values between –1 and 1 are generally regarded as acceptable. Values less than 1 indicate a flatter (platykurtic) curve and values greater than 1 indicate a more peaked (leptokurtic) distribution. (See *Normal distribution* and *Skewness*)

Lambda (λ): A proportional reduction in error (PRE) measure of association for nominal variables. Where the independent variable allows an accurate prediction of all values of the dependent variable, lambda will achieve a value of 1 (a perfect association); where knowledge of the independent variable provides no help in predicting the dependent variable Lambda will equal zero. SPSS produces both symmetric and asymmetric versions of Lambda. You should use the symmetric value if you are unable to make a decision as to which of your variables is dependent/independent. (See *Gamma, Goodman and Kruskal's tau, Proportional reduction in error* and *Somer's D*)

Levels of measurement: Central to statistical analysis, the concept of levels (or scales) of measurement helps to determine the types of statistical analysis procedures that may be carried out on particular variables. There are four levels of measurement, determined according to the amount of information inherent within a variable:

- *Nominal or Categorical*: The 'lowest' level of measurement that only allows one to differentiate between categories of the variable. We cannot place these categories in any meaningful order — although numbers may be assigned to the categories when variables are coded, these are merely labels and have no intrinsic meaning (e.g., Marital status: (1) Always single; (2) Married; (3) Living as married; (4) Separated; (5) Divorced; (6) Widowed) (See *Binary variable*);
- *Ordinal*: Ordinal variables differ from nominal variables in that their categories can be arranged into a meaningful order (e.g., from highest to lowest), however, one cannot determine the degree of difference between the categories (e.g., an ordinal scale of Pain: (1) Feels nothing; (2) Tickles; (3) Uncomfortable; (4) Hurts; (5) Agony);
- *Interval*: For variables measured at the interval level it is possible to measure the precise distance between each of the categories. However, the interval scale does not have an absolute zero point and it is therefore inappropriate to compute ratios between two values measured on this scale;
- *Ratio*: The highest level of measurement as it possesses all the features of the other three and, in addition has an absolute zero. Ratio statements can be meaningfully made about such variables (e.g., €20 is twice as much as €10).

For all practical purposes the distinction between interval and ratio scales has little significance in terms of statistical procedures – SPSS lumps both together and calls them 'scalar'. Sometimes they are also termed 'quantitative', 'metric' or 'continuous' data.

Levene's test for equality of variances: A test as to whether the variance of two groups differs significantly. (See *t-test*)

Linear assumption: A link between two variables in which the relationship can be depicted as a line. (See *Curvilinear relationship*)

Line chart: A diagram with one or more lines in which each line indicates the frequencies of a variable as they change across categories.

'Listwise' missing values: SPSS will exclude values indicated as 'missing' from any statistical analysis. If the 'listwise' option is taken in a multivariate analysis, a case will be excluded if any of the variables involved are missing for that case. (See *Missing values* and *Pairwise missing values*)

Logical operators: Links used in conjunction with Boolean logic in IF-type statements: 'Greater than' (>); 'Equals' (=); 'Not equal' (~=); 'Less than' (<). (See *Boolean logic* and *IF*)

Logistic regression: A form of regression in which the dependent variable is categorical (either binomial categories or multinomial). (See *Regression*)

Logit: A form of loglinear analysis in which the primary goal is to establish the effects of each independent variable on a single dependent variable. (See *Loglinear analysis*)

Loglinear analysis: A multivariate technique for categorical data. The basic goal of most loglinear analyses is to find the simplest possible model that can explain the interactions between the variables. (See *Gross effect, Logit, Marginal effect* and *Model selection*)

Marginals: In a crosstabulation table, the sum of the values in a row or the sum of the values in a column. The values used to calculate row or column per cents or the expected frequencies in any cell. (See *Crosstabulation* and *Loglinear analysis*)

Marginal effect: Rows or columns with a relatively larger number of cases will on average be expected to have more cases in each cell than rows or columns with relatively fewer cases. (See *Chi-square, Crosstabulation and Loglinear Analysis*)

Mean: The central point for interval/ratio data. Found by adding together the values in a batch and then dividing by the total number of cases. (See *Central tendency*)

Median: The central point for ordinal data. Found by ordering the cases from highest to lowest and finding the 50% midpoint in the ordering where half of the cases are below and half are above. (See *Central tendency* and *Quartiles*)

Missing values: A coding that indicates a valid value does not exist for a variable; e.g., codings for 'Refused to answer', 'Unknown', 'Spoiled answer', 'Question not applicable' etc. SPSS will exclude values indicated as 'missing' from any statistical analysis. Missing values should be given as obviously 'impossible' codes so that they do not inadvertently become included in an analysis.` (See *Listwise missing values* and *Pairwise missing values*)

Mode: The central point for categorical/nominal data. The value for which there are more cases than any other value. (See *Bimodal, Central tendency* and *Multimodal*)

Model selection: A procedure in loglinear analysis in which progressively simpler models are chosen by a process of systematic elimination until the simplest possible model that still 'fits' the observed cell distributions is found. (See *Loglinear analysis*)

Multicollinearity: Two or more independent variables being highly correlated with each other. A problem for interpreting the valid unique effect of each variable on a dependent variable.

Multimodal: A distribution of scalar values with three or more distinct modes or 'humps'. (See *Bimodal* and *Mode*)

Multiple response sets: Special variables where SPSS combines the responses to a range of variables.

Multivariate: Involving more than two variables, opposed to *Univariate* (one variable) and *Bivariate* (two variables)

Negative relationship: A link between two variables where, when the values of one variable rise, the values of the second variable will tend to *fall*. (See *Positive relationship*)

Nominal data or variable: (See *Levels of measurement*)

Normal distribution: The tendency for data to cluster around a central point in a predictable and symmetric way: 'the bell-shaped curve'.

Null Hypothesis: The logical opposite of the Hypothesis. The Null Hypothesis typically takes the form of predicting no *difference* between groups or no *relationship* between variables. The accuracy of the statement is evaluated by statistical analysis.

Oblique rotation: Where the axes in a factor analysis are allowed to correlate with each other after rotation. (See *Factor analysis* and *Orthogonal rotation*)

Operationalisation: Developing variables to represent conceptual abstractions or theories in order to apply them in an analysis. (See *Deduction, Durkheim, Empiricism, Induction* and *Positivism*)

One-tailed test: A statistical test of a hypothesis that predicts the direction of a difference or relationship. (See *Hypothesis* and *Two-tailed test*)

Ordinal data or variable: (See *Levels of measurement*)

Orthogonal rotation: Where the axes in a factor analysis are constrained to be at right angles to (uncorrelated with) each other after rotation. (See *Factor analysis* and *Oblique rotation*)

Outlier: A datum that is extremely different (i.e., much larger or much higher) from most of the other data in a batch. (See *Box plot* and *Exploratory data analysis*)

'Pairwise' missing values: SPSS will exclude values indicated as 'missing' from any statistical analysis. If the 'pairwise' option is taken in a multivariate analysis, a case will be excluded only from those parts of the analysis where a missing value found is directly included in a calculation. (See *Missing values* and *Listwise missing values*)

Parametric test: A statistical test utilising interval or ratio data that is based on the assumption that the data have a Normal distribution. (See *Normal distribution*)

Pie chart: A diagram in which the relative sizes of the categories of a variable are depicted as 'slices' of a 'pie'.

Population parameter: A figure that is based upon the whole population. (See contrast to *Sample estimate*)

Positive relationship: A link between two variables where, when the values of one variable rise, the values of the second variable also tend to rise. (See *Negative relationship*)

Positivism: The analysis of quantitative data in which the primary goal is to evaluate a pre-existing theory or concept. (See *Deduction, Durkheim, Empiricism, Induction* and *Operationalisation*)

Post-hoc test: A test to see which groups differ significantly after an overall difference is found between the groups. (See *Analysis of Variance*)

Phi (ϕ): An appropriate measure of association when the variables in a crosstabulation table are categorical. It is closely related to Chi-square and easily calculated by dividing the Chi-square result by the sample size and obtaining the square root. Values are bounded between 0 and 1, with 0 representing no association and 1 signifying a perfect association. Phi is suitable for 2 by 2 tables only as with larger tables it may produce values greater than 1. Cramer's V should be used for tables exceeding 2 rows and 2 columns. (See *Chi-square, Cramer's V* and *Crosstabulation*)

Power: The extent to which a given statistic accurately summarises the characteristics of a batch of data and avoids rejecting a hypothesis that is true or accepting a hypothesis that is false. (See *Type I* and *Type II Errors*)

Proportional reduction in error (PRE): A family of statistics that calculate the degree to which the values of a dependent variable can be estimated when the values of an independent variable are known. (See *Gamma, Goodman and Kruskal's tau, Lambda* and *Somer's D*)

Quartiles: The quarter points for ordinal data. Found by ordering the cases from highest to lowest and finding the 25% points in the ordering. The upper quartile is the 75% point where three-quarters of the cases are below and one quarter is above. The lower quartile is the 25% point above one quarter of the cases and below three-quarters of the cases. (See *Median*)

Range: The difference between the highest and lowest values in a batch of data. (See *Dispersion*)

Ratio data or variable: (See *Levels of measurement*)

Recode: A SPSS data transformation procedure in which a code or range of codes are given different values.

Record: (*See Case*)

Regression: A group of statistical procedures in which the effect of one or more independent variables on a dependent variable are estimated. The general form of a multivariate regression equation is $y = a + b_1x_1 + b_2x_2 + \ldots + b_nx_n$. Where 'y' is the predicted value of the dependent variable, 'a' is a constant that sets the level of 'y', 'x' represents the independent variables and 'b' represents the amount of change in 'y' that is predicted by the change of one unit in 'x'.

Reliability: The ability of an instrument or statistic to give consistently the same results when the underlying characteristic being measured has not altered. (See *Validity*)

Residual: The difference between an observed value and the value that is predicted or expected. The extent to which a statistical result depicts the actual features of a batch of data is termed its 'fit'. The 'leftover' which the statistic does not depict or explain is the 'residual'. (See *Goodness of fit*)

Rotation: 'Spinning' the axes of the components in a factor analysis so that each component comes closer to the factors that 'load' on it. There are two basic types of rotation: orthogonal rotation, where the axes are constrained to be at right angles to (uncorrelated with) each other, and oblique rotation where the axes are allowed to correlate with each other. After rotation, it is more common to refer to the components as 'factors'. (See *Factor analysis, Oblique rotation* and *Orthogonal rotation*)

Sample estimate: A figure that is based upon a sample from a population and hence is an estimate of the true *population parameter*. (See *Population parameter*)

Scaling: (*See Levels of measurement*)

Scattergram: A diagram that is the plot of points for individual cases in a batch of data which are determined by two variables where one variable makes up the 'x' axis and the other variable makes up the 'y' axis.

Scheffe test: A test used in Analysis of Variance to establish which categories of a group differ significantly from each other. (See *Analysis of Variance* and *Post-hoc test*)

Significance level: The probability that the result of a statistical test is due to chance rather than being a genuine phenomenon. The conventional 'cut-off' points are odds of: 1 in 20 of a chance result ($p < 0.05$); 1 in 100 of a chance result ($p < 0.01$); 1 in 1,000 of a chance result ($p < 0.001$). (See *Degrees of freedom*)

Skewness: The extent to which a distribution has a long upward skew (a 'positive skew', represented by a positive number) or a long downward skew (a 'negative skew', represented by a negative number). A Normal distribution is not skewed, and its measure of 'skewness' is zero. (See *Normal distribution* and *Kurtosis*)

Social fact: Regularities in social phenomena that are purported to exist at a higher level than individual consciousness or the simple aggregation of individual behaviour. (See *Durkheim*)

Spearman's Rho correlation coefficient: A measure of association between two ordinal variables, ranging between -1.00 (strong negative association), 0.00 (no association) and $+1.00$ (strong positive association). (See *Correlation coefficient, Pearson's product moment*)

Somer's D: A measure of association for ordinal variables in a crosstabulation table that takes into account tied cases for the dependent variable. SPSS calculates symmetric and asymmetric versions of this statistic. (The symmetric version is used if you cannot decide which variable is dependent and which variable is independent.) (See *Gamma, Goodman and Kruskal's tau* and *Lambda*)

Standard deviation: The measure of dispersion around the mean in an interval/ratio batch of data. The square root of the *variance* (the sum of the squared differences from the mean of each individual value). (See *Variance*)

Standardisation: Removing the effects of level and distribution from batches of data. (Effected for interval/ratio data by subtracting the mean and dividing by the standard deviation; effected for ordinal data by subtracting the median and dividing by the interquartile deviation.) All standardized batches of data have a central point (mean or median) of zero and a measure of dispersion (standard or interquartile deviation) of one. Standardized correlation or regression coefficients will range between –1.00 and +1.00.

Statistical significance: (See *Significance level*)

Stem and leaf diagram: A diagram which provides a visual depiction of the shape of the batch's distribution while retaining the individual data values. The values are broken down into two significant figures, one representing the stem and the other the leaf. (See *Exploratory data analysis*)

Syntax: Statements written in a computer program's command language.

Transforming values: (*See Data manipulation*)

t-test: A set of statistical tests that assess whether the distribution of values for groups or batches can be considered to come from the same population or not. (See *Levene's test for equality of variances*)

Two-tailed test: A statistical test of a hypothesis in which the hypothesis predicts a difference or a relationship but not the direction of the difference or relationship). (See *Hypothesis* and *One-tailed test*)

Type I error: Accepting a hypothesis as true when in fact it is false.

Type II error: Rejecting a hypothesis as incorrect when in fact it is correct.

Univariate: (see *Multivariate*)

Validity: The extent to which a measure actually measures or represents that which it purports to measure. (See *Reliability*)

Value label: A short description of a number coding of a variable. The value label has no analytic function but appears with the numeric coding to help the human interpret output. (See *Variable label* and *Variable name*)

Variable: A single item of data that can take a number of values (i.e., that can *vary*). (See *Case*)

Variable label: A short description of a variable that is attached to it. The variable label has no analytic function but appears with the variable name to help the human interpret output. (See *Value label* and *Variable name*)

Variable name: A unique combination of letters and numbers that is the identifier of each variable in an SPSS dataset. (See *Value label* and *Variable label*)

Variable View: The data window that shows the characteristics of each variable in a SPSS dataset. (See *Data view*)

Variance: A measure of the extent that a batch of data range around its central point. For a mean, the variance is the sum of the squared differences from the mean of each individual value. (See *Standard deviation*)

Wald statistic: A ratio of the beta coefficient in logistic regression to its standard error. Used to estimate the relative significance of the effect of different independent variables upon the dependent variable.

Weighting: 'Counting' individual cases more or less than 1 in an analysis. Commonly used to rectify under- or over-sampling. (See *Data selection*)

References

Clegg, Francis. (1990). *Simple Statistics*. Cambridge: Cambridge University Press.

Comrey, A.L. (1973). *A First Course in Factor Analysis*. San Diego: Academic Press.

De Vaus, D. (1991). *Surveys in Social Research*. London: Allen and Unwin.

Erickson, B.H. and Nosanchuk, T.A. (1992). *Understanding Data*. Buckingham: Open University Press.

Ganzeboom, Harry B.G. and Treiman, Donald J. (1996). "Internationally Comparable Measures of Occupational Status for the 1988 International Standard Classification of Occupations". *Social Science Research* 25: 201–39.

Kuhn, Thomas S (1962). *The Structure of Scientific Revolutions*. Chicago and London: The University of Chicago Press.

Lin, Nan (1976). *Foundations of Social Research*. New York: McGraw-Hill Book Company.

Loether, H.J. and McTavish, D.G. (1974). *Descriptive Statistics for Sociologists*. Boston: Allyn and Bacon.

Norusis, Marija M.J. (1999). *Guide to Data Analysis*. New Jersey: Prentice-Hall.

Norusis, M.J. (2008). *16.0 Guide to Data Analysis*. New Jersey: Prentice-Hall.

Tukey, John W. (1977). *Exploratory Data Analysis*. Reading, MA: Addison-Wesley.

Weisberg, Herbert H.F. (1992). *Central Tendency and Variability*. Newbury Park: Sage.

Index